Nabokov

*Criticism,
reminiscences,
translations and
tributes*

*edited by
Alfred Appel, Jr. &
Charles Newman*

A Clarion Book

*Published by
Simon and Schuster*

A Clarion Book
Published by Simon and Schuster
Rockefeller Center, 630 Fifth Avenue
New York, New York 10020

First Simon and Schuster paperback printing 1970

SBN 671-20786-5

Manufactured in the United States of America

[1. Criticism]

[2. Reminiscences]

[3. Translator/translations

[4. Tributes]

[*Nabokov*]

Nabokov and Chekhov: the lesser Russian tradition

SIMON KARLINSKY

In the late 1880's Anton Chekhov, M.D., until then known to readers of Russian humorous magazines for his light and entertaining literary miniatures, turned to more serious kinds of writing and produced his first mature and important stories. A large segment of the reading public and such major older writers as Lev Tolstoy and Leskov were quick to realize the value and the originality of the new kind of literary art discovered by Chekhov. But the powerful Populist-oriented Russian literary critics of the day were united in their determined hostility. To them, Chekhov was a gifted, even brilliant writer whose art had no discernible aim or direction, who was indifferent to the joys and sufferings

7

of the people he portrayed and who, in his more humorous moments, was an amusing but mindless literary clown. A frequent charge that Russian critics of the 1880's and -90's leveled against Chekhov was his supposed disregard of the humanitarian traditions of his native literature.

Some forty years later, in the late 1920's, Vladimir Nabokov, lepidopterist and chess expert, until then mainly known for his facile and prolific verse which appeared in Russian émigré newspapers in Berlin and Paris (and as the translator of *Alice in Wonderland* into Russian), turned to writing serious short stories and novels. The more literate segment of the Russians living abroad and such important exiled writers as Zamyatin and Khodasevich were quick to acclaim Nabokov as the most significant and stimulating of the younger Russian writers of the day. But the various factions of émigré literary criticism, usually at odds with each other's views, were soon united in proclaiming that the brilliance of Nabokov's style was a façade that covered up the emptiness of his content. The conventionally realistic émigré novelist Mikhail Osorgin described Nabokov as a writer who is not only "almost entirely divorced from current Russian problems, but whose place is outside of any direct influence of the Russian classical literature." The metaphysical-minded and very influential émigré critic Georgii Adamovich (caricatured by Nabokov in *The Gift* as Christopher Mortus and mentioned in the earlier version of *Speak, Memory* as the leader of the Adamites) wrote that the novelty of Nabokov's writing was only apparent, since it was a matter of "novelty of narrative technique and not of a novel perception of life." Like Osorgin, Adamovich emphasized Nabokov's supposed un-Russianness. "All of our native traditions are severed in him," he wrote in 1934.[1]

The misgivings about Nabokov's Russian authenticity, sounded by émigré critics in the 1930's, are now taken up in the infrequent references to him made by members of the Soviet literary establishment in the 1960's. The Soviet novelist Yurii Bondarev, during his visit to the Berkeley campus in 1965, refused to admit that Nabokov was any kind of Russian writer at all. For Bondarev, Nabokov's Russian writings were the work of a foreigner who happens to write fluently in Russian. It was not the fact of Nabokov's emigration, Bondarev made clear, that made him so un-Russian, for the Soviet novelist was quite prepared to accept the émigré writers Ivan Bunin and Boris Zaitsev as authentically Russian.

We cannot imagine a French or an American novelist proclaimed non-French or non-American because of the style or the content of his work (or by virtue of his residence in another country). Obviously, then, there is some element in Nabokov's writing that is equally and instinctively felt as a violation of their native literary tradition by a Russian "academic" realist (Osorgin), by the sophisticated inheritor of Russian Symbolist and Acmeist poetics (Adamovich) and by a moderately iconoclastic, post-Stalinist Soviet writer (Bondarev).

Since the Soviet novelist's acceptance of Bunin and rejection of Nabokov as Russian has been mentioned, we might turn to the relations between these two writers in our search for an explanation of this Russian attitude toward Nabokov. In his autobiography, Nabokov describes how Bunin, soon after receiving his Nobel prize for literature, invited him to dinner. The dinner party was not a success, which Nabokov blames on his own refusal to engage in "heart-to-heart talks, confessions in the Dostoevskian manner or discussions of eschatological matters." Mutual boredom at the end of the meal was the result (this episode has been quoted by Aleksandr Tvardovsky in his introduction to the recent Soviet edition of Bunin's works as proof of Bunin's Russian authenticity and of the snobbish and heartless character of Nabokov). At the end of that unfortunate dinner, Bunin was quoted by Nabokov as remarking, "You will die in dreadful pain and complete isolation." [2]

Bunin's remark offers us a very interesting clue. In his own memoir about his friendship with Anton Chekhov, Bunin tells us that the one critical comment that had ever really hurt Chekhov was the remark of the Populist critic Skabichevsky in the

1880's that Chekhov would eventually die drunk in the gutter, forgotten by everyone.[3] A coincidence, perhaps? But it has implications of considerable relevance. Bunin's unconscious reminiscence of Skabichevsky's taunt of Chekhov is only one example of the frequent similarity of the critical reactions of writers steeped in the traditions of Russian 19th-century intelligentsia to Chekhov and to Nabokov, a similarity all the more unexpected because the literary debuts of these two writers are separated by a period of 40 years, by two major political revolutions and by the almost equally momentous cultural revolution of the Symbolist era. And yet when we read the Populist critic Mikhailovsky's charges that Chekhov's *The Steppe* is a stroll of a mindless young giant who has no idea where he is going or why; or the numerous allusions to Chekhov's indifference to his characters and to his cold inhumanity, covered up by technical mastery (this was in the 1880's and -90's, before the dreadful later cliché of Chekhov as the poet of twilight Russia had been devised); when we read all those indignant reviews with which Chekhov was greeted at the time when his literary art was at its peak; and when we then turn to some of the articles about the Russian novels of Vladimir Nabokov written by various liberal-minded or metaphysical-minded Russian émigrés in the Russian journals that were published in Paris in the 1930's, we are astounded by the numerous correspondences. The basic criticism is almost the same: that originality and novelty of the writer's craftsmanship serve no discernible human purpose and are probably a mask covering up his indifference to his fellow humans.

Now, we know that Chekhov and Nabokov are not particularly alike as writers (Chekhov is, however, one of the few Russian prose writers whom Nabokov unconditionally admires). Still, are all those critics of two different epochs and of very dissimilar ideological orientation so very wrong to have reacted in such an identical manner? No, not really. There is, in fact, a set of profound basic similarities between Chekhov and Nabokov which separates them from most other Russian writers and certainly from the Soviet ones. To begin with, Chekhov and

Nabokov have a tremendous respect for their chosen art form, quite independently of what ideological ends it may serve. In this they are on the side of Pushkin. On the other hand, Gogol, Tolstoy, Turgenev, Dostoevsky, Blok, Mayakovsky, Solzhenitsyn and a host of lesser lights could not conceive of their art as divorced from some educational, proselytizing, religious, civic or some other extra-literary goal to which the writer subscribes.

The impulse that underlies most of Russian 19th-century prose (and certainly the Soviet prose of recent decades) is similar in nature to the impulse that underlies the social sciences. Human behavior, or rather the means of improving it, is the central focus of interest. The literary art of Chekhov and Nabokov (as was also probably the case with Pushkin) springs from a different sort of impulse, which for the purpose of demonstrating the contrast can be said to be comparable to the impulse behind the biological sciences.

Chekhov is of course very much involved with the biological sciences. Not only his degree in medicine points to this, but also his constant and pervasive interest in nature conservation, expressed in such stories as "The Flute" and in the plays *The Wood Demon* and *Uncle Vanya*. Charles Darwin was one of Chekhov's favorite writers; he described his sensation when reading Darwin rather unexpectedly as "voluptuous." One of Chekhov's close friends was the zoologist Wagner (some of whose ideas were reflected in the ideas of the zoologist von Koren in *The Duel*). Chekhov and Wagner investigated together the conditions at the Moscow zoo in the early 1890's and, as a result, Chekhov wrote the devastating and very funny critique of the way the zoo was run, which he published under the title "The Charlatans" ("Fokusniki") and under an assumed name. If the readers now usually have an image of Chekhov rather at variance with a man so closely involved with biology and zoology, it is due to decades of criticism that had sentimentalized this writer or had imposed on him the traditional sociological values of Russian 19th-century intelligentsia.

Thus, we can understand the distorted reputation acquired

by Chekhov's longest single work, the book of travel impressions entitled *The Island of Sakhalin*. In the course of their debate on the writer's political obligations, which appeared in *The New Leader* some years ago, the critic Irving Howe and the novelist Ralph Ellison both referred to this work of Chekhov as an impassioned political document and commended Chekhov on the high civic courage he displayed in his indictment of the Czarist mistreatment of political prisoners. It is a safe bet that neither Mr. Howe nor Mr. Ellison had read Chekhov's book at the time (it was published in English several years after their exchange in what is probably the most spectacularly inept and clumsy translation ever printed). What these two American writers described was the sort of thing they *would expect* a Russian writer to write about a Czarist penal colony.

As a matter of plain fact, *The Island of Sakhalin* is not about political prisoners at all (there were very few of these on the island and Chekhov was not allowed to see them). Most of the book is a very thoroughly researched ethnographic and demographic study of a colony of common criminals, forced to settle in an inhospitable environment which the Russian government was trying to colonize. In addition to the convict settlers, Chekhov was interested in the plight of the mistreated and vanishing native populations of the area (the Gilyaks and the Ainus) and the mistreated and vanishing local fauna, especially the salmon. The passage on the barbarous mismanagement of salmon fishing resulting from the ignorance of its life cycle is a set piece that no other major 19th-century Russian writer could have written, and that very few of them would be interested to read. We do not minimize Chekhov's artistry, or his very genuine human compassion and concern, if we say that his preoccupation with biology colors all of his mature work. Read from this angle, "The Dreary Story," *The Duel* or *The Cherry Orchard* would yield any number of surprises.

Nabokov's interest in animal and plant life, his lepidoptery, his aesthetic delight in butterfly collecting are not as easy to overlook as Chekhov's biological preoccupations. Nabokov himself calls our attention to that aspect of his art and systematically exploits this theme in his fiction. In an early Russian poem that bears the English title "Biology" [4] (the opening sentence reads: "My Muse does not blame me: in the study of life's quivers, all is beauty"), Nabokov describes himself in a Cambridge laboratory, examining a linden leaf under a microscope and admiring the anatomy of a dissected frog. At the end of the poem, the poet is joyously anticipating his return home, where his volume of verse and a pipe the Muse filled for him await him. This initial point of departure, enunciated in a poem written before 1923, has remained basic to Nabokov's art ever since; much of Ada's and Van's biological commentary can be seen as a lavish and baroque apotheosis of this particular component, found in smaller quantities almost everywhere else in Nabokov. It is his training in lepidoptery that gives this writer the precision of observation and the science-derived caution in interpreting his findings which he, like Chekhov, applies to his study of human and social predicaments and situations.

This very precision of observation and restraint in evaluation is what makes Chekhov's picture of turn-of-the-century Russian village life in "The Peasants" or in "In the Ravine" and Nabokov's depiction of the American motel civilization in Lolita so overwhelmingly and irresistibly believable. If we compare these utterly convincing *fictional* descriptions to Fyodor Dostoevsky's *nonfictional* London (in "Winter Notes on Summer Impressions"), so deeply experienced and so utterly false because a few slanted observations have obviously been put at the service of a preconceived nationalistic and philosophical scheme, we get the precise nature of the difference. Dostoevsky in this case is indeed within the prevailing tradition of Russian literature, the tradition that places the writer's interest in the moral or religious implications of man's interrelationship with other men above interest in studying what is actually taking place or how this actuality can be reflected in the writer's art. Gogol, Tolstoy, and Mayakovsky at the end of their respective literary careers were mainly preoccupied with how they could best place their creative talent at the service of their chosen ideology. Their literary output itself became merely a tool with which to serve the ideology. Pushkin, Chekhov and, in his way, Nabokov, however, are more interested in observing, recording and diagnosing than in teaching, indoctrinating or prescribing a cure. It was Chekhov who praised Pushkin's *Eugene Onegin* for refraining from offering any solutions to problems raised, and settling instead for a beautifully clear ("correct") statement of those problems.

Pushkin's name fits into this scheme of a biology-oriented literary tradition quite naturally. On closer scrutiny, he can also be recognized as a writer within this lesser Russian tradition of objectivity and precision. Again a nonfictional work will serve to emphasize the extent of such objectivity. Pushkin's *Journey to Arzrum,* for example, when placed side by side with Chekhov's *The Island of Sakhalin,* will reveal that there is a certain kinship in the writer's method: the writer describes what he sees and refrains from sweeping conclusions or generalizations. The Russian landscape in *Eugene Onegin* charms us with its sobriety and precision, while Tolstoy's Caucasus in *The Cossacks,* intended by the author to depict the real Caucasus stripped of all romantic associations, ends up being a personalized *paysage d'âme* in comparison. One of Pushkin's very last prose works is his essay "John Tanner," based on the memoirs of a man who spent many years living among the North American Indians. In this work Pushkin dwells at length and in detail on the behavior and habits of the American moose (as depicted in his source)—a psychologically revealing detail, for that passage on the moose is sure to have greatly interested Chekhov and Nabokov, just as it certainly would have puzzled and bored Gogol or Dostoevsky. This interest in man's natural environment that is so typical of the Russian objective tradition in no way precludes the author's concern with social, human or even metaphysical issues. But it does change his basic attitude from that of a religious reformer or a labor organizer to that of a biological researcher, an anthropologist or a surgeon. Argument is possible as to which outlook is more humane in the long run; it is the quality of the writer's concern rather than its degree that makes the difference.

A century of socially and politically oriented literary criticism has obscured many of the relevant aspects of Pushkin in the Russian cultural tradition and has prevented the Soviet and Western critics from seeing Anton Chekhov as a writer very much at variance with the prevailing Russian notions of what literature is all about. The tradition of objective and independent literary art, not subservient to ideology, nationalism or religion, did exist in the 19th century (one can cite A. K. Tolstoy as another example), but it was so little perceived that when Nabokov did appear, the reaction of many of the émigré critics was as described: he was proclaimed un-Russian. It was in his novel *The Gift,* first published in serialized form in 1938, that Nabokov finally and fully revealed how deeply he is steeped in the Russian literary tradition and how much he himself is a part of it. The novel *The Gift* is a hybrid literary form; while being a conventional novel about fictional characters, it is also a literary polemic and a fairly detailed history of Russian literary criticism and of Russian literature in general. The ostensibly satirical but in fact enormously serious biography of Nikolai Chernyshevsky, which forms one of the chapters of *The Gift,* touches on some of the most basic and hidden mainsprings of 19th-century Russian literature in such a direct and daring manner that the chapter in question could not be included at the time of the novel's first publication. The editors of the émigré journal in which it was being serialized felt that it blasphemed against the things which to many literate Russians have become sacred and undebatable. The issue was not so much the literary reputation of Chernyshevsky as the very basic assumptions on the uses of literary art as such.

In the face of *The Gift, The Event* and *Ada,* all permeated with references and allusions to Russian literature and culture, in the face of the gigantic commentary to *Eugene Onegin,* the question of whether Nabokov is or is not a Russian writer appears pointless indeed. But the émigré critics who raised the issue in the first place direct our attention to an important basic fact of Russian literature: the existence of a hitherto unperceived lineage of biological humanitarianism in the Russian tradition, in contradistinction to the more evident ideological humanitarianism.

This may be of concern primarily to literary critics; as for major Russian writers, they have usually been able to value literary art, even when practiced by a contemporary of a different temperament or orientation. Thus, Gogol could venerate Pushkin, despite the enormous differences in their moral values and views on the uses of art. Lev Tolstoy could perceive and acclaim Chekhov's originality, even though there probably was not a single moral or aesthetic issue on which these two writers could agree. Similarly, at the time when the émigré journals were debating whether Nabokov was humanitarian and/or Russian, it was Ivan Bunin, the most important of Nabokov's senior colleagues abroad, who, on November 2, 1930 (i.e., some years before the dinner Nabokov described), remarked to a close friend that Nabokov had introduced "a new kind of literary art" and discovered "a whole new universe for which one can only be grateful to him." [5]

Notes

1. The comments of Osorgin, Adamovich and numerous other adverse émigré critics are quoted in Gleb Struve, *Russkaia literatura v izgnanii,* New York, 1956, pp. 278-90.

2. *Speak, Memory,* New York, 1966, p. 286.

3. *A. P. Chekhov v vospominaniakh sovremennikov,* Moscow, 1960, p. 525 and editorial note on p. 767. The original Russian idiom used by Skabichevsky and quoted by Bunin was "to die drunk under some fence."

4. "Biology," in *Gornii put' (The Empyrean Path),* Berlin, 1923, p. 155.

5. Galina Kuznetsova, *Grasskii dnevnik,* Washington, 1967, p. 184.

[1. Criticism]

Backgrounds of *Lolita*

ALFRED APPEL, JR.

Critics too often treat Nabokov's twelfth novel as a special case quite apart from the rest of his work, when actually it concerns, profoundly and in their darkest and yet most comic form, the themes which have always preoccupied him. Although *Lolita* may still be a shocking novel to several aging non-readers, the exact circumstances of its troubled publication and reception may not be familiar to younger readers. After four American publishers refused it, Madame Ergaz, of Bureau Littéraire Clairouin, Paris, submitted *Lolita* to Maurice Girodias' Olympia Press in Paris.[1] Although Girodias must be credited with the publication of several estimable if controversial works by writers

---

This essay will appear in somewhat different form as part of the introduction to *The Annotated Lolita*.

such as Jean Genet, his main fare was the infamous Travellers Companion series, the green-backed books once so familiar and dear to the eagle-eyed inspectors of the U.S. Customs. But Nabokov did not know this, and because of one of Girodias' previous publishing ventures, the "Editions du Chêne," thought him to be a publisher of "fine editions." Cast in two volumes and bound in the requisite green, *Lolita* was quietly published in Paris in September 1955.

Because it seemed to confirm the judgment of those nervous American publishers, the Girodias imprimatur became one more obstacle for *Lolita* to overcome, though the problem of its alleged pornography indeed seems remote today, and was definitively settled in France not long after its publication. I was Nabokov's student at Cornell in 1953-54, at a time when most undergraduates did not know that he was a writer. Drafted into the army a year later, I was sent overseas to France. On my first pass to Paris I naturally went browsing in a Left Bank bookstore. An array of Olympia Press books, daringly displayed above the counter, seemed most inviting—and there, between copies of *Until She Screams* and *The Sexual Life of Robinson Crusoe,* I found *Lolita*. Although I thought I knew all of Nabokov's works in English (and had searched through out-of-print stores to buy each of them), this title was new to me, and its context and format were more than surprising, even if in those innocent pre-Grove Press days the semi-literate wags on fraternity row had dubbed Nabokov's Literature 311-312 lecture course "Dirty Lit" because of such readings as *Ulysses* and *Madame Bovary* (the keenest campus wits invariably dropped the *B* when mentioning the latter). I brought *Lolita* back to my base, which was situated out in the woods. Passes were hard to get and new Olympia titles were always in demand in the barracks. The appearance of a new girl in town thus caused a minor clamor. "Hey, lemme read your dirty book, man!" insisted "Stockade Clyde" Carr, who had justly earned his sobriquet, and to whose request I acceded at once. "Read it aloud, Stockade," someone called, and, skipping the Foreword, Stockade

18

Clyde began to make his remedial way through the opening paragraph. "Lo . . . lita, light . . . of my life, fire of my . . . loins. My sin, my soul . . . Lo-lee-ta: The . . . tip of the . . . tongue . . . taking . . . a trip . . . *Damn!"* yelled Stockade, throwing the book against the wall, *"It's God-damn Litachure!!"* Thus the Instant Pornography Test, known in psychological testing circles as the "IPT." Although infallible, it has never to my knowledge been used in any court case.

At a double remove from the usual review media, *Lolita* went generally unnoticed during its first six months. But in the winter of 1956 Graham Greene in England recommended *Lolita* as one of the best books of 1955, incurring the immediate wrath of a columnist in the *Sunday Express,* which moved Greene to respond in *The Spectator.* Under the heading of "Albion" (suggesting a quaint tempest in an old teapot), the *New York Times Book Review* of February 26, 1956, alluded briefly to this exchange, calling *Lolita* "a long French novel," and not mentioning Nabokov by name. Two weeks later, noting "that our mention of it created a flurry of mail," the *Times* devoted two-thirds of a column to the subject, quoting Greene at some length. Thus began the underground existence of *Lolita,* which became public in the summer of 1957 when the *Anchor Review* in New York devoted 112 of its pages to Nabokov, including an excellent introduction by F. W. Dupee, a long excerpt from the novel, and Nabokov's Afterword, "On a Book Entitled *Lolita."* When Putnam's brought out the American edition in 1958 they were able to dignify their full-page advertisements with an array of statements by respectable and even distinguished literary names, though *Lolita's* fast climb to the top of the best-seller list was not exclusively the result of their endorsements or the novel's artistry. "Hurricane/Lolita swept from Florida to Maine" (to quote John Shade in *Pale Fire* [line 680]), also creating storms in England and Italy, and in France, where it was banned on three separate occasions. Although it never ran afoul of the law in this country, there were predictably some outraged protests, including an editorial in *The New Republic,* but since these at best belong to social rather than literary history, they need not be detailed here, with one exception. Orville Prescott's review in the daily *New York Times* of August 18, 1958, has a charm that should be preserved: " 'Lolita,' then, is undeniably news in the world of books. Unfortunately, it is bad news. There are two equally serious reasons why it isn't worth any adult reader's attention. The first is that it is dull, dull, dull in a pretentious, florid and archly fatuous fashion. The second is that it is repulsive." * Prescott's remarks complement those of an anonymous reviewer in *The Southern Quarterly Review* (January 1852), who found an earlier, somewhat different treatment of the quest theme no less intolerable: "the book is sad stuff, dull and dreary, or ridiculous. Mr. Melville's Quakers are the wretchedest dolts and drivellers, and his Mad Captain, who pursues his personal revenges against the fish who has taken off his leg, at the expense of ship, crew and owners, is a monstrous bore. . . ."

Not surprisingly, Humbert Humbert's obsession has moved commentators to search for equivalent situations in Nabokov's earlier work, and they have not been disappointed. In *The Gift* (written between 1935 and 1937), some manuscript pages on the desk of the young poet Fyodor move a character to say:

Ah, if only I had a tick or two, what a novel I'd whip off! From real life. Imagine this kind of thing: an old dog—but still in his prime, fiery, thirsting for happiness—gets to know a widow, and she has a daughter, still quite a little girl—you know what I mean—when nothing is formed yet but already she has a way of walking that drives you out of your mind— A slip of a girl, very fair, pale, with blue under the eyes—and of course she doesn't even look at the old goat. What to do? Well, not long thinking, he ups and marries the widow. Okay. They settle down, the three of them. Here you can go on indefinitely—the temptation, the eternal torment, the itch, the mad hopes. And the upshot—a miscalculation. Time flies, he

---

*In a manner similar to Joyce's, Nabokov four years later paid his respects to Prescott, though not by name, by having the assassin Gradus carefully read *The New York Times:* "A hack reviewer of new books for tourists, reviewing his own tour through Norway, said that the fjords were too famous to need (his) description, and that all Scandinavians loved flowers" (*Pale Fire*, 1962, p. 275). This was actually culled from the newspaper.

gets older, she blossoms out—and not a sausage. Just walks by and scorches you with a look of contempt. Eh? D'you feel here a kind of Dostoevskian tragedy? That story, you see, happened to a great friend of mine, once upon a time in fairyland when Old King Cole was a merry old soul. . . .

Although the passage [2] seems to anticipate *Lolita* ("It's queer, I seem to remember my future works," says Fyodor), *Laughter in the Dark* (1932) is mentioned most often in this regard, since Albinus Kretschmar sacrifices everything, including his eyesight, for a girl, and loses her to a hack artist, Axel Rex. "Yes," agrees Nabokov, "some affinities between Rex and Quilty exist, as they do between Margot and Lo. Actually, of course, Margot was a common young whore, not an unfortunate little Lolita [and, technically speaking, no nymphet at all—A.A.]. Anyway I do not think that those recurrent sexual oddities and morbidities are of much interest or importance. My Lolita has been compared to Emmie in *Invitation,* to Mariette in *Bend Sinister,* and even to Colette in *Speak, Memory . . ."* (*Wisconsin Studies* interview). Nabokov is justly impatient with those who hunt for Ur-Lolitas; for a preoccupation with specific "sexual morbidities" obscures the more general context in which these oddities should be seen, and his Afterword, "On a Book Entitled *Lolita,"* offers an urgent corrective.

"The first little throb of *Lolita,"* he writes in the Afterword, "went through me late in 1939 or early in 1940, in Paris, at a time when I was laid up with a severe attack of intercostal neuralgia. As far as I can recall, the initial shiver of inspiration was somehow prompted by a newspaper story about an ape in the Jardin des Plantes who, after months of coaxing by a scientist, produced the first drawing ever charcoaled by an animal: this sketch showed the bars of the poor creature's cage" (p. 313).* This account does not allow for that passage in *The Gift,* but it does offer a brilliant summary image: Humbert, the "aging ape" writing from prison, whose impossible love metaphorically con-

*The parenthetical page references are to the hardcover edition (New York, 1958).

21

nects him with that imprisoned animal, learns the language, in his fashion, and records his "imprisonment," and his narrative is the "picture" of the bars of the poor creature's cage. The Jardin des Plantes *donnée* also connects Humbert with the characters in Nabokov's Russian novels. Writing about Sirin [himself] in *Conclusive Evidence* (1951), in a sentence omitted from the second edition (*Speak, Memory*), Nabokov says, "His best works are those in which he condemns his people to the solitary confinement of their souls."

That "initial shiver of inspiration" resulted in a short story, "The Magician" ("Volshebnik"), written in Russian in 1939. "The man was a Central European, the anonymous nymphet was French, and the loci were Paris and Provence," writes Nabokov. "I had him marry the little girl's sick mother who soon died [of natural causes], and after a thwarted attempt to take advantage of the orphan in a hotel room, Arthur (for that was his name) threw himself under the wheels of a truck" (p. 314). Although Nabokov thought he had destroyed "The Magician" (as he says in the Afterword), it unexpectedly turned up among his papers in 1964, a fifty-four page typescript rather than the thirty pages of memory (but he says he will surely never publish it). Nabokov excerpted two passages for Andrew Field's critical study.[3] In the first, the magician sees the young girl for the first time in the Tuileries Gardens:

A girl of twelve (he determined age with an unerring eye), dressed in a violet frock, was moving step by step her roller skates, which did not work on the gravel—lifting each in turn and bringing it down with a crunch—as she advanced at a kind of Japanese tread, through the striped rapture of the sun, toward his bench. Later (as long as that "later" endured) it would seem to him that right then, at one glance he had taken her measure from head to foot: the animation of her reddish-brown curls which had been recently trimmed, the lightness of her large vacant eyes which somehow brought to mind a semi-translucent gooseberry, the gay warm color of her face, her pink mouth, just barely open so that her two large front teeth were resting lightly on the cushion of her lower lip, the summer tan of her bare arms with sleek fox-like little hairs running along the forearms, the vague tenderness of her still narrow but already not at all flat chest, the movement of the folds in her skirt, their short sweep and light fall back into place, the slenderness and glow of her careless legs, the sturdy straps of her roller skates. She stopped in front of the amiable woman sitting beside him who, turning to rummage in something which she had by her right hand side, found and held out to the little girl a piece of chocolate on a piece of bread. Chewing rapidly, she undid the straps with her free hand, shook off all the heaviness of steel soles on solid wheels—and, descending to us on earth, having straightened up with a sudden sensation of heavenly nakedness which took a moment to grow aware of being shaped by shoes and socks, she rushed off.

According to Field, Arthur makes no sexual advances until almost the final page, soon after the girl's mother has died:

"Is this where I sleep?" the little girl asked indifferently, and when, struggling with the shutters so as to further close the slits between them, he answered, yes, she looked at her cap which she was holding in her hand and limply tossed it onto the broad bed.

"Well," he said after the old porter who had lugged in their suitcases had left, and there remained only the beating of his heart and the distant shiver of the night, "Well . . . Now to bed."

Unsteady in her drowsiness, she stumbled against the edge of the armchair, and, then, simultaneously sitting down, he drew her to him by encircling her hip; she, arching her body, grew up like an angel, strained all her muscles for a moment, took still another half-step, and then lightly sank down in his lap. "My darling, my poor little girl," he murmured in a sort of general mist of pity, tenderness, and desire, observing her sleepiness, fuzziness, her wan smile, fondling her through her dark dress, feeling the stripe of the orphan's garter through its thin wool, thinking about her defenselessness, her state of abandonment, her warmth, enjoying the animated weight of her legs which sprawled loose and then again, with an ever so light bodily rustle, hunched themselves up higher—and she slowly wound one dreamy tight-sleeved arm around the back of his neck, immersing him in the chestnut odor of her soft hair.

But Arthur fails as both a magician and lover, and soon afterwards dies in a manner which Nabokov will transfer to Charlotte Haze. While the scene clearly foreshadows the first night at the Enchanted Hunters hotel, its straightforward action and solemn tone are quite different, and it compresses into a few paragraphs what will later occupy almost two chapters (pp. 121-135).

Arthur's enjoyment of the girl's "animated weight" suggests the considerably more combustible lap scene in *Lolita* (pp. 60-63), perhaps the most erotic interlude in the novel—but it only suggests it. Aside from such echoes, one must assume, on the evidence of these two long passages, that little beyond the basic idea of the tale subsists in *Lolita;* and the telling is quite literally a world apart.

"The Magician" went unpublished not because of the forbidding subject matter but rather, says Nabokov, because the girl possessed little "semblance of reality." In 1949, after moving from Wellesley to Cornell, he became involved in a "new treatment of the theme, this time in English." Although *Lolita* "developed slowly," taking five years to complete, Nabokov had everything in mind quite early. As is customary with him, however, he did not write it in exact chronological sequence. Humbert's confessional diary was composed at the outset of this "new treatment," and was followed by Humbert's and Lolita's first journey westward, and the climactic scene in which Quilty is killed ("His death had to be clear in my mind in order to control his earlier appearances," says Nabokov). Nabokov next filled in the gaps of Humbert's early life, and then proceeded ahead with the rest of the action, more or less in chronological order. Humbert's final interview with Lolita was composed at the very end, in 1954, followed only by John Ray's Foreword.

Especially new in this treatment was the shift from the third person to the first person, which created—obviously—the always formidable narrative problem of having an obsessed and even mad character meaningfully relate his own experience, a problem compounded in this specific instance by the understandable element of self-justification which his perversion would necessarily occasion, and by the fact that Humbert is a dying man. One wonders whether Thomas Mann would have been able to make *Death in Venice* an allegory about art and the artist if Aschenbach had been its narrator. While many of Nabokov's principal characters are victims (Luzhin, Pnin, Albinus), none of them tells his own story, and it is only Humbert who is both victim and victimizer, thus making him unique among Nabokov's first-person narrators (discounting Hermann, the mad and murderous narrator of *Despair,* who is too patently criminal to qualify properly as victim). By having Humbert tell the tale, Nabokov created for himself the kind of challenge best described in Chapter Fourteen of *Speak, Memory* when, in a passage written concurrently with the early stages of *Lolita,* he compares the composition of a chess problem to "the writing of one of those incredible novels where the author, in a fit of lucid madness, has set himself certain unique rules that he observes, certain nightmare obstacles that he surmounts, with the zest of a deity building a live world from the most unlikely ingredients—rocks, and carbon, and blind throbbings."

In addition to such obstacles, the novel also developed slowly because of an abundance of materials as unfamiliar as they were unlikely. It had been difficult enough to "invent Russia and Western Europe," let alone America, and at the age of fifty Nabokov now had to set about obtaining "such local ingredients as would allow me to inject a modicum of average 'reality' (one of the few words which mean nothing without quotes) into the brew of individual fancy." "What was most difficult," he recently told an interviewer, "was putting myself . . . I am a normal man, you see." [4] Research was thus called for, and in scholarly fashion Nabokov followed newspaper stories involving pedophilia (incorporating some into the novel), read case studies and, like Margaret Mead coming home to roost, even did research in the field: "I travelled in school buses to listen to the talk of the schoolgirls. I went to school on the pretext of placing our daughter. We have no daughter. For Lolita, I took one arm of a little girl who used to come to see Dmitri [his son], one kneecap of another," and thus a nymphet was born.[5]

Perspicacious "research" aside, it was a remarkable imaginative feat for a European émigré to have re-created America so brilliantly, and in so doing to have become an American writer. Of course, those critics and readers who marvel at Nabokov's accomplishment may not realize that he physically knows America better than most of them. As he says in *Speak, Memory*, his adventures as a "lepist" carried him through two hundred motel rooms in forty-six states, that is, along all the roads traveled by Humbert and Lolita. Yet of all of Nabokov's novels, *Lolita* is the most unlikely one for him to have written, given his background and the rarefied nature of his art and avocations. "It was hardly foreseeable," writes Anthony Burgess, "that so exquisite and scholarly an artist should become America's greatest literary glory, but now it seems wholly just and inevitable." [6] It was even less foreseeable that Nabokov would realize better than any contemporary the hopes expressed by Constance Rourke in *American Humor* (1931) for a literature that would achieve an instinctive alliance between native materials and old world traditions, though the literal alliance in *Lolita* is perhaps more intimate than even Miss Rourke might have wished. But to know Nabokov at all personally is first of all to be impressed by his intense and immense curiosity, his uninhibited and imaginative response to everything around him. To paraphrase Henry James' famous definition of the artist, Nabokov is truly a man on whom nothing is lost, except that in Nabokov's instance it is *true*, whereas James and many American literary intellectuals after him have been so self-conscious in their mandarin "seriousness" and consequently so narrow in the range of their responses that they have often overlooked the sometimes extraordinarily uncommon qualities of the commonplace.

Nabokov's responsiveness is characterized for me by the last evening of my first visit to Montreux in September 1966. During my two hours of conversation with the Nabokovs in their suite after dinner, Nabokov tried to imagine what the history of painting might have been like if photography had been invented in the Middle Ages; spoke about science fiction; asked me if I had noticed what was happening in *Li'l Abner*, and then compared it, in learned fashion, with an analogous episode of a dozen years back; noted that a deodorant stick had been found among the many days' siege provisions which the Texas sniper had with him on the tower; discoursed on a monstrous howler

in the translation of Bely's *St. Petersburg;* showed me a beautifully illustrated book on hummingbirds, and then discussed the
birdlife of Lake Geneva; talked admiringly and often wittily
of the work of Borges, Updike, Salinger, Genet, Andrei Sin-
yavsky ("Abram Tertz"), Burgess and Graham Greene, always
making precise critical discriminations; recalled his experiences
in Hollywood while working on the screenplay of *Lolita,* and
his having met Marilyn Monroe at a party ("A delightful actress. Delightful," he said. "Which is your favorite Monroe
film?"); talked of the Soviet writers he admired, summarizing
their stratagems for survival; and defined for me exactly what
kind of a beetle Kafka's Gregor Samsa was in *The Metamorphosis* ("It was a domed beetle, a scarab beetle with wing-sheaths,
and neither Gregor nor his maker realized that when the room
was being made by the maid, and the window was open, he
could have flown out and escaped and joined the other happy
dung beetles rolling the dung balls on rural paths"). And did I
know how a dung beetle laid its eggs? Since I did not, Nabokov rose, and imitated the process, bending his head toward his
waist as he walked slowly across the room, making a dung-
rolling motion with his hands until his head was buried in them
and the eggs were laid. When Lenny Bruce's name somehow
came up, both Nabokov and his wife commented on how sad
they had been to hear of Bruce's death; he had been a favorite
of theirs. But they disagreed about where it was they had last
seen Bruce; Mrs. Nabokov thought it had been on the Jack
Paar show, while her husband—the scientist, linguist and author
of fifteen novels, who has written and published in three languages, and whose vast erudition is most clearly evidenced by
the four-volume translation of Pushkin's *Eugene Onegin,* with its
two volumes of annotations and one-hundred-page "Note on
Prosody"—held out for the Ed Sullivan show.

Not only is nothing lost on Nabokov, but, like the title character in Borges' story "Funes the Memorious," he seems to
remember everything. At dinner the first evening of my 1966
visit, we reminisced about Cornell and his courses there, which

were extraordinary and thoroughly Nabokovian, even in the smallest ways (witness the "bonus system" employed in examinations, allowing students two extra points per effort whenever they could garnish an answer with a substantial and accurate quotation ["a gem"] drawn from the text in question). Skeptically enough, I asked Nabokov if he remembered my wife, Nina, who had taken his Literature 312 course in 1955, and I mentioned that she had received a grade of 96. Indeed, he did, since he had always asked to meet the students who performed well, and he described her accurately (seeing her in person in 1968, he remembered where she had sat in the lecture hall). On the night of my departure I asked Nabokov to inscribe my Olympia Press first edition of *Lolita*. With great rapidity he not only signed and dated it, but added two elegant drawings of recently discovered butterflies, one identified as *"Flammea pallida"* ("Pale Fire") and, below it, a considerably smaller species, labeled "Bonus bonus." [7] Delighted but in part mystified, I inquired, "Why 'Bonus bonus'?" Wrinkling his brow and peering over his eyeglasses, a parody of a professor, Nabokov replied in a mock-stentorian voice, "Now your wife has 100!" After four days and some twelve hours of conversation, and within an instant of my seemingly unrelated request, my prideful but passing comment had come leaping out of storage. So too has Nabokov's memory been able to draw on a lifetime of reading—a lifetime in the most literal sense, for Humbert invokes the most distant of Nabokov's enthusiasms: lines from Verlaine or Poe, a detective story read in early youth, a tennis match seen at Wimbledon forty years before. All are clear in his mind, and recorded in *Lolita,* memory negates time.

When queried about Nabokov, friends and former colleagues at Cornell invariably comment on the seemingly paradoxical manner in which the encyclopedic Nabokov mind could be enthralled by the trivial as well as the serious. One professor, at least twenty years Nabokov's junior and an instructor when he was there, remembers how Nabokov once asked him if he had ever watched a certain soap opera on television. Soap operas are of course ultimately comic if not fantastic in the way they characterize the life of the typical middle-class housewife as an uninterrupted series of crises and disasters; but missing the point altogether, suspecting a deadly leg-pull and supposing that with either answer he would lose (one making him a fool, the other a snob), Nabokov's young colleague had been reduced to a fit of wordless throat-clearing. Recalling it ten years later, he seemed disarmed all over again. On easier terms with Nabokov was Professor M. H. Abrams, who warmly recalls how Nabokov came into a living room where a faculty child was absorbed in a television western. Immediately engaged by the program, Nabokov was soon quaking with laughter over the furiously climactic fight scene. Just such idle moments, if not literally this one, inform the hilarious burlesque of the comparable "obligatory scene" in *Lolita,* the tussle of Humbert and Quilty which leaves them "panting as the cowman and the sheepman never do after their battle" (p. 301).

Even though he had academic tenure at Cornell, the Nabokovs never owned a house, and instead always rented, moving from year to year, a mobility he bestowed on refugee Humbert. Professor Morris Bishop, Nabokov's best friend at Cornell, who was responsible for his shift from Wellesley to Ithaca, recalls visiting them just after they had moved into the appallingly vulgar and garish home of an absent Professor of Agriculture. "I couldn't have lived in a place like that," says Bishop, "but it delighted him. He seemed to relish every awful detail." Although Bishop didn't realize it then, Nabokov was learning about Charlotte Haze by renting her house, so to speak, by reading her books and living with her pictures and "wooden thingamabob[s] of commercial Mexican origin." These annual moves, however dismal in their circumstances, constituted a field trip enabling entomologist Nabokov to study the natural habitat of Humbert's prey. Bishop also remembers that Nabokov read the New York *Daily News* for its crime stories,* and for an even more con-

---

*In *Pale Fire,* Charles Kinbote spies John Shade seated in his car, "reading a tabloid newspaper which I had thought no poet would deign to touch" (p. 22).

centrated dose of bizarrerie, Father Divine's newspaper, *New Day*—all of which should recall James Joyce, with whom Nabokov has so much else in common. Joyce regularly read *The Police Gazette*, the shoddy magazine *Titbits* (as does Bloom), and all the Dublin papers, attended burlesque shows, knew by heart most of the vulgar and comically obscene songs of the day, and was almost as familiar with the work of the execrable lady lending-library novelists of the *fin de siècle* as he was with the classics, and when he was living in Trieste and Paris and writing *Ulysses*, relied on his Aunt Josephine to keep him supplied with the necessary sub-literary materials. Of course, Joyce's art depends far more than Nabokov's on the vast residue of erudition and trivia which Joyce's insatiable and equally encyclopedic mind was able to store.

Nabokov is very selective, whereas Joyce collected almost at random and then ordered in art the flotsam and jetsam of everyday life. That Nabokov does not equal the older writer in this respect surely points to a conscious choice on Nabokov's part, as his Cornell lectures on *Ulysses* suggest.* In singling out flaws in what is to him the greatest novel of the century, Nabokov stressed the "needless obscurities baffling to the less-than-brilliant reader," such as "local idiosyncrasies" and "untraceable references." Yet Nabokov has also practiced the art of assemblage, incorporating in the rich textures of *Bend Sinister, Lolita, Pale Fire,* and *Ada* a most "Joycean" profusion of rags, tags and oddments, both high and low, culled from books or drawn from "real life." Whatever the respective scale of their efforts in this direction, Nabokov and Joyce are (with Queneau and Borges) among the few modern fiction writers who have made aesthetic capital out of their learning. Both include in their novels the compendious

---

* The course in question is Literature 311-312, "Masterpieces of European Fiction," MWF, 12 (first term: Jane Austen's *Mansfield Park*, Gogol's *Dead Souls*, Dickens' *Bleak House*, Flaubert's *Madame Bovary*, and Tolstoy's *The Death of Ivan Ilyich;* second term: Tolstoy's *Anna Karenina*, Stevenson's *Dr. Jekyll and Mr. Hyde*, Gogol's *The Overcoat*, Kafka's *The Metamorphosis*, Proust's *Swann's Way*, and *Ulysses*, in that order).

stuff one associates with the bedside library, the great literary anatomies such as Burton's *Anatomy of Melancholy* or Dr. Johnson's *Dictionary,* or those unclassifiable masterpieces such as *Moby-Dick, Tristram Shandy,* and *Gargantua and Pantagruel,* in which the writer makes fictive use of all kinds of learning, and exercises the anatomist's penchant for the collage effected out of verbal trash and bizarre juxtapositions—for the digression, the catalogue, the puzzle, pun, and parody, the gratuitous bit of lore included for the pleasure it can evoke, and for the quirky detail that does not contribute to the book's verisimilar design but nevertheless communicates vividly a sense of what it was like to be alive at a given moment in time. A hostile review of Nabokov's *Eugene Onegin* offered as typical of the Commentary's absurdities its mention of the fact that France exported to Russia some 150,000 bottles of champagne per annum; but the detail happens to telescope brilliantly the Francophilia of early nineteenth-century Russia, and is an excellent example of the anatomist's imaginative absorption of significant trivia and a justification of his methods. M. H. Abrams recalls how early one Monday morning he met Nabokov entering the Cornell Library, staggering beneath a run of *The Edinburgh Review,* which Nabokov had pored over all weekend in Pushkin's behalf. "Marvelous ads!" explained Nabokov, "simply marvelous!" It was this spirit that enabled Nabokov to create in the two volumes of *Onegin* Commentary a marvelous literary anatomy in the tradition of Johnson, Sterne, and Joyce—an insomniac's delight, a monumental, wildly inclusive, yet somehow elegantly ordered ragbag of humane discourse, in its own right a transcending work of imagination.

Nabokov was making expressive use of unlikely bits and pieces in his novels as early as *The Defense* (1930), as when Luzhin's means of suicide is suggested by a movie still, lying on the Veritas film company's display table, showing "a white-faced man with his lifeless features and big American glasses, hanging by his hands from the ledge of a skyscraper—just about to fall off into the abyss"—a famous scene from Harold Lloyd's 1923 silent film, *Safety Last.* Although present throughout his work of the nineteen-thirties, and culminating logically in *The Gift,* his last novel in Russian, Nabokov's penchant for literary anatomy was not fully realized until after he had been exposed to the polar extremes of American culture and American university libraries. Thus the richly variegated but sometimes crowded texture of *Bend Sinister* (1947), Nabokov's first truly "American" novel,* looks forward to *Lolita,* his next novel. *Bend Sinister'*s literary pastiche is by turns broad and hermetic. Titles by Remarque and Sholokov are combined to produce *All Quiet on the Don,* and Chapter Twelve offers this "famous American poem":

> A curious sight—these bashful bears,
> These timid warrior whalemen
>
> And now the time of tide has come;
> The ship casts off her cables
>
> It is not shown on any map;
> True places never are
>
> This lovely light, it lights not me;
> All loveliness is anguish—

No poem at all, it is formed, says Nabokov, by random "iambic incidents culled from the prose of *Moby-Dick.*" Such effects receive their fullest orchestration in *Lolita,* as the Notes to *The Annotated Lolita* will suggest.

If the *Onegin* Commentary (1964) is the culmination, then *Lolita* represents the apogee in fiction of Nabokov's proclivities as anatomist, and as such is a further reminder that the novel extends and develops themes and methods present in his work all along. Ranging from Dante to *Dick Tracy,* the allusions, puns, parodies, and pastiches in *Lolita* are controlled with a mastery unequaled by any writer since Joyce (who died in 1941).

---

* Although published in New York in 1941, a year after Nabokov's emigration, *The Real Life of Sebastian Knight* was in fact written in Paris in 1938 (in English). Students of chronology should also note that *Lolita* precedes *Pnin* (1957). The date of the former's American publication (1958) has proved misleading.

Readers should not be disarmed by the presence of so many kinds of "real" materials in a novel by a writer who believes so passionately in the primacy of the imagination; as Kinbote says in *Pale Fire,* " 'reality' is neither the subject nor the object of true art which creates its own special reality having nothing to do with the average 'reality' perceived by the communal eye."

By his example, Nabokov has reminded younger American writers of the fictional nature of reality. When Terry Southern in *The Magic Christian* (1960) lampoons the myth of American masculinity and its attendant deification of the athlete by having his multimillionaire trickster, Guy Grand, fix the heavyweight championship fight so that the boxers grotesquely enact in the ring a prancing and mincing charade of homosexuality, causing considerable psychic injury to the audience, his art, such as it is, is quite late in imitating life. A famous athlete of the 'twenties was well-known as an invert, and Humbert mentions him twice, never by his real name, though he does call him "Ned Litam" (p. 234)—a simple anagram of "Ma Tilden"—which turns out to be one of the actual pseudonyms chosen by Tilden himself, under which he wrote stories and articles. Like the literary anatomists who have preceded him, Nabokov knows that what is so extraordinary about "reality" is that too often even the blackest of imaginations could not have invented it, and by taking advantage of this fact in *Lolita* he has, along with Nathanael West, defined with absolute authority the inevitable mode, the dominant dark tonalities—if not the contents—of the American comic novel.

Although Humbert clearly delights in many of the absurdities around him, the anatomist's characteristic vivacity is gone from the pages which concern Charlotte Haze, and not only because she is repugnant to Humbert in terms of "plot," but rather because to Nabokov she is the definitive artsy-craftsy suburban lady —the culture-vulture, that travesty of Woman, Love, and Sexuality. In short, she is the essence of American *poshlust,* to use the "one pitiless [Russian] word" which, writes Nabokov in

Gogol, is able to express "the idea of a certain widespread defect for which the other three European languages I happen to know possess no special term." *Poshlust:* the "sound of the 'o' is as big as the plop of an elephant falling into a muddy pond and as round as the bosom of a bathing beauty on a German picture postcard" (p. 63). More precisely, it "is not only the obviously trashy but also the falsely important, the falsely beautiful, the falsely clever, the falsely attractive" (p. 70).[8] It is an amalgam of pretentiousness and philistine vulgarity. In the spirit of Mark Twain describing the contents of the Grangerford household in *Huckleberry Finn* (earlier American *poshlust*), Humbert eviscerates the muddlecrass (to wax Joycean) world of Charlotte and her friends, reminding us that Humbert's long view of America is not an altogether genial one.

In the course of showing us our landscape in all its natural beauty, Humbert satirizes American songs, ads, movies, magazines, brand names, tourist attractions, summer camps, dude ranches, hotels, and motels, as well as the Good Housekeeping Syndrome (*Your Home Is You* is one of Charlotte Haze's essential volumes) and the cant of progressive educationists and child guidance pontificators.* Nabokov offers us a grotesque parody of a "good relationship," for Humbert and Lo are "pals" with a vengeance; *Know Your Own Daughter* is one of the books which Humbert consults (the title exists). Yet Humbert's terrible demands notwithstanding, she is as insensitive as children are to their actual parents; sexuality aside, she demands anxious parental placation in a too typically American way, and, since it is Lolita "to whom ads were dedicated: the ideal consumer, the subject and object of every foul poster" (p. 150), she affords Nabokov an ideal opportunity to comment on the Teen and Sub-Teen Tyranny. "Tristram in Movielove," remarks Humbert, and Nabo-

---

* Satirized too is the romantic myth of the child, extending from Wordsworth to Salinger. "The McCoo girl?" responds Lolita kindly. "Ginny McCoo? Oh, she's a fright. And mean. And lame. Nearly died of polio." If the origin of modern sentimentality about the child's innocence can be dated at 1760, with the publication of *Mother Goose's Melodies*, then surely *Lolita* marks its death in 1955.

34

kov has responded to those various travesties of behavior which too many Americans recognize as tenable examples of reality. A gloss on this aspect of *Lolita* is provided by "Ode to a Model," a poem which Nabokov published the same year as the Olympia Press edition of *Lolita* (1955):

> I have followed you, model,
> in magazine ads through all seasons,
> from dead leaf on the sod
> to red leaf on the breeze,
>
> from your lily-white armpit
> to the tip of your butterfly eyelash,
> charming and pitiful,
> silly and stylish.
>
> Or in kneesocks and tartan
> standing there like some fabulous symbol,
> parted feet pointing outward
> —pedal form of akimbo.
>
> On a lawn, in a parody
> of Spring and its cherry-tree,
> near a vase and a parapet,
> virgin practicing archery.
>
> Ballerina, black-masked,
> near a parapet of alabaster.
> "Can one—somebody asked—
> rhyme 'star' and 'disaster'?"
>
> Can one picture a blackbird
> as the negative of a small firebird?
> Can a record, run backward,
> turn "repaid" into "diaper"?
>
> Can one marry a model?
> Kill your past, make you real, raise a family,
> by removing you bodily
> from back numbers of Sham? [9]

35

Although Nabokov has called attention to the elements of parody in his work, he has repeatedly denied the relevance of satire. One can understand why he says, "I have neither the intent nor the temperament of a moral or social satirist" (*Playboy* interview), for he eschews the overtly moral stance of the satirist who offers "to mend the world." Humbert's "satires" are too often effected with an almost loving care. Lolita is indeed an "ideal consumer," but she herself is consumed, pitifully, and there is, as Nabokov has said, "a queer, tender charm about that mythical nymphet." Moreover, since Humbert's desperate tourism is undertaken in order to distract and amuse Lolita and to outdistance his enemies, real and imagined, the "invented" American landscape also serves a quite functional, thematic purpose, for it helps to dramatize Humbert's total and terrible isolation. In their ways Humbert and Lolita are captives each of the other, imprisoned together in a succession of bedrooms and cars, but so distant from one another that they can share nothing of what they see, making Humbert seem as alone during the first trip west as he will be on the second, when she has left him and the car is an empty cell.

Nabokov's denials notwithstanding, however, many of Humbert's observations of American morals and mores *are* satirical, the product of his maker's moral sensibility, though the novel's greatness does not depend on the profundity or extent of its "satire," which is overemphasized by readers who fail to recognize the extent of the parody, its full implications, or the operative distinction made by Nabokov: "Satire is a lesson, parody is a game."

To stress the satiric elements of *Lolita* above all others is as limited a response as to stop short with its sexual content. "Sex as an institution, sex as a general notion, sex as a problem, sex as a platitude—all this is something I find too tedious for words," Nabokov told an interviewer from *Playboy,* and his Cornell lectures on Joyce further indicate that he is not interested in sexual oddities for their own sake. On May 10, 1954, in his opening lecture on *Ulysses* (delivered, as it turns out, at the time he was completing *Lolita*), Nabokov said of Leopold Bloom: "Joyce intended the portrait of an ordinary person. [His] sexual deportment [is] extremely perverse. . . . Bloom indulges in acts and dreams subnormal in an evolutionary sense, affecting both individual and species. . . . In Bloom's (and Joyce's) mind, the theme of sex is mixed with theme of latrine. Supposed to be ordinary citizen: mind of ordinary citizen does not dwell where Bloom's does. Sexual affairs reap indecency upon indecency. . . ." Coming from the creator of Humbert Humbert, the fervent tone and the rather old-fashioned sense of "normalcy" may seem unexpected. On May 28, the last class of the term and concluding lecture on Joyce, he discussed the flaws in *Ulysses,* complaining that there is an "Obnoxious, overdone preoccupation with sex organs, as illustrated in Molly's stream-of-consciousness. Perverse attitudes exhibited." * In spite of the transcriptions in notebookese, one gets a firm idea of Nabokov's attitude toward the explicit detailing of sexuality, and his remarks imply a good deal about his intentions in *Lolita*.

These intentions are underscored in the Afterword, "On a Book Entitled *Lolita,*" where Nabokov lists, without explanatory comment, "the nerves of the novel . . . the secret points, the subliminal co-ordinates by means of which the book is plotted" (p. 318). They include the "class list of Ramsdale School" (where, among other things, Irving Flashman suffers quietly, the only Jew in a room of Gentiles); "Lolita in slow motion advancing toward Humbert's gifts" (she is remembered as an illusory creature in a dream, rather than as the object of Humbert's foul lust, and the allusion to his gifts recalls his desperate bribery, as well as its results); "the pictures decorating the stylized garret of Gaston Godin" (a pantheon of homosexual artists); "the Kasbeam barber" (he talks of his son, dead for thirty years, as though he were still alive); "Lolita playing tennis" (if ever Humbert

---

* From the present writer's class notes, 1953-54.

37

succeeds in capturing her ineffable grace, it is in this scene [pp. 234-236]); "the hospital at Elphinstone" (where Quilty "steals" Lo); and, lastly, "the tinkling sounds of the valley town coming up the mountain trail (on which I caught the first known female of *Lycaeides sublivens* Nabokov)." None of these "secret points" is exclusively sexual. Rather, the images and characters all formulate varying states of isolation, loss, obsession, and ecstasy which generalize Humbert's consuming passion; the concluding "co-ordinate," after all, places in their midst the author, butterfly net firmly in hand.

That the seemingly inscrutable Nabokov would even write this essay, let alone reprint it in magazines and append it to the twenty-five translations of *Lolita,* surely suggests the dismay he must have felt to see how many readers, including some old friends, had taken the book solely on an erotic level. Those exposed "nerves" should make it clear that insofar as it has a definable subject, *Lolita* is not merely about pedophilia. As Humbert says, rather than describe the details of the seduction at the Enchanted Hunters hotel, "Anybody can imagine those elements of animality. A greater endeavor lures me on: to fix once for all the perilous magic of nymphets" (p. 136). Humbert's desires are those of a poet as well as a pervert, and not surprisingly, since they reflect, darkly, in a crooked enough mirror, the artistic desires of his creator.

Humbert's is a nightmare vision of the ineffable bliss variously sought by one Nabokov character after another. For a resonant summary phrase, one turns to *Agaspher* (1923), a verse drama written when Nabokov was twenty-four. An adaptation of the legend of the Wandering Jew, only its Prologue was published. Tormented by "dreams of earthly beauty," Nabokov's wanderer exclaims, "I shall catch you/catch you, Maria my inexpressible dream/from age to age!" [10] Near the end of another early work, the novel *King, Queen, Knave* (1928), an itinerant photographer walks down the street, ignored by the crowd, "yelling into the wind: 'The artist is coming! The divinely favored, *der gottbegna-*

dete artist is coming!' "—a yell that ironically refers to the novel's unrealized artist, businessman Dreyer, and anticipates and announces the arrival of such future avatars of the artist as the chess player Luzhin in *The Defense* (1930), the butterfly collector Pilgrim in "The Aurelian" (1931), the daydreaming art dealer and critic Albinus Kretschmar in *Laughter in the Dark* (1932), the imprisoned and doomed Cincinnatus in *Invitation to a Beheading* (1935-36), who struggles to write, the inventor Salvator Waltz in *The Waltz Invention* (1938), and the philosopher Krug in *Bend Sinister* (1947), as well as poets *manqués* such as Humbert Humbert in *Lolita* (1955), and such genuine yet only partially fulfilled artists as Fyodor in *The Gift* (1938), Sebastian Knight in *The Real Life of Sebastian Knight* (1941), and John Shade in *Pale Fire* (1962).[11] When perceived by the reader, the involuted design of each novel reveals that these characters all exist in a universe of fiction arrayed around the consciousness of Vladimir Nabokov, the only artist of major stature who appears in Nabokov's work.

Some readers, however, may feel that works that are in part about themselves are limited in range and significance, too special, too hermetic. But the creative process is fundamental; perhaps nothing is *more* personal by implication and hence more relevant than fictions concerning fiction; identity, after all, is a kind of artistic construct, however imperfect the created product. If the artist does indeed embody in himself and formulate in his work the fears and needs and desires of the race, then a "story" about his mastery of form, his triumph in art is but a heightened emblem of all of our own efforts to confront, order and structure the chaos of life, and to endure, if not master, the demons within and around us. "I am thinking of aurochs and angels, the secret of durable pigments, prophetic sonnets, the refuge of art," says Humbert in the closing moments of *Lolita,* and he speaks for more than one of Nabokov's characters.

Notes

1. See Nabokov's article, *"Lolita* and Mr. Girodias," *Evergreen Review,* XI (February 1967), 37-41.

2. Also pointed out by Andrew Field in *Nabokov: His Life in Art* (Boston, 1967), p. 325, and Carl R. Proffer, *Keys to Lolita* (Bloomington, 1968), p. 3.

3. Field, *op. cit.,* pp. 328-29.

4. Penelope Gilliatt, "Nabokov," *Vogue,* No. 2170 (December 1966), 280.

5. *Ibid.*

6. Anthony Burgess, "Poet and Pedant," *The Spectator,* March 24, 1967, p. 336. Reprinted in *Urgent Copy* (New York, 1969).

7. A photograph of these drawings appears in *Time,* May 23, 1969, p. 83.

8. For Nabokov's most recent description of *poshlost* (as he now transliterates it), see his interview, *Paris Review,* No. 41 (Summer-Fall 1967), 103-4.

9. Vladimir Nabokov, *Poems* (New York, 1959), p. 35.

10. Translated and quoted by Field, *op. cit.,* p. 79.

11. Continually held in apposition to these characters and serving as their foils and/or antagonists is a grotesque gallery of bad artists, meretricious writers, hack scholars, and tendentious theorizers—perverters of the imagination all. They include the nameless, personified inventor of automatons in *King, Queen, Knave* (and the sculptor and professor of physiology who assist him); the chess impresario Valentinov in *The Defense;* Axel Rex, the cartoonist and forger of Old Masters in *Laughter in the Dark;* Paduk, the dictator in *Bend Sinister;* Professor Hamm, belletristic implementer of the Ekwilist philosophy; and Clare Quilty, the dramatist, scenarist, and pornographer in *Lolita;* N. G. Chernyshevski, the social revolutionary, whose biography constitutes Chapter Four in *The Gift* (several other actual Russian writers may be included with Fyodor as heroes of the novel); the futurist poet Alexis Pan and the journalist-biographer Mr. Goodman in *The Real Life of Sebastian Knight;* and editor-annotator Kinbote in *Pale Fire.* Hermann, the murderous narrator of *Despair,* represents a unique departure from this pattern: the only instance where, save for the authorial presence, the "bad artist" has the novel entirely to himself.

Invitation to a Beheading: Nabokov and the art of politics

ROBERT ALTER

> The logical result of Fascism is the introduction of aesthetics into politics. . . . Mankind's self-alienation has reached such a degree that it can experience its own destruction as an aesthetic pleasure of the first order.
>
> —WALTER BENJAMIN,
> "The Work of Art in the Age of Mechanical Reproduction"

Because *Invitation to a Beheading* is in many ways the most explicit of Nabokov's fictions of ostentatious artifice, it at once lucidly illustrates his conception of the novel and puts to the test the limits of that conception. Over the past few years, with the publication in English of most of Nabokov's Russian fiction, and with a growing body of intelligent American criticism on his novels, the brilliance of his technical virtuosity has come to be widely appreciated, but a suspicion persists in some critical circles that his achievement is mere technical virtuosity, that the intricately convoluted designs of his novels make them self-enclosed, sterile, and therefore finally "minor." What is at issue is not just a critical commitment to realism—a literary convention toward which Nabokov has shown both lofty disdain and impish mockery—but an expectation of moral seriousness in literature which goes back in English criticism to figures like Matthew Arnold and Samuel Johnson. For American and British critics deriving from this tradition, the novel, though it may and perhaps even should delight, must above all teach us something—about the social, political, and spiritual spheres we inhabit, about the nature of moral choice and character, about the complexities of our psychological makeup. The obviously centripetal direction, then, of Nabokov's imagination, whirling all social, political, and psychological materials into a circumscribed inner concern with art and the artist, is construed as a failure of the novelist to engage the larger world of human experience, would seem to confess his ultimate lack of seriousness. *Invitation to a Beheading* is surely an extreme instance of this general centripetal movement. Written in Berlin in 1935, it takes the ugliest, most disturbing of modern political actualities, the totalitarian state, and uses it, one gathers, merely as a dramatically convenient background for the recurrent Nabokovian theme, which is, to borrow Simon Karlinsky's apt formulation, "the nature of the creative imagination and the solitary, freak-like role into which a man gifted with such imagination is inevitably cast in any society." [1]

The narrator of *Invitation to a Beheading* plays so continually and conspicuously with the status of his narration as artifice that the general point hardly needs critical elaboration. The first paragraph of the novel informs us that the protagonist has been sentenced to die, and immediately the narrator pauses to remind us that we are reading a book, and a rather peculiar one, at that: "So we are nearing the end. The right-hand, still untasted part of the novel . . . has suddenly, for no reason at all, become quite meager: a few minutes of quick reading, already downhill, and—O horrible!" [2] In the conventional novel of imprisonment, in the conventional fictional pattern of crime and punishment, the sentencing of the hero would of course take place toward the end, after a long and arduous development, so we are put on notice at once that conventional expectations will be subverted in the particular fiction before us. As we move on, Nabokov takes pains to remind us repeatedly that each scene has been arranged by a theatrical stage manager: again and again, visual descriptions are conveyed in explicitly painterly terms, even made to seem two-dimensional painted backdrops; if there is an atmospheric disturbance, it has to be reported as "a summer thunderstorm, simply yet tastefully staged, . . . performed outside" (p. 129); and time itself, as Cincinnatus points out, is not a continuous flow, like time in the "real" world, but purely a series of conventional indications within a represented action: "note the clock in the corridor. The dial is blank; however, every hour the watchman washes off the old hand and daubs on a new one—and that's how we live, by tarbrush time" (p. 135). And so the novel proceeds, through dozens of ingenious variations on this one underlying idea down to the grand finale when the daubed-in perspective slips out of kilter, the scenery totters, the painted rows of spectators come crashing down, and Cincinnatus goes striding off toward what we hope is a more human world.

All this flaunted artifice is clear enough in the novel, and it makes good thematic sense in relation to the hero, whose unspeakable sin of "gnostic turpitude" consists, after all, in imagining the world as an artist and in wanting to become what the world he exists in cannot by its nature tolerate, a true writer. It is precisely this continuous concern, however, with the artist's predicament, that the devotees of high seriousness object to in Nabokov. Hasn't the writer shirked his responsibilities by converting totalitarianism into the stuff of a fable about art and artifice? Can there be anything but frivolous self-indulgence in his decision finally to collapse the totalitarian state into mere discarded stage machinery, at the very moment in history when all civilized values were threatened by Stalinist terror and Nazi bestiality?

Such objections, it seems to me, conceive in far too narrow terms the ways in which fiction may "engage the world of experience," or are predicated on rather restrictive notions of what is involved in experience—even political experience. I would argue on the contrary that there is an important inner connection between the special emphasis on ostentatious artifice in *Invitation to a Beheading* and the totalitarian world which is the setting of the novel, and that Nabokov, precisely through his concern for art and the fate of the artist, is able to illuminate a central aspect of the supposedly human condition in an era of police states and totalitarian terrors. Two years after writing *Invitation to a Beheading,* Nabokov included in *The Gift* a kind of meditation about the meaning of executions that could serve as a useful gloss on the entire nature of political and social reality in the earlier novel:

Fyodor recalled his father saying that innate in every man is the feeling of something insuperably abnormal about the death penalty, something like the uncanny reversal of action in a looking-glass that makes everyone left-handed: not for nothing is everything reversed for the executioner: the horse-collar is put on upside down when the robber Razin is taken to the scaffold; wine is poured for the headsman not with a natural turn of the wrist but backhandedly; and if, according to the Swabian code, an insulted actor was permitted to seek satisfaction by striking the *shadow* **of the offender, in China it was precisely an actor—a shadow— who fulfilled the duties of the executioner, all responsibility being as it were lifted from the world of men and transformed into the inside-out one of mirrors.**[3]

Now, in order to make sense of this seemingly fanciful notion, we shall have to raise the tactless question of what, in fact, Nabokov conceives reality to be. This would appear to be particularly foolish to ask of a writer who has warned that reality is a word never to be used except within quotation marks, but

I believe it is of the utmost relevance to Nabokov's whole literary enterprise, the ultimate concerns of which are epistemological and metaphysical—like those of his great English precursor in the fiction of ostentatious artifice, Laurence Sterne. Nabokov, like Sterne, is continually bemused by the mystery through which individual consciousness in a subtle and at times perverse alchemic process transmutes the brute data of experience into the "reality" that each of us inhabits. The key to any sense of reality, certainly for Nabokov and probably for all of us, is the perception of pattern. Consciousness needs at least the illusion that it can control some of the data it encounters, seeing in them orderly sequence, recurrence, analogy, cause and effect, to be able to believe in their reality: the sun sets, the sun also rises, says the Preacher, but if it never rose again, if it came up as a thousand incandescent fireballs or a great gleaming poppy-seed cake, we would be in a nightmare or a fun-house fantasy, not in what most of us would call the real world. For Nabokov, as consciousness achieves a condition of acrobatic poise and elastic strength, integrating more and more into meaningful patterns, it encounters more reality, or rather makes the world around it at last real. That is why Cincinnatus, trapped in a world which he repeatedly reminds us is a mad jumble of "senseless visions, bad dreams, dregs of delirium, the drivel of nightmares" (p. 36), is not an escapist but a defiant rebel when he envisages another existence comprised of perfect, endlessly delighting pattern: "*There, tam, là-bas,* the gaze of men glows with inimitable understanding; *there* the freaks that are tortured here walk unmolested; *there* time takes shape according to one's pleasure, like a figured rug whose folds can be gathered in such a way that two designs will meet" (p. 94). The most prominent literary echo here is of course Baudelaire's vision of perfected art and pleasure in "L'Invitation au Voyage"—"*Là tout n'est qu'ordre et beauté,/Luxe, calme et volupté*" *—while those artfully gathered folds of patterned time nicely characterize Nabokov's subsequent treatment of time in *Speak, Memory,* his attempt to fix through art the

* "There, all is pure order and beauty, / Sumptuousness, calm, and pleasure."

reality of his personal experience. What may seem peculiar is the obtrusion into Cincinnatus's vision of aesthetic bliss of an explicitly moral idea, that in the harmonious world elsewhere the poor tormented freaks of his own flawed world will be left unharmed. To begin to understand this interweaving of moral and aesthetic, we must return to the shadowy headsman of Fyodor's father's reflections, who stands still unexplained in his backhanded, inside-out realm of mirrors.

If consciousness is the medium through which reality comes into being, the sudden and final obliteration of consciousness through mechanical means is the supreme affirmation by human agents—the executioners—of the principle of irreality. For the mind's ability to perceive freely or create patterns and delight in them is what makes man's life human, but in the appointed executioner mind is focused down to guiding the motions that will blot out all pattern in another human mind, man in a grim farce pretending that he is not a sentient being but something like a falling tree or an avalanche, a stupid instrument of blind murderous forces. Execution is the central rite of Cincinnatus's world, realizing its utmost possibilities, because that world, in all its institutional arrangements and daily social relations, is explicitly contrived to numb, cloud, cripple, and finally extirpate individual consciousness. It therefore must remain a relentlessly incredible world from the viewpoint of any genuinely human consciousness —its halls filled with trick mirrors producing meretricious effects, its personages crudely painted clowns more papier-mâché than flesh, even the conventional spider in its prison cell turning out to be a rubber facsimile, the shoddy practical joke of a dime-store mentality. Here, as elsewhere, Nabokov's anti-realist method has the effect of probing to the roots of real experience: his totalitarian state is not in any sense a disguised description of an actual regime, but the lineaments of his fictional fantasy, drawn with a rigorous sense of self-consistency (and not freely improvised like the fictions of some fashionable American "fantasts"), reveal the ultimate implications of the totalitarian principle, constitute a kind of ideal model of totalitarian possibilities. Thus, one critic could with considerable justice see in this novel a prophetic insight into the underlying operative assumption in Hitler's enterprise of mass-manufactured death: "the unspoken, vile, dehumanizing assumption that the guiltless victim must collaborate in his own torture and death, must enter into the corruption of his tormentors and depart this world robbed of life, integrity and individuality alike." [4] What must be added is that this world of ultimate obscenity is deliberately, justifiably, held at a comic distance so that the horror does not overwhelm, so that the whole insidious mechanism can be examined by a humane critical intelligence that affirms its own power to prevail through its constant presence in the cunning concern of the narrator for the embattled humanity of his protagonist. If the observer is able to preserve an intelligent sense of the possibilities of consciousness, then a society based on a universal collusion to surrender consciousness must seem to him a grotesque and improbable farce, a congeries of "specters, werewolves, parodies" (p. 40) that is sinister in both senses of the word—menacing, and belonging to a left-handed, inverted realm of mere negation.

It is worth examining more closely the relation between the theme of art in the foreground and the political background of the novel. Sartre's dictum that "a novelist's aesthetic always sends us back to his metaphysic" is eminently applicable here, and I think it is also relevant to keep in mind Sartre's rather special sense of "metaphysic," which implies not merely a conceptual grasp of reality but a moral posture toward it. Even what seems to be a preoccupation with the mechanics of technique on Nabokov's part has a strict thematic function, and this is especially true of a recurrent peculiarity of *Invitation to a Beheading*—that so many of its scenes are conceived as formal exercises in vision. Here, for example, is a brief description of the prisoner futilely attempting to see out of his cell window:

Cincinnatus was standing on tiptoe, holding the iron bars with his small hands, which were all white from the strain, and half of his face was covered with a sunny grating, and the gold of his left mustache shone, and there was a tiny golden cage in each of his mirrorlike pupils,

while below, from behind, his heels rose out of the too-large slippers. (p. 29)

The physical image of Cincinnatus is of course sharply and meticulously defined, made to seem very "real"—and not only the physical image, because through that final, telling detail of the oversize slippers we get a sense of the sad, touching, pathetic, vaguely funny nature of this trapped figure. What is important to note is that virtually every phrase of the description makes us aware of the cunning artificer, framing, selecting, eliciting pattern. Nabokov in effect invites us to participate in the perception of how a painter (a Flemish realist, let us say) and, by implication, a novelist, goes about "realizing" a scene. Each of the minute details, the small hands white with gripping, the gleaming half-mustache, the bars reflected in the pupils, is strategically chosen to make us see the whole figure caught in a particular light and a particular posture. We are led simultaneously to envisage Cincinnatus as a human being in a moment of anguish and as a formal study in dark and light contrasts, symmetrically divided by shadow. The reflecting surface is of course an invaluable resource in such studies of the possibilities of representation—one recalls the mirrors in Van Eyck interiors—because it allows the artist to duplicate forms and objects on a different scale, from a different angle, or even to smuggle new presences into the scene. The golden cages, however, in Cincinnatus's eyes are more than a device of visual preciosity, for in our very awareness of their paradoxical beauty we are led back to the terror of Cincinnatus's entrapment: is the cage in fact inside his head, a function of his own mode of vision, or, alternately, has an actual imprisonment cut him off from reality, reducing vision to an infinite regress of unyielding bars, so that, as for Rilke's caged panther, *"Ihm ist, als ob es tausend Stäbe gäbe,/Und hinter tausend Stäben keine Welt"?* *

Let us look at another, more elaborate instance of these exercises in vision. Cincinnatus frequently thinks back to the shreds

---

* "For him, it's as though there were a thousand bars / And behind a thousand bars no world."

of happiness he was able to grasp in the Tamara Gardens; it is the one place in which he can imagine concretely something like a human environment. But it should be noted that even in nostalgia he does not simply recall the Gardens, he explicitly *envisages* them. At one point he is brought out by his captors onto the turret of the prison and looks down on the town below:

Our travelers found themselves on a broad terrace at the top of a tower, whence there was a breathtaking view, since not only was the tower huge, but the whole fortress towered hugely on the crest of a huge cliff, of which it seemed to be a monstrous outgrowth. Far below one could see the almost vertical vineyards, and the creamy road that wound down to the dry river bed; a tiny person in red was crossing the convex bridge; the speck running in front of him was most likely a dog.

Further away the sun-flooded town described an ample hemicycle: some of the varicolored houses proceeded in even rows, accompanied by round trees, while others, awry, crept down slopes, stepping on their own shadows; one could distinguish the traffic moving on First Boulevard, and an amethystine shimmer at the end, where the famous fountain played; and still further, toward the hazy folds of the hills that formed the horizon, there was the dark stipple of oak groves, with, here and there, a pond gleaming like a hand mirror, while other bright ovals of water gathered, glowing through the tender mist, over there to the west, where the serpentine Strop had its source. Cincinnatus, his palm pressed to his cheek, in motionless, ineffably vague and perhaps even blissful despair, gazed at the glimmer and haze of the Tamara Gardens and at the dove-blue melting hills beyond them—oh, it was a long time before he could take his eyes away. . . . (pp. 42-43)

If the passage demonstrates a rigorous adherence to consistent point of view, it is point of view more in the sense of a Breughel than a Henry James. The paradoxical effectiveness of the description, like that of Cincinnatus clinging to the bars, depends on our awareness that the scene seems real precisely because it is a scrupulously ordered artistic composition. As we look down on the scene with Cincinnatus, we are taken into the magic of its presence by being made to see it as a painting. The foreground is defined, in a painterly repetition of form, as a duplication in outline with diminished scale—a huge tower on a fortress towering hugely on a cliff. The eye is then led down through the most careful arrangement of perspective along the winding road (formally duplicated further down in the serpentine line of the river), past the tiny human figure on the convex bridge and the indistinguishable speck which is "most likely a dog," on to the town itself and the bluish haze of the hills at the horizon. Effects of color and light are nicely balanced in painterly fashion and conveyed to us in a vocabulary that suggests the artist's nuanced choice of pigments and even something of the way he applies them to his canvas: we move from the "creamy" road to the red figure, then into the "sun-flooded" town with its "varicolored" houses, set off by the "hazy folds of the hills" in the distance and the "dark stipple" of the woods just below the hills. The vocabulary of color is not only precise in its distinctions but also designed to communicate a sense of the pleasure—an almost sensual delight in the opulence of beauty—that informs aesthetic experience: this is why the road is "creamy," the distant fountain an "amethystine shimmer" in the sunlight, the horizon an inviting vision of "dove-blue melting hills." Inevitably, there are reflecting surfaces in the picture, those ponds seen gleaming like hand mirrors in the park far below, the mirror here serving the rather simple function of illustrating the artist's exquisite ordering of effects of light and perspective in the scene. Finally, there is one detail in the landscape that goes beyond the decorum of painterly terms, the houses creeping down the slope, "stepping on their own shadows." The graphic personification, however, seems perfectly right because it suggests how a scene done with painstaking art begins to transcend the limits of its own medium, assuming an elusive life that is more than color and line, plane and texture.

Such passages offer ample evidence of Nabokov's virtuosity, but looking at them, as we have so far, out of context, we have not yet answered the question of what it is all for. These scenes actually stand in a relation of dialectic tension to the world of the novel in which they occur, and one clear indication of that is the artful placement of mirrors within them. Fyodor's father, we recall, uses mirrors in a negative sense, connecting them with death and irreality, but in *Invitation to a Beheading* there are good and bad uses of mirrors, just as there is good and bad art. Nabokov invokes a whole spectrum of traditional symbolic associations suggested by mirrors—the mirror of art held to nature; the mirror of consciousness "reflecting" reality (or does it only reflect itself, we are at least led to wonder; is Cincinnatus's prison merely a house of mirrors?); the mirror as a depthless, inverted, unreal, mocking imitation of the real world. The most striking development of the mirror idea in the novel is appropriately ambiguous, Nabokov's memorable parable of imagination and reality, the crazily rippled "*nonnon* mirrors" which, when set opposite complementarily shapeless lumps, reflect beautifully "real" forms, the two negatives making a positive. Is this a model for the alchemy that the imagination works on formless reality, or does it rather illustrate the kind of mountebank's trick that has come to serve as a manufactured substitute for art, a merely illusionistic amusement for the masses? The former alternative, in which one can see the distorted magical mirrors as an image of Nabokov's own art, is clearly the more attractive of the two, but the fact that the device of the *nonnons* is reported to us by Cincinnatus's mother, herself the tricky insubstantial creature of a dimensionless world, at any rate leaves a teasing residue of doubt in our minds.

Elsewhere in the novel, the contexts in which mirrors appear are more clearly negative. For the insidious M'sieur Pierre, they are the implements of a self-admiring, self-absorbed hedonism: "there is nothing more pleasant," he tells Cincinnatus, laying claim to a background of subtle sexual expertise, "than to surround oneself with mirrors and watch the good work going on there" (p. 145). For Marthe, Cincinnatus's inexhaustibly promiscuous wife, the mirror is the most patently fake stage-prop in her factitious world of theatrical (or rather farcical) deceptions: as part of the domestic scenery which she has temporarily moved into Cincinnatus's cell, "There came a mirrored wardrobe, bringing with it its own private reflection (namely, a corner of the connubial bedroom with a stripe of sunlight across the floor, a dropped glove, and an open door in the distance)" (p. 99). More ambiguously, Cincinnatus himself adopts the tricky role of the mirror as a stratagem of survival: a mirror is of course a transparent surface with an opaque backing, and Cincinnatus, an opaque figure in a world of mutually transparent souls, learns to "feign translucence, employing a complex system of optical illusions, as it were" (p. 24), that is, reflecting to those around him a fleeting simulacrum of translucence from the surface of his immutable opacity.

It is precisely the association of mirrors with both art and consciousness that justifies this range of ambiguities in their appearance in the novel. For while Cincinnatus dreams of, and at certain moments his creator pointedly exercises, a beautifully patterned art, the most essential quality of the world that imprisons him is cheap, false, meretricious, mechanical art. More succinctly, Nabokov's ideal model of the totalitarian state is, to invoke the embracing Russian term he explains so elaborately in his study of Gogol, a world of *poshlust*. The leering, inane faces of *poshlust* are everywhere in *Invitation to a Beheading,* but I will try briefly to review some of the most symptomatic instances. The act of murder by state decree is imagined by its perpetrators as a work of art. M'sieur Pierre fancies himself an *artiste,* carrying his headsman's ax in a velvet-lined case like a musical instrument. In his person and manner M'sieur Pierre is obviously the embodiment of quintessential *poshlust,* often with excruciating detail, as in the two illusionistic green leaves he has tattooed around his left nipple to make it seem "a rosebud . . . of marchpane and candied angelica" (p. 160). The eve of Cincinnatus's execution is marked by a grandiose ceremony that smacks of a crucifixion staged in Radio City Music Hall with a thousand dancing Rockettes. A million varicolored light bulbs are planted "artfully" (the narrator's word) in the grass to form a monogram of the initials of the headsman and his victim. The chief ingredients of this "art" are monstrous quantity and mechanical means; appropriately, the production is sloppily arranged and doesn't quite come off.

Bad art, in fact, is the ubiquitous instrument of torture for the imprisoned Cincinnatus. Thus, in a niche in the prison corridor, he sees what he imagines is a window through which he will be able to look down on the longed-for Tamara Gardens in the town below, but when he approaches, he discovers that it is a crude trompe l'oeil painting: "This landscape, daubed in several layers of distance, executed in blurry green hues and illuminated by concealed bulbs, was reminiscent . . . of the backdrop in front of which a wind orchestra toils and puffs" (p. 76). The colors are drab, the treetops stirless, the lighting torpid, in short the painting is in every respect the exact opposite of that artfully composed view of the town and the Gardens which Cincinnatus had enjoyed earlier from the prison tower.

The use of hidden light bulbs as part of an unconvincingly illusionistic effect is significant because the substitution of mechanical device for imagination is the key to most of the bad art in the novel. Thus, the art par excellence of this world of *poshlust* is photography. It is essential to the grand production on the eve of the beheading that Cincinnatus and his executioner be photographed together by flash-bulb light (predictably, with hideous results). At the beginning of the novel, the prisoner is brought the two local newspapers with two weirdly complementary color photographs of his house on the front page (and one should keep in mind, of course, the inevitably false, blurry, bleeding quality of color photographs reproduced on newsprint). One picture shows the facade of the house, with the photographer from the second paper peering out of Marthe's bedroom window. The other, taken from that window, shows the garden and gate with the first photographer shooting the facade of the house. The circularity of the two photographs is just the reverse of Nabokov's practice of introducing hints of his own presence as artificer into his fictions. Here each of the photographers is inadvertently caught by the other in the act of using his mechanical black box to snap the scene, and the tawdry nature of the whole procedure is emphasized by the clear hint of still another sexual betrayal by Marthe in the presence of the photographer in her bedroom (p. 23).

The culminating example of the mechanical art of photography as the instrument of *poshlust* is the "photohoroscope" devised by M'sieur Pierre. Using retouched snapshots of Emmie, the young daughter of the warden, placing her face in montage with photographs of older people in other circumstances, he offers a chronological record of a hypothetical woman's life, from childhood to old age and death (pp. 167-71). The simulation of a life is of course utterly unconvincing, and there is something vaguely obscene about this face of a little girl faked up as the face of a mature woman, then of an old lady. The photohoroscope is an ultimate achievement of anti-art, using purely mechanical means to produce a patently false contrivance, impotent to cope with the rich enigma of experience in time, blind to the dimension of consciousness, profaning the mystery of human life. The companion-piece to M'sieur Pierre's album is the novel *Quercus* that Cincinnatus takes out of the prison library. This three-thousand-page tome on the life of an oak tree, "considered to be the acme of modern thought," is Nabokov's *reductio ad absurdum* of the naturalistic novel and of the principle of exhaustive documentary realism:

It seemed as though the author were sitting with his camera somewhere among the topmost branches of the Quercus, spying out and catching his prey. Various images of life would come and go, pausing among the green macules of light. The normal periods of inaction were filled with scientific descriptions of the oak itself, from the viewpoints of dendrology, ornithology, coleopterology, mythology—or popular descriptions, with touches of folk humor. (p. 123)

Such photographic realism, in other words, is mindless, formless, pointless, infinitely tedious, devoid of humanity. It denies imagination, spontaneity, the shaping power of human consciousness; subverting everything art should be, it produces the perfect novel of a totalitarian world.

At this point seekers of high seriousness might be moved to object: a merely *aesthetic* critique of totalitarianism, an objection to it on the grounds of its bad taste? This novel does offer an aesthetic critique of the totalitarian idea, but it is not "merely" that because so much more than good taste is implied by art for Nabokov. As I shall now try to make clear, Nabokov's aesthetic in fact leads us back to a metaphysic, and one with ultimately moral implications. In his discussion of *poshlust* apropos of *Dead Souls,* Nabokov remarks parenthetically that it is a quality "which yawns universally at times of revolution or war." [5] I am tempted to see a Popean pun in "yawns," like the great apocalyptic pun near the end of the *Dunciad* in which Dulness yawns—both announcing the soporific reign of universal tedium and threatening to engulf civilization. In any case, the world of Pope's *Dunciad* offers a suggestive analogy to that of *Invitation to a Beheading,* being a hilarious yet ominous farce that represents a general breakdown of humanistic values, where the intellect is put to such widespread perverted use that art and thinking become impossible. What needs emphasis, however, is that Nabokov notes the prevalence of *poshlust* under conditions of political absolutism not merely because it is an observable and offensive aspect of revolutionary and militant regimes— from Stalinist statuary to Mussolinian murals—but because he recognizes in it an indispensable principle of such regimes, a necessary expression of their inner nature.

If we look across from literature to the evidence of history, the gratuitous gestures of the totalitarian state may provide us a clue precisely because they are made out of inner necessity, not from the need to achieve practical ends. Thus, it was the compulsion of their moving spirit, not real utility, which led the Nazis to welcome their unspeakable trainloads of doomed human cattle with brass bands at the railroad sidings blaring cheery patriotic songs. This is totalitarian *poshlust* in the purest form

55

of its moral and aesthetic obscenity; it takes little effort to imagine M'sieur Pierre waving the baton for such a grisly band, a vaguely beery smile playing over his lips. *Poshlust* is indispensable to totalitarianism because it is the natural expression of a deadened consciousness persuaded it is devoted to lofty ends, and at the same time it is the means of foisting sham values, anesthetizing still human imaginations until they are incapable of making sane distinctions: ugly becomes beautiful, death becomes life, and over the portals of a man-made hell one affixes an ostensibly noble sentiment like *Arbeit macht frei*. "Sentimentality," Norman Mailer has written, "is the emotional promiscuity of those who have no sentiment"; this is why it is in a hideously trashy sentimentalism that the totalitarian spirit comes to full, festering florescence.

There is one passage in *Invitation to a Beheading* that finely illuminates this whole question of the essential, inexorable antagonism between totalitarianism and authentic art. It provides an especially forceful example of how art for Nabokov is inevitably connected with a larger vision of man because here he also deals with the limits of art. We are observing Cincinnatus in his cell once more, though from whose viewpoint we are not informed until the sudden, unsettling turn near the end of the paragraph. Again we are given a portrait composed of precisely selected details—the texture of his skin and hair, the state of his clothing, the movement of his eyes—with abundant indications that these are the details of a carefully executed painting. All these minute particulars, we are told, "completed a picture" that was made up

of a thousand barely noticeable, overlapping trifles: of the light outline of his lips, seemingly not quite fully drawn but touched by a master of masters; of the fluttering movements of his empty, not-yet-shaded-in hands; of the dispersing and again gathering rays in his animated eyes; but even all of this, analyzed and studied, still could not fully explain Cincinnatus: it was as if one side of his being slid into another dimension, as all the complexity of a tree's foliage passes from shade into radiance, so that you cannot distinguish just where begins the submergence into the shimmer of a different element. It seemed as though at any moment, in the course of his movements about the limited space of the haphazardly invented cell, Cincinnatus would step in such a way as to slip naturally and effortlessly through some chink of the air into its unknown coulisses to disappear there with the same easy smoothness with which the reflection of a rotated mirror moves across every object in the room and suddenly vanishes, as if beyond the air, in some new depth of ether. At the same time, everything about him breathed with a delicate, drowsy, but in reality exceptionally strong, ardent and independent life: his veins of the bluest blue pulsated; crystal-clear saliva moistened his lips; the skin quivered on his cheeks and his forehead, which was edged with dissolved light . . . and all this so teased the observer as to make him long to tear apart, cut to shreds, destroy utterly this brazen elusive flesh, and all that it implied and expressed, all that impossible, dazzling freedom—enough, enough—do not walk any more, Cincinnatus, lie down on your cot, so you will not arouse, will not irritate . . . And in truth Cincinnatus would become aware of the predatory eye in the peephole following him and lie down or sit at the table and open a book. (pp. 121-22)

The opposing attitudes toward human life of the artist and the totalitarian are beautifully dramatized in the contrasted responses to ultimate frustration of the painter's eye at the beginning of the passage and the jailer's eye at the end. Elsewhere in the novel, we have seen how the cunning artist celebrates the power of art to fix reality in arresting pattern; here, however, the narrator confesses the final impotence-in-power of art before the stubborn mystery of an individual human life. In other passages, we noted the use of mirrors as reflecting and perspectivistic devices which demonstrated the magisterial control of the artist over his materials; here, by contrast, there is no actual mirror in the scene: instead, the mirror is introduced as a simile, a fragment of visual experience used figuratively with paradoxical effectiveness to define the limits of visual representation. Partial readings of Nabokov's novels have sometimes led to the inference that the world they portray is fundamentally a world of aesthetic solipsism, but this passage makes clear that it is life rather than art alone that is inexhaustible, and that art's ability to renew itself, to be infinitely various and captivating, finally depends upon its necessary inadequacy in the face of the inexhaustible enigma of conscious life. The artist's human subject here glimmers, shimmers, slides into a hidden dimension beyond visualization, but the very frustration of the artist's purpose brings him back to his subject with a sense of loving wonder—all that ardent, independent life pulsing through the bluest of blue veins —the inevitability of partial failure spurring him to attempt again and again the impossible magic of comprehending life in art.

With the transition indicated in the text of the novel by the first set of suspension points, the eye at the keyhole changes from the artist-observer's to the jailer's, and immediately the radical elusiveness of the prisoner becomes an infuriating taunt, an outrageous provocation to mayhem. For the artistic consciousness, the two essential activities are wonder and delight; for the totalitarian mentality, the one essential activity is control, manipulation—and therefore mysteries are intolerable, all souls must be "transparent" like the moving parts in a display-motor encased in clear plastic, so that they can at all times be completely accessible to control. Worse than opaque, Cincinnatus is seen here in defiant iridescence, continuing to exercise the inner freedom that his jailers have long since renounced because it was too dizzying, too difficult, interfered in too many complicated ways with the simple, stupefying gratifications of mutual manipulation. One can see why all "freaks," all who are different, must be tortured in this world, and why it is an essential quality of the perfected world of art là-bas to leave such creatures wholly unmolested.

The peculiarly generalized nature of Cincinnatus as a character serves the purpose of making him function in the novel as an embodiment of the generic possibilities of human freedom. Although this is a novel about art, it is not, in the conventional sense, a literary portrait of the artist because the artist here is conceived as an everyman, a paradigm of that life of consciousness which is common, at least in potential, to all human beings. Cincinnatus in his cell determines to become a writer not because there is a streak of the aesthete in him but because, finding himself a creature with consciousness in an existence that offers nothing to explain that incredible fact, he envisages art as the fullest, most human response to his own human condition. In the passage we have been considering, Nabokov offers us an external view of the mystery of individual life. Elsewhere, in the pages quoted from Cincinnatus's journal, we get an eloquent statement of that same mystery felt from within. The prisoner contemplates himself issuing from unknowable burning blackness, spinning like a top, headed he knows not where, and he wants desperately to be able to capture in words that crazy, tormenting, somehow stirring condition. "I have no desires, save the desire to express myself—in defiance of all the world's muteness. How frightened I am. How sick with fright. But no one shall take me away from myself" (p. 91). The perspective of *Invitation to a Beheading* is, I think, finally political in Aristotle's sense of the term, not Machiavelli's: by emphasizing an an elaborately self-conscious art both as its medium and its moral model, the novel affirms the tough persistence of humanity in a world that is progressively more brutal and more subtle in its attempts to take us away from ourselves.

Notes

1. Simon Karlinsky, "Illusion, Reality, and Parody in Nabokov's Plays," *Wisconsin Studies in Contemporary Literature,* VIII, 2 (Spring 1967), p. 268.

2. Vladimir Nabokov, *Invitation to a Beheading,* tr. by Dimitri Nabokov in collaboration with the author (New York, 1959), p. 12. Subsequent references in the text are to this edition.

3. Vladimir Nabokov, *The Gift,* tr. Dimitri Nabokov (New York, 1963), p. 215.

4. Julian Moynahan, "A Russian Preface for Nabokov's *Beheading*," *Novel,* I, 1 (Fall 1967), p. 16.

5. Vladimir Nabokov, *Nikolai Gogol* (Norfolk, Conn., 1944), p. 65.

The Handle:
Invitation to a Beheading and *Bend Sinister*

STANLEY EDGAR HYMAN

In his Foreword to the English translation of *Invitation to a Beheading* in 1959, Vladimir Nabokov writes: "No doubt, there do exist certain stylistic links between this book and, say, my earlier stories (or my later *Bend Sinister*)." Precisely what he meant by stylistic links is puzzling, since the books are radically different in style, at least in English, but, as many have noticed, they do have a theme in common, what we might call the vulgarity of power, and they make a fascinating study in conjunction.

Invitation to a Beheading was written in Russian in Berlin in 1934 and 1935, and published in Paris in 1938 as *Priglashenie na kazn'*. It is the story of Cincinnatus C., who is sentenced to beheading for "gnostical turpitude" by a comic-opera totalitarian state on the first page, and beheaded on the next to last page, after spending the intervening time in a prison that is at once horribly funny and horrible.

Cincinnatus is the weakest and most fragile of heroes, and the author properly calls him "My poor little Cincinnatus." When he hears the sentence, Nabokov writes:

He was calm; however, he had to be supported during the journey through the long corridor, since he planted his feet unsteadily, like a child who has just learned to walk, or as if he were about to fall through like a man who has dreamt that he is walking on water only to have a sudden doubt: but is this possible?

Cincinnatus is "light as a leaf," and so small that his wife Marthe "used to say that his shoes were too tight for her." He is illegitimate, never having known his father and scarcely knowing his mother. Cincinnatus is brave in fantasy—at one point his imaginary double steps on the jailer's face—but in reality he is a coward, dying "anew every morning" as he awaits his execution. He cries in his cell; when he is finally led to his execution his hands tremble uncontrollably, and he feels "only one thing—fear, fear, shameful, futile fear." His marriage with Marthe consisted of her tireless cuckolding of him, telling him about it "in a soft cooing voice" each time, and neither of her awful children is his. Finally, he is wishfully gullible: when his lawyer brings him a petition to obtain printed copies of the speeches made at his trial, and Cincinnatus bravely tears it up, the lawyer has only to suggest that the envelope may have contained a pardon, and Cincinnatus is down on the floor, trying to put together the scraps.

Yet with all these physical and moral weaknesses, Cincinnatus has certain strengths. When he is shorn of all other resources, like Ransom's Captain Carpenter, he still has his valiant tongue. Cincinnatus tells his jailers: "I obey you, specters, werewolves, parodies"; he announces to the prison director: "I thank you, rag doll, coachman, painted swine"; he curtly dismisses a monologue by M'sieur Pierre, his fellow inmate who turns out to be the headsman, as "Dreary, obtrusive nonsense." Beyond that, he has two further strengths: he feels "a fierce longing for freedom, the most ordinary, physical, physically feasible kind of freedom"; and he accepts the solitary human condition, so that during all the stages of the execution, Cincinnatus keeps affirming: "By myself, by myself."

The prison and the prison experience are fantastic, phantasmagoric. At one point Cincinnatus moves a table in his cell and stands on a chair on it in order to look out the window; at another point he discovers that the table has been bolted to the floor "for ages," and could never have been moved. Later the cell bulges and floods, Cincinnatus's cot becomes a boat, and he falls into the water and would have drowned except that he is fished out. Throughout the jail experience, the prison director, the doctor, the jailer, and Cincinnatus's lawyer keep turning into each other. At one point, when M'sieur Pierre is doing acrobatic tricks, the cell turns into a circus, and the prison director becomes the ringmaster. Increasingly, everything turns into a theatrical production. "A summer thunderstorm, simply and tastefully staged, was performed outside." When Cincinnatus's mother visits him, he charges that she is "a clever parody of a mother," notes that her raincoat is wet although her shoes are dry, and adds, "Tell the prop man for me." When Emmie, the prison director's young daughter, visits Cincinnatus in his cell, she whispers moistly into his ear, then flies off on a trapeze, leaving his ear wet and singing. The cell spider that has been his companion turns out to be spurious, made of plush with spring legs, and the jailer had built its web for it.

As Cincinnatus leaves the prison for his execution, it disintegrates: first his cell disappears as he leaves it, then other cells crumble, next the whole fortress starts to come apart. The same clouds go by over and over again, clearly a stage setting. There is "something wrong with the sun, and a section of the sky was shaking," behind the first rows, the crowds at the execution are painted on the backdrop, and the poplars around the square

topple one by one. By the book's last paragraph, it has all
disintegrated:

Little was left of the square. The platform had long since collapsed
in a cloud of reddish dust. The last to rush past was a woman in a
black shawl, carrying the tiny executioner like a larva in her arms. The
fallen trees lay flat and reliefless, while those that were still standing,
also two-dimensional, with a lateral shading of the trunk to suggest
roundness, barely held on with their branches to the ripping mesh of
the sky. Everything was coming apart. Everything was falling. A spinning
wind was picking up and whirling: dust, rags, chips of painted wood, bits
of gilded plaster, pasteboard bricks, posters, an arid gloom fleeted.

The microcosm of this macrocosmic unreality is a series of
cruelly funny sadistic tricks played on Cincinnatus while he is
in jail. Early in the novel Cincinnatus finds everything un-
guarded and walks out of the jail. He walks through the town,
gets to his house, runs up the stairs to his apartment, opens the
door and finds himself back in his cell. The prison director
promises him a visit from his wife and family and, as Cincinnatus
quivers with joy and anticipation, ushers in M'sieur Pierre instead
In the cruelest of all the tricks, Cincinnatus hears another prisoner
tunneling to him, he taps rhythmically to communicate with the
tunneler, makes sounds to mask the sounds of digging from the
guards—finally the tunnel breaks through into the wall of his
cell, and M'sieur Pierre and the prison director climb out of the
hole, shaking "with unrestrained laughter, with all the transitions
from guffaw to chuckle and back again, with piteous squeals in
the intervals between outbursts, all the while nudging each other,
falling over each other." Cincinnatus's reaction to this kindly
practical joke is "such terrible unmitigated dejection that . . .
he would have lain down and died then and there." Later he
escapes again and gets out on the hillside below the fortress,
where he meets Emmie, who had promised to help him to freedom and promptly leads him to her father's apartment, where
the prison director and M'sieur Pierre are having tea. Just before the execution, Cincinnatus makes a list of all the things
that have tricked him:

"Everything has fallen into place," he wrote, "that is, everything has duped me—all of this theatrical, pathetic stuff—the promises of a volatile maiden, a mother's moist gaze, the knocking on the wall, a neighbor's friendliness, and, finally, those hills which broke out in a deadly rash."

But Cincinnatus has one ultimate strength, which foreshadows his final triumph: his absolute isolation. He writes:

. . . in the end the logical thing would be to give up and I would give up if I were laboring for a reader existing today, but as there is in the world not a single human who can speak my language; or, more simply, not a single human; I must think only of myself, of that force which urges me to express myself.

At the end, after he is beheaded, he stands up and walks away, as a tiny figure who is both his lawyer and the prison director reproaches him; then, "amidst the dust, and the falling things, and the flapping scenery, Cincinnatus made his way in that direction where, to judge by the voices, stood beings akin to him."

Bend Sinister was written in English and first published in the United States in 1947. It tells the story of Adam Krug, distinguished philosopher and professor in an unnamed small Slavic country, who refuses his assent to the new dictator, who was his schoolfellow, and the increasing pressures that are brought on Krug until he is finally delivered by madness and death. The title is mysterious. "Bend Sinister" is a turn to the left (in *The Real Life of Sebastian Knight,* the narrator speaks of "following the bends of his life"); it is the mark of a bastard in heraldry, and it has the dangerous suggestions of the English "sinister." I think I have some idea what the title means, but I will postpone discussion of it until later.

Krug is as visibly strong as Cincinnatus is visibly weak. He is an enormous man, confident and self-assured. When the President of his university presents a petition of support for the dictator to his faculty, only Krug refuses to sign, remarking disdainfully: "Legal documents excepted, and not all of them at that, I have never signed, nor ever shall sign, anything not written by myself." When the dictator, Paduk, whose schoolboy name was "the Toad," has Krug in for an interview, and asks rhetorically why he wanted to see Krug, Krug replies: "Because I am the only person who can stand on the other end of the seesaw and make your end rise." When he is finally brought to agree to sign a statement of support in hopes of saving his young son, the news of his son's death frees the old Krug, and he tears up the papers and tries to strangle the nearest clerk. Krug is further strengthened by his international fame: he is the only celebrity that his country has produced in modern times. He has a number of loyal and incorruptible friends, one described as "as reliable as iron and oak." He is devoted to the ideal of freedom and collects inanities of the dictatorship for the "delight of free humorists" of the future. He has an exceptionally powerful brain, an unusual virility, and is so much a man of action that he not only tries to strangle the clerk, but earlier punches a government official in the mouth. Most of all, he is deeply loving, devoted to his wife, who dies early in the book following an unsuccessful kidney operation, and to his young son David.

Many of Krug's strengths turn out to be weaknesses in the morally inverted world of the dictatorship. His intellectual pride, which leads him to regard most people as "imbeciles," makes him unable to take the dictator and his popular support seriously. The philosophical complexity of his mind leads him to hesitate and delay, so that he does not escape the country when he could. His powerful imagination leads him to picture David endlessly tortured and suffering. His loyal friends are ways that pressure can be put on him, and his consuming love for David, now that his wife is dead, is his ultimate vulnerability: "And what agony, thought Krug the thinker, to love so madly a little creature."

Bend Sinister has some of the shoddy institutional trickery of *Invitation to a Beheading*. When Ember, the first of Krug's friends to be arrested to put pressure on Krug, is seized, it is not by uniformed security police with carbines, but by "A handsome lady in a dove-gray tailor-made suit and a gentleman with a glossy red tulip in the buttonhole of his cutaway coat." The gentleman explains to Krug: "But headquarters knew that Mr.

Ember was an artist, a poet, a sensitive soul, and it was thought that something a little dainty and uncommon in the way of arrests, an atmosphere of high life, flowers, the perfume of feminine beauty, might sweeten the ordeal." As M'sieur Pierre does card tricks and gymnastics, and tries to coax Cincinnatus into endless games, so Krug finds in the dictator's waiting room "various games of skill." Paduk has in fact turned the country's public ceremonials into reproductions of his school life.

A denial of reality comparable to that of *Invitation to a Beheading* runs through *Bend Sinister*. Describing Paduk, the author interrupts to say: "It is not a difficult part but still the actor must be careful not to overdo what Graaf somewhere calls 'villainous deliberation.'" As for Krug, receiving his prepared speech from Paduk: "The actor playing the recipient should be taught not to look at his hand while he takes the papers *very slowly* (keeping those lateral jaw muscles in movement, please) but to stare straight at the giver: in short, look at the giver first, *then* lower your eyes to the gift." At one point, when Krug gets home and goes into the bathroom, he finds Mariette, the maid who is a police spy and has been trying to seduce him, standing naked in the tub soaping herself. He then orders dinner from a caterer, and "She was still in the bathroom when the man from the Angliskii Club brought a meat pie, a rice pudding, and her adolescent buttocks." In Krug's notes for philosophical articles, there is "the instantaneous disintegration of stone and ivy composing the circular dungeon," as at the end of *Invitation to a Beheading,* but here it is either a metaphor for death as the instantaneous gaining of perfect knowledge or for death as absolute nothingness.

The author is obtrusive in *Invitation to a Beheading,* calling his hero "My poor little Cincinnatus" and such, but in *Bend Sinister* he is a godlike chess player who controls all the pieces on both sides. Krug has the selective mishearing of the preoccupied: when the President of the university makes a speech and says, "when an animal has lost his feet in the aging ocean," Krug is mishearing "when an admiral has lost his fleet in the raging ocean"; when Krug reads in the speech written for him that "the State has created central organs for providing the country with all the most important products which are to be distributed at fixed prices in a playful manner," he then realizes it is a "planful" manner and corrects himself. But perhaps the original versions were right: the animal who lost his feet, or at least his toes, is Lear's Pobble, whose Aunt Jobiska could have saved Krug from a lot of his difficulty, and a "playful manner" is exactly the way the never-grown-up schoolboy Paduk would distribute goods.

The book begins with Krug seeing a curious oblong puddle on the asphalt, and ends with the author seeing it, observing that Krug had somehow perceived it earlier, and translating it into a symbol of the imprint left by a human life. Krug recalls his dead wife, as a young girl, carrying a hawk moth into the house to show her aunt, and in his vision he directs and redirects the scene. Later, Peter Quist, a police agent who is pretending to help Krug flee the country, shows him a beautiful plate of a hawk moth. At the book's end, as Krug dies, shot by the dictator's gunmen, the author hears a hawk moth, perhaps Krug's soul, strike the netting of his window. The last words of the book are: "Twang. A good night for mothing." Earlier, when Krug's son David is seized, Krug threatens "All six of you, all six will be tortured and shot if my child gets hurt." It is the emptiest of threats, with no authority behind it but the force of rhetoric, but it has the power of fate and doom: when David is killed, all six of them are precisely tortured and shot. Finally, the author explains his direct intervention in the story as a Greek *deus ex machina*. David is dead and Krug is locked in jail, awakening from a dream. The narrator writes:

It was at that moment, just after Krug had fallen through the bottom of a confused dream and sat up on the straw with a gasp—and just before his reality, his remembered hideous misfortune could pounce upon him— it was then that I felt a pang of pity for Adam and slid towards him along an inclined beam of pale light—causing instantaneous madness, but at least saving him from the senseless agony of his logical fate.

It is thus mad that Krug attacks Paduk (heroically, insanely?) and is gunned down.

Cincinnatus and Krug, in short, have different sorts of commitment to the world. Their families are a case in point. Cincinnatus, who has no family of his own other than the mother he has seen once or twice in his life, is finally visited by Marthe's family in his cell. They arrive with all their furniture and set up domestic life there: Marthe's maternal grandfather, so old that he is transparent, exhibits a portrait of his mother as a young woman, in turn holding a portrait; Marthe's father curses Cincinnatus "in detail and with relish"; one of Marthe's brothers wears a crepe arm band and makes up word games to remind Cincinnatus of his coming fate; Marthe is accompanied by a young suitor perfumed with violet scent; Cincinnatus's subnormal non-daughter Pauline hides, and his lame non-son Diomedon strangles the cat. In contrast to this disgusting family, to whom one could feel no attachment, Krug's wife was a paragon of gaiety and charm (she once hung a Chardin in his study "to ozonize your dreadful lair") and his son is all that anyone could want in a son.

This contrast comes through most clearly in parallel images of disintegration in the book. On one occasion in his cell Cincinnatus starts to undress and comes apart:

He stood up and took off the dressing gown, the skullcap, the slippers. He took off the linen trousers and shirt. He took off his head like a toupee, took off his collarbones like shoulder straps, took off his rib cage like a hauberk. He took off his hips and his legs, he took off his arms like gauntlets and threw them in a corner. What was left of him gradually dissolved, hardly coloring the air. At first Cincinnatus simply reveled in the coolness; then, fully immersed in his secret medium, he began freely and happily to . . . The iron thunderclap of the bolt resounded, and Cincinnatus instantly grew all that he had cast off, the skullcap included.

When Krug has a comparable fantasy it is not free and joyous but a horrible nightmare about his late wife:

Olga was revealed sitting before her mirror and taking off her jewels after the ball. Still clad in cherry-red velvet, her strong gleaming elbows thrown back and lifted like wings, she had begun to unclasp at the back of her neck her dazzling dog collar. He knew it would come off together with her vertebrae—that in fact it was the crystal of her vertebrae —and he experienced an agonizing sense of impropriety at the thought that everybody in the room would observe and take down in writing her inevitable, pitiful, innocent disintegration. There was a flash, a click: with both hands she removed her beautiful head and, not looking at it, carefully, carefully, dear, smiling a dim smile of amused recollection (who could have guessed at the dance that the real jewels were pawned?), she placed the beautiful imitation upon the marble ledge of her toilet table. Then he knew that all the rest would come off too, the rings together with the fingers, the bronze slippers with the toes, the breasts with the lace that cupped them . . . his pity and shame reached their climax, and at the ultimate gesture of the tall cold strip-teaser, prowling pumalike up and down the stage, with a horrible qualm Krug awoke.

The difference, in a word, is that Cincinnatus is free because he has no hostages to fortune, and Krug, at least until David is murdered, is the prisoner of his ties to others. "Will no one save me?" Cincinnatus suddenly cries out in his cell, "opening his pauper's hands, showing that he had nothing." Since no one *will* save him, he can blithely save himself. In all his time in jail he receives only two gifts: his mother brings him a pound of candy to suck, which he ignores, and Marthe brings him a bunch of cornflowers, which she refers to as poppies. Krug, however, has real human ties: deep down inside him "a dead wife and a sleeping child," and his loyal friends who risk (and lose) their lives for him. But the key to his vulnerability is David. Near the end of his interview with Paduk, the dictator says: "All we want of you is that little part where the handle is." "There is none," Krug answers firmly, "and hit the side of the table with his fist." When the police agent Quist discovers that Krug will not leave the country without David, he realizes that *David* is the handle, and knows that the discovery will result in his promotion. "They have found the handle," the author comments when the police seize David, and in truth Krug is soon in the prison office, offering to "speak, sign, swear—anything the Government wants. But I will do all this, and more, only if my child is brought here, to this room, at once."

What the title finally means, I think, after all its obvious meanings, is the curve of that handle. "Krug" in German means some sort of liquid measure or tankard (it means "circle" in Russian), and at first it is brimming with blessings, but the bend of the handle is its dangerous vulnerability.

Beyond that, Krug is of the world, committed to its things and values, whereas Cincinnatus is in it but not of it. Cincinnatus's trade is that of a doll-maker, and the unreality (or other-reality) of his work is a further source of strength. "I am an expert in dolls," he says to M'sieur Pierre at one point, "I shall not yield." But Krug's professorship anchors him firmly to this world, in that his work relates him to real people: students, colleagues, readers. Even the tiny details of their torments by the state contrast: in his cell Cincinnatus is served toast "with tortoiseshell burns," giving the simple food a kind of elegance. But when Krug looks at a railroad track and pictures escape, here is his vision: "On some bricks nearby the mournful detective assigned to his house and an organ-grinder of sorts sat playing *chemin de fer;* a soiled nine of spades lay on the ashstrewn ground at their feet, and, with a pang of impatient desire, he visualized a railway platform and glanced at a playing card and bits of orange peel enlivening the coal dust between the rails under a Pullman car which was still waiting for him."

In his Foreword to the English translation of *Invitation to a Beheading,* Nabokov says that the book may have been effected by his seeing both the Bolshevist and the Nazi regimes "in terms of one dull beastly farce." Neither book is farce, but there are scenes in both that fit the "dull beastly" description very well. In *Invitation to a Beheading,* M'sieur Pierre's monologue on sex while he plays his atrocious chess with Cincinnatus, and the final public banquet for Cincinnatus on the night before his execution, where the town park is lighted by a million bulbs producing a grandiose monogram of the entwined initials of Pierre and

Cincinnatus, have the proper quality; in *Bend Sinister,* they are matched by a scene in which Paduk the Toad, disguised as Mad Tom, appears at night in Krug's cell in a final effort to break him down, or by David's disgusting death, torn to pieces by hoodlums as part of a state project for their rehabilitation.

The last word on both books comes from, of all people, Cincinnatus's quasi-mother. On her visit to his cell, she inexplicably tries to explain some toys of her childhood, consisting of a "crazy mirror" and a collection of shapeless, distorted, and disgusting objects. The mirror distorted ordinary objects, but when the distorted *"nonnons"* were seen in it they "became in the mirror a wonderful, sensible, image; flowers, a ship, a person, a landscape." The world of dictatorship, of vulgar power and dull beastly farce, is those misshapen *"nonnons,"* but in the crazy mirror of Nabokov's art—and the mirror has been the most obsessive motif in his work from first to last—it takes on the shapeliness of art. Nabokov believes (or believed in the 1930's and 1940's) that in a world of tyranny, one is strongest if he has no hostages to fortune, if he neither loves nor is loved. Beyond that he is (or was) deeply Gnostic, insisting that one must be in the world but not of it. But then it is probably absurd to draw morals from his books. As the narrator says at the conclusion of *The Real Life of Sebastian Knight,* "the old conjuror waits in the wings with his hidden rabbit," and Nabokov's next rabbit may squeak, "Commitment, commitment." Vladimir Nabokov is our greatest living writer, and if he has written, in the conjunction of *Invitation to a Beheading* and *Bend Sinister,* a fable about the vulnerability of having a handle, he himself seems to have no handle at all, not even a ghostly lapel by which we could seize hold of him for a moment.

Laughter in the Dark: dimensions of parody

DABNEY STUART

I. The novel as motion picture

The structure of almost all of Vladimir Nabokov's works of fiction (the *possible* exception is *The Eye*) is dependent on their author's use of modes of artistic perception not usually associated with the form we traditionally label "the novel." *Invitation to a Beheading,* for instance, is structured according to the formal attributes of a stage-play; *The Gift* responds structurally to the demands of both a book of literary history and a biography, the latter of which also informs *Pnin*. Sometimes the form of a particular kind of "novel" is employed for purposes other than, and beyond, those for which it is normally intended: in *The Real Life of Sebastian Knight* the detective story is used as, to quote Knight, "a springboard to higher regions of emotion." [1] The effect—and,

I would guess, because of the consistency with which Nabokov employs the technique, the intention—of this is, broadly speaking, twofold: continually to remind the reader, through the form of the book that he is reading, that he is reading a book, and to embed in the form of the book itself the possibilities of parody that are more immediately obvious in particular details, character gestures, and diction. In terms of the conception of fiction as a literary mode, the major implication of the use of this technique to produce these effects is that one can see fiction as nothing else, by its very nature, but parody, regardless of how intensely the writer seems to be concerned with verisimilitude. Thus, from this perspective, a work—say *Germinal,* or *Sister Carrie,* for instance —of the most obvious "naturalistic" intentions is no less a parody than *Lolita,* a parody, of course, of the life it tries to reproduce. One implication (among others) that I find central to Nabokov's fiction is that, since any fiction is a parody of life, the best fiction, or the fiction that is most consciously itself, is the fiction that acknowledges as completely as it can be made to do its own parodic nature. To put this in terms which have traditionally riddled reviews of and commentaries on fiction, particularly novels, the last thing a writer should try to do is bamboozle his readers into "identifying with," or "sympathizing with," his characters. The object, on the contrary, is to keep the reader at a substantial distance from not only the characters but the book in which they appear, to put him as much as possible in the place of the author, to give him a sense of participating in the game of composition, to remind him, in short, of the nature of the experience he is involved in; that is, reading, confronting an imaginative creation that has its own principles of reality that do not ask to be viewed from the same perspective one views other aspects of his life.[2] It may be, in fact, that one result of reading Nabokov's books is to force the reader into considering other aspects of his life from the perspective the novel seeks to create; it may also be that this possibility is part of the cause of what seems to be a widespread resistance to his work. As he has said, "There are people whom parody upsets." [3]

Whatever the theoretical directions one tries to follow, the fact of the technique seems to me unarguable. And the most frequent mode of artistic perception Nabokov employs by means of which to structure his "novels" is the motion picture; [4] it shows up in *King, Queen, Knave* and *Lolita* particularly, but in both those books it coexists with other modes. The novel whose structure, and meaning, depends most pervasively on the motion picture as a form through which the experience of the book is to be perceived and evaluated is *Laughter in the Dark,* which I would like to discuss in some detail.

Even a casual reading of *Laughter in the Dark* reveals that motion pictures play a central part in the novel, at least as far as the characters themselves are interested in them. Margot Peters dreams from her adolescence in her family's squalid tenement of becoming a film star; after she has set up shop on her own she tries, on the strength of bravura alone, to make connections with a producer. She meets Albinus while she is working as an usher in a movie house, and once she has hooked him she persuades him to finance a picture in which she has the second female lead, a picture which is produced and the reader views in chapter 23. Moreover, Axel Rex has spent some of his devious artistic energy making cartoons, and it is he whom Albinus requests to consider helping to animate certain paintings by old masters. In fact, the novel opens with this idea: "It had to do with colored animated drawings . . . How fascinating it would be, he [Albinus] thought, if one could use this method for having some well-known picture . . . perfectly reproduced on the screen in vivid colors and then brought to life—movement and gesture graphically developed in complete harmony with their static state in the picture . . . little by little bringing the figures and the light into the [original] order, settling them down, so to speak, and ending it all with the first picture." [5] Albinus broaches the idea to Rex, but apparently, as the novel progresses, drops it and has to settle for his part in the production of the miserable film in which Margot has a role.

This surface concern is so presented, however, that very soon one becomes aware that much more is at stake, that Albinus' idea, Rex's possible collaboration in its fulfillment, and Margot's having a part in a movie are all determining factors in a pattern that involves their total experience with each other, not just their superficial interest in the cinema.

That the mode of the telling of the story is more important than the salient events of the story is focused in the first two paragraphs of chapter one.

Once upon a time there lived in Berlin, Germany, a man called Albinus. He was rich, respectable, happy; one day he abandoned his wife for the sake of a youthful mistress; he loved; was not loved; and his life ended in disaster.

This is the whole of the story and we might have left it at that had there not been profit and pleasure in the telling; and although there is plenty of space on a gravestone to contain, bound in moss, the abridged version of a man's life, detail is always welcome.

The next five paragraphs (through page 11) are given to the development of Albinus' idea of the animation of paintings by old masters, thus keying the form in which "welcome detail" is to be presented; it will be animated still-life, or motion picture, and the paragraph in which Albinus seems to relinquish his idea is intended rather to signal the transmutation of that idea into the structural principle on which the rest of the novel depends.

Upon a certain day in March Albinus got a long letter from him [Axel Rex, who is interested in helping Albinus], but *its arrival coincided with a sudden crisis in Albinus' private—very private—life,* so that the beautiful idea, which otherwise would have lingered on and perhaps found a wall on which to cling and blossom, had strangely faded and shriveled in the course of the last week. (11, italics mine)

The "sudden crisis" is, of course, Albinus' having met (or more accurately, seen and been impressed by) Margot Peters, who happened to be the usher on duty in a movie house to which he had gone to pass an hour before a business appointment. That the letter from Rex expressing interest in Albinus' nascent project coincides with Albinus' first visions of Margot deepens the "crisis"; Rex will perform the function of animator, though not in the way Albinus initially desired. Rex has, in fact, written in his letter that he would accept "a fee of so much (a startling sum) . . . for designing say a Breughel film—the 'Proverbs' for instance, or anything else Albinus might like to have him set in motion" (11). The metaphor of motion begins to become resonant at the end of the chapter; Albinus thinks:

"What the devil do I care for this fellow Rex, this idiotic conversation, this chocolate cream . . . ? I'm going mad and nobody knows it. And _I can't stop,_ it's hopeless trying, and tomorrow I'll go there [to the movie house] again and sit like a fool in that darkness." (13, italics mine)

Already Nabokov has begun to suggest the moral implications of the use of the motion picture as the mode through which the novel is to be perceived: it has to do with madness and the way in which an irresponsible desire can turn on the person who entertains it, finally controlling him as though he were indeed no more than an actor in a film whose role, as it were, plays him. And the chapter closes with Albinus' thinking in the most traditional melodramatic terms about the possible conclusion of the enmeshings of a love triangle: "No, you can't take a pistol and plug a girl you don't even know, simply because she attracts you" (13). The foreshadowing of the novel's conclusion is obvious.

The second chapter is equally suggestive. It is basically concerned with the contrast between the nature of Albinus' marriage and his desire for some other liaison. All the details given about his relationship with his wife, Elisabeth, are of a piece, suggesting, essentially, inertness. Albinus has a "slowish mind," he speaks with a "very slight hesitation"; his former affairs (before his marriage) have been "tedious," "of the heavyweight variety," involving women who were "cold" and "dreary." The summary adjective in the description is "feeble," and those girls of whom he has dreamed but has not known have "just slid past him." The woman he finally marries is pale and delicate, "a clinging little soul, docile and gentle," whose love, with rare exceptions, is "of the lily variety." If one combines with this focus on sluggishness, inertia, and docility the name "Albinus," one begins to take seriously the notion that before his meeting with Margot, his idea about animation, and his correspondence with Rex, Albinus has been living a still life.

The other aspect of the polarity chapter two presents is Albinus' desire for something else, and this desire is focused on his brief visit to the movie house, where he first sees Margot. (The pivot on which the two aspects of chapter two turn is the birth of Albinus' daughter, Irma.)[6] Again the description Nabokov employs is important. There is motion within the cinema as well as on the screen. Margot is dressed in black (no lily), and she is, suggestively, his guide. It is in this chapter that the motion picture in which the characters in the novel act their roles can be said to begin. There is the location of Albinus' meeting with Margot in the movie house, the bringing together of the black and white (Albinus himself as well as the nature of his life up to this point, and the black usher leading him to his seat in the darkness) as though a negative has been created, and the introduction of motion into Albinus' life. But what is crucial are the two brief snippets from the movie Albinus watches after he sits down. He sees

a girl . . . receding among tumbled furniture before a masked man with a gun

and

a car . . spinning down a smooth road with hairpin turns between cliff and abyss.

For Albinus, and the reader at this point, "there was no interest whatever in watching happenings which he could not understand since he had not yet seen their beginning," but once the reader finishes the novel the importance of these two scenes, and the care with which they have been placed, becomes clear, though neither the importance nor the care dawns on Albinus. These two brief scenes are from Albinus' experience later in the novel:

the drive away from the hotel at Rouginard, on a winding road between cliff and abyss, which ends in the accident that causes Albinus' blindness, and the last full scene of the book in which he tries to murder Margot. Albinus is watching scenes from the motion picture that will become his life, and the ungentle, though subtle, irony of his not understanding these scenes "since he had not yet seen their beginning" is lost on him: he is at that precise moment involved in the first scenes of the film he watches. That this is so is intensified by another sentence: "Had he not gone there that second time he might perhaps have been able to forget this ghost of an adventure, but now it was too late." The inevitability of his involvement is clear, but what is added is the nature of what he is involved in: *the ghost of an adventure,* which may be considered a concise definition of any particular instance of the celluloid art.[7]

Chapter three, which seems (and is) on the surface of the narrative merely a flashback designed to fill one in on Margot Peters' past, is made to perform more interesting functions. First, the description of Margot is done in terms that serve to intensify the contrast, already implied, between her and Albinus' wife. She is, to use one phrase as representative, "bright and high-spirited," an animated foil to the passive Elisabeth. Moreover, the crucial event in her past is her truncated affair with Axel Rex. Their fated[8] combined activity in Albinus' life, already suggested by the "coincidence" in Albinus' "very private life" in chapter one, has begun a good deal earlier than the present time of the novel. And Nabokov treats their initial affair in his usual skillful way. It seems that the "career" of Margot, in whose beginning Axel Rex is instrumental, will be nothing more than that of expensive whore. But there is more to it than that; the details of their relationship are carefully fitted into the pattern of cinematic experience that informs the whole novel. Margot's liaison with Rex is inseparable, first, from art: she poses (I suppose one could say professionally) for art classes, and Rex's last gesture before he leaves is to sketch her lying on the bed. In addition, the whole chapter is laden with Margot's visions of herself as a movie star:

So the days passed and Margot had only a very vague idea of what she was really aiming at, though there was always that vision of herself as a screen beauty in gorgeous furs being helped out of a gorgeous car by a gorgeous hotel porter under a giant umbrella. (30)

Finally, the apparent downward course of her ambition (from posing, to being rebuffed by film producers, to working as an usher in a cinema) is in reality a progression toward the one movie in which she will star, the love triangle of Peters, Rex, and Albinus. The chapter closes with her first direct meeting with Albinus, their first exchange of words, and the first reel of Nabokov's ghost of an adventure is under way.

There are two other particular items worth noting about the third chapter. First, Margot's vision of her gorgeous self as screen star is fulfilled, though not in the terms she uses when she envisions it. The night she meets Albinus it is raining.

"You're drenched," she said with a smile. He took the umbrella out of her hand; she pressed still closer to him. (43)

Presumably, since there is nothing to indicate the contrary, Albinus has seen the same movie each time he has come to the cinema during this first, crucial week. It is the movie in which he is unwittingly one of the stars and in whose beginning he is currently involved. The repetition of the detail of the umbrella, significantly deflated from Margot's vision of it, is part of the pattern by which Nabokov signals the nature of the book. Second, the progression of Margot's "artistic" activities echoes Albinus' original idea of animating paintings. She is first sketched, as it were, anonymously, by art students, then by the man whom Albinus requests to assist in the animation project, Axel Rex. Then she meets Albinus in the opening scenes of the motion picture that is the novel.

I have gone into some detail with the first three chapters of *Laughter in the Dark* to try to show how thoroughly, from its beginning, Nabokov has committed the novel's form to the mode of the film. I will continue to follow this direction, but without maintaining as strict an allegiance to the chapter by chapter development of the book.

Throughout the rest of the novel Nabokov continues to employ phrases whose chief purpose seems to be to keep the reader alerted to the basic mode of perception through which he is being asked to view the experiences of its characters. Margot, for instance, often makes "all sorts of wonderful faces for the benefit of her dressing-chest mirror or recoil[s] before the barrel of an imaginary gun" (69), the latter of which activities again figures in the end of the book. Before his wife discovers his infidelity and leaves him, Albinus covers frequent absences from home by saying his evenings out are "spent with some artists interested in the cinema idea of his" (70), a statement he considers a lie, but the unsettling truth of which the reader should be well aware. At the close of the scene in which Albinus leaves his otherwise deserted apartment, Frieda, the maid, sobs "in the wings" (89); among the erotic gestures of Margot which please Albinus is the "gradual dimming of her eyes (as if they were being slowly extinguished like the lights in a theater)" (92); at the beach, Margot's bathing suit is "too short to be true" (112); Margot views the sort of life Albinus could offer her as "full of the glamor of a first-class film with rocking palm trees and shuddering roses (for it is always windy in filmland)" (118); at the Swiss villa Rex eats "like a silent film diner" (162); and during one of the dinners which Axel and Margot share with Albinus this passage occurs:

As she sat between these two men who were sharing her life, she felt as though she were the chief actress in a mysterious and passionate film-drama—so she tried to behave accordingly; smiling absently, drooping her eyelashes, tenderly laying her hand on Albinus' sleeve, as she asked him to pass the fruit, and casting a fleeting, indifferent glance at her former lover. (147)

But perhaps the best of these fillips to the reader's awareness occurs in chapter 15, as Nabokov is describing the first days Margot spends in Albinus' flat.

> Late one night, as he was soaping Margot's back after a dance and she was amusing herself by standing in the full bath upon her enormous sponge (bubbles coming up as in a glass of champagne), she suddenly asked him whether he did not think she could become a film actress. (122)

The image of the actress in the glass of champagne, delightfully undercut, is straight out of the golden age of the cinema, or, in a metaphoric mixture true to the nature of that age, the silver screen. And it appears here not only as a part of the pattern of cinematic experience that is the core of the book's meaning, but also in connection with Margot's broaching to Albinus the possibility that he finance a film in which she would act, which turns out to be a film within the film that is the novel.

It is with such an image that one begins to get the taste of parody, and to detect the implications of the use of the mode of motion pictures as the form by which the novel is structured. The "real-life" actress whom Nabokov refers to indicates the sort of movie he wants his reader to have in mind; that is, the mode of the film as a way of perceiving the meaning of the book is used both generally and specifically. The actress is Garbo, and the specific kind of film that comes to mind is the melodramatic tragedy of romantic intrigue.[9] The first suggestion of this possibility occurs in a sentence describing Margot's activity as an usher in the movie house: "She stood in the darkness leaning against the wall and watched Greta Garbo" (42). The focus is sharpened in chapter eight, in which Albinus makes his first entrance into the rooms Margot has rented and furnished at his expense. On his way to the flat, whose location he has learned by cutting through some of the lies Margot has told him about her past, he notices his surroundings.

> It was half past seven. Lights were being put on, and their soft orange glow looked very lovely in the pale dusk. The sky was still quite blue, with a single salmon-colored cloud in the distance, and all this unsteady balance between light and dusk made Albinus feel giddy.

"In another moment I shall be in paradise," he thought, as he sped in a taxi over the whistling asphalt. (77)

The concatenation of suggestions in the passage is very effective. The hour is the hour when couples go to the cinema; the lights are soft, as in a theater before the film begins; Albinus uses a taxi, as per advertisements intended to appeal to lighthearted lovers on an evening out in a big city (and this is Berlin). There is the traditional mindless sunset for sentimentalists mushing up the sky. Added to these suggestions, which are easy enough, is the effect his surroundings have on Albinus: the combination of light and dark makes him "giddy," and, as the thought he has suggests, his giddiness involves his perception, not just his physical equilibrium. That his perception, his taste, his aesthetic preferences, and his moral sense are indeed unsteady, is, as it were, proved by his being able to accept the apartment when he enters it.

Margot was lying in a kimono on a dreadful chintz-covered sofa, her arms crossed behind her head. On her stomach an open book was poised, cover upward. (77-78)

The confusion over the letter Margot has sent Albinus, which is being delivered even as the two lovers talk about it, the perplexity this causes Albinus, Margot's cool indifference to his dilemma, and Albinus' futile dash across Berlin to intercept the letter are all of a piece with the best (or worst) of the frantic stylized melodrama of the cinema of the twenties. In addition to the caricatured scene there are two details which deepen one's sense of the mode Nabokov is using to condition the reader's perception of the chapter. First, as Albinus ends his trip to try to intercept the ominous letter:

He arrived, he jumped out, he paid as men do in films—blindly thrusting out a coin. (80)

Second, as Margot reacts to Albinus' potential hysteria:

She shrugged her shoulders, picked up the book and turned her back on him. On the right-hand page was a photographic study of Greta Garbo. (79)

82

And the chapter ends this way:

She let the book slip to the floor and smiled as she looked at his downcast twitching face. *It was time to act, she supposed.*

Margot stretched herself out, was aware of a pleasant tingling in her slim body, and said, gazing up at the ceiling, "Come here."

He came, sat down on the edge of the couch and shook his head despondently.

"Kiss me," she said, closing her eyes. "I'll comfort you." (82, italics mine)

Fadeout. The whole chapter seems to me superbly done, uniting for the first time in the novel the mode of the cinema as the perspective from which the novel is to be viewed, the essential parodic intention of the use of the mode, and the moral suggestions implicit in the parody. Albinus, caught in the exaggerated melodrama of the film experience he is in part the creator of, is quite blind long before the automobile accident puts him in the condition which physically acknowledges the moral fact.

As with the series of details I listed earlier in connection with Nabokov's continual reminders to the reader of the perceptual mode of the novel, so in connection with the parodic importance of the same mode: in a scene of reconciliation between Margot and Albinus we read, " 'And you don't really despise me?' she asked, smiling through her tears, which was difficult, seeing there were no tears to smile through" (100); when Albinus, still with his secret more or less intact, converses with his brother-in-law, the narrator says, "Indeed, there was a fine flavor of parody about this talk" (105); and, later, when Rex gets a button on his jacket caught in the lace of Margot's dress while he is trying to kiss her before Albinus returns to the room:

Rex was about to raise himself, but at the same moment he noticed that a button of his coat was caught in the lace on Margot's shoulder. Margot tried to disentangle it swiftly. Rex tugged, but the lace refused to give way. Margot grunted in dismay, as she pulled at the knot with her sharp shiny nails. At that moment Albinus swept into the room.

"No, I'm not embracing Fraulein Peters," said Rex coolly. "I was only making her comfortable and got entangled, you see."

Margot was still worrying the lace without raising her lashes. The situation was farcical in the extreme and Rex was enjoying it hugely.

Albinus silently drew out a fat penknife with a dozen blades and opened what turned out to be a small file. He tried again and broke his nail. The burlesque was developing nicely. (164-65)

The terms "farcical" and "burlesque," along with Rex's awareness of the nature of the scene in which he is snagged, leads one to the passages dealing directly with the subject of caricature, passages in which the novel theorizes about itself. Rex is, basically, a caricaturist himself, and, "to say the least of it, a cynic" (142).

As a child he had poured oil over live mice, set fire to them and watched them dart about for a few seconds like flaming meteors. And it is best not to inquire into the things he did to cats. Then, in riper years, when his artistic talent developed, he tried in more subtle ways to satiate his curiosity, for it was not anything morbid with a medical name—oh, not at all—just cold, wide-eyed curiosity, just the marginal notes supplied by life to his art. It amused him immensely to see life made to look silly, as it slid helplessly into caricature. He despised practical jokes: he liked them to happen by themselves with perchance now and then just that little touch on his part which would send the wheel running downhill. (142-43)

The paradigmatic "practical joke" Nabokov gives as representative of the sort of humor that appeals to Rex is revealing as it reverberates among the actual happenings of the experience Rex is involved in in the novel.

Thus goes the Hegelian syllogism of humor. Thesis: Uncle made himself up as a burglar (a laugh for the children); antithesis: it *was* a burglar (a laugh for the reader); synthesis: it still was Uncle (fooling the reader). (143)

This brief dialectic loosely parallels the structure of the "joke" that happens to Albinus, in which Rex adds his "little touch": Albinus dresses himself up as lover in a film; it *is* a lover in a film; it is, as the bullet enters the flesh, still Albinus. In the transmutation of the paradigm into Albinus' experience the moral implications of the "joke" become somewhat more apparent. The thesis involves an irresponsible sense of becoming involved in a game which has no consequences: one can fool oneself at the outset by thinking one has control over the outcome, as Albinus attempts to do when he considers "plugging" the chick before he has even spoken to her. In fact, after he is committed to the affair, Albinus is still able to consider the easy way out: "She is still my wife and I love her, and I shall, of course, shoot myself if she dies by my fault" (91). The antithesis involves the reader's seeing how completely the film role engulfs Albinus, and he is fooled by the synthesis in the sense that, having congratulated himself on seeing the cinematic nature of Albinus' experience he forgets the "real" Albinus, who does, indeed, for all practical purposes, shoot himself.[10] The structure of the book is such, in other words, that the reader may tend to forget the *actor in the role*, and pay attention to only the role itself, as Albinus himself does: the Rexian joke, then, is on both Albinus and the reader.

I am not sure how far one can push such an analogy; I do think, however, the general relationship is there, and it is stressed almost immediately in the text by this sentence:

The art of caricature, as Rex understood it, was thus based (apart from its synthetic, fooled-again nature) on the contrast between cruelty on the one side and credulity on the other. (144)

The simple connection here is Rex-cruelty, Albinus-credulity; the more complicated implications of the pairings I will discuss in Part II.

The dependence of the novel's parodic intention on the presence of the mode of the motion picture as conditioning the perspective from which it is to be viewed, and the implications suggested by the parody, which are given a theoretical base in the comments on Rex's ideas about caricature, are focused in three notable instances.

First in Albinus' recollection of the accident: "A sharp jerk of the steering wheel to avoid [the cyclists]—and up the car dashed, mounting a pile of stones on the right, and in the next fraction of that second, a telegraph post loomed in front of the windscreen. Margot's outstretched arm had flown across the picture—and the next moment the magic lantern went out" (240). The terminology by which Albinus' perception is presented is part of the film mode of the novel, and the association of the magic lantern with Albinus' consciousness makes clear one metaphorical direction in which the film mode is to be taken. One would expect the movie to end when the lantern goes out, but the dark chamber suggested by the Russian title of the novel, *Kamera Obskura,* works against this allegorical limitation. It is also quite fitting, in terms of the sense of moral fate the novel is partly concerned with, that Nabokov suggest here that the movie has taken over Albinus' experience; if it has not been clear before, it is obvious after the accident that any idea Albinus had about controlling his own destiny is pure illusion. And there is a corollary to this. One might expect that since his credulous vision had gotten Albinus into his predicament, perhaps the removal of that vision would bring with it some kind of insight: the trite idea of a blind man knowing himself, and "reality," better than the man whose ability to see helps him keep appearances between himself and the truth. But it doesn't happen this way: Albinus "could not always succeed in convincing himself that physical blindness was spiritual vision; in vain did he try to cheat himself with the fancy that his life with Margot was now happier, deeper and purer, and in vain did he concentrate on the thought of her touching devotion" (257-58).

Which leads into the second point; the following passage occurs in the context of the statements about physical and spiritual blindness:

Albinus now became conscious that he had not really been different from a certain narrow specialist at whom he used to scoff: from the workman who knows only his tools, or the virtuoso who is only a fleshy accessory of his violin. Albinus' specialty had been his passion for art; his most brilliant discovery had been Margot. But now, all that was left of her was a voice, a rustle and a perfume; it was as though she had returned to the darkness of the little cinema from which he had once withdrawn her. (257)

In terms of the book's structure, this is exactly what has happened. One of the scenes—the car on the winding road—that Albinus saw in the movie which was playing at the cinema where he first saw Margot has already been realized in his own life; the book is turning back on itself. And the darkness inside which he moves becomes, again fittingly, the darkness of a cinema. It is in great part his own perception, his imaginative way of making his shabby and irresponsible affair with Margot take on the sheen of a Garbo movie, which has got him where he is. Again, his loss of eyesight is a physical acknowledgment of a moral fact.

The third such instance in which the implications of the parody are focused is the viewing of Margot's film, which occupies the whole of chapter 23. Everyone at the viewing except Albinus is able to see what a horrid actress Margot is. Seeing the film could have been a key to Margot's "real" nature for Albinus, but a blind man can't see. And while the screening of Margot's film is in progress Rex, who is bored, "closed his eyes, saw the little colored caricatures he had been doing lately for Albinus, and meditated over the fascinating though quite simple problem of how to suck some more cash out of him" (190). Margot acts in the film as she acts in the affair with Albinus, and Rex's thought about the caricatures serves to focus the association between the two contexts, as well as to suggest Albinus' thorough credulity.

To return, finally, to Irma's birth, which I mentioned previously as the pivot on which the polarity of chapter two turns, I would like to make one or two suggestions about the way in which the perceptual mode of the novel, the film, is made to include characters other than the members of the triangle. First of all, Albinus' thoughts while he waits in the hospital for the baby to be born are presented in terms that set his perception of the event in the cinematic basis of the rest of his experience. Just as the doctor announces the birth, "before Albinus' eyes there appeared a fine dark rain, like the flickering of some very old film (1910, a brisk jerky funeral procession with legs moving too fast)" (18). The doctor's announcement has been, to say the least, enigmatical: "At length the assistant surgeon emerged and said gloomily: 'Well, it's all over'" (18). That might, indeed, make a prospective father, haggard and worried, think of a funeral, but only an art historian and restorer of paintings who has a tendency to view his life as though it were a motion picture would respond in the terms Albinus does.

This is interesting in itself, since it reveals Albinus' penchant for the distancing of reality through art before he begins his liaison with Margot, but Albinus echoes the doctor's words later in the novel, making Irma's birth resonant with his death. He says, after the bullet penetrates his side, "So that's all" (291). It is as though the process of viewing life—all of it, not just the affair with Margot—as a motion picture began with the birth of Irma; and, further, that Albinus' death occurred at Irma's birth.[11] I mean that figuratively, of course: once Albinus began to conceive his life as a film then he began to live a parody of himself, which could be said to be a kind of death the rest of the novel fulfills. Elisabeth herself, when she is first described, may be seen, then, through Albinus' eyes as part of a motion picture. The black and white contrast between her and Margot adds to this possibility, as does the inclusion of Paul in a conversation that has about it "a fine flavor of parody." Thus, the whole world of the novel, as seen by Albinus, and not simply his relationship with Rex and Margot, is conceived in the mode of the film.

II. Albinus Rex

Nabokov has said that "Satire is a lesson, parody is a game."[12] *Laughter in the Dark* is no less a game than any other fiction he has written; I hope the sense of that game, of details placed as pieces in a puzzle, of echoes and interpenetrations, has been apparent in my comments thus far. At the same time, as I have been trying to show, the game is so played as to imply certain moral, aesthetic and perceptual concerns; Nabokov's novels and stories are by no means moralizing—far from it, and that is part of one's delight in reading them—but they are involved with moral predicaments on which their very structure comments.

He has also said, "There are no 'real' doubles in my novels," and, speaking of *Laughter* specifically, "A lover can be viewed as the betrayed party's double but that is pointless." [13] What I want to do now, in the teeth of those remarks, is discuss the relationship implied between Albinus and Axel Rex in *Laughter;* the problem set by Nabokov's comments becomes to talk about that relationship without slipping into the traditional—a la Dostoevsky, for instance, or Melville—assumption of the existence of "real" doubles.

One might begin with a passage to which I have already referred:

Thus the art of caricature, as Rex understood it, was based . . . on the contrast between cruelty on the one side and credulity on the other.

This in itself suggests only a kind of pairing, not doubling; Rex is cruel, Albinus credulous. And when ones takes the passage in the context of Albinus' idea of the animation of still life, and that idea's fulfillment in the novel, one can see that both Rex and Albinus are necessary to its realization: Albinus has the idea, Rex supplies the motion. This mutual dependence is further suggested by the names of the two characters: Albinus, a pale and passive man, Rex, a masterful, active one; Albinus in some sense a freak snared in the trap of inertia, Axel Rex, both king and that around which motion is centered.[14] Further, there is a foiling of the professional functions of the two men: Albinus is a restorer of old paintings, Rex a forger of them.

None of these details points toward doubling of characters in any sense, but when they are seen in concert with other suggestions made in the course of the novel one has to go farther with the possibility. In regard to the name Albinus, for instance, we are told in the first paragraph "Once upon a time there lived . . . a man called Albinus." Well, since no one *in* the novel calls him Albinus (the characters call him Albert, the name of a king famous enough to be on tobacco tins) one wonders who *does* call him that. His creator? And why? Possibly to suggest, among the other possibilities I've mentioned, by the Latin ending of his name a connection with the Latin word that serves as the name of his rival? Add to this the manner in which the narrator describes the general response Margot has to the two men: "And she liked Miller enormously" (35), "And she quite liked Albinus" (68); the point at which "Albinus marveled at his own divided nature" (46); and this rather unignorable passage in chapter 27: "she [Margot] needed only one man—Rex. And Rex was Albinus' shadow" (207-8). Add these instances to the possible connection suggested in the use of Latin words for the two characters' names, and I think one has to admit that something beyond simple foiling is at stake.

If this were all, one could possibly drop the matter. But it isn't. There are two other aspects of the way the two men are treated that make the problem (if it's a problem) impossible to evade. First, Margot discovers Albinus' address by getting his last name from the lining of his hat and finding it in the telephone book under "R." Second, and most convincing of all, is the fact that both Rex and Albinus adopt, independently of each other (but not of their creator), the same pseudonym when they try to disguise their identity from Margot—Miller, which Albinus embroiders to Schiffermiller.[15] It is, in fact, the use of the name Schiffermiller to designate someone Margot wants to assist her with her luggage in chapter 39 that thoroughly complicates the whole idea of possible doubles. Who is this last Schiffermiller? Rex? Why does Margot call him that? Is there a character named Schiffermiller independent of the two men who have used the sound pseudonymously? It is very difficult to tell, and it is indeed possible that Nabokov intends the reader of the novel to make a fool of himself, after the manner of Rex's idea of the effect of caricature, as I am doing now, by seeking the resolution of a pattern where no resolution is possible. A skillful detective story writer knows red herrings are as important as real clues.[16]

There is no doubt that Axel Rex is a character who exists separately from Albinus (as, for instance, Smurov is *not* physically separate from the "I" of *The Eye*); but there also seems to me to be no doubt that one is intended at least to entertain the possibility that Rex and Albinus interpenetrate in some way.

There seems to be at least the chance that one is intended to see Rex as embodying qualities which Albinus would himself like to possess, particularly Rex's mobility and his success with women. And perhaps this toying with the possibility of their being doubles is a means to intensify the mutual dependence that is absolutely necessary for the fulfillment of their functions as characters in the inexorable *formal* destiny of the novel.

This latter possibility brings one to the edge of another dimension of *Laughter in the Dark* which further complicates it, and turns its parodic implications back upon itself.

III. Udo Conrad

I have been talking about the idea of animating paintings by old masters as though it originated with Albinus. It did not.

It so happened that one night Albinus had a beautiful idea. True, it was not quite his own, as it had been suggested by a phrase in Conrad (not the famous Pole, but Udo Conrad who wrote the *Memoirs of a Forgetful Man* and that other thing about the old conjuror who spirited himself away at his farewell performance.) (7, third paragraph of the novel)

The latter of those two books by Udo Conrad is mentioned again, by title, when authorial techniques are discussed at a party in Albinus' flat. The whole passage is revealing.

"I don't know, gentlemen, what you think of Udo Conrad," said Albinus, joining in the fray. "It would seem to me that he is that type of author with exquisite vision and a divine style which might please you, Herr Rex, and that if he isn't a great writer it is because—and here, Herr Baum, I am with you—he has a contempt for social problems which, in this age of social upheavals, is disgraceful and, let me add, sinful. I knew him well in my student days, as we used to meet now and then. I consider his best book to be *The Vanishing Trick,* the first chapter of which, as a matter of fact, he read here, at this table—I mean—well—at a similar table. . . ." (132-33)

Udo Conrad is, to use a figure appropriate to the controlling focus of *Laughter in the Dark,* an ectype of Vladimir Nabokov. The original of Conrad's *Memoirs* is Nabokov's *Speak, Memory;* [17] *Invitation to a Beheading,* of all his books the one Nabokov holds in "greatest esteem," [18] lurks behind Conrad's *The Vanishing Trick*. The "similar table" probably still exists somewhere in an anonymous room in Berlin, with an almost palpable ghost still seated at it, if Nabokov doesn't have it in his rooms in Montreux. Further, Albinus' critical remarks reproduce in small, as do the criticisms of Sebastian Knight's books in that novel, the two most frequent judgments made about Nabokov's fiction;[19] the phrases "exquisite vision" and "divine style" are more than dinner table effusions, suggesting as they do Nabokov's constant concern with the nature of perception and the author's relationship to the books he writes.

The concern with this relationship, and the attempt to make it a conscious part of the experience of a given novel, was not new for Nabokov when he wrote the Russian original of *Laughter* in 1931. He, as Blavdak Vinomori (and his wife), had made "visits of inspection" in the last two chapters of *King, Queen, Knave* (1928),[20] and in that same novel he had not only appeared in another anagrammatical disguise—as Mr. Vivian Badlook, the photographer—but also in the ectypes of Goldemar (the author of a play and screenplay called *King, Queen, Knave*), old Enricht (Franz's landlord), and both the professor who created the mannikins and Mr. Ritter, who contracted to buy them.[21] And he has continued to use the technique, the most obvious examples being Vivian Darkbloom in *Lolita* and Vivian Bloodmark in *Speak, Memory*.

These figures are *not* Nabokov—none of them are complex enough, for one thing—but signals of the presence of the authorial control without which no fiction is, or can be, written. In the case of *Laughter* Conrad's presence immediately makes one aware that no idea originates with the characters in a novel; thus one knows, or should know, from the beginning of the book that an important part of reading the novel is the reader's consciousness of what I would call the authorial presence, the controlling intelligence that is at work in every facet of the book. Things happen because the author makes them happen; the challenge for the author, in which he asks the reader to participate, is to make them happen according to an inexorable logic implanted in the structure of the book. Everything is not permitted—the author is not an aesthetic anarchist—and he asks the reader to test the formal demands of the composition even as he experiences them, to replay the game of composition the author has played in the initial writing of the book.

With this in mind, then, one sees that Conrad's personal appearances (in chapters 27, 28, and 29) perform a parodic function, directing the overall parody of the novel toward the novel itself, and the authorial control over the novel. For Nabokov has a technical problem to solve in the chapters in which Conrad appears: it is time for Albinus to discover that he is being betrayed by Margot and Rex, and the author needs some way of communicating to him the truth of the situation about which he is deluded. Who knows the truth besides Margot and Rex, neither of whom could be expected to spoil a good thing by tattling? The author. So *he* appears, or more accurately through Udo Conrad acknowledges his presence, and himself imparts to Albinus the crucial information. The formal machinery of the novel, in short, is uncovered at this point: what saves it from creaking is Nabokov's integration of the problem into the meaning of the novel, or the experience of reading the novel. He extends the parody that is being directed toward the characters in the novel to include the author (and the reader) of the novel. To use the terms with which I began this essay, he acknowledges, as part of this particular book's fiber, the essentially parodic nature of fiction itself.

Conrad's appearance, and the function he performs, reminds the reader of his involvement in artifice, in an imaginative experience that can be, by its nature, nothing except parody. It is no wonder that there are people whom parody upsets; I would guess that the more conscious the person the greater the possible upset, and the more possibly creative and rewarding it might be. If, as this novel implies, human perception is inevitably imaginative, then one is faced with the deduction that all perceptual constructions, whether they are embodied in a novel or not, are parodies, and that the assumption that a human being lives in and can apprehend a comfortable "factual" reality is the most disturbing parody of all.

Notes

1. See my "Angles of Perception" (*MLQ*, Sept. 1968) and "All the Mind's a Stage" (*U. of Windsor Review*, Spring 1969).

2. Nabokov has been explicit about this in interviews with Herbert Gold (*Paris Review*, #41, Summer-Fall 1967): "My characters are galley slaves" (p. 96); and Alfred Appel, Jr. (*Wisconsin Studies in Contemporary Literature*, Spring 1967): "I think that what I would welcome at the close of a book of mine is a sensation of its world receding in the distance and stopping somewhere there suspended afar like a picture in a picture" (p. 136); and in various places in *Speak, Memory* (revised edition, New York, 1966), of which the following is representative: "It should be understood that competition in chess problems is not really between Black and White but between the composer and hypothetical solver (just as in a first-rate work of fiction the real clash is not between the characters but between the author and the world)" (p. 290). See also note 16, below.

3. Appel interview, *op. cit.*, p. 139.

4. The only things more recurrent in his fiction are butterflies (with the accompanying suggestion that human life may be instaric) and chess. See note 15, below.

5. *Laughter in the Dark*, A New Directions Book (new edition, 1960), pp. 8-9. All further quotations from this edition are noted in parentheses following the passages.

6. I will discuss the implications of this at the close of Part I.

7. Other aspects of the novel seem conceived in line with the use of the film as the mode through which it is to be perceived. The profusion of chapters, their varied lengths, and especially the very brief ones, suggest a scenario. There are stage directions not only for the last scene but also on p. 150. Twice the fictional technique suggests the use of a subliminal frame in a motion picture: the flash to the hockey game on p. 170, when Rex meets Paul in the entrance to Albinus' apartment house, and in Margot's quick memory of Rex locking Frau Levandovsky in the lavatory as she (Margot) locks Albinus in his bedroom, on p. 62. The first three chapters make the past present by flashback, and the point of view from which the accident is handled (chapter 32) suggests the cinematic technique of panning.

8. By the novelist. See Part III of this essay.

9. Because of the fun made with the name—Dorianna Karenina—of the leading lady in the film that Albinus finances, one might guess even more specifically that a particular movie is to be invoked, Garbo's *Anna Karenina*.

10. See Carol T. Williams' comments on this pattern ("Nabokov's Dialectical Structure," *Wisconsin Studies in Contemporary Literature*, Spring 1967). Rex's "burglar" joke is itself echoed in the body of the novel when Albinus tries to explain Margot's presence in his apartment to Paul by saying a burglar had locked him in the bathroom. In keeping with the paradigm of Hegelian dialectic, Margot *does* become a burglar in effect, as she and Rex rapidly reduce Albinus' bank account after the accident.

11. Chapters 20 and 21, which deal with Irma's death, expand this focus somewhat, suggesting as they do that Margot is, for Albinus, among her other aspects, also a child, a substitute for Irma. The dialogue which opens chapter

22 sharpens this possibility: Albinus says to Margot, "You're a child yourself" (180). Margot has turned the nursery in Albinus' flat into a ping-pong room, which suggests something about the way Albinus' life has been transformed into a game whose rules have nothing to do with paternal responsibility. As he stands in the ping-pong room, almost at the point of giving up his affair and returning to his wife, he "listlessly took up a small celluloid ball and let it bounce, but instead of thinking of his child he saw another figure, a graceful, lively, wanton girl, laughing, one heel raised, as she thrust out her ping-pong bat" (178). Further, as Albinus tries to console Margot during her tantrums over her bad performance in the film, he "used the very words with which he had once comforted Irma when he kissed a bruise—words which now, after Irma's death, were vacant" (192). The Englishwoman's comment when she sees Albinus and Margot frolicking on the beach—"Look at that German romping about with his daughter"—also seems part of this pattern.

12. Appel interview, *op. cit.*, p. 138.

13. *Ibid.*, p. 145.

14. There are two spots where the Axel-axle association—axle as a moving center causing radiant motion—is suggested beyond the audial hint: "Margot suddenly gave a sob and turned away. [Rex] pulled her by the sleeve, but she turned away still farther. They revolved in one spot" (135); "He despised practical jokes: he liked them to happen by themselves with perchance now and then just that little touch on his part which would send the wheel running downhill" (143).

15. There is a good possibility that lepidoptera are involved in the pattern of the novel's meaning: a miller is a kind of moth. I don't have the equipment to develop this. Nor can I do anything more than point out the chance that the Black-White drama between the two kings of a chess game is operating in the play between Rex, Albinus, and the reader.

16. Nabokov speaks of nature and art as games "of intricate enchantment and deception"; see *Speak, Memory*, pages 125 and 290-91.

17. There may be a problem here. *Kamera Obskura* was written in 1931, and the first English version, translated by Winifred Roy—"insufficiently revised by me," Nabokov has said (Appel interview, *op. cit.*, p. 144)—appeared in 1936, the year in which Nabokov established the order of chapters for *Speak, Memory*, and wrote and published the first of these, "Mademoiselle O," chapter five of the finished work (see the foreword to *SM*). Nabokov himself "Englished" *Laughter* for Bobbs-Merrill in 1938, and the edition I'm using was brought out by New Directions in 1960. Given Nabokov's gamesmanship, it is quite likely that, as early as the 1936 English version of the novel, he is referring to one of his own books, although at that time only one chapter of it had been completed.

18. Appel interview, *op. cit.*, p. 152.

19. See (on pages 287-88 of *Speak, Memory*) Nabokov's remarks about the critical response among Russian émigrés in Berlin to the work of V. Sirin, which is to say himself.

20. See the foreword to the novel (McGraw-Hill, New York, 1968), p. viii.

21. Two of the characters from *King, Queen, Knave* play the shortest of phantomic parts in *Laughter*: when Albinus returns to his flat after his family has departed, he finds in the mail "an invitation for lunch from the Dreyers" (86).

[1. Criticism]

On Sirin
VLADISLAV KHODASEVICH

Art cannot be reduced to form, but without form it has no existence and, consequently, no meaning. Therefore the analysis of a work of art is unthinkable without an analysis of form.

Analysis of form would be a proper way of beginning every

"On Sirin" was written by the major Russian émigré poet and literary critic Khodasevich in 1937. In the 1930's Khodasevich was one of the most perceptive and constant champions of Nabokov's ("Sirin's") work. Written before Khodasevich had a chance to read *The Gift*, the essay is as pertinent to Nabokov's later novels as it was to his earlier ones, to which it refers.

The first four pages of the essay establish the connection between the art of fiction on the one hand and the display of freaks at sideshows and performing of conjuring tricks on the other, the common elements being the display of craftsmanship and the desire to startle and to divert. The opening passages on craftsmanship are couched in the form of a complex set of references to several Pushkin poems. Since the full understanding of Khodasevich's implications presupposes the knowledge of complete Pushkin texts and their interrelationship with certain poems by Horace and by Derzhavin, even the most exact translation of these four pages would be meaningless without extensive commentary. They are, accordingly, omitted from the present translation. [Simon Karlinsky] judgment about an author, every account of him. But formal analysis is so cumbersome and complicated that, in speaking of Sirin, I should not venture to suggest that you enter into that region with me. Besides, even I have not produced a true and sufficiently complete analysis of Sirin's form, real work in criticism under present conditions being impossible. All the same, I have made certain observations—and I shall permit myself to share the results.

Under thorough scrutiny Sirin proves for the most part to be an artist of form, of the writer's device, and not only in that well-known and universally recognized sense in which the formal aspect of his writing is distinguished by exceptional diversity, complexity, brilliance and novelty. All this is recognized and known precisely because it catches everyone's eye. But it catches the eye because Sirin not only does not mask, does not hide his devices, as is most frequently done by others (and in which, for example, Dostoevsky attained startling perfection) but, on the contrary, because Sirin himself places them in full view like a magician who, having amazed his audience, reveals on the very spot the laboratory of his miracles. This, it seems to me, is the key to all of Sirin. His works are populated not only with the characters, but with an infinite number of devices which, like elves or gnomes, scurry back and forth among the characters and perform an enormous amount of work. They saw and carve and nail and paint, in front of the audience, setting up and clearing away those stage sets amid which the play is performed. They construct the world of the book and they function as indispensably important characters. Sirin does not hide them because one of his major tasks is just that—to show how the devices live and work.

Sirin has a novel built entirely on the play of autonomous devices. *Invitation to a Beheading* is nothing more than a chain of arabesques, patterns and images, subordinated not to an ideological, but only to a stylistic unity (which, by the way, constitutes one of the "ideas" of the work). In *Invitation to a Beheading* there is no real life, as there are no real characters with the

97

exception of Cincinnatus. All else is merely the play of the stage-hand elves, the play of devices and images that fill the creative consciousness or, rather, the creative delirium of Cincinnatus. With the termination of their playing the story comes to an abrupt end. Cincinnatus is not beheaded and is not not-beheaded, since through the length of the entire story we see him in an imaginary world where no real events of any kind are possible. In the concluding lines, the two-dimensional painted world of Cincinnatus caves in over the collapsed backdrop: "Cincinnatus made his way," says Sirin, "amidst the dust, and falling things, and the flapping scenery, in that direction where, to judge by the voices, stood beings akin to him." Here, of course, is depicted the return of the artist from creative work to reality. If you wish, the beheading is carried out at that moment, but not the same one nor in the same sense as that expected by the hero and the reader: with the return into the world of "beings akin to him," the existence of Cincinnatus the artist is cut off.

Peculiar to Sirin is the realization, or perhaps only a deeply felt conviction, that the world of literary creativity, the true world of the artist, conjured through the action of images and devices out of apparent simulacra of the real world, consists in fact of a completely different material—so different that the passage from one world into the other, in whichever direction it is accomplished, is akin to death. And it is portrayed by Sirin in the form of death. If Cincinnatus dies, passing from the crea-tive world into the real one, then conversely, the hero of the story "Terra Incognita" dies at that instant when he finally plunges completely into the world of imagination. And although the transitions are accomplished in diametrically opposed direc-tions, both are equally depicted by Sirin in the form of a disin-tegration of the stage set. Both worlds, in their relationship one to the other, are for Sirin illusory.

In exactly the same way the butterfly dealer, Pilgram, in the story "The Aurelian," is dead for his wife, for his customers, for the whole world, at that moment when he finally sets out for Spain—a country not coincident with the real Spain, because it has been created by his fancy. In exactly the same way Luzhin dies at that moment when, throwing himself out of the window onto the pale and dark squares of a Berlin courtyard, he once and for all slips out of reality and plunges into the world of his chess creation—there where there are no wife, no acquaintances, no apartment, but where there are only the pure, abstract relationships of creative devices.

If "The Aurelian," "Terra Incognita" and *Invitation to a Beheading* are wholly devoted to the theme of the interrelationship of worlds, then *The Defense* is the first work in which Sirin rose to the full stature of his talent (because here, perhaps for the first time, he found the basic themes of his work)—then *The Defense,* belonging as it does to the same cycle, at the same time contains a transition to the second series of Sirin's writings, where the author poses different problems for himself—invariably, however, connected with the theme of a creative work and the creative personality. These problems are of a somewhat more limited—one could even say professional—character. In Luzhin's person the very horror of such professionalism is shown; it is shown that a permanent residence in the creative world, if the artist is a man of talent and not of genius, will, as it were, suck out his human blood, turning him into an automaton which is not adapted to reality and which perishes from contact with it.

The Eye depicts a charlatan of the arts, an impostor—a man without gift and by nature a stranger to creative work, but endeavoring to pass for an artist. Several mistakes committed by him are his ruin, although he of course does not die, but only changes his profession, for he, after all, has never been in the world of creative work and there is in his story no passage from one world into the other. However, in *The Eye* the theme is already set forth and it becomes central in *Despair,* one of Sirin's best novels. Here are shown the sufferings of a genuine, self-critical artist. He perishes because of a single mistake, because of a single slip allowed in a work which devoured all of his creative ability. In the process of creation he allowed for the possibility that the public, humanity, might not be able to understand and value his creation—and he was ready to suffer proudly from lack of recognition. His despair is brought about by the fact that he himself turns out to be guilty of his downfall, because he is only a man of talent and not of genius.

The life of the artist and the life of a device in the consciousness of the artist—this is Sirin's theme, revealing itself to some degree or other in almost every one of his writings, beginning with *The Defense*. However, the artist (and more concretely speaking, the writer) is never shown by him directly, but always behind a mask: a chess-player, a businessman, etc. The reasons for this are, I believe, manifold. Foremost among them is that here, too, we have to do with a device, though quite an ordinary one. Russian formalists call it "making it strange." It consists in showing the object in unexpected surroundings, which place it in a new position, reveal new aspects of it, and force a more direct perception of it. But there are also other reasons. Had he represented his heroes directly as writers, Sirin would have had, in depicting their creative work, to place a novel inside a story or a story within a story, which would excessively complicate the plot and necessitate on the part of the reader a certain knowledge of the writer's craft. The very same would come about, but with some other difficulties, if Sirin had made them painters, sculptors or actors. He deprives them of professional artistic attributes, but Luzhin works on his chess problems and Hermann on plotting a crime in exactly the same manner that an artist works on his creations. Finally, one should take into consideration the fact that, except for the hero of *The Eye,* all of Sirin's heroes are genuine, inspired artists. Among them, Luzhin and Hermann, as I mentioned, are only gifted men and not geniuses, but even they cannot be denied a deep artistic nature. Cincinnatus, Pilgram and the nameless hero of "Terra Incognita" do not possess those detrimental traits with which Luzhin and Hermann are marked. Consequently, all of them, being shown without masks as undisguised artists, would become (expressed in the language of teachers of literature) positive types, which, as is known, creates exceptional and, in the present instance, unwarranted difficulties for the author. Moreover, in such a case it would be too difficult for the author to deliver them from that pompous and sugary tone which almost inevitably accompanies literary portrayals of true artists. Only the hero of *The Eye* could have been made a man of letters by Sirin while avoiding these difficulties, for the simple reason that that hero is a fake writer. However, I think—I am even almost convinced—that Sirin, who has at his disposal a wide range of caustic observations, will some day give himself rein and favor us with a merciless satiric portrayal of a writer. Such a portrayal would be a natural development in the unfolding of the basic theme with which he is obsessed.

translation by Michael H. Walker,
edited by Simon Karlinsky and Robert P. Hughes

The revival of allegory
P. M. BITSILLI

I. A. Bunin wrote me concerning my article "Remarks on Tolstoy" (*Sovremennye Zapiski,* LX) that he had never read Tolstoy's "The Devil" and was struck by the similarity of parallel passages in that story and in [Bunin's] "Mitya's Love" which I cited. Bunin's testimony is exceptionally important and valuable. It confirms the fact that having common "birthmarks" is not always an indication of the direct dependence of one author upon another. This does not, of course, mean that the method of investigating such "birthmarks" should be excluded. That

"The Revival of Allegory" appeared in *Sovremennye Zapiski,* LXI, 1936. P. M. Bitsilli (1879-1953) was a Russian literary scholar and critic who resided in Bulgaria between the two World Wars. His work appeared in Russian émigré and Bulgarian academic publications and was apparently never collected or published in book form. He is the author of excellent studies of Pushkin and Dostoevsky (see Brown University Slavic Reprint IV), as well as one of the finest (and least known) monographs on Chekhov (see Yearbooks of the University of Sofia, 1941-42, Vol. 6).

would be to renounce any attempt to reconstruct the genesis of literary works, or for that matter of any manifestation of human endeavor—i.e., to renounce history in general. The whole task of the historian is reducible, after all, to the very same thing, for, unlike the naturalist, the historian—rather like a detective—is deprived of the only means of establishing anything for certain: he is denied the possibility of experimenting. The fact attested by Bunin testifies to something else: the existence of the Hegelian "objective spirit." This, understandably, merely extends the possibilities of applying a method of investigating "birthmarks," a method not in the least limited to the fact that, employing it, we are in a position to make more or less plausible conjectures about the sources of a particular literary work. The detection of such sources in itself affords interest only at a high level of specialization, but it is important insofar as it brings us closer to understanding an author's initial creative conception.[1] The origin of identical "birthmarks" encountered in two, or several, authors is not important. Whether they testify to so-to-speak "physical kinship" or are the result of coincidence, their presence is caused by the similarity of their spiritual experience. Authors compared in this manner would seem to shed some light on each other, that we might catch that "uncommon" facial expression of which Baratynsky wrote and see just what features go into making up this distinctive appearance.

I have said enough to clarify the goal of the experiment which I now propose that the reader perform—not on the authors which will be the subject of the discussion, for this is impossible, but on himself. Here is a description of a certain martial "campaign," during which someone betrayed the commanding officer and replaced many of his real soldiers with tin ones: The attack begins . . . the little tin soldiers do not budge from the spot, "and since their facial features were merely painted on in outline form, and moreover very haphazardly, from a distance it seemed that the little soldiers were smiling ironically." But then something extraordinary occurred: right before everyone's eyes the little soldiers (tin ones) began one by one to be filled with blood. "Their

103

eyes, hitherto motionless, suddenly began to roll around in expressions of anger; their moustaches, painted on randomly, moved to their proper places and began to twitch; their lips, thin rosy lines almost washed off by past rain, began to protrude, expressing their intention to pronounce something. Nostrils appeared, where there had been none before, and began to flare, revealing the soldiers' impatience."

Here is another episode from the same source (I shall henceforth camouflage the names in order not to put the reader on the trail): "X, a good trencherman, became enticed by Y's head. He kept sniffing at it, as if it were something edible. Finally, finding himself alone with Y, he became resolute. 'A little bite,' he moaned to Y, alertly observing the expression in the eyes of his chosen victim. At the first sound of the request so decisively formulated, a shiver ran through Y. His position immediately appeared to him with that irrevocable clarity in the light of which all negotiations become useless. He glanced timidly at his attacker and, meeting his resolute gaze, fell in a state of boundless anguish. Nevertheless, he still made a feeble attempt to repulse him. A struggle ensued, but X flew into a rage and became ecstatic with desire. His eyes flashed and his belly grumbled sweetly. He was panting, and moaning, and calling Y 'darling,' . . . 'honey,' he was licking and sniffing him, and so forth. Finally, with unheard of frenzy, X threw himself upon his victim, cut off a slice of his head with a knife, and swallowed it on the spot. One slice led to another, then another, until not a crumb remained. Then Y suddenly leapt up and began to wipe off with his paws the parts of his body which X had doused with vinegar. Then he began to twirl round and round in one place and suddenly he crashed with his whole hulk onto the floor." It turned out his head was full of stuffing.

Here is a passage from another story by the same author: A certain young man falls into the clutches of two swindlers. They invite him to join them at a restaurant, promising to treat him. Having gotten him drunk and having stolen his topcoat, they disappear—without paying the bill, naturally. He has no money, so the police are called, and he is taken away to the station. The "boss-man," addresses him reproachfully: "His speech was simple and artless, like truth itself. It was not, however, devoid of some spice, and from this angle it resembled fiction, being a majestic synthesis of truth mingled with fable, simplicity mingled with fancy, embellished with gems of poetry. 'Ah, young man, young man!' said the 'boss-man.' 'Reflect on what you've done! Try to come to grips with your deed. . . . Don't just skim the surface, search the very depths of your conscience. Ah, young man, young man!' "

I suggest that the reader pause here without looking further and ask himself where these passages came from and what they call to mind. I am sure that everyone will answer that they are from some stories by Sirin, or from early drafts for *Invitation to a Beheading*. In reality, this is from Saltykov. The first two passages are from "History of a Town," the last one from "A Confused Affair." This last episode ought to have been quoted in full, to reveal how Ivan Samoilych gets caught, how passersby heckle him as he is led away (" 'Well, perhaps m'lord would please to take a stroll? . . . Hee-hee-hee!' rang out the voice of a girl Ivan Samoilych knew, who worked for her living. 'Our compliments to you,' chimed in a fair-haired student standing nearby"), how they have either brought him in, or are in the process of bringing him in ("reality" continually alternates with delirium). The similarity to corresponding episodes in *Invitation to a Beheading* is striking.

One more experiment, in reverse, might be performed on me. If before I had read *Invitation to a Beheading* someone had read to me the passage from it in which the books in the public library begin to rot from dampness, since it is located on a barge (whereupon it becomes necessary to reroute the river), I would have thought this was some incident in "History of a Town" that I had forgotten.

Saltykov, a genius but a practically unreadable one, is now forgotten by nearly everyone. This is perhaps why when people write about Sirin they recall that Gogol was his forefather, but never recall Saltykov. Sirin's closeness to Gogol is indisputable. I shall pause once more over the details—the "birthmarks": ". . . they are often accompanied by a very young girl, a silent, taciturn, sometimes comely creature; a nasty little lapdog; and a wall-clock with a pendulum which ticks away mournfully." Where does this come from? At first glance it seems to be something by Sirin. Actually it is from "The Portrait" [by Gogol]. Gogol's enumerations of "things" are based on the same scheme.[2] It is very probable that Sirin borrowed this device from him. Thus, in *Despair,* the hero "takes inventory of [his] spiritual possessions": "I have a foolish, but attractive . . . wife, a nice little flat, excellent digestion, and a dark-blue automobile." [Translated from the original Russian version of *Otchaianie*]. "The monotonous . . . eternally ordered and, as it were, buttoned-up faces of clerks . . ." ("The Portrait"). Cf. the description of Rodrig Ivanovich's external appearance in *Invitation to a Beheading.*

But Gogol is incomparably more careful, more restrained, and more "classical" in his use of "romantic irony." Saltykov and Sirin go much further than Gogol in adopting these stylistic figures, which are based on an intentional lack of distinction between "live" and "dead," and which aim at emphasizing the inanimation of the "animate" and the divisibility of the "indivisible" in an individual: "When Ivan Samoilych appeared in the dining room, the whole crowd was present. Right before everyone the tar-black moustache of the birthday celebrant protruded; also present, as an inescapable adjunct, the figure of Charlotte Gottliebovna popped up gaunt and straight as a stick. Around them there stood . . ." and so on. This passage from "A Confused Affair" is amazingly similar in tone to the passage in which Cincinnatus's relatives visit him. If one reads Gogol after reading *Invitation to a Beheading* and "History of a Town," then his "dead souls" begin to seem alive. It isn't just that Kovalyov is driven to despair over the loss of his nose, while the governors of Glupov carry on their lives unperturbed, one with a musical clock in his head which he removes at night, another with a stuffed head. Nor is it simply that Gogolian heroes always preserve their identity, while Rodrig Ivanovich is lowered in status to Rodion every now and then. The point is the verbal suggestions through which the reader is given a view of the world through the eyes of Gogol, Saltykov, and Sirin. Gogol would not have said that the governor began to "wipe his head with his little paws," as Saltykov did (see above), and as Sirin would (there are any number of analogous expressions in Sirin's works). Furthermore, there is that mixture, alien to Gogol's speech but so characteristic of Saltykov's and Sirin's, of the "scholarly," coldly majestic, or elevated style, and the "trivialities," which enhance the deathly weirdness and grotesque deformity of Saltykov's and Sirin's images. In Gogol's language there are fewer elements of ridicule, mockery, and parody than in that of Saltykov or Sirin.

All the comparisons made thus far have been in the realm of stylistics; they testify to an affinity of temperament, "tone," and "coloring" that exists between Saltykov and Sirin. These are still hardly birthmarks. But here is one passage from *The Golovlyov Family* which might be ascribed to this category. Little Judas's brother, Pavel, dies. His mother imagines to herself how little Judas will appear at the funeral, how he will pretend to be mourning, and how he will go about verifying the inheritance—"And how alive was the voice of Little Judas which rang in her ears as he addressed her: 'But remember, dear Mama, brother had some little gold cuff-links . . . such good ones that he only wore them on holidays . . . only where have those cuff-links disappeared to?—I just can't imagine!'" And in *Invitation to a Beheading,* just after Cincinnatus has been sentenced to death, his lawyer, worried and agitated, runs to his cell: he has just lost a cuff-link! What is this? Coincidence? Unconscious reminiscence? I cannot decide. I was not expecting to happen upon all these traits of Sirin in Saltykov; then, when I reread *Despair* after *Invitation to a Beheading,* a passage from *The Golovlyov Family* suddenly came to mind, practically the only one I still remembered from reading Saltykov long ago: how little Judas, arriving at the last stage of his spiritual decline, surrenders himself to "a binge of idle speculation," to "intellectual dissipation": "having locked himself up in the study . . . he languished over a fantastic task: he constructed every possible unrealizable proposition, taking himself into account, he conversed with imagined company and created entire scenes in which the first chance personality which came into his mind became a character." I recalled this passage when I realized that Felix, Hermann's "double," is no other than this "chance personality which came into his head" and which he does not actually meet. (Ardalion is right: in the real world there are not any "doubles" [3]). And this gave me the key to understanding not only *Despair,* but indeed Sirin's whole *oeuvre,* so that what seemed to me up to this point to be affected virtuosity on his part, a flaunting of his verbal mastery, or at best an extravagant expenditure of creative strength, now struck me as a strictly regulated overall plan, artistically justified and necessary.

If *Despair* is regarded as an ordinary novel, as fiction (i.e., something invented, but real all the same), then it can be interpreted in various ways, each of them just as "real." Hermann does actually meet Felix, who looks exactly like him; he really does not guess, despite the evidence, that his wife is having an affair with Ardalion; and he contrives the crime in order to secure his "happiness" once and for all. Or: Hermann knows about his wife's infidelity, but does not want to admit it to himself. He decides to murder Felix in the hope that this will restore "his hearth and home." Or else: in despair over his wife's infidelity, he ends up creating Felix in his imagination, along with everything that follows. If so, then this is a bad novel, for real-life relationships cannot be reduced to an indefinite equation, no matter how complex they be, and no matter how much they may abound in inner contradictions. All this has validity, however, provided Hermann is a real human being. But what if he is a "Little Judas"? Little Judas is a moral idiot, in the literal meaning of the word (an "idiot" being a man who exists spiritually in and for himself, outside his surroundings, in empty space, i.e., not a human being). He is characterized by that "epistomological vileness," that "impenetrability," for which Cincinnatus was sentenced to death. For such a non-human being there is no difference between real people and figments of the imagination. They all, including him, are located for him on a plane of life in which laws of logic no longer function. No one has depicted this state of mind better than Saltykov: "His existence [Little Judas's] was so complete and independent that he had nothing more to desire. The whole world was at his feet . . . he could vary each protozoan motif endlessly, he could attack each one afresh, reworking it in a new fashion each time." This is because Little Judas the idiot does not suspect the existence of that which, albeit unconsciously, lies at the basis of each real human being's consciousness: the irreversibility of the life-flow, the uniqueness of each moment, resulting from the interactions mentioned by Tolstoy. Such result is *necessary,* it is *inevitable,* even though the interactions themselves be (from an ordinary, workaday point of view) accidental and thus invested with a *meaning* of their own. The pseudo-life led by Little Judas and Hermann in an empty, illusory world has, like authentic life, its own special laws, its own kind of idiotic, wild logic incomprehensible to us. It was not by chance that, having begun to reread Saltykov with the passage which can be considered the starting point of Little Judas's spiritual trajectory, I fell straightway upon the trail seemingly left by one of Sirin's characters. There is no need to assert that Sirin is under the influence of Saltykov. A single "birthmark" (cufflinks) is far from sufficient to prove this, however. Here, coincidences could be brought about by the equally deep penetration of both writers into the substance of this pseudo-life and its pseudo-logic.

This can be substantiated by yet another observation. Saltykov has a work the conception of which would seem to have nothing in common with anything by Sirin: "The Diary of a Provincial in Petersburg." It begins like something of a real diary, in the Saltykov manner naturally, i.e., constantly lapsing into Swiftian satire, wherein caricature is intentionally brought to the very edge of improbability. The "provincial" is made a victim of some kind of mystification which muddles his senses. The real world for him changes into an illusory one: "Now, after two farces played on me, I cannot sit down without thinking: 'But what if this chair collapses under me!' I cannot step on the floorboard without the thought vexing me that perhaps this floorboard is not a floorboard at all, but only the likeness of one. Do I exist or do I not? Do I live in a hotel, or not in a hotel? Are these walls surrounding me, or only some likeness of walls?' . . ." (How much this tone reminds us of Sirin!) There follows a description of one such mystification: "the International Statistics Congress," which turned out to be a meeting of political conspirators. They were caught and are being tried. The judge (who was impersonating a *preses*) addresses the defendants: "Gentlemen! You are guilty of a very serious crime, and only completely wholehearted repentance can mitigate your fate. Our responsibilities regarding you are not very pleasant, but we are sustained by our sense of duty, and we shall remain true to it. . . . Nevertheless we are fully aware that your position is not the most enviable, and therefore we shall do everything possible to mitigate it. Until you have been convicted by law, you are our guests, messieurs! [The "pleading" takes place at the Hôtel du Nord. P.B.]. . . . Now the official in charge will take you . . . to your own rooms and will have some tea served to you. . . ." There follows an interrogation and a new session: " . . . the doors opened and we were invited into the room, where there was a table set for forty persons, in accordance with the number of judges and prisoners. 'Well, gentlemen,' said the pseudo-*preses,* 'we have fulfilled our duty, and you have fulfilled yours. But we shall not forget that you are people just like us. More than that, you are our guests, and we are obliged to see to it that you be not entirely bored. Now, after a piece of juicy roast beef and a glass of good wine, we should be able to abandon ourselves entirely without care to a discussion of those very schemes for which you are on trial. Waiter! Dinner! And plenty of champagne!' " Need one be reminded of Cincinnatus's conversation with M'sieur Pierre concerning the "feast in his honor" given by the "city fathers" on the eve of his execution? In "The Diary of a Provincial" there are many other passages which, if not in subject matter then at least in tone, correspond strikingly to various episodes in *Invitation to a Beheading*. It is this tone, which reflects Saltykov's and Sirin's common intuition and the delirious state of their characters' psyches ("The Diary" gradually evolves into real delirium), which appears to be the theme, in a broad sense of the word, from which their works grow.

Every genuine work of art is conceived and composed in the artist's mind more or less unconsciously; thus, Poe's celebrated Foreword to "The Raven" must be considered as none other than a conscious, *post factum* reconstruction of an unconscious creative process. But, to be sure, another course is also conceivable: one can begin with a reflection about his intuition and then construct, through a line of reasoning, a system of symbols that would most tangibly embody the idea of a world perceived by the consciousness. A work created in this manner will be artistically deficient, devoid of those elements which cause a work of art to first win us over, and only then be rationally grasped or "deciphered" by our consciousness. And yet, the schemes of symbols that result would be identical to the ones intuited by the true artist.

As proof we may use a comparison of Sirin's work with *Journey to the End of the Night* by Céline. Céline is a writer of great intellect, but one completely lacking in Sirin's gift of creating, through verbal relationships, the illusion of reality. This in itself is enough to disprove the proposition that Sirin's last works were influenced by *Voyage au bout de la nuit*. Besides, the first of them, *Camera Obscura*, was published simultaneously with *Voyage* (1932), and there are no fewer similarities between these two than between *Voyage* and *Despair* or *Invitation to a Beheading*. The point of departure here is the same: some spe-

111

cial, terrifying, spiritual experience, a revelation, that reveals
. . . nothing! "At such moments," says Céline's "hero," "everything aggravates your loathsome ennui, forces you to see things,
people, the future, such as they really are, i.e. as skeletons [there
is something quite similar to this in one of Turgenev's "Poems
in Prose"], as nothing—and still you must love these nothings,
value them, imagine them to be animate, as if they really existed." (Cf. Sirin's "Terror," published in *Sovremennye Zapiski*
as early as 1926, a brief story which could be quoted here in
entirety.) Such a spiritual experience turns the one who under-
went it into a nothing. Could Céline's Bardamu or Sirin's Cincinnatus be a son or have a mother? And what constitutes a
mother in this world of theirs? "If," says Bardamu, "I were lying on the executioner's block, my mother would scold me for
not wearing a neckerchief." Compare the farewell between Cincinnatus and Cecilia C.: all her attention is directed to the disorder in his cell. The disappearance of the world from the field
of consciousness, self-isolation, the breakdown of personality—
such are the mutually resultant aspects of this spiritual experience. Hence the spontaneous appearance of "The Double." Did
Céline read Dostoevsky? His "double," as distinguished from
Goliadkin's or Hermann's, is not a "double" in the exact sense
of the word. Leon Robinson, whom Bardamu encounters for
the first time during the war, is in no way similar to him. His
"double-hood" amounts to the fact that he turns up with Bardamu at every state of the latter's "journey," and no matter how
much Bardamu feels his presence as a burden, he is unable to
get away from him. Robinson simultaneously repels him and
attracts him. How? Why? This is left unexplained, and it could
not be explained. Robinson does not need Bardamu, nor does
Bardamu need him. There is nothing in common between them.
And still, each time they are separated, Robinson waits for
Bardamu, searches for him, and vice versa. The Bardamu-Robin-
son "double-hood" is underscored by the fact that when Robinson is temporarily blinded, they acquire a mistress in common

—a striking parallel with *Camera Obscura,* in which the loss-of-sight motif develops with such symbolic profundity. Madelon, abandoned by Robinson, murders him. Bardamu accompanies the body to the grave. This is the last stage of his own "journey"; he has reached the "edge of the night." Robinson's death marks the end of Bardamu's earthly wanderings. Not because he loved Robinson—this was not the case—rather because his "double" had at least some goal in life, even though it was the most pitiful and despicable one: to "set himself up" by murdering old woman Henrouille (however, when Robinson has gained his end, he refuses, apparently without any reason, to profit by it). Robinson was, as it were, the intermediary link between Bardamu, who desired nothing and was unable to desire, and life. Robinson is something like Hermann in *Despair:* Bardamu is Cincinnatus, the eternal recluse for whom life amounts to an unnecessary and inane postponement of death. When Macbeth learns of his wife's death, he says: "She should have died hereafter: there would have been time for such a word. To-morrow, and to-morrow, and to-morrow creeps in this petty pace from day to day, to the last syllable of recorded time. . . . Life's but a walking shadow. . . . It is a tale told by an idiot . . . signifying nothing." The end of *Invitation to a Beheading* provokes the reader's bewilderment: was Cincinnatus deprived of his life or not? It would seem not. But then, why should the three Parcae appear at the scaffold? Did Sirin not abuse his art here in order to intrigue or simply dupe the reader? Actually this represents a reversal, of sheer genius, of the "cliff-hanging ending," the ending customarily followed by the statement "to be continued in the next issue." Such sequel would then provide the solution of the riddle which has been posed to the reader. But here everything ends with the "cliff-hanging." The point is that there can be no answer to the question, for the question itself cannot be phrased. Death is the end of life. But can we call that state in which Cincinnatus lived "life"? Is it not all the same whether he was decapitated or not? Real life is movement directed to-

113

ward some goal, toward self-discovery in intercourse and in strife with real people. Death is the completion of life. Life is the thesis—death the antithesis; after which human consciousness expects some kind of synthesis—some final, extratemporal realization of the sense of a completed life. But if nothing is asserted in life, if life does not propose any thesis, then how can there be an antithesis, and how then is a synthesis possible? All that Cincinnatus can expect after the execution is to go where "beings akin to him" are waiting. This is the "immortality" which terrifies the hero of *Despair,* the endless continuation of what there was here in this "life": "Indeed," said Hermann, "imagine yourself just dead—and suddenly wide awake in Paradise where, wreathed in smiles, your dear dead welcome you. Now tell me, please, what guarantee do you possess that these beloved ghosts are genuine; that it is really your dear dead mother and not some petty demon mystifying you, masked as your mother and impersonating her with consummate art and naturalness?"

No matter how much literary schools, tastes, devices, and styles may differ among themselves, one immutable law has always existed in art, the law of rhythm, i.e., of life itself. The alternation of light and shading, *andante* and *allegro,* strong and weak syllables, consonance and dissonance, and so forth—all this is but an expression of the alternation of tension and relaxation, joy and despondency, and finally life and death. In fiction, the law of rhythm is realized above all in the alternation of episodes: of cheerful and sad ones, comic, or idyllic, and tragic ones, and of minor and significant ones. Fielding, Stendhal, Dickens, and Tolstoy achieved the greatest mastery in this. A narrative about life must reproduce life's movement. In Sirin there is not a trace of this, and for this reason a first reading of his works produces an impression of an absence of rhythm, i.e., of artistic imperfection and lawlessness.

There are works, however, which belong to the category of fiction by virtue of their external form only. *Dead Souls* and Dostoevsky's novels are dramas by their internal structure rather than novels. In this realm, the law of rhythm is implemented primarily in the juxtaposition of images and characters, and not necessarily in the alternation of greater and lesser tension in their struggles. In Dostoevsky, for example, tension is always drawn up to a maximum point. In Sirin there is none of this, because there are no characters. Each of his personages is the "everyman" of ancient English mystery-plays, but an "everyman" seen in his own way. Each of them is blind and deaf, absolutely "impenetrable"—each a caricature of Leibnitz's "windowless" monad. Relationships among them consist of purely mechanical attractions and repulsions. But these creatures want to live. They seem to remember now and then the possibility of feeling as a human would, of having contact with one another; and these efforts of theirs to regain sight, to awaken, efforts hopelessly doomed to fail, are the most terrifying of all. This rhythm of life as depicted by Sirin (using the word "life" approximately, for lack of any other word) corresponds to the tone of his narration: all the time it seems that just around the corner we shall hear human speech, but hardly have its faint syllables begun to be heard when it lapses once again into parody.

Artistic perfection provides conclusive evidence that a work fully expresses an idea conceived in an author's mind. The nature of the idea itself is determined by the author's individuality. This is clear in itself and is, properly speaking, tautological. However, it does not follow from this that an author's creative conception is but "sublimation" of this or that complex he has. Nor does it follow that the images he creates are significant as autobiographical evidence. Although Gogol declared that he himself was Khlestakov and Chichikov it is best simply to ignore this, for it could have been the result of self-hypnosis or hypochondria, and we are not in a position to ascertain whether he was right or wrong in saying it. If Goethe said that there was no crime of which he was not capable, then he wanted of course to express by this his ability to comprehend everything. The spiritual experience in Gogol, Saltykov, and Sirin should be regarded as one in which a certain aspect, not of their own personalities but of man or life in general, is revealed. The theme of human "impenetrability" is an eternal one. The fact that it has in our time been developed with such unprecedented artistic thoroughness, and that in the course of this development, as we have seen, two authors as diverse in character and the scope of their creative gifts as Sirin and Céline seemed to walk in stride, proves that this theme is the theme of our very epoch, an epoch of individualism still persisting, driven to excess, which corrodes the personality, but also an epoch of depersonalizing, dehumanizing, soulless collectivism. Those remaining *au-dessus de la mêlée* no longer have, and those drawn into the *mêlée* do not yet have, any objectively meaningful governing factors, i.e., any religion in the broadest sense of the word. Some believe what they are conditioned to believe, others consciously disavow any faith because it is commonly accepted. "There is yet another reason why I cannot, nor wish to, believe in God:" the hero of *Despair* exclaims, "the fairy tale about him is not really mine, it belongs to strangers, to all men; it is soaked through by the evil-smelling effluvia of millions of other souls that have spun a little under the sun and then burst." I notice, incidentally, that there is a passage remotely parallel to this one in *The Golovlyov Family:* "There are enough such people in the world, and they live by themselves . . . breaking toward the end like rain bubbles."

Some see in *Invitation to a Beheading* a kind of utopia turned wrong side out, a sort of Wellsian image of the future totally deformed by various kinds of worldly "progress." This, of course, is a mistake. In such a utopia Cincinnatus would be taken to his execution in an automobile or airplane—not in a carriage. This is a u-topia in the literal sense of the word and simultaneously a "u-chronia." This is the world in general, just as Cincinnatus is man in general—everyman. Sirin intertwines everyday absurdities in the most artful fashion to emphasize this, as does André

Gide in *Voyage d'Urien*. The bearers of eternal "human" qualities, of qualities which pertain to the "inhuman" in human nature; Sirin's "men in general," like Gogol's and Saltykov's heroes, as well as Dostoevsky's supermen, can never and nowhere, not in any epoch, be real, concrete people. They are allegorical figures—incarnations of "ideas." In *Voyage au bout de la nuit,* where everything that might create the illusion of reality is reduced to a minimum, where people are depicted in a crudely schematic manner, the overall pattern of allegory becomes conspicuous. Allegory has come to be considered a kind of pseudo-art. But even the *Divine Comedy* could be taken for "pseudo-art." If a work of art leaves an integral impression, it is artistically justified. (This does not always come easily: one has to give up the customary demands made of the novel, the painting, etc.) Such are Sirin's works, and still they are allegorical and not symbolic. Symbolic art is not "allegorical"—the symbol is an adequate expression of a concept. If one were to attempt to paraphrase some poem by Blok or Annensky "in one's own words," nothing would be left of the original. But *Invitation to a Beheading* and *Despair* can be and must be paraphrased—that was what Céline did without suspecting it.

Our time would seem to be characterized by a revival of allegorical art, a genre long ago fallen into disuse and forgotten. This art's prerequisite is a certain estrangement from life. Allegory is connected to life as a kind of "alter-existence." Allegorical art flourished during the time of crisis in the Middle Ages, when an old culture was dying and a new one had not yet come into being. In our time old allegorical motifs in fiction are being revived (for example the "wandering soul" motif of *Voyage au bout de la nuit* and *Voyage d'Urien*). In reading Sirin we recollect images beloved by authors of the late Middle Ages, such as apocalyptic horsemen and dancing skeletons. The tone and style are the same: a combination of the ridiculous and the horrible, a "grotesque." Berdyaev dubbed our era "a new Middle Ages," with reference to its inherent tendencies toward the restoration of more organic social forms. But history progresses dialectically through a series of endlessly arising contradictions. The new arises as a result of the disintegration of the old, and from this point of view the title "Autumn of the Middle Ages" might well be applied to our age, just as it was coined by one historian [4] for the period experienced by Europe in the fourteenth and fifteenth centuries.

translated by Dwight Stephens

Notes

1. Cf. A. Bem, "U istokov tvorchestva Dostoevskago" (1936), Foreword, for the proper treatment of this question.

2. In "The Nose" the Doctor "had resin-black side-whiskers and a robust healthy doctor's wife."

3. Cf. Goliadkin's conversation with his servant Petrushka in *The Double:* " . . . . good people . . . live without hypocrisy, and they never occur in pairs. . . ." The connection between Dostoevsky's story and "The Nose" is only too well known (Cf., Bem, *ibid.*) The nose in Dostoevsky's version becomes its owner's double. Sirin, following in Dostoevsky's footsteps, develops the Gogolian theme in the same direction.

4. J. Huizinga, *Herbst des Mittelalters.*

Extraterritorial

GEORGE STEINER

Romantic theory argues that, of all men, the writer most obviously incarnates the genius, *Geist,* quiddity of his native speech. Each language crystallizes, as it were, the inner history, the specific world-view of the *Volk* or nation. This theory is a natural part of romantic historicism and the nineteenth-century discovery of the shaping power of linguistic development. Indo-European philology seemed not only a road into the otherwise unrecapturable past, into the time of the roots of consciousness, but also a uniquely penetrative approach to the matter of ethnic quality. These notions, eloquent in Herder, Michelet, Humboldt, seem to match common sense. The writer is a special master of the language. In him the energies of idiomatic usage, of etymological implication, declare themselves with obvious force. He may, as D. W. Harding says in a well-known passage, bring "language to bear on the incipient thought at an earlier stage of its development" than do ordinary speakers. But it is *his* language he brings to bear; it is his familiarity with it, somnambular, genetic, that makes the bearing radical and inventive. The life of the language, in turn, reflects the writer's presence more than it does that of any other métier: "We must be free or die, who speak the tongue /That Shakespeare spake."

Hence the *a priori* strangeness of the idea of a writer linguistically "unhoused," of a poet, novelist, playwright not thoroughly at home in the language of his production, but displaced or hesitant at the frontier. Yet this sense of strangeness is more recent than one might think. Much of European vulgate literature has behind it the active pressure of more than one language. I would argue that a good deal of poetry from Petrarch to Hölderlin is "classical" in a very material sense: it represents a long act of *imitatio,* an inner translation into the relevant vernacular of Greek and Latin modes of statement and feeling. Literal currents of Greek, Latin and Italian move through Milton's English. Racine's perfect economy depends, in part, on the completing echo of the passage from Euripides—an echo fully present in the poet's mind and assumed to be so, in some degree at least, in that of his literate public. Bi-lingualism, in the sense of an equal expressive fluency in one's own language and in Latin and/or French was the rule rather than the exception among the European élite until the latter eighteenth century. Quite often, in fact, the writer felt more at ease in Latin or in French than he did in his own tongue: Alfieri's *Memoirs* tell of his long struggle to acquire natural authority in Italian. Latin poetry continues to be produced until almost our own time.

Nevertheless, there is more than nationalist mystique to the notion of the writer *enraciné.* Latin was, after all, a very special case, a sacramental and cultural interlingua preserving its function precisely because the European vernaculars were moving apart in deepening self-consciousness. The language of Shakespeare, of Montaigne, of Luther, embodies an extreme local strength, an assertion of specific, "untranslatable" identity. For the writer to become bi- or multi-lingual in the modern way, genuine shifts of sensibility and personal status had to occur. These are visible, for the first time perhaps, in Heine. Binary values characterize his life. He was a Jew with a Christian upbringing and a Voltairian view of both traditions. His poetry modulates continually between a romantic-conservative and a radical, satiric stress. Politics and personal mood made him a commuter in Europe. This condition determined his equal currency in French and in German and gave to his German poetry a particular genius. "The fluency and clarity which Heine appropriated from current speech," says T. W. Adorno, "is the very opposite of native 'at-homeness' *(Geborgenheit)*. Only he who is not truly at home inside a language uses it as an instrument." The bi-lingual virtuosity of Oscar Wilde may have had even subtler roots. There is the Anglo-Irish relation with its traditional bias toward an eccentric, exhibitionist mastery over English; there is also the Irish use of France as a counter to English values and Wilde's own use of French thought and writing to strengthen his aesthetic, liberating polemics against Victorian standards. But I wonder whether the linguistic display which allowed Wilde to write *Salomé* in French (or which inspired the Latin verse of Lionel Johnson) does not point deeper. We know absurdly little about the vital congruence of eros and language. Oscar Wilde's bi-lingualism may be an expressive enactment of sexual duality, a speech-symbol for the new rights of experiment and instability he claimed for the life of the artist. Here, as at other important points, Wilde seems to me one of the true sources of the modern tone.

The links with Samuel Beckett are obvious. Another Irishman fantastically proficient in both French and English, rootless because so variously at home. For a good deal of Beckett's work we do not know whether the English or the French version came first. His parallel texts have an uncanny brilliance. Both language-currents seem simultaneously active in Beckett's inter- and intra-lingual composition; translating his own jokes, puns, acrostics, he seems to find in the other language the unique, natural analogue. It is as if the initial job of invention was done in a crypto-language, compounded equally of French, English, Anglo-Irish and totally private phonemes. Though he does not, so far as I know, publish poetry or parables outside Spanish, Borges is another of the new "esperantists." His intimacy with French, German and, particularly, with English is profound. Very often an English text—Blake, Stevenson, Coleridge, De Quincey—underlies the Spanish statement. The other language "shines through," giving to Borges's verse and to his *Fictions* a quality of lightness, of universality. He uses the vulgate and mythology of Argentina to ballast what might otherwise be almost too abstract, too peregrine an imagination.

As it happens, these multi-linguists (Ezra Pound has his place in this context) are among the foremost writers of the age. The equation of a single pivot of language, of native deep-rootedness, with poetic authority is again in doubt. And if we except Latin, perhaps in real doubt for the first time. This is a decisive aspect of Nabokov.

The Nabokov bibliography is full of traps and obscurities. But it seems established that he has produced original work in at least *three* languages. I say "at least" because it may be that one story, "O.," taken up in *Speak, Memory* (1951) and later in *Nabokov's Dozen* (1958), first appeared under the same title, in French, in *Mesures* (Paris, 1939).

This is only one facet of Nabokov's multi-lingual nature. His translations, re-translations, pastiches, cross-linguistic imitations, etc., form a dizzying cat's-cradle. No bibliographer has, until now, fully unraveled it. Nabokov has translated poems of Ronsard, Verlaine, Supervielle, Baudelaire, Musset, Rimbaud from French into Russian. Nabokov has translated the following English and Irish poets into Russian: Rupert Brooke, Seumas O'Sullivan, Tennyson, Yeats, Byron, Keats and Shakespeare. His Russian version of *Alice in Wonderland* (Berlin, 1923) has long been recognized as one of the keys to the whole Nabokov *oeuvre*. Among Russian writers whom Nabokov has translated into French and English are Lermontov, Tiutchev, Afanasi Fet and the Anonymous of *The Song of Igor's Campaign*. His *Eugene One-*

gin, in four volumes with mammoth textual apparatus and commentary, may prove to be his (perverse) *magnum opus.* Nabokov has published a Russian text of the Prologue to Goethe's *Faust.* One of his most bizarre feats is a re-translation back into English of Konstantin Bal'mont's "wretched but famous" (Andrew Field: *Nabokov,* p. 372) Russian version of Edgar Allan Poe's *The Bells.* Shades of Borges's Pierre Menard!

Equally important, if not more than these translations, mimes, canonic inversions and pastiches of other writers—darting to and fro between Russian, French, German, English and American —are Nabokov's multi-lingual recastings of Nabokov. Not only is he, together with his son Dimitri Nabokov, the principal translator into English of his own early Russian novels and tales, but he has translated (?) *Lolita* back (?) into Russian, and there are those who consider this version, published in New York in 1967, to be Nabokov's crowning feat.

I have no hesitation in arguing that this poly-linguistic matrix is the determining fact of Nabokov's life and art or, as Field more aptly phrases it, "life in art." Nabokov's passions for entomology (a branch of the theory of classification) and chess— particularly chess problems—are "meta-linguistic" parallels to his principal obsession. This obsession is, of course, not wholly of Nabokov's choosing. As he points out with tireless, aggrieved insistence, the political barbarism of the century made him an exile, a wanderer, a *Hotelmensch,* not only from his Russian homeland but from the matchless Russian tongue in which his genius would have found its unforced idiom. This is obviously the case. But whereas so many other language exiles clung desperately to the artifice of their native tongue or fell silent, Nabokov moved into successive languages like a traveling potentate. Banished from Fialta, he has built for himself a house of words. To be specific: the multi-lingual, cross-linguistic situation is both the matter and form of Nabokov's work (the two are, no doubt, inseparable and *Pale Fire* is the parable of their fusion).

It would be by no means eccentric to read the major part of Nabokov's opus as a meditation—lyric, ironic, technical, parodistic—on the nature of human language, on the enigmatic co-existence of different, linguistically generated world visions and of a deep current underlying, and at moments obscurely conjoining, the multitude of diverse tongues. *The Gift, Lolita* and *Ada* are tales of the complex erotic relations between speaker and speech and, more precisely, laments, often as formal and plangent as the funeral orations of the baroque, for Nabokov's separation from the one true beloved, "my Russian language." It is with two other masters of the language, Pushkin and Gogol, and with his predecessor in exile, Bunin, that Nabokov feels himself to be essentially contemporary. The theme haunts *Speak, Memory,* to me the most humane and modest of Nabokov's books. It comes through penetratingly even in the more didactic, explicitly technical of Nabokov's pronouncements. As he told his Wellesley students in 1945: "You can, and should, speak Russian with a permanent broad smile." In Russian a vowel is an orange, in English a mere lemon. This also, I would judge, is the source of the motif of incest, so prevalent throughout Nabokov's fiction and central in *Ada.* Incest is a trope through which Nabokov dramatizes his abiding devotion to Russian, the dazzling infidelities which exile has forced on him, and the unique intimacy he has achieved with his own writings as begetter, translator and re-translator. Mirrors, incest and a constant meshing of languages are the cognate centers of Nabokov's art.

This leads, inevitably, to the question of "Nabokese," the Anglo-American interlingua in which Nabokov has produced the bulk of his work since the early forties. There are those who regard the language of *Lolita* and its successors as a wonder of invention, elegance and wit (cf. *Time*: "the greatest living writer of English fiction"). To other ears Nabokov's prose is a macaronic, precious, maddeningly opaque and self-conscious piece of candy-floss. It is alien not only in details of lexical usage, but in its primary rhythms which go against the natural grain of English and American speech. In the main, this kind of disagreement is a matter of olives: one has the taste or one doesn't. At a first reading *Ada* (in so many ways a variation on the themes of *Pale Fire*) seems to me self-indulgent and at many points irredeemably overwritten. The Newspeak of Ardor is often on the same predictable level of ingenuity as double-acrostics. The mixture of English, French, Russian and private esperanto is labored. It is as if Nabokov had been mastered by that multilingual dilemma which has, until now, been so notably in his control. But with a writer of this reach, first readings are always inadequate. Lived with, the layer cake in *Ada* may prove a culinary find. It is, I feel, less profitable at this stage to debate over the merits or vices of "Nabokese" than it is to throw light on its sources and fabric.

We need really detailed study of the quality and degree of pressure which Russian puts on Nabokov's Anglo-American. How often are his English sentences "meta-translations" of Russian? To what extent do Russian semantic associations initiate the images and contour of the English phrase? Especially, we need an authoritative concordance of Nabokov's Russian poetry and English prose. I suspect that many of the characteristic motions of style in Nabokov's fiction since *Sebastian Knight* embody a resurrection of or variation on the poetry which Nabokov produced in Russian from 1914 to 1939. Whole episodes in *Lolita* and *Ada,* as well as the Augustan mock-epic pastiche in *Pale Fire,* seem to have precise roots in Russian poems some of which go back to the early 1920's. Is a good deal of Nabokov's English a piece of smuggling, an illicit conveyance across the frontier of Russian verse now captive in a society he contemns?

We also require careful analysis of the local and literary background of Nabokov's English. Its aesthetics, its particular rhetoric, the ideals of exact profusion and ironic pedantry it aims at, can be placed. We find them in the Cambridge which Nabokov attended as an undergraduate and in related Bloomsbury. Allowing for all that the book owes to Gogol, I find it difficult to dissociate *Lolita* from the English versions of *art nouveau,* from the colorations of Beardsley, Wilde and Firbank. The

125

lordly asperities and *glissandos* of condescension which are so distinctive of the Nabokov tone can be paralleled in Lytton Strachey, Max Beerbohm and the early Evelyn Waugh. Indeed the whole stance of the amateur/*amatore* of genius, marvelously at ease in a dozen branches of arcane learning, always turning toward the golden afternoons and vintages of the past, is demonstrably late Edwardian and Georgian. That Nabokov's earliest translations and vignettes should concern Rupert Brooke and Cambridge is indicative. Much in his art, and much that now seems most idiosyncratic or original, is a re-invention of that lost world of white flannels and honey for tea. In the England of Virginia Woolf, Nabokov found interwoven the two principal "topics" of his sensibility: the lilac summers of a lost, high bourgeois order, and the erotic ambiguities of Lewis Carroll. One would want to know also what forms of American vulgate and American literature (if he read any) bore in on Nabokov after 1941.

All these would be preliminary lines of inquiry toward getting right the "strangeness," the polysemic nature of Nabokov's uses of language[s]. They would clarify not only his own prodigious talent, but such larger questions as the condition of multi-lingual imagining, of internalized translation, of the possible existence of a private mixed idiom "beneath," "coming before" the localization of different languages in the articulate brain. Like Borges—whom he cheaply and self-betrayingly mocks in *Ada*—Nabokov is a writer who seems to me to work very near the intricate threshold of syntax; he experiences linguistic forms in a state of manifold potentiality and, moving across vernaculars, is able to keep words and phrases in a charged, unstable mode of vitality. Beyond the personal case, moreover, we find the representative stance, or rather motion. A great writer driven from language to language by social upheaval and war is an apt symbol for the age of the refugee. No exile is more radical, no feat of adaptation and new life more demanding. It seems proper that those who create art in a civilization of quasi-barbarism which has made so many homeless, which has torn up tongues and peoples by the root, should themselves be poets unhoused and wanderers across language. Eccentric, aloof, nostalgic, deliberately untimely as he aspires to be and so often is, Nabokov remains, by virtue of his extraterritoriality, profoundly of our time, and one of its spokesmen.

Vanessa atalanta, genus *Nymphalidae,* the Red Admirable (or Admiral) butterfly, which figures throughout Nabokov's work. "My dark Vanessa, Crimson-barred, my blest / My Admirable butterfly!" exclaims John Shade in the poem *Pale Fire* (lines 270-271), and a Red Admirable alights on his arm the minute before he is killed (see lines 993-995 and Kinbote's note for them). In the final chapter of *Speak, Memory* Nabokov recalls seeing in Paris, just before the war, a live Red Admirable being promenaded on a leash of thread by a little girl; in *Lolita,* "Vanessa van Ness" is the maiden name of the mother of Humbert's first fatal love, Annabel Leigh, and Lolita herself is of course a prominent member of the *Nymphalidae* family.

"Spring in Fialta": the choice that mimics chance

BARBARA HELDT MONTER

"Spring in Fialta," dated Paris, 1938, became the title story of two collections of Nabokov's short stories published in the United States, one in Russian and the other a paperback version in English. The latter includes three stories written originally in Russian; "Spring in Fialta" is one of these. Nabokov mentions it twice in *Ada,* and indeed "Spring in Fialta" resembles Nabokov's latest book in its openness, in its description of memory's triumph over time and space. The period from 1937 to 1940 contains both the peak and the finale of Nabokov's achievement as a writer in Russian. During those years he produced two plays, *The Event* and *The Waltz Invention,* and published the book version of

Invitation to a Beheading, The Gift (his greatest novel of this period), and *The Eye* (a collection of short stories). In 1941 Nabokov published his first novel in English, *The Real Life of Sebastian Knight,* after he had come to the United States—now no longer really an émigré, but a refugee. The period immediately following would be Nabokov's darkest and most sparse; *Bend Sinister* was published in 1947. Now that Nabokov has matched and surpassed his early peaks of creativity, we can note with delight in the story "Spring in Fialta" all the most important Nabokovian artistic preoccupations and stylistic traits packed into a mere score of pages. It is as clear a masterpiece among Nabokov's short stories as *Lolita* and *Pale Fire* among his novels.

The protagonist-narrator of the story undertakes a quest similar to that which forms the structure of so many works by Nabokov. It is a journey without direction, unplanned and with an uncertain goal. Movement—through the ever-diminishing space of Russia, European capitals and finally the one small town of Fialta, and through a time made magical by the past being forever repeated in a résumé and brought up short by the present—leads finally not to something found but to an awareness of loss, the loss of a woman scarcely loved. The story begins and ends in the present and concerns a man who takes a short respite from a business trip, meets a woman he has met casually on several distant occasions, in several equally distant places, a woman married, like him, and always surrounded by "friends." The woman, Nina, is consistently generous and casual in giving herself to the narrator and to others. The chance meetings between Nina and the narrator recur outside of the continuity of their separate lives, which form an almost irrelevant background. The narrator has a premonition during their "seemingly carefree, but really hopeless meetings" that "something lovely, delicate, and unrepeatable was being wasted: something which I abused by snapping off poor bright bits in gross haste . . ." (Lolita is similarly "wasted"). Immediately after this last meeting in Fialta, Nina is killed in an automobile crash.

The author himself makes a signature appearance in the story as a big Englishman who at one point steps from chair to window-sill to capture a "compact furry moth," analogous in its finished perfection to the work of art itself. This is not a playful quirk but a serious warning for the reader not to mistake the narrator for the author. The Englishman-author is bent on capturing one precise thing; the narrator is less sure of the object of his quest. Even if we did not know that a moth or a butterfly is the sign of lepidopterist Nabokov's presence, we would be aware that the Englishman's detachment from the events of the story contrasts markedly with the narrator's increasing involvement with them.

The appearance of the Englishman is a small detail which serves a special purpose, in a story where no detail is irrelevant. With Nabokov, detail can be savored even before it begins to form the inevitable complicated pattern of the work. Virginia Woolf writes of how certain scenes in the novels of the great classical writers give a finality of effect and lie "apart from the story, beyond the reach of change." * With Nabokov not scenes but smaller units—images, phrases, even isolated words—seem to have the completeness of, for instance, the scene of the wolf-hunt in *War and Peace*. If enjoyment of the separate details of fiction apart from the total fiction were immoral, Nabokov would be one of the most immoral writers ever.

When Nabokov changes some details from Russian into English, he of course makes the detail more appropriate to the particular language, but he often strengthens the thrust of the whole story. The opening paragraphs, heavy with descriptive detail, set down the bright pieces that will compose the mosaic of the story (the poster of a visiting circus into whose truck Nina will crash in the final sentence, or the yellow bit of unripe orange peel which is echoed by her yellow scarf and yellow car). The narrator is ready for understanding, for he walks with all his "senses wide open." For Nabokov visual perception especially reveals what the lower senses, touch or taste, reveal for Proust; they

* Virginia Woolf, *Collected Essays*, New York, Harcourt, Brace and World, 1967, I, 262.

provide a key to memory and ultimately to understanding of past and present alike. From Russian to English, Nabokov changes none of these basic images, but he does heighten the intensity of some phrases, because English suggests new linguistic possibilities. Thus the "sea rococo of shells" becomes in English the "mantelpiece dreams of sea shells," the "frozen carousel" becomes a "sorry-go-round," the "eye" of the Russian becomes "all my senses." The name Fialta is toyed with even more lovingly in English. In Russian it reminds the narrator of violets (described, but not named) and of the sound of Yalta; in English violets become "violaceous syllables," a viola appears, and the real place name (too prosaic-sounding perhaps after the Conference) becomes a more suggestive "lovely Crimean town."

On the other hand, nothing in English can replace the grammatical contrasts which in Russian underline the interplay of past and present that constitutes the essence of the story. In Russian the imperfective and perfective aspects of the verb alternate, often within the same sentence. The imperfective is used whenever the narrator recalls a past repeated and enduring. In English the verb itself cannot carry these qualities ("Every time I *had met* her . . . , she *had not seemed to recognize* me at once . . ."). The perfective aspect is used for the more abrupt narrative or historical present ("and this time too she *remained* quite still *for a moment*"), briefer and less enduring. (All italics mine.)

The key device of all Nabokov's art, from his early Russian works to his latest English ones, is his calling attention to the difference between art and life. Thus the "life" of fiction is purposely made to appear artistic. At least once in translating from Russian to English Nabokov reinforces the idea that the meetings of the two protagonists are staged. Whereas the Russian text just states: "I met Nina very long ago," the English reads: "My introductory scene with Nina had been laid in Russia quite a long time ago." The narrator of this story thus becomes a kind of sub-creator with his awareness that his life is staged, just as Humbert Humbert is aware of McFate pursuing him. The narrator says: "This time we had met in warm and misty Fialta, and

I could not have celebrated the occasion with greater art, could not have adorned with higher vignettes the list of fate's former services, even if I had known that this was to be the last one. . . ." Nabokov makes the reader laud both the artifices of the author and the wonderment of the narrator who strives to grasp the full pattern of the mosaic in which he himself is depicted. There is in this story a sense of finality, of "that final appointment" set by fate. It is the finality not of life, but of art. Only in the English version does Nabokov mention "a fading memory of ancient mosaic design" on the sidewalk, another clue to the design of the story itself.

Every work of art is based upon choice and coincidence, but authors deal variously with the problem of how much of it to reveal. In *War and Peace* meetings and partings are so long delayed, so prepared by lifelike detail that they often seem no more coincidental than those of life itself. In *Doctor Zhivago* the thick network of coincidence must be taken on faith, as part of the work's symbolism. In the works of Laurence Sterne coincidence is rhetorically marveled at. Nabokov is closest to Sterne. He knows that the hand of the author can never be totally disguised, so he uses it as part of the fiction itself. Not God, but the author creates the events of fiction. His protagonist is aware of being manipulated, but this fact only enhances the suspense of the quest and the blinding flash of recognition at the end. The reader is aware of the author's task not only because the latter appears in the guise of an Englishman, but also because he is contrasted with a briefly appearing "Franco-Hungarian writer," a man who only wanted to weave words inventively. The narrator objects: "Were I a writer, I should allow only my heart to have imagination, and for the rest rely upon memory, that long-drawn sunset shadow of one's personal truth." The two would-be writer-characters add up to the author, who does both. But why not let the story itself prove this? Why break in with a polemic on art? Why let the narrator himself be a sub-artist, using such metaphors as "again and again she hurriedly appeared in the margins of my life, without influencing in the least its basic text." One answer is that in any case we are aware that fiction is fiction, and it is a feat of authorial skill when we see the hand of the artist in the process of sketching the outline of human faces, bringing them to life. Nabokov lets us witness the process of creation and the creation itself simultaneously.

Ultimately, however, only the creation itself matters. With Nabokov the strategy of skill is appropriate to a story about the necessity for skill, for application, in unraveling the threads of one's own existence. To some extent, then, within the framework of Nabokov's total creation, the narrator himself strives to create, but on another level he is part of the author's creation. There exists in almost any reader a resistance to the fact that the sound of a word may determine its meaning and therefore its very existence, as in the name Fialta. It is perhaps the same resistance we feel when we see fate determining character, a character suddenly become aware that he is caught in the plot of a fiction. These things must be yielded to in Nabokov, not in some mysterious way as in Pasternak's novel, but in order that mere illusion of unreality may never become a prop for the reader's emotion. Nabokov weaves a tougher web of illusion, an illusion of *unreality*.

Nabokov's sentences exist to be looked at as well as through. When each image has been seen, it must be connected, counterposed to its kindred images in order to complete the mosaic. Often similarities are neighbors: Nabokov is as fond of the catalogue (often a catalogue of grotesques, for instance that of the habitués of a café) as was Pushkin. The catalogue device brings objects from disparate fields into contrasting juxtaposition. Again, it lends a kind of blatant virtuosity to the narration itself. But more often the connections between details are not made, for the details of his world are taken by the narrator to be clues to the mystery that can be solved only by his own memory. As the reader makes sense of the story, so, in a parallel fashion, the narrator makes sense of the meaning of his meetings with Nina. The reader is ahead in one sense, for in spite of all his sophistication he always expects a love story, which this turns out to be.

But the narrator who is aware of the nature of his love only at the end makes more use of the clues, and leads the reader in the knowledge of memory's power to create understanding of the present through a reenactment of the past.

In the story, as in a religious ritual, the repetition of events and gestures abolishes time. The protagonists meet repeatedly, always in different places and never twice in a single year. All the settings are "trite" and unworthy except for the first and the last. The first meeting occurred around 1917 in the whiteness of a mythical Russian winter at a country estate, where the narrator kissed Nina before knowing her name. At the other meetings they are both émigrés, in transit, "acting out . . . (their) own aimless destiny." With Nabokov, Russian émigrés are a metaphor for any men in search of their own personal truth, and Russia is his metaphor for the mythical past, never to be recaptured except by the arduous effort of memory. Their final meeting takes place in the story's immediate past, in Fialta where the old and new towns symbolize the interlacing of present and past. Fialta seems reluctant to reveal anything (the story opens with the words: "Spring in Fialta is cloudy and dull"), but soon bright pieces of color begin to form the mosaic of memory: "a yellow bit of unripe orange peel on the old, slate-blue sidewalk, which retained here and there a fading memory of ancient mosaic design." While most of the clues in the story are colored, memory itself is white, as in the flash of understanding at the end. The white snow of Russia becomes a white sky and sun, as the whole movement of the story turns into the crescendo-diminuendo of the long final sentence:

But the stone was as warm as flesh, and suddenly I understood something I had been seeing without understanding—why a piece of tin foil had sparkled so on the pavement, why the gleam of a glass had trembled on a tablecloth, why the sea was ashimmer: somehow, by imperceptible degrees, the white sky above Fialta had got saturated with sunshine, and now it was sun-pervaded throughout, and this brimming white radiance grew broader and broader, all dissolved in it, all vanished, all passed, and I stood on the station platform of Mlech with a freshly bought newspaper, which told me that the yellow car I had seen under the plane trees had suffered a crash beyond Fialta, having run at full speed into the truck

of a travelling circus entering the town, a crash from which Ferdinand and his friend, those invulnerable rogues, those salamanders of fate, those basilisks of good fortune, had escaped with local and temporary injury to their scales, while Nina, in spite of her long-standing, faithful imitation of them, had turned out after all to be mortal.

The tinfoil, the glass and the sea, all details which had appeared before, are all reflectors, reflecting two ways, back into the past and forward from the past into the present. Each present meeting with Nina had brought a summary of all their past meetings, but the reason for this and the understanding that memory always comes too late appears in a white radiance at the end. Seeing had not been understanding until then. The narrator had assumed Nina to be a chameleon personality, like the protagonists in *The Eye* and in *The Real Life of Sebastian Knight,* because of her seemingly infinite adaptability and acquiescence. But chameleons, salamanders and basilisks are invulnerable species because of their very lowness on the evolutionary scale. The highest forms of life are the most transitory, and Nina proved finally to be ephemeral. The narrator had had premonitions of disaster, ones always centered on Nina herself. His fears that "something lovely, delicate, and unrepeatable was being wasted" are separated, until the end, from any feeling of his own final loss. Only then is the mosaic complete.

Nabokov is more interested in mosaics than in natural scenes, so of course the flash of understanding is as patterned as the "lives" preceding it. The reader of common sense again protests that life itself would not be structured thus, but Nabokov peers at precisely the kind of mimicry Nina displayed, in an effort to penetrate life's secrets. Like an eccentric librarian in one of his own later stories, "The Vane Sisters," Nabokov seeks in life— in words and in lepidoptery—"the chance that mimics choice, the flaw that looks like a flower." The very expression of the idea, as in this phrase the very letters of the words, yields patterns of mimicry. But art, of course, is really the opposite; it is the *choice* that mimics *chance.* Few writers other than Nabokov have dazzled us more thoroughly into a permanent awareness of this double truth.

In place of lost time: *Ada*
JEFFREY LEONARD

Ever since Zeno, philosophers have been attacking our conventional belief in the "reality" of chronometric Time. Van Veen's *The Texture of Time* represents the first full-scale attack of this sort so far launched by an inhabitant of Antiterra. But, unlike his counterparts on this planet, Van's writings, though lacking in philosophical completeness, are boundlessly optimistic, attempting to replace lost Time with a more satisfactory notion of Remembered Time, or "Pure Time," or "Perceptual Time." *Ada* is an affirmative book and "Veen's Time" is an affirmative philosophy that achieves, despite a number of formal errors, a workable resolution to the problem of Time, at least as it is faced by the artist.

Conventional Time is a dead-end street, ending in death; it is, unfortunately, also designated "one-way" by that comedy villain, fate. Conventional Time is a function of space and motion, since the only way we can measure it, or even perceive it, is through linear progression. It is easily grasped by the practical intellect in that reasoning itself is based upon the space-time principle of consecutive order. But for the artist, or for anyone, in fact, who wishes to avoid being steamrollered into oblivion, conventional Time is the archenemy.

Nabokov is not the first writer to seek a way out. He owes a debt at least to Jorge Luis Borges, whom he acknowledges, in not very flattering terms, by his anagrammatic reference in *Ada* to an Osberg, author of "pretentious fairy tales." But Nabokov is more ambitious than Borges. In an interview in an appropriately named magazine,* Nabokov says of the Argentine writer: "At first Vera and I were delighted by reading him. We felt we were on a portico, but we have learned there was no house." Borges does indeed build porticos on nonexistent houses, but Nabokov gives us the house. In "Avatars of the Tortoise" and "A New Refutation of Time," Borges, like Van Veen, undermines the validity of chronometric Time and unlocks the prison from which the artist must escape. But Borges, content merely to appreciate his vertiginous paradoxes, does not replace lost Time. "Veen's Time" provides the same imaginative freedom, which Nabokov then uses to create *Ada,* his house of art in the arbors and ardors of Ardis.

Escape from conventional Time is the artist's problem. Nabokov's ingenious solution is to deny chronometric Time and to create a new Time which, for him, has "texture" instead of linear progression. Van delights "sensually in time, in its stuff and spread, in the very impalpability of its grayish gauze, in the coolness of its continuum." Through textured time, the art of *Ada* becomes possible: "*The Texture of Time* is only the central rose-web of a much larger and ampler novel," said Nabokov, early in *Ada*'s composition.[1] For Nabokov, conventional Time consists of "numbers and rows and series—the nightmare and malediction harrowing pure thought and pure time" and "mathematical formulas, which immediately blind one's brain." Con-

* *Time,* May 23, 1969.

ventional Time destroys the past, reduces the present to "an instant of zero-duration," is ruled by the destructive movement of space through space (the "rent in the canvas"), renders meaningless those "immortal moments" captured in the artist's mind. A Time caressing and caressed by the memory and imagination is the only medium for Nabokov's art. Time must be an "ever-ever land," a "flowering of the present." This is not to say that such a Time exists in "reality." Physically the artist may be caught in the spherical prison of space-time, but his imagination is free to create a world in which Time is not the ruler but the ruled.

In everyday life, we don't "feel" Time. We only objectively note its passing, through measurement. In the imagination and the memory, however, there is something akin to a "texture" of Time, a certain feel to it. It is independent of any sequence of events. Events are located in past Time, but, if one examines his own memory, he discovers no sense of "flowing" from one event to another. The events, recalled at random, seem to have a "texture" of Time about them, a texture of "smooth" Time or of "dimpled" Time, but with no sense of "flow." This kind of Time, Nabokov's, is immobile; it enhances rather than devalues the recollection. It is the Time-medium of art. "Pure Time, Perceptual Time, Tangible Time, free of content, context and running commentary—this is *my* time and theme," says Veen. "All the rest is numerical symbol or some aspect of space." We still die, but in the flowering present, the past is eternalized. The memory and imagination obey Perceptual, not physical, Time.

Since the connection between Time and space is intimate, there must be, along with a new notion of Time, a corresponding change in the nature of space. Antiterra is, of course, the representation (but not the symbolic representation) of that new space. History (Time) and geography (space) are rearranged to suit Nabokov's imagination. Van and Ada are the spies sent out by Nabokov to explore the new Space-Time: ". . . it's fun to be two secret agents in another country," says Van. "Spies from Terra?" asks Ada. Sometimes space on Antiterra becomes almost a plaything of the imagination. There are flying carpets and Van's Mascodagama act, both excellent examples of Nabokov's working his way between what he calls his "own truth and the parody of it." The intimate connection between Time and space is broken. Space ceases to be the comic villain. "No one shall make me believe," says Van, "that the movement of matter (say, a pointer) across a carved-out area of Space (say, a dial) is by nature identical with the 'passing' of time. Movement of matter merely spans an extension of some other palpable matter, against which it is measured, but tells us nothing about the actual structure of impalpable Time." Space ceases to chronometrically violate Time. Within the memory and imagination (again, examining anyone's imagination, even if he isn't a genius), space is essentially passive, nondestructive, in Nabokovian terms. There is no rent in the canvas. Whereas in physical reality "the blind finger of space probe[s] and tear[s] the texture." Anti-terra is a remembered land, an imagined land; here space is less malicious than on Terra. Space-Time is both anti-terror and anti-tyrannical.

Van Veen may have started out to be a philosopher but he realizes that he is, instead, an artist. (To be sure, this realization comes a little late, but there is every indication that Van suspected it all along.)

One afternoon in 1957 . . . it suddenly occurred to our old polemicist that all his published works . . . were not epistemic tasks set to himself by a savant, but buoyant and bellicose exercises in literary style. He was asked why, then, did he not let himself go, why did he not choose a big background for the match between Inspiration and Design; and with one thing leading to another it was resolved that he would write his memoirs— to be published posthumously.

This statement, flippantly parodying the genesis of the work, is related to a more serious one some hundred pages earlier: "He knew he was not quite a savant, but completely an artist." The reader has already reached this conclusion for himself. In Van's writing true genius is revealed not in "ideas" but in his style and use of metaphor. Van himself seems to have been rather slow in realizing it: "[my] philosophic work, so oddly impeded by its own virtue—by that originality of literary style which constitutes the only real honesty of a writer." As an artist, reconstructing his past, Van's style is hardly an impediment.

In his own memoir, *Speak, Memory,* Nabokov was faced with the same problem of Time and solved it in much the same way as Van. In that work, he didn't outline a theory of Time, as Van does, but, conversely, he stated the need for one, in terms of art, more clearly, more eloquently:

> **The cradle rocks above an abyss and common sense tells us that our existence is but a brief crack of light between two eternities of darkness. . . . Nature expects a full-grown man to accept the two black voids, fore and aft, as stolidly as he accepts the extraordinary visions in between. Imagination, the supreme delight of the immortal and immature, should be limited. . . . I rebel against this state of affairs. I feel the urge to take my rebellion outside and picket nature. . . . That this darkness is caused merely by the walls of time separating me from the free world of time- lessness is a belief I gladly share with the most gaudily painted savage.[2]**

Van, approaching the problem initially as a philosopher, states the problem in this way to the unfortunate Philip Rack, who is about to die:

> **The mind of man, by nature a monist, cannot accept two nothings; he knows there has been one marking his biological inexistence in the infinite past, for which his memory is utterly blank, and that nothingness, being as it were, past, is not too hard to endure. But a second nothing is logically unacceptable.**

Vengeful Van is, of course, about to use this argument to prove to Rack that all of eternity for him will be a rack of pain, but the argument parallels Nabokov's complaint in *Speak, Memory.* Before either memoir is possible, Time must be rethought and tamed. The triumph in each book is the direct association of Time and consciousness resulting in an imaginative freedom which molds the sensory data of memory into new life. Or, as Page Stegner put it, Nabokov "escapes the spherical prison of time by creating in his art a subjective world that spirals out of chronometric time."[3] Nabokov once described his existence as a colored spiral within a glass sphere. The glass sphere is "real" life, in which Time ultimately can neither be comprehended nor transcended. Within that prison, however, exists the spiral, the solution to the vicious circle, composed equally of memory and imagination, constituting art through the miracle of language.

Ada, unlike *Speak, Memory,* attempts to bring this artistic concept of Time as close to the level of theory as it can without ceasing to be art. *Ada* asserts, more than suggests, a central theme of Nabokov. In an interview with Alfred Appel, Nabokov said, "When we speak of a vivid individual recollection we are paying a compliment not to our capacity of retention but to Mnemosyne's mysterious foresight in having stored up this or that element which creative imagination may use when combining it with later recollection and inventions. In this sense, both memory and imagination are a negation of time." [4] They are a negation, anyway, of conventional Time and, in *Ada,* are the source of "Pure Time." Their power is illustrated by Van's ability to almost relive the past: "Hammock and honey: eighty years later he could still recall with the young pang of the original joy his falling in love with Ada. Memory met imagination halfway in the hammock of his boyhood's dawns." All the principles expounded in "Veen's Time" are centered on the ability of memory to perceive Time as texture, rather than progression. Corollaries to the theory include the separation of space from Time; the past as accumulation of senses; the nonexistence of the third "panel" of Time, the future. But finally, "Veen's Time" is a function of memory: "Time is but memory in the making." The importance of memory as the true key to past ("ever existing in my mind") and the present ("to which my mind gives duration and therefore 'reality'" *) is brilliantly underscored by Nabokov's use of Kim Beauharnais' still photographs. For Van, and Nabokov, these stills can only corrupt the "reality" of the past that is truly captured only by memory and imagination. In the photographs Van's and Ada's past has been "spoofed and condemned" by their static, untextured unreality. The photo-

* This is Nabokov's refutation of the present as an instant of "zero-duration."

graphs are "trivial," turning moments of magic immortality into glossy, senseless, insensate parodies of significance. On the other hand, the sequences of Ada in *Don Juan's Last Fling* are a "complete refutation of odious Kim's odious stills," not because they attempt to reproduce an actual moment of the past, but because, by affording Van fleeting glimpses of Ada's elusive beauty, they stimulate his imagination to recreate the Ada he knew. In comparison to camera technology, "memory is a photo studio deluxe on an infinite Fifth Power Avenue."

"Veen's Time" is but the theoretical rose-web of what is more comprehensively the artist's Time or "Ada Time." "Veen's Time" expounds the principles, but before the principles become alive as art, they must be incorporated as metaphor and style and structure into the texture of *Ada*. In his National Educational Television interview (1965), Nabokov said that in his new work, *The Texture of Time,* the figures of speech used to describe Time would begin to come alive and participate as characters in a story. That Nabokov has succeeded in this rather misty undertaking, or that *Ada* actually represents such an attempt, seems to me highly unlikely. But the sense of Nabokov's pronouncement cannot be mistaken. If not as characters, the metaphors of Time must nevertheless somehow be a part of the artistic experience and of the blooming of the artistic experience in language. "Veen's Time" is an element in the original event itself, a perceptual quality, a certain texture; it figures as metaphor in the language that transforms the event into art; and it affects the structural design of the work. Beyond doubt, the most elusive of these three aspects of Time is the first. It is the hardest to describe, as Van discovers in his attempts to "philosophize" the phenomenon. It is, perhaps, misleading to say that Time is an element in the original event; more precisely, it *becomes* an element in the original event when that event is recalled, when it becomes the property of memory. Since everything the artist has to work with is something from the past, however recent, all events are infused with memory and memory's sense of Time. Van comes closest to describing this when he says, ". . . the rapture of her identity, when placed under the microscope of reality (which is the only reality) shows a complex system of those subtle bridges which the senses traverse . . . between membrane and brain, and which always was and is a form of memory, even at the moment of its perception." Just as the moment remembered is *felt,* so is the Time which suffused it *felt.* Time sometimes can be felt as pain. A verbal slip (Nabokovian, not Freudian) on the next to last page reveals Van's awareness of Time as pain: ". . . a work he had never written, though planned to write many pains. There was no pain to do it now—and high pain for *Ada* to be completed." Time also drives Aqua Durmanov painfully mad. The sensation of Time was likened by Van to hollows and "dim pits." These are Aqua's tormentors: "It was the forming of soft black pits in her mind, between the dimming sculptures of thought and recollection, that tormented her phenomenally." And Van as a psychologist studies countless cases of chrono-madness. Time is painful because a cherished recollection is, in the memory, surrounded by a sense of loss associated with Time. But Van, who earlier in his life—before the loss of Ada—had "fanatically denounced the existence of physical pain in all worlds," can "delight sensually in time." He is a "lover of time." He wishes "to caress time." This, more than pain, is the kind of Time experienced by the artist. Time as pain, succumbed to occasionally even by Van, is, in a sense, a capitulation to chronometric Time, even though it still obeys the memory. Time that can be caressed, on the other hand, is "Pure Time," *Ada* Time. It is what Van is aware of in the finest passages of the book, or, rather, what ninety-year-old Van is aware of when he writes the passages. Between the event and the recollection, Time becomes a factor. It is this Time that can be felt, sometimes as pain but more often as bliss. When Ada calls Van by telephone at the end of their seventeen-year separation:

It was the timbre of the past as if the past had put through the call, a miraculous connection . . . that telephone voice, by resurrecting the past and linking it up with the present, with the darkening slate-blue mountains beyond the lake, with the spangles of the sun dancing through

the poplars, formed the centerpiece in his deepest perception of tangible time, the glittering "now" that was the only reality of time's texture.

"Veen's Time" can also be experienced as the area between and around the bright points of memory; as the hollow between rhythmic beats, in which Pure Time "lurks" (the gray gap between black beats, the Tender Interval, "Veen's Hollow"); and as the intervals between events ("twin dimples, each brimming with a kind of smooth, grayish mist, and a faint suggestion of old confetti"); and all of us experience the shiver of déjà vu, which, for Van, becomes a twin shiver of "two-fold déjà-vu."

In Van's, Nabokov's, or in any art, the poetic experience and the language used to describe it are interrelated. In a sense, the experience is not truly perceived until it becomes language. Language not only conveys but qualifies the content of art. Insofar as Perceptual Time participates in Van's experience of art, it also participates, as metaphor, in the language of art. Describing the unique thrills of his Mascodagama Act, Van writes:

> The essence of the satisfaction belonged rather to the same order as the one he later derived from the self-imposed, extravagantly difficult, seemingly absurd tasks when V.V. sought to express something, which *until* expressed, had only a twilight being (or even none at all—nothing but the illusion of the backward shadow of its imminent impression). It was Ada's Castle of Cards. It was the standing of metaphor on its head not for the sake of the trick's difficulty, but in order to perceive an ascending waterfall or a sunrise in reverse: a triumph, in a sense, over the ardis of time. Thus the rapture young Mascodagama derived from overcoming gravity was akin to that of artistic revelation in the sense utterly and naturally unknown to the innocents of critical appraisal.

In like manner, "Veen's Time" has only a twilight being until it is expressed in the texture of *Ada*. Neither we nor Van can comprehend it as philosophy but it becomes "real" when it appears as metaphor in the context of the memory and the memoir. Thus, on the morning before disaster, Van "looks forward to another day of increasing happiness (with yet another uncomfortable little edge smoothed away, another raw kink in the past so refashioned as to fit into a new pattern of radiance). . . ."

The meaning of Time and the sense in which Van experiences it begin to come clear in figures such as this, whereas the mind resists the philosophical assertion. Such phrases as "the heights and hollows of time" and "the static gray time," "chance crease in the texture of time," "overlappings of time" occur throughout and elucidate the meaning and nature of Time as an artist's tool. *Ada*, on Van's level, is a vast recapturing and restructuring of the past, a heroic exercise in total recall. Time is the obedient servant of memory, following the valleys and vales, the creases and crevasses of the mind's terrain.

For V.V. himself Time is, moreover, the plaything of design; it can be folded like a map (though Van, ironically, has some trouble with that trick), punctured like a canvas, superimposed upon itself, and stood upon its head. The structure of *Ada*, therefore, like the language, has much to do with Perceptual Time. Van's memoir is an effort to eternalize the ardors of Ardis, the perilous joy of his and Ada's youth. The structure of *Ada* telescopes toward a past some eighty years distant in Time. As chronometric Time lengthens, Perceptual Time foreshortens; each succeeding Part, though comprising more years, is composed of less Pure Time. Events are removed from their conventional Time sequence, juxtaposed, or arranged antiphonally.

When, in the middle of the twentieth century, Van started to reconstruct his deepest past, he soon noticed that such details of his infancy as really mattered (for the special purpose the reconstruction pursued) could be best treated, could not seldom be *only* treated, when reappearing at various later stages of his boyhood and youth, as sudden juxtapositions that revived the part while vivifying the whole. This is why his first love has precedence here over his first bad hurt or bad dream.

Imagination can, in a sense, control the history of Time. Characteristically, Nabokov carries this notion to a parodic extreme. Van, recalling several alternative actions he might have taken after Demon discovers his relationship with Ada, writes them as if they had happened, concluding Part Two with "There are other possible forkings and continuations that occur to the dream-mind, but these will do." *Ada* is the creation of Van, who is, in turn, the creation of Vladimir Nabokov. In this doubly controlled work of art, Time becomes the servant of two master memories.

Even art, however, has its limitations. There is, in *Ada*, inescapably, a note of sadness. Though the imaginative power of the artistic "spiral" seems endless, that spiral still exists within the glass "sphere," the prison of everyday Time. Memory's hold on the past is tenuous, as the aging Van becomes more and more aware. As the memory fails, chronometric Time begins to assert itself over Perceptual Time. But still, within the context of art, Ada and ardor are, in the words of Alfred Appel, "constants that unify past and present and deny the encroachments of 'the end' " [5] and Nabokov himself seems unwilling to give up "the ineffable hereafter that both our young people mutely and shyly believed in."

Notes

1. Alfred Appel, Jr., "An Interview with Vladimir Nabokov," *Nabokov: The Man and His Work,* ed. L. S. Dembo (Madison, 1967), p. 43.

2. Vladimir Nabokov, *Speak, Memory*, rev. ed. (New York, 1966), pp. 13-14.

3. Page Stegner, *The Art of Vladimir Nabokov: Escape into Aesthetics* (New York, 1966), p. 50.

4. Appel, "Interview," p. 32.

5. Alfred Appel, Jr., *"Ada,"* *New York Times Book Review*, Section 7, Part 1 (May 4, 1969), p. 1.

The mechanics of *Pale Fire*

NINA BERBEROVA

1.

Everybody would probably agree that when a novel, a story, a poem has two levels, realistic and symbolic, the realistic is obvious while the symbolic requires a certain effort of the reader to be understood and appreciated. We follow the story of Ivan Ivanovich, in love with Marya Petrovna, and slowly somewhere between the lines Theseus and Ariadne start flickering. A terrible epidemic devastates a city but this is only the surface: we are being told about the absurdity and purposelessness of the entire world.

There is in *Pale Fire* a structural surprise: the symbolic level, the fantastic, the poetic, lies on its surface and is obvious, while the factual, the realistic is only slightly hinted at, and may be approached as a riddle. The realistic level is hidden by the symbolic one which has nothing enigmatic in it and is immediately clear to the reader. To know the real facts is another story and a tricky one. Here they are:

Two men were living in the United States near a university campus. One of them, John Shade, was a famous poet; the other, Professor Charles Kinbote, had recently arrived from Europe. Kinbote had rented a house in the poet's neighborhood; his landlord happened to be Judge Goldsworth. Some time ago, Judge Goldsworth had put an assassin in a lunatic asylum; this man had recently escaped and was searching for the judge to avenge himself. On one summer evening Kinbote and Shade were walking between their houses. The killer appeared, mistook Shade in the darkness for the judge (they were slightly alike) and shot him.

From this well-hidden factual level let us go to the obvious fantastic one:

Kinbote is not a "displaced person," he is a "displaced soul." In the past he has been the King of a lost Kingdom. His grandfather and his father were rulers of a remote Nordic peninsula, a country called Zembla. He lived in a palace (or castle) making love to young lads; he married, ascended the throne, and was nicknamed Charles the Beloved. A day came when a riot at the glass factory started. Charles was kicked out of his palace and put in a tower, but he escaped, having found—according to tradition—a secret exit. We are told that he escaped not in the attire of a nun (as nasty tongues have gossiped) but in royal purple, that is to say, in a bright red undershirt. The anti-karlists, backed by their powerful neighbor, took over his marvelous land. But this was not enough: they sent Gradus the Killer to the United States to chastise Kinbote, the "international scholar." The powerful neighbor gloomily watched the development of events, overbrimming with "congested nationalism and provincial sense of inferiority."

When Charles now looks back he sees a magical quality to everything in his lost land: his reign had been "peaceful and elegant," the climate had been improved from year to year, and the tax system gradually became a thing of beauty. All the Zemblan boys were incredibly beautiful and healthy, they had pink cheeks and dreamy eyes. "Dear Marcel and dear Gide" would have appreciated these young "faunlets" if only they could have known them!

Kinbote calls Zembla "my fabulous Kingdom" and his boyhood—"tender and terrible." "The dazzling Zembla burns in my brain," writes Kinbote recalling the "Crystal Kingdom" where acrobats and actors were the delight of the courtiers, where there were such manly customs. . . . We are also told that the famous Zemblan folk epic of the XII c. had been written in 1798, that Zemblans drink vodka, and that the empire of the powerful Sosed could be seen on the other shore of the Gulf of Surprises in fair weather.

We already know that Kinbote lives next door to the famous Shade because in his "legendary land" (where he buried his crown and scepter) he decided to tell the immortal story of his Zembla and his own drama to the poet. He found Shade, he gave him the "marvelous material," and Shade—he has no doubt about it—will make him immortal: he and his Zembla will never die. One of the recurrent themes of Shade's poem is the mirror reflecting Shade himself in the process of shaving: he looks at his face, before starting to work on a 24-hour beard, from the point of view of a geographical map—between his nose and his upper lip he imagines that strange land, that unknown Zembla of which his beloved Alexander Pope has said once:

At Greenland, Zembla, or the Lord knows where

and Shade mentions the legendary land for the first (and last) time:

Old Zembla's fields where my gray stubble grows.

Here on that upper lip the climate is rough but "the slaves make hay between my mouth and nose."

This is the unique mention of the marvelous peninsula in

Shade's poem. But Kinbote doesn't stop here: he reads the poems a second time, looks for oblique allusions and, although he finds some, is ultimately disappointed. He realizes that he has given Shade *everything* including the title of the poem *(Solus Rex)* but Shade has invented his own title *(Pale Fire)*—taking it from nowhere. This was probably the "pale fire" (muses Kinbote) that consumed the variants of Shade's poem when the old witch Sybil Shade deployed her intrigues. Kinbote is now trying to write his own variants but they are anemic, unnecessary, they have no place in the poem. There are some blurred data in the Index at the end of the book about who wrote what. It is obvious that Charles the Beloved is doomed to await a new Gradus who—he firmly hopes—some day won't miss *him*. Perhaps he is already on his way?

Banished forever from paradise, Charles Kinbote lives the life of a lonely man: no one needs him, he has no roots, only memories of his absurdly blissful past. In these memories there is a corner of a dark room with an empty locked trunk and the relic of a sewing machine. A masculine mother (or aunt) and a stupid paralytic father (or uncle) were the guardians of his early years. We are told about a castle or palace but we can hardly believe this: Kinbote still continues to call his middle-class rented house a castle, a palace, a humble shack, a log cabin with a tiled bathroom, a cave. "Dear Jesus, do something" —comes the howl one night when music booms around Kinbote's cabin and brings on an unbearable headache. (He is now living in a new place where he is busy writing the commentary to Shade's manuscript.)

We see the slightly comic and pathetic reality of his past that certainly could not have led to anything immortal, poetical, and beautiful. The whole book is about not being needed. And he thought he was so important, so fascinating!

2.

Comic effects are important: they hold together the structure of the novel. They can be divided in two groups: the first one consists of semantic comical elements; the second—of comical puns and word play. Here are some examples of the first group; the comic element is tightly interwoven with the sense of the sentence:

A lackey *takes off* the King's *slippers,* then *takes them away,* then comes back again, *takes them away, brings them back,* again *takes them away* . . . Kinbote's memory fails: was Shade's daughter *six days* in the barn or was it *six years?* In another instance during a nonchalant run of a sun-tanned Ganymede-Antinous across a Swiss garden we are told that he was dressed in a "leopard spotted loin cloth," "in black bathing trunks," "in white tennis shorts," "in a Tarzan brief." When Gradus comes to Nice and sees the promenade des Anglais he is enchanted by *beautiful trucks* and *motorcycles* (and also by cars). The anti-karlists write their notes on *tasty paper* which is *swallowed* later with gusto for the sake of conspiracy. Two Russian advisers that are sent from the other side of the Gulf of Surprises are called *Andronnikov* and *Niagarov* but later become *Andron and Niagarushka.* Kinbote spies on Shade and knows how much he writes each evening of "our poem," the mathematics are simple: 1,000 minutes produce 50 lines, which means that Shade writes "one syllable a minute." And on the campus there is Professor Pnin, not in person, but when the strange figure of Gradus the Villain appears, people hearing his Zemblan accent and noticing his strange behavior think that this is the new assistant of Pnin, a new member of the Russian Department.

The second group are the puns. Wordsworth and Goldsmith are divided in half: Wordsmith is the name of the university where Kinbote pursues his academic career, Goldsworth—the name of his landlord, the judge, who looks like the old waitress, who in her turn looks like a Medusa, or like Shade himself. The Institute of Preparation for the Hereafter is called IPH or IF and its president is Dr. Macaber. What of Gradus himself? He is of course Leningardus, D'Argus, De Grey, and about him we hear the following:

> **Leningrad-*us*-ed to be Petrograd,**
> **A prig-*rad*-*us* (Obsolete past of *read*).**

The famous Russian joke about His Majesty's coronation has its exact counterpart in English when the Blessed Sovereign solemnly puts on his head, instead of a *crown*, first a *crow* and then a *cow*, etc.

In the range of literary devices one also finds Nabokov's direct address to the reader. In *Lolita* the author-narrator-hero addresses himself not only to the buyer of his book but also to the jury that will some day judge him, and to the typesetter. In *Pale Fire* one of the persons Kinbote addresses is the Doctor who obviously will soon start visiting Kinbote (or perhaps is visiting him now). This is casual, and comes at the end of the Commentary ("We may concede, Doctor . . ."). After this a sentence in the Introduction takes a meaning: in introducing the reader to his analysis of Shade's poem Kinbote gave his first comment on its four Cantos: the First "with all those amusing birds," etc.; the Second "your favorite." . . . Until we come to page 279 where we find the Doctor, we might surmise that "your" means either Kinbote's wife, Diza, or Kinbote's archenemy, Sybil Shade (the poet's wife), or perhaps even "Vera" to whom the novel is dedicated. But after "We may concede, Doctor" no doubts are possible: the first address has also been made to the Doctor, present or future. Kinbote appeals to him from his "de profundis" like Gogol's Madman: "Mother, have pity on your sick child!"

Who this Doctor is and where he comes from no one knows. But like the Gendarme in the *Revizor* he will soon put an order into things. The ordeal has to have an end, "and damn that music!" The solemn tone of Kinbote suddenly breaks up, the mixture of pseudo-scientific pedantry, Pnin's academic tradition, and the verbosity of a madman come to an end. The tone collapses when on the last page in one sentence the real face of Kinbote appears:

"—Well folks, I guess many in this fine hall are as hungry and thirsty as me and I'd better stop, folks, right here."

This spontaneous speech is the nearest we can get to the

atmosphere of the locked trunk and the old sewing machine that are hidden in the far corner of Kinbote's past.

I have spoken at length elsewhere about the autoreminiscences of Nabokov and how he uses them. I called them at that time his "recurrent imagery." Perhaps it would be more appropriate to call them a chain of symbols where relations between tenor and vehicle are the same for nearly forty years.

They could yield the chemistry of Nabokov's creative process. In *Pale Fire* they are again there: butterflies, the chess game, tennis, mirrors, words read in reverse, the likeness of people, the conjurer with a dove flying out of his hat or his sleeve, the noise of running water muffling the noise of illicit love, a Nordic land —image of paradise lost.

There are other symbols, those that hold the whole structure together, and among the most important is "Zoorlandia" from an early novel by Nabokov, *Exploit (Podvig,* 1932). This strange land has moved since 1932 across many novels and most of the poems to its last and greatest incarnation in *Pale Fire.* This land both exists and does not, it has been and is no more, memory deliberately or unintentionally distorts it, makes it more magnificent and pathetic than it has ever been, gives it grandeur and pettiness, beautifies it and ridicules it, makes it more tragic and more comic than it ever was. There are moods and feelings about which one cannot speak in dead seriousness but only obliquely and ironically. A contemporary Baudelaire must laugh in his "Belgian hell." In chess we know that the King left alone in a corner of the chessboard has no chance to come back to his throne but the Knight who jumps in all directions, over everyone else, sometimes is able to project his movements beyond the chessboard: hadn't Nabokov made clear in *The Defense* the fact that the borderline between the 64 squares and reality might disappear and the figures move into "real life"? This reality where chess figures feel at home is not quite an ordinary one: there the likeness of people is not something casual and ordinary, and the resemblance between people becomes a controversial phenomenon: one man thinks that that jobless workman in

Zwickau looks like his twin brother, but others do not notice it. Gradus looks like the madman but this nobody will ever know. Shade is taken for the judge although it would have been easier to take for Shade the waitress at the campus cafeteria. And young Gordon, sun-tanned in Switzerland, will remind one of Lolita.

And here is another device: the dissolved epigraph which was used with such virtuosity in *Lolita*. There Poe's "Annabel Lee" was dissolved; in *Pale Fire* it is a Shakespearean tragedy. The royal uncle's translation into Zemblan of *Timon of Athens* was taken by Charles the Beloved on his journey out of a cupboard smelling of naphthalene. Not having handy the English original he squeezes every drop out of it to feed his despair. But let us look into the Zemblan translation (there were a total of 32 volumes, we are told). Thus we will have a glimpse into Zemblan Shakespeare.

In the original we read:

> **The sun's a thief, and with his great attraction**
> **Robs the vast sea: the moon's an arrant thief**
> **And her** *pale fire* **she snatches from the sun!**
>
> **The sea's a thief, whose liquid surge resolves**
> **The moon into salt tears; the earth's a thief**
> **That feeds and breeds by a composture stolen**
> **From general excrement: each thing's a thief.**
>
> (Act 4, scene 3)

The uncle whose translation the Zemblan Academy was not permitted to criticize did the following with it:

> **The sun is a thief: she lures the sea**
> **And robs it. The moon is a thief:**
> **He seals his silvery light from the sun.**
> **The sea is a thief: it dissolves the moon.**

It wasn't only Shakespeare that got lost but the title of Shade's poem too. For Kinbote the commentator and scholar *pale fire* has only one association: the burning of the precious variants, where his story has perished.

Let us now turn to *Timon of Athens*.

Timon lives in his palace surrounded by servants and feasts

with Athenian friends who flatter him and sponge on him. He lavishes on them gifts, money, precious stones, and they praise him. But there comes a day when everything has been given away and Timon sends his servants to his friends for money. But his friends are not willing to part with their money and Timon exiles himself from Athens; he lives in the woods, eating roots and berries, and is full of hatred toward the world. *"I am a misanthropus."* Nabokov securely hides behind comical effects so as not to give a name to what destroyed Kinbote (which is, of course, homesickness).

Timon chases away the Philosopher who comes to see him and also his devoted servant who wants to share his fate. Even gold that he finds in the soil does not console him—he does not need it now. Before dying he composes his own epitaph.

An exile, a misanthrope, he is a man of "moonlight" with all its implications and associations, including, of course, its reflection as "pale fire." He loves Athens and he hates Athens, he loves Alcibiades and he offends him, he gives everything to friendship and he chases friends out of his house, slapping their faces. Proud and angry, a beggar on a heap of new gold, he is alone and doesn't need anyone, he feeds on his misanthropia.

3.

Thus the theme of *Timon of Athens* has been dissolved in *Pale Fire,* in the tragi-comic destiny of the Beloved King exiled from his Zembla, from his Zoorlandia. A Solus Rex—but who is Solus Rex? What do we know about this lonely chess figure?

Solus Rex was the title of a Russian novel by Nabokov which he started just before the Second World War, in Russian. The first part of it was published in the last issue of an émigré quarterly in Paris, *Sovremennye Zapiski,* Spring 1940. *Pale Fire,* written in English and published in 1962, grew out of this early novel.

In *Solus Rex* the distant land is an island, it became a peninsula later. It doesn't exist any more, but was a legendary mythological Kingdom whose King is mentioned as K (no dot)

—as in chess games. The regime is obsolete, rotten, the ministers are morons, trustworthy people are few. The plotters are old-fashioned, too; they hide their cloaks and daggers somewhere and their clandestine meetings oddly resemble the gatherings of the Decembrists: swords, oaths, dice throwing, and punch drinking. K lives amid an unreal setting as if borrowed from a theater stage, or from a dream, or from a book. The royal family consists of idiots and revelers: an uncle, an aunt, a cousin. There is an old morning gown, worn slippers, coffee for breakfast. The stupid uncle and the crazy aunt, the vulgar prankster, the cousin live in a humdrum. The atmosphere is sticky; the old trunk and the sewing machine would undoubtedly have belonged here. K is forced to leave, he is ousted from his palace, from the capital. Dreadful, degrading flight! Life becomes petty, poor, middle class, and nothing saves it: neither the cloud of mystery upon it nor the myth of buried family treasures. The language of the dialogues is full of "Russisms"—popular, low-brow expressions, anachronistic pretentious Slavonicisms, a mixture of high-falutin neologisms, with colloquialisms, ridiculous clichés. They are put together in a harum-scarum way (by the dramatis personae) and in an intricate pattern of assonances and alliterations (by Nabokov); they have interior rhymes, they form puns that play as large a part in *Solus Rex* as in *Pale Fire,* and strike the same notes in Russian as they strike in English. But what is even more important, we see in *Solus Rex* a projection into the past of Charles the Beloved, his life before he became Kinbote. Under the window of his dingy room there is a heap of garbage: chicken feathers, broken chamber pots, empty cans. The ceiling in his room has a crack, the furniture has dusty slipcovers and the interior of the Victorian cupboard stinks. A basket full of soiled linen and the ironing board take all the space, an old barometer "indicates by memory non-existing weather," and the clock has stopped long ago. On an iron bed in a long nightshirt sits . . . the son of a notary public, Dimitri Nikolaevich Sineusov * and

* This name can be found in a short story of the early 1940's, *Ultima Thule,* loosely connected with *Solus Rex.*

around the house roars and rattles a huge city strangely reminding one of a Paris of Russian émigrés in the 1930's. A neon sign blinks in the window, the dark staircase leads to the narrow street.

Uncle and nephew are talking:

"—Atta boy! Isn't it queer how he's beginning to take after his mother, my poor sister? . . . I am too poor, child, to present you with a riding horse but I still have a lovely little whip. This is an interesting object, a historical thing. . . . But positively no riding horse: I keep a last pair of old nags for my hearse, don't be angry. . . ." †

The past and the present run into each other and merge. K looks at the garbage, at the dusty cupboard, and recalls the way it looked in his Kingdom. There one silly event followed another: scientists blew up the valley to make a new mountain range in the middle of the island; someone got a patent for portable domestic gallows. Dilapidation, disorder, frustration cannot be transfigured, "a slice of rough and humble life" (Sologub) cannot be transmuted into a "sweet legend." The hero secretly plays with the idea that it might be possible. What will follow is clear to everyone: someday there will be a new "ward number such and such."

Out of the nonsensical, ludicrous past a couple of odd objects, a couple of forgotten gestures survived: a silver basin, a ceremonious bow, a snapshot of a grandee on a horse with a blurred tail, perhaps one of those Rogfrieds or Guildrases (names invented according to the same principles as Wordsmith and Goldsworth) who climbed on the throne of the Kingdom, calling it a barrel in the midst of an ocean on which it was uncomfortable to sit because of hemorrhoids.

What puts *Solus Rex* so near to the fabrics and mechanics of *Pale Fire* are the innumerable combinations of unusual clusters of adjectives and nouns where each of them has a strong functional potential colored by ironic effect: red-cheeked cans of preserves, unused volcanos, juicy casualness, mossy brains,

† My translation.

monotonous miracles, liberal illiteracy, spotty reputation, and many others, most of them having in Russian an interesting sound-effect bonus. Of similar interest are Nabokov's stylistic peculiarities: combinations of nouns, adjectives and direct (or indirect) objects that have an even stronger metaphorical potential spiced with a comical effect: the deafness of an old servant cut off from the world by the cotton of his old age; the egg-shaped basket put here by an unknown Columbus; a parliament that flickers and cracks like a dim candle; the industrious satisfaction of desires, and many others.

Among some other literary devices of Nabokov I would like to mention his masterly resurrection of old metaphors, his rejuvenation of accepted clichés, his galvanization of a dead word with, of course, an ironic effect: a man with an abject little *mustache* that goes his way *picking* at life; or the statement that we all go *feeding* on the *nipples* of *Virtue* although they might turn out to be furuncles; or the *cup* of *patience overflowing* with early breakfast coffee.

There are also some interesting parodies of Russian and foreign classics most inconspicuously put into the text for sophisticated readers only. There is Shakespeare: (as the story of K goes on, we are told that) the heather in the forest was so dense that it tangled up the stirrups of the plotters and did not let the army go through. There is Pushkin (in the structure of the sentence as a translation from the French): "We are apt to give our past some features. . . . Slaves of a bondage, we are endeavoring. . . . Looking back we see the road and are convinced. . . ." There is Bunin: "On the day of the picnic the weather was cold and breezy, the skies were of a mother-of-pearl color and flying, willow bushes were bending down in the ravine, horses' hoofs splattered splashes out of fat pools onto a chocolate colored track, the crows were croaking; and later after passing the bridge, the horsemen turned and went at a trot amidst the dark heath, here and there interspersed by fine birch trees already starting to turn to yellow." And here is Nabokov himself parodied by Nabokov: "The wind beckoned to the honeysuckle,"

"The trees in a coach-and-four manner moved beyond the clouds," "The hardest principles adjusted themselves to the frailest abstractions."

Solus Rex was interrupted by the war and never finished. Nabokov's Russian period ended. To his new country (and language) he nevertheless did bring intact his main theme with all its multiple side effects, its outgrowths, and the basic features of his narrative style, i.e., a perfectly balanced dose of the serious and satiro-ironico-comical elements. For forty years his theme has held together and has given a wholeness to his entire work. There is no possible understanding of all the intricacies of *Pale Fire* without first looking into *Solus Rex*. Kinbote as well as K are both trying "to restore their lost connection with reality" but both are compelled "to be satisfied with some ad hoc knocked together passageways." As for the Author, there is no danger that he will lose connection with reality: in his ancestral mansion, his palace, or his garret, he will firmly grasp it, and thus through him we also will have it at hand.

"Botkin." Snowbound gravestone, Columbus, Ohio, 1968.
(Photo by Anthony Libby)

Ada described

ALFRED APPEL, JR.

At Cornell University, where he taught for a decade (1948-58), Vladimir Nabokov would always begin his first lecture by saying, "Great novels are above all great fairy tales . . . literature does not tell the truth but makes it up." *Ada,* Nabokov's fifteenth novel, thirty-fifth book, and first new novel since *Pale Fire* (1962), is a great fairy tale, a supremely original work of the imagination. Published two weeks after Nabokov's seventieth birthday, it provides further evidence that he is a peer of Kafka, Proust, and Joyce, those earlier masters of totally unique universes of fiction.

Ada, or Ardor: A Family Chronicle (its full title) is a love story, an erotic masterpiece, an Edenic fantasy, a philosophical investigation into the nature of time. Almost twice as long as any

Parts of this article first appeared in *The New York Times Book Review,* © 1969 by The New York Times Company and reprinted by permission.

previous Nabokov novel, its rich and variegated prose moves from the darkest to the lightest of sonorities as Nabokov sensually evokes the widest range of delights. Nabokov has said that as a writer he is "half-painter, half-naturalist," and was "born a landscape painter." [1] He has never "painted" more luminously than in *Ada*. It is an extraordinarily visual book, teeming with allusions to painters and paintings.[2] Since "Remembrance, like Rembrandt, is dark but festive" (p. 103), Nabokov often favors the glowing tonalities of the Dutch Old Masters, though for his most terrifying visions he moves south to the Flemish hells of Bosch (see pp. 435-36).[3] Many scenes in *Ada* are veritable *tableaux vivants* of works ranging from Beardsley's illustrations for *Lysistrata* to the idyllic and sunny landscapes of Lorrain and Renoir, Monet and Prendergast. "Whose brush was it now?" asks the narrator at the end of a love scene. "A titillant Titian? A drunken Palma Vecchio? No, she was anything but a Venetian blonde. Dosso Dossi, perhaps? Faun Exhausted by Nymph? Swooning Satyr? . . . A moment later the Dutch took over: Girl stepping into a pool under the little cascade to wash her tresses, and accompanying the immemorial gesture of wringing them out by making wringing–out mouths—immemorial too" (p. 141). But *Ada* is a kind of museum in more ways than one. As the family chronicle to end all such chronicles, it is also a museum of the novel, and it employs parody to rehearse its own history.

Spanning one hundred years and replete with a prefatory Family Tree, *Ada* is presented as the memoir of Dr. Ivan (Van) Veen, psychologist, professor of philosophy, author, libertine, and student of time, who chronicles his lifelong love for his "cousin," Ada Veen. To speed-readers, Ada and Van may remain "first cousins," but genealogically speaking, the story of the affluent, wide-ranging, and ingrown Veen family is not a simple one, and the novel's first three chapters are difficult reading, as the author well realizes ("The modest narrator has to remind the rereader of all this," he remarks at one point [p. 19]). Walter D. (Demon) Veen and Walter D. (Dan) Veen, first cousins born the same year, have married twin sisters, Aqua and Marina Durmanov, descendants of "a Russian princely race." While Dan reappears briefly throughout the novel, desperate Aqua goes mad and commits suicide in the third chapter. Dan's and Marina's putative offspring are Ada (b. 1872) and Lucette (b. 1876), but it becomes clear that Demon has fathered Ada. Demon's and Aqua's sole child would seem to be Van Veen (b. 1870), but he too is the result of Demon's and Marina's continuing affair, and was substituted for Aqua's stillborn baby. Submitted to the looking–glass universe of *Ada* (Lewis Carroll is invoked often), the staid Family Tree thus becomes a fun-house jumble.

Several reviewers identified Van as Ada's half-brother, rather than full brother, which should warn *Ada*'s readers and critics to proceed more modestly than not. Because of the novel's amplitude and complexity, its allusiveness, elusiveness, and gradual accretion of significant detail, my purpose here is to label, rather than "interpret," its contents and contours, an intention fully in the spirit of Van Veen and his maker. When Van is pressed for a psychiatric explanation of two delusions, he doubtless speaks too for Nabokov the lepidopterist, teacher, and translator and annotator of *Eugene Onegin:* "in my works, I try not to 'explain' anything, I merely describe" (p. 519).

Told mainly in the third person, *Ada* is divided into five parts. Part One occupies almost half of the novel, and details Van's youth, travels, and incestuous romance with Ada at Arcadian Ardis Hall, the opulent country estate of his uncle. The agony caused by Ada's infidelity turns out to be a creative force and as Part One concludes, Van is "pregnant" with his first book. Part Two ends with Van forsaking Ada, following his father's implorations. In Part Three, after many amorous vicissitudes, Ada gets married and Van loses her for seventeen years, finally regaining her in 1922 in Part Four, while he is working on his book, *The Texture of Time.* Part Five, a kind of coda, finds them together, with a small entourage, celebrating Van's ninety-seventh birthday and the virtual completion of the memoir at hand, which is to be published posthumously. Ada and Van no longer exist as we read *Ada*—and indeed they do not, since they are fictional.

Van's manuscript has been seen through the press by one of their entourage, Ronald Oranger, a considerably more self-effacing editor than *Lolita*'s John Ray, Jr., or *Pale Fire*'s Charles Kinbote. The book is preceded by a brief note from Oranger, modestly signed "Ed." Oranger has assiduously indicated Van's changes in the text, but his proofreading is a disaster. He has failed to delete his many parenthetical directions to the printer, accidentally incorporated in the text by a typesetter even less talented than the editor—"(thus in MS)," "Sic! Ed.)"—and a very moving insertion, made by Van in his old age, is comically marred by the chapter-concluding editorial gaffe, "Insert" (p. 221). Although Oranger is but fleetingly present at the end of *Ada* and is never described, these errors invest the poor, well-intentioned fellow with a strangely immediate, human dimension —quite appropriate, since Mr. and Mrs. Oranger are, "With the exception of . . . a few incidental figures, and some non-American citizens" (p. 1), the only people named in the book who are still alive.

More to Oranger's credit is his preservation of the running commentaries which Van and Ada have addressed to one another, dramatic marginalia alternately sarcastic and loving, condescending and tender. Ada is not only Van Veen's muse, desire, tormentor, and alter ego ("Vaniada"), but his severest critic and collaborator as well, sometimes even taking Van's place to write a page or two. Having shared so many years with him since the beginning of their love at Ardis Hall (he was fourteen, she twelve), Ada assists him unceasingly in his efforts to recollect and order the past, and the struggle takes place before the reader's eyes. Instead of the pathos of time, however, Nabokov gives us the comedy of their attempts to recapitulate it, and the joyousness of their success.

In addition to writing a memoir, philosopher Veen is trying to describe the nature of time. He incorporates in Part Four twenty of the preliminary pages of *The Texture of Time*. Van tries to divorce Time from tyrannic Space and thus deny the Future, recognizing the inherent paradoxes. No doubt with Zeno in mind, he notes "that we cannot enjoy the *true* present, which is an instant of zero duration" (p. 550). "To be eternal the Present must depend on the conscious spanning of an infinite expansure" (p. 551), and that expanse—"The flowering of the Present"—is equated with love.

Van speaks of "The direction of Time, the ardis of Time," and at the end of Part One, Ada poetically evokes Ardis Hall as ". . . jacarandas at Arrowhead/In supernatural bloom" (p. 324). The jacaranda is a tropical American tree, while "Ardisia" is a genus of tropical evergreen shrubs and trees, from *ardis,* Greek for "the point of the arrow:—alluding to the acute lobes of the corolla" (the petals of a flower). "The arrow," writes Hans Meyerhoff, "in its flight through space and time, is, at any given moment or 'now,' always standing still—which seems to make mockery of our common-sense notions of flying through space and time." [4] Ada and the ardor of Ardis are the constants that unify past and present and deny the encroachments of "the end." Working with metaphors, rather than mathematics, Van knows that his "didactic" efforts are a trap, an endless maze, and just as he is about to give up, he gets a letter from Ada saying that her husband is dead and she is on her way to rejoin him. Ardis restored, the Present flowers and Van is able to complete *The Texture of Time* (1924), a great literary success and his most famous book until now.

Ada's return also contributes to the creation of *Ada,* since Van does not undertake his memoirs until 1957. The entire book can be said to spiral out of Part Four, and the "earlier" work, *The Texture of Time.** As Part Four concludes, Ada sympathizes with Van's efforts: "We can know the time, we can know a time. We can never know Time. Our senses are simply not meant to perceive it. It is like—" (p. 563). Part Four ends with Ada in

---

* Like Quilty's death scene in *Lolita* and the poem *Pale Fire*, this crucial section seems to have been written at or near the outset of the novel's composition. *Ada*'s initial working title was *The Texture of Time*, and in a National Educational Television interview filmed in 1965, Nabokov discusses what is now Part Four, though he makes it sound like the beginning of the book.

mid-sentence, and her phrase "It is like—" points back to the novel's first page, for the similes and metaphors she is about to grope for comprise the novel's first 532 pages, a considerably extended metaphor, a vast and enchanting fantasia. If *Ada* is a "philosophical novel" (and Van uses those qualifying quotation marks when thus describing his first book, *Letters from Terra*), it is one in which the novelist has found an aesthetic form and poetic equivalent for the "philosophy," a correlative for Ardis' eternal realm.

Most of *Ada* is set in an antiworld. The idea of an imaginary land and/or language has long concerned Nabokov. Self-propelled out of Russia with urgent force in 1919, he has been on the move ever since, giving him ample time to consider the nature of space. To émigrés such as Pnin and Humbert Humbert, America seems an invented land, and incontrovertibly imaginary lands extend from five of Nabokov's untranslated Russian works (1924-1940) to Padukgrad in *Bend Sinister* (1947), to Zembla in *Pale Fire* (1962), reaching an apotheosis in *Ada,* where the entire universe has been re-imagined, including Space-Time. God is called "Log" in *Ada,* and the universe consists of two sibling planets, "Anti-terra" (or "Demonia"), on which the action is set, and "Terra," the subject of endless debate. Only deranged minds accept the notion of Terra, and when in her madness Aqua Veen envisages a "minor hymnist's paradise," her delusions depict life in our modern cities (p. 21). A distorted version of Van Veen's first book, the speculative and totally ignored *Letters from Terra* (1891),* is fifty years later (Part Five) made into a horrific science fiction farce that clearly rehearses the first half of twentieth-century history. Although Veen and the reader have by now literally and figuratively returned to earth, thousands of people "believed in the secret Government-concealed identity of Terra and Antiterra" (p. 582)—a brilliant stroke, unhappily enough, since history is indeed a mad dream, a bad movie, and

* It is published under the appropriate pseudonym of "Voltemand," from *Volte,* German for "sleight-of-hand." See pp. 338-46 for a summary of the book.

World War II a mythical happening or pop extravaganza, as anyone in touch with the under-thirties generation knows, since "Casablanca" exists for them, but not Auschwitz.

Van, whose favorite sport is dancing on his hands, extends his stunt and turns time upside down. Antiterra follows "Veen's Time," while on "Terra the Fair" some objective order of time prevails. Except for certain literary matters, there is a variable gap of from fifty to one hundred years between Antiterra and the " 'distortive glass of our distortive glebe,' as a scholar who desires to remain unnamed has put it with such euphonic wit" (p. 18),* and in the first three parts of *Ada* Nabokov has neatly folded back time. Details from life on Terra are anachronistically refracted in another "nineteenth century" on Antiterra. Dates as we know them are meaningless; although Nabokov does not put them in quotation marks, the reader would be well-advised to do so. These details are drawn from Terra's future, as well as its earlier periods, since "1895" on Antiterra could equal 1995 on Terra. Thus the characters in *Ada* casually utilize such conveniences as "automatic dorophones," "hydrodynamic telephones," "hydrograms," and "jiggers" (flying carpets). Familiar machines have different names ("petroloplanes" and "Sonorolas" [radios]), and the glories of recent periods on Terra are enjoyed in Antiterra's "nineteenth century," including Cokes, bikinis, movies, Proust, Joyce, comic strips, and the Villa Venus, a chain of one hundred luxurious brothels serving every need, as though the chaste Playboy Clubs were to be managed by Aristophanes.

This description makes *Ada* sound like science fiction, and in part it is. Nabokov has long been an admirer of H. G. Wells's science fiction (Van Veen alludes to *The War of the Worlds* [p. 19] and *The Invisible Man* [pp. 133 and 203]). Van's first book is SF, appropriately, since Nabokov himself has written several works of "physics fiction," as Van Veen prefers to call his *Letters from Terra,* to distinguish it from trashy space-operas

---

* Glebe: *archaic and poetic*: soil; also land owned by the church. The joke refers, of course, to Antiterran faith in a heavenly Terra. Milton used the word, and he is alluded to on the same page ("Abraham Milton").

and "topical utopias" (distinctions not made by the many critics who too quickly dismiss all science fiction). Like several contemporary writers (notably Anthony Burgess and J. L. Borges), Nabokov has employed inimitably many of the themes, modes, and conventions of SF: time travel ("The Tragedy of Mister Morn," 1924 [untranslated], and "Time and Ebb," 1945); automata (*King, Queen, Knave,* 1928); identity transfer, telekinesis, and invisibility (*The Eye,* 1930); the futuristic dystopia (*Invitation to a Beheading,* 1936, and *Bend Sinister,* 1947); the infernal machine ("The Waltz Invention," 1938); teleportation ("The Visit to the Museum," 1939); space and time travel ("Lance," 1952); and psychic phenomena ("The Vane Sisters," 1959). Nabokov's SF strain culminates in the physics fiction that is *Ada,* and it is only just (and a grand gesture) that the Moon Walk was scheduled for July 21, Ada Veen's birthday.

Antiterra's startling geographic boundaries are the result of Nabokov's unique version of the "What *if*—?" mode of SF—the story that is based on an imaginary and dramatic reversal of history. There are several such turns in *Ada*. Paramount is the fact that on Antiterra the Tartars were not defeated at the battle of Kulikovo in 1380, and their great empire did not disintegrate in the next century. Instead, hordes of Russians have been driven into North America, or "Estoty," an American province extending from the Arctic Circle to the U.S. proper. Their descendants now live happily throughout the united "Amerussia" governed by Abraham Milton. More specifically, the "Seven Tories" is a protectorate "still lovingly called 'Russian' Estoty" (Alaska) which commingles with " 'Russian' Canady, otherwise 'French' Estoty, where not only French, but Macedonian and Bavarian [and Swedish] settlers enjoy a halycon climate under our Stars and Stripes" (p. 3). Punning place names reflect this particular melting-pot: Le Bras d'Or, Akapulkovo, Goluba University [Columbia plus the Russian word for "pigeon"], and elegant New Cheshire [Catskills]. On Terra, Van tells us, Amerussia was of course "split into its components, with tangible water and ice separating the political, rather than poetical notions of 'America' and 'Russia' " (p. 18). Elsewhere on Antiterra, Britain, having annexed France in 1815, has extended its Commonwealth from "Scoto-Scandinavia to the Riviera" (p. 19), the Balkans and Indias are Anglo-American protectorates, and the situation in the Middle East is hinted at by Cairo's Cohnritz hotel. Menacing all, however, is "Tartary, an independent inferno, which . . . spread from the Baltic and Black Seas to the Pacific Ocean, [and] was touristically unavailable" (p. 20).

Ada's most intricate anachronisms are linguistic and literary. Like almost everything else, clichés are reversed (" 'That's very black of you, Dad,' said pleased Van" [p. 241]), and the use of contemporary slang at Ardis proves charming ("I goofed"). Given their circumstances, the characters are quite naturally trilingual; faithful to verisimilitude, Nabokov includes some Russian and French. The former is transliterated and usually translated parenthetically, the latter is not translated. But the French affords no problem, since there is not much more of it than one would find in the average, run-of-the-mill Tolstoy novel. Just as Russian literature is collectively one of the heroes of *The Gift* (1937), Nabokov's last Russian novel, so too is Count Tolstoy one of the heroes of *Ada,* and Nabokov pays him abundant tribute.

Tolstoy appears frequently in both the text and texture of *Ada*. In part a Tolstoyan capriccio, it celebrates through parody the master's novelistic plenitude, his style and technique. Van Veen often invokes Tolstoy by name, familiarly and endearingly ("Lyovin," "old Leo," "naughty old Leo"), and Demon Veen even reveals an apt family connection, quite removed: "my aunt Kitty . . . married the banker Bolenski after divorcing that dreadful old wencher Lyovka Tolstoy, the writer" (p. 240). On his travels, student Van is shown "the peasant-bare footprint of Tolstoy preserved in the clay of a motor court in Utah where he had written the tale of Murat, the Navajo chieftain, a French general's bastard, shot by Cora Day in his swimming pool" (p. 171). In spite of such Antiterran transmutations, a good many of Tolstoy's unadulterated Russian footprints are nevertheless visible in *Ada*.

The novel's opening sentence quotes an inept translator's unintentionally comic reversal of the famous beginning of *Anna Karenina.** However confused things may be in *that* novel's unhappy family, they are certainly worse in the opening pages of *Ada,* a parodic extension of old Leo's first page. Before Aqua commits suicide, her thoughts are "rather 'Kareninian' " (p. 28), and later her sister Marina, suffering her own Kareninian despair, "walked to the end of the platform in Tolstoy's novel. First exponent of the inner monologue," adds Van, a critical point original to Nabokov, emphasized in his Cornell lectures on Tolstoy and Joyce, and, for pedagogical purposes, repeated several times in *Ada.* Van then burlesques the interior monologue which prefigures and counterpoints Anna's death (pp. 299-300). Vronsky turns up in *Ada* as the film director who has an affair with Marina, and like Kitty and Levin, Ada and Van exchange coded messages. Van acknowledges that their trysts are rendered less covertly than some that come to mind: "Aleksey and Anna may have asterisked here!" (p. 521). Unlikely scenes from Tolstoy are transformed into startling and unsettling similes. Aqua's "panic and pain, like a pair of children in a boisterous game, emitted one last shriek of laughter and ran away to manipulate each other behind a bush as in Count Tolstoy's *Anna Karenin,* a novel" (p. 25). *The Texture of Time* is included near the end of the novel in order to parallel the placement of Tolstoy's didactic digression on history in *War and Peace* ("let us shift to the didactic metaphorism of Chekhov's friend, Count Tolstoy," remarks Van [p. 430]), and it is no coincidence that Demon Veen marries Aqua in 1869, the year which saw the publication of the last

* " 'All happy families are more or less dissimilar; all unhappy ones are more or less alike,' says a great Russian writer in the beginning of a famous novel (*Anna Arkadievitch Karenina,* transfigured into English by R. G. Stonelower, Mount Tabor Ltd., 1880)." Stonelower, of course, is invented. The Garnettized version reads: "Happy families are all alike; every unhappy family is unhappy in its own way." Stonelower's *Arkadievitch* is also wrong; the correct feminine form would be *Arkadievna.* In his *Eugene Onegin* Commentary, Nabokov conjectures that "Mount Abora," in Coleridge's "Kubla Khan," may be Mount Tabor, "an amba (natural citadel), some 300 feet high in the Siré district of the Tigré . . ." (Vol. III, p. 441). Translator Stonelower would be better employed on top of that mount, following the trade implicit in his name.

volume of *War and Peace*. "The end of an extraordinary epoch coincides with Van's no less extraordinary boyhood," writes Van in the novel's concluding mock-blurb, summarizing the confluence of Van's youth and Tolstoy's artistic zenith. "Nothing in world literature," Van quickly continues, "save maybe Count Tolstoy's reminiscences, can vie in pure joyousness . . . with the 'Ardis' part of the book."

The allusions to Tolstoy's *Childhood, Boyhood, and Youth* made by Van on the first and last pages of *Ada* are of no small significance.* *Ada,* like Tolstoy's trilogy, is cast as an autobiographical novel. Van's short chapters, the relaxed pace of his narrative, and many of the lovingly described scenic details mimic Tolstoy's manner (and manor). Moments from Tolstoy become dazzling set pieces in Veen: the first kiss, the fateful letter, the tearful farewell. The Tolstoyan tears flow freely where they should, at the end of a chapter. Van does not hesitate to discuss in *Ada* what Tolstoy exiled to his private diaries (his amorous adventures, his self-abuse), and where in his reminiscences Tolstoy was vague about his father's amours, Van is more than candid; after all, he is the result of one of them. At the end of *Youth,* Tolstoy looks forward to narrating "the second and happier half of my youth," but he never wrote the last volume of his projected tetralogy. Nabokov once supplied an ending for Pushkin's unfinished "The River Nymph," and Part One of *Ada,* in itself book-length, is by way of Nabokov's completion of Tolstoy's reminiscences. As such, it is the last nineteenth-century Russian novel, just as the entire book is the first and only classic of "Amerussian" literature.

Tributes notwithstanding, the nineteenth-century novel has not survived the time warp in *Ada*. At the end of an early chapter, "Ada and Van met in the passage, and would have kissed at some earlier stage of the Novel's Evolution in the History of Literature" (p. 96). Nabokov confronts nothing less than that

---

* The initial reference to "another Tolstoy work, *Detstvo i Otrochestvo* (*Childhood and Fatherland*, Pontius Press, 1858)," constitutes another joke about bad translations, since *Otrochestvo* means "boyhood" or "girlhood," not fatherland. The latter is *Otechestvo.*

evolution, and *Ada* is a self-contained survey course, a completion of the syllabus (Literature 311-312, "The Novel: Austen to Nabokov," MWF, 12). Like those other great protean modernists, Picasso and Joyce (who appears in *Ada*'s Family Tree in the person of Van's grandfather Dedalus Veen), Nabokov uses parody to re-investigate the fundamental problems of his art. "Old storytelling devices . . . may be parodied only by very great and inhuman artists," says Van modestly and not altogether accurately (p. 248), as he simultaneously celebrates Tolstoy's achievement and, in a manner far more human and humane than Grandfather Joyce's in "Oxen of the Sun," surveys the nearly exhausted possibilities of the novel and the assumptions of its practitioners.

Van ponders "Empty formulas befitting the solemn novelists of former days who thought they could explain everything" (p. 475). Although Nabokov has not gone as far as Robbe-Grillet, he would agree with him that characters in a fiction cannot be definitively understood or studied like X-ray pictures. But since most readers still want packaged and clearly labeled explanations, especially of human behavior, Nabokov parodies their expectations. Early in *Ada,* Nabokov interrupts the narrative to pose some "Questions for study and discussion," such as, "Was Van's adult incapacity to 'shrug' things off only physical or did it 'correspond' to some archetypal character of his 'undersoul'?" (p. 83). The first three chapters, so thorny as exposition, surely parody the reassuring initial pages of those traditional novels—so anachronistic to Nabokov—which prepare the reader for the story about to unfold by supplying him with the neat and complete psychological, social, and moral pre-histories of fictional characters. In his concluding blurb, Van appreciates "the many intricacies of plot and psychology" in his memoir. *Psychology?* How frustrating to encounter a story about a psychologist's incest that offers no "psychological" explanations, but an abundance of "philosophy." Even more unsettling is the fact that Van's darkest feelings involve betrayal, not guilt, and that Van and his sister live happily ever after, to use the apt fairy-tale phrase. Tolstoy the moralist would certainly not approve, as Nabokov well knows, and one can only imagine how "old Dusty" (Dostoevsky), a titan who means something less to Nabokov, would have treated the ostensible story of *Ada*. Civic leaders, scoutmasters, ministers, and parents (none of whose vigils should cease) may wonder "What is Nabokov's moral attitude toward incest?" He would no doubt grant that it does complicate matters in a good many ways, but that prose fiction should do more than make such easy judgments.

While Van in the early chapters is waiting to be born (shades of *Tristram Shandy*), so too is the great age of the novel, a painful birth. Van's enthusiastic concluding blurb notes that "the story proceeds at a spanking pace," but the pace is sometimes purposefully slow, befitting an infancy of sorts, as Veen plots time's texture and parodies the realist's efforts to limn "reality." On his first tour of Ardis Hall, Van announces "The Attic. This is the attic. Welcome to the attic," thus undermining the possibility that an examination of old novelistic furniture could reveal very much (p. 44), though he does catalog a goodly number of antiques before Part One is over. When Van first approaches Ardis Hall, "the romantic mansion appeared on the gentle eminence of old novels" (p. 35), and he observes "rows of stylized saplings" (p. 35) and "an artificial cascade borrowed from some brook or book" (p. 44). A coachman drinking tea "came straight from a pretzel-string of old novels" (p. 154), Lucette returns to her bag "the balled handkerchief of many an old romance" (p. 369), a scene in the library "might have become a chapter in one of the old novels on its own shelves" (p. 137), and Ada wishes she could ring for the maid, as "in Georgian novels," but, sadly, there is no electricity at Ardis (p. 118). "They had one moment to plan things," complains Van, "it was all, historically speaking, at the dawn of the novel which was still in the hands of parsonage ladies and French academicians, so such moments were precious" (p. 127).

Van is conscious of every kind of novelistic locution and technique: "as Jane Austen might have said"; " 'Reader, ride by' . . . as Turgenev wrote" (p. 43); "as a French writer of an earlier century might have . . . called [it]" (p. 10); ". . . to use a hoary narrational turn" (p. 242); *"On fait son grand Joyce* after doing one's *petit Proust,"* notes Ada (p. 169); "poor Stream of Consciousness, *marée noire* by now," interjects Van in the midst of one (p. 300)—all of which should suggest that to write a novel today after the example of the great nineteenth-century realists or the no less classic modernists of fifty years ago is as anachronistic as finding characters reading Joyce in "1870," or driving away from a Chekhovian duel scene in a shiny new convertible (as happens at Ardis).

Nabokov allows Van Veen to write his first book only upon the completion of Part One and his principal museum tour of "the Novel's Evolution," thereby suggesting the efficacy of parody. Having leisurely rehearsed the novel's past, Nabokov then points to its future, and the book at hand, by doing some bravura handstands of his own. The opening chapters of Part Two successively offer an assemblage of letters; a physics fiction within the physics fiction that is the entire novel; a fantastic parody; a classroom lecture; and a description of photographs. Nabokov almost seems to stage this kaleidoscopic array of narrative possibilities for the benefit of Part One's numerous figures of parody, a miraculously animated gallery who, from their confines in Part One, watch the Maestro perform, as in Picasso's recent etchings in *Gravures 347,* which picture several Old Masters standing behind the modern master, who bedazzles them at his easel.

"Only in the tritest of terms can I describe Lo's features," says Humbert Humbert, summarizing Nabokov's sense of the challenge faced by the contemporary writer. "I might say her hair is auburn, and her lips are red as licked red candy . . . oh, that I were a lady writer who could have her pose naked in a naked light!" But Nabokov is not alone in thinking that an artist's efforts to articulate unique, if not all but ineffable, states of mind and feeling are unhappily circumscribed by the conventions of language and literature. "Oh I wish there were some words in the world that were not the words I always hear!" bemoans Snow White, in Donald Barthelme's novel of that name. "Everything has been

173

said before," says the computer in Jean-Luc Godard's film, *Alphaville*. "Everything's been said already, over and over," echoes John Barth in "Title," one of the tales in his collection, *Lost in the Funhouse*. "I'm as sick of this as you are; there's nothing to say." This is of course not so, as novels such as *Lolita*, *Pale Fire*, and *Ada* demonstrate; as always, the writer must find new modes of expression, though Nabokov succeeds only because he is always so acutely aware of the risks involved in telling what may be, after all, an old story indeed.

"Old storytelling devices" are but one of Nabokov's concerns. Through parody and self-parody, he exorcises the trite terms inherent in each story he chooses to tell, and by parodying the reader's conception of "story"—his stereotyped expectations and preoccupation with "plot" machinations—Nabokov frees him to experience a fiction intellectually, aesthetically, ecstatically. Nabokov refuses to allow the reader to be distracted by a tyrannic concern with "What Happens Next?" The denouement of Ada's and Van's story is made apparent by Ada's parenthetical interjections ("Van, thank goodness, is ninety now—in Ada's hand" [p. 104]), which challenge the old-fashioned reader's idea of "story"; to reveal the outcome before the story is barely underway is of course to ruin it. After explaining the code Ada and Van use in writing to each other, Nabokov unexpectedly employs it:

> **Van plunged into the dense undergrowth. He wore a silk shirt, a velvet jacket, black breeches, riding boots with star spurs—and this attire was hardly convenient for making *klv zdB AoyvBno wkh gwzxm dqg kzwAAqvo a gwttp vq wjfhm* [his way through the brush and crossing a brook to reach—A.A.] Ada in a natural bower of aspens, *xlic mujzikml* [they embraced—A.A.] after which she said . . . (p. 157).**

The decoded passages are anticlimactic enough; the joke is at the expense of those who hope that the action is too incendiary to print as is, or believe that the "meaning" of a story rests in the linear development of its narrative.

Writers, as well as readers, are not always willing to admit or even recognize that a story has been told before. The ludicrous

literary activities of Mlle Larivière, the Veens' grotesque gover-
ness, are a case in point. Guy de Maupassant must exist only on
Terra, for Mlle Larivière "thinks that in some former Hindooish
state she was a boulevardier in Paris; and writes accordingly"
(p. 53), which enables her to fashion *La Rivière de Diamants*
("The Diamond Necklace"):

**The pretty and refined wife of a seedy clerk borrows a necklace from
a wealthy woman friend. On the way home from the office party she loses
it. For thirty or forty horrible years the unfortunate husband and wife
labor and economize to repay the debts they accumulated in the purchase
of a half-million-franc necklace which they had secretly substituted for
the lost one when returning the jewelbox to Mme F. Oh, how Mathilde's
heart fluttered—would Jeanne open the box? She did not. When decrepit
but victorious (he, half-paralyzed by a half-century of *copie* in the *mansarde,*
she, unrecognizably coarsened by the washing of floors *à grand eau*), they
confess everything to a white-haired but still young-looking Mme F. the
latter tells them, in the last phrase of the tale: "But, my poor Mathilde,
the necklace was false; it cost only five hundred francs!" (p. 83)**

It is obviously, with a few changes of detail, Maupassant's famous
story *La Parure* (Mlle Larivière is once called "Mlle Laparure"
[p. 87]). The story "become[s] a classic in girls' schools," and
under her "gorgeous pseudonym" of "Guillaume de Monpar-
nasse," Mlle Larivière grows rich and famous (p. 194). Her name
also alludes to the very distinguished Dr. Larivière in *Madame
Bovary,* who is brought to Emma's bedside by Homais and her
two physicians, Bovary and Carnivet (Part III, chapter eight).
Madame Bovary cannot be saved, even by Larivière, just as
Madame Bovary should not be revived as such, though writers on
our own terra firma persist in rewriting stories and novels that
already exist.

Ada too seems to have its precursors, and Nabokov offers some
of the most famous poetical evocations of sisters, including those
of Byron, Baudelaire, the Bible, and Chateaubriand. Several telling references to Eden and the first siblings occur early in Part
One, while the allusions to Byron should recall his incest with his
half-sister Augusta and the fact that his daughter was named

Augusta Ada, addressed simply as "Ada" in *Childe Harold's Pilgrimage*. Byron's Ada was gifted mathematically, whereas Nabokov's Ada pursues the natural sciences. "Ada . . . liked crossing orchids," says Van as he does some crossing of his own: *"Mon enfant, ma soeur, / Songe à l'épaisseur / Du grand chêne à Tagne . . . [p. 106]"* ("My child, my sister, / Dream of the thickness / Of the great oak at Tagne"). The opening of Baudelaire's *L'Invitation au voyage* (*"Mon enfant, ma soeur, / Songe à la douceur"*) has been combined with *"le grand chêne,"* a phrase drawn from *Le Montagnard émigré* ("The Exiled Mountaineer"), one of Chateaubriand's *romances* (a sentimental ballad or song). That phrase is repeated again, along with other lines from the same *romance,* in the twenty-two-line verse pastiche which begins chapter twenty-two [!] of *Ada:*

My sister, do you still recall
The blue Ladore and Ardis Hall?

Don't you remember any more
That castle bathed by the Ladore?

Ma soeur, te souvient-il encore
Du château que baignait la Dore?

My sister, do you still recall
The Ladore-washed old castle wall?

Sestra moya, tï pomnish' goru,
I dub vïsokiy, i Ladoru?

My sister, you remember still
The spreading oak tree and my hill?

Oh! qui me rendra mon Aline
Et le grand chêne et ma colline?

Oh, who will give me back my Jill
And the big oak tree and my hill?

Oh! qui me rendra, mon Adèle,
Et ma montagne et l'hirondelle?

Oh! qui me rendra ma Lucile,
La Dore et l'hirondelle agile?

Oh, who will render in our tongue
The tender things he loved and sung?

(pp. 138-139)

The most important stanza (three) is quoted directly from Chateaubriand, and his lines *"Qu'effleuroit l'hirondelle agile"* and *"Oh! qui me rendra mon Hélène, / Et ma montagne, et le grand chêne?"* are variously adapted by Van, whose substitution of *"Lucile"* for *"Hélène"* in the penultimate stanza underscores the sister theme once more, since Chateaubriand's sister was named Lucile.

Like Chateaubriand, who first celebrated it (line six), "la Dore" is omnipresent at Ardis; county, town, and river are named after it. One is often reminded that the hill overlooking the adored Ladore River is dominated by the black ruins of Bryant's Castle, or Château Bryant (a punningly anglicized Chateaubriand).[5] The French writer was deeply affected by the ocean during his boyhood at St. Malô, and the Romantic iconography of the sea is prominent in his work; thematically, the Chateaubriandesque waters flow throughout *Ada*. Van's two mothers, Aqua and Marina, are well-named, and Lucette, whose name echoes that of Chateaubriand's sister, drowns herself after her half-brother has spurned her advances, an experience she may well have had in common with Lucile de Chateaubriand, who retreated to a convent and inspired her brother to write *René*. The association is underlined when "Lucette, one fist on her hip, sang a St. Malô fisher-song" (p. 81).

Because there are forty-three chapters in Part One, the pastiche of *Le Montagnard émigré* which frames chapter twenty-two is literally and figuratively central to the Ardis section.* *Le Montagnard émigré* was first published in *Mercure français* in 1806, and later included in Chateaubriand's story *Les Aventures du dernier Abencerage* ("The Adventures of the Last Abencerage"), where the now untitled verses are sung by a young French prisoner of war as his own composition. Van knows them in the

---

* See p. 141 for the chapter-ending quotation, and for other echoes, pp. 192, 241, 428, and 530.

latter context, as a subsequent hint suggests; his pseudonymous *Letters from Terra* is published in Manhattan by the "bogus house" of "Abencerage," to which news Ada adds, in one of her characteristic parentheses, "Had I happened to see a copy I would have recognized Chateaubriand's *lapochka* and hence your little paw, *at once*" (p. 342). The story, however, is not about incest, but no matter, since any and all of the Chateaubriand allusions coalesce to fix Ada's and Van's story in the Romantic tradition (or so it would seem), and the evocation of *"Ma soeur,"* transcribed, translated, and transmuted, points to *René*, Chateaubriand's most famous work.

René, ou les effets des passions, a separately published episode from Chateaubriand's *Le Génie du Christianisme*, was to France what *The Sorrows of Young Werther* and *Childe Harold* were to Germany and England, respectively. In his *Onegin* Commentary, Nabokov calls the story of René and his sister Amélie "a work of genius by the greatest French writer of his time" (Vol. III, p. 98). He notes that "A subtle perfume of incest permeates their relationship: 'cher et trop cher René.'" Ada reads at age nine or ten "a story by Chateaubriand about a pair of romantic siblings" (p. 133), and "she sometimes . . . in gentle jest" calls Van *"cher, trop cher René"* (p. 131). Riding the crest of her success, Mlle Larivière writes *Les Enfants Maudits* ("The Accursed Children"), a novel and film scenario "about mysterious children doing strange things in old parks" (p. 249); its hero is named "René" (or "Renny") and its setting, naturally, is "Bryant's château" (p. 205). Ada even has a small part in the film version (see pp. 197-206), and Marina is supposed to play the mother, though she backs down when the script degenerates (pp. 424-25).* *René* was conceived under the same elm in Middlesex, England, where Byron *"s'abandonnait aux caprices de son âge,"* claims Chateaubriand in *Mémoires d'outre-tombe* (which, like Veen's, were published posthumously). One of the footmen at Ardis is named Middlesex, and Van, lying near an immense elm, reads

---

* *Les Enfants Maudits* is also the occasion for another parody of bad translations; see p. 217.

Ada's copy of *Atala* (p. 89), another episode from *Le Génie* (and one that is often printed in tandem with *René*). An earlier love story also set in the lush, light-dappled landscapes of a fantasized America,[6] *Atala* chronicles the doomed love of Chactas the Natchez and Atala, a Christianized Indian princess. Its overtones of incest are not usually commented upon, but Atala's father turns out to have been old Lopez, the Castilian who had once adopted Chactas, who henceforth insists on calling Atala "sister." To complete the circuit of synthetic incest, the unmarried Lopez lives with his sister.

The network of Chateaubriand allusions, Ada's abiding interest in natural and unnatural history, and the resonant theme of memory and desire all cohere. Early in the novel, verbally gifted Ada anagrammatically links "scient," "nicest," "incest," and "insect" (p. 85), and then Van, recollecting their first sexual intimacies at Ardis, relates how "During the last week of July, there emerged, with diabolical regularity, the female of Chateaubriand's mosquito"—named after Charles Chateaubriand, however, who "was not related to the great poet and memoirist born between Paris and Tagne" (p. 106). He "had not been the first to be bitten by it . . . but the first to bottle the offender," says Van of Chateaubriand the entomologist, though his remarks can of course be taken in more ways than one. Chateaubriand's mosquito is "characterized by an insatiable and reckless appetite for Ada's and Ardelia's, Lucette and Lucile's [!] . . . blood" (p. 106). Its thirst for Ada is so great, and "The girl's pale skin, so excitingly delicate to Van's eye, [is] so vulnerable to the beast's needle," that Van must virtually compete with the mosquitoes to possess her. He wildly kisses her while her five fingers try "to quench the lust of her precious [bitten] skin, leaving at first pearly, then ruby, stripes along her enchanting leg and briefly attaining a drugged beatitude into which, as into a vacuum, the ferocity of the itch would rush with renewed strength" (p. 107). When the jaded and faded Veens are finally reunited almost forty years later, at the end of Part Four, deep desire only stirs when Van sees Ada on a balcony below, "her white neck and arms, the pale flowers on her flimsy peignoir, her bare legs, her high-heeled silver slippers. Pensively, youngly, voluptuously, she was scratching her thigh at the rise of the right buttock: Ladore's pink signature on vellum at mosquito dusk. Would she look up?" She does, and greets him with the most Romantic of flourishes: "All her flowers turned up to him, beaming, and she made the royal-grant gesture of lifting and offering him the mountains, the mist and the lake with three swans" (p. 562).

Although the allusions seem to define *Ada* as a period piece (to pun in a manner not unknown to Van Veen), they finally serve as an ironic foil. Morbid and melancholy René recoils from Amélie when he recognizes the nature of her attachment, and after she enters a convent, he loses himself in the wilds of Louisiana, where he dies. Nor is Ada's behavior to be confused with that of either Amélie or Atala, who commits suicide over her loss of virtue. "All art is a game," says Van,* and the Chateaubriand allusions in part constitute a series of delusive moves, setting up the expectation—and hope?—that *Ada* will somehow be a tale of remorse and retribution; Nabokov well knows that some readers, very poor losers, are bound to be disappointed.† By thoroughly enjoying their caprices in *Ada's* veritable bed of allusions, Nabokov's "children of Venus" assume a literary life of their own.

Mlle Larivière, of all people, telescopes Nabokov's achievement. Even though Chateaubriand, unlike Maupassant, exists on Antiterra, one suspects that *Les Enfants Maudits* will be a complete steal from *René,* but it is not. Instead, she "had two adolescents, in a French castle, poison their widowed mother who had

---

* "I can never understand their games and little secrets," says Marina to Demon, speaking of Van and Ada and voicing a common complaint against their maker (p. 249).
† Chateaubriand and Byron are to *Ada* what Poe and Mérimée are to *Lolita.* Humbert continually calls Lolita "Carmen," and at tender and crucial moments quotes from Mérimée, a trap for the reader who concludes that Humbert will surely kill the deceitful enchantress, since José killed his Carmen. "A damned good fool I have made of someone," says the narrator of Nabokov's *Despair.* "Who is he? Gentle reader, look at yourself in the mirror."

seduced a young neighbor, the lover of one of her twins." By the time the much rewritten film script reaches the screen as a western, *The Young and the Doomed*, it "had now become the story of a murder in Arizona, the victim being a widower about to marry an alcoholic prostitute, whom Marina, quite sensibly, refused to impersonate" (p. 424). However trite her results, Mlle Larivière has avoided copying *René*, just as Nabokov has recast, remade, and transcended it in *Ada*.

Van may call himself "a romantic character" (p. 193), but Nabokov undermines our hero's estimation of himself. Van is hardly an *"homme fatal,"* and as presented in *Ada*, the unfettered self is not always a joy to behold; the ego is seen as the monster it often is, calmly and coldly transfixed by an anti-Freudian writer who offers no redeeming causation. In addition to the artist's suffering, we witness the suffering he causes others, something the *Bildungsroman* has never stressed. Thus Ada and Van contribute to Lucette's self-destruction, and her suicide movingly records the high price their freedom exacts. Van enjoys two hundred women, the same number Byron is alleged to have had, and during the ocean voyage on which Lucette takes her life, she and Van together see a film called *Don Juan's Last Fling*. Much to Lucette's chagrin, Ada appears on the screen in the role of the gypsy girl whom the dashing Don rescues, somewhat anticlimactically:

The Don rides past three windmills, whirling black against an ominous sunset, and saves her from the miller who accuses her of stealing a fistful of flour and tears her thin dress. Wheezy but still game, Juan carries her across a brook (her bare toe acrobatically tickling his face) and sets her down, top up, on the turf of an olive grove. Now they stand facing each other. She fingers voluptuously the jeweled pommel of his sword, she rubs her firm girl belly against his embroidered tights, and all at once the grimace of a premature spasm writhes across the poor Don's expressive face. He angrily disentangles himself and staggers back to his steed (p. 489).

Ada's and Van's eroticism is meaningful elsewhere only because Van's "Byronic" libertinism has been burlesqued throughout the novel, and Ada's bravura gesture on the balcony is so incandescent a moment because "a touch of parody [has given] its theme the comic relief of life" (p. 137).

A reviewer who saw in reunited Ada and Van an image of Nabokov's own married life drew an angry response from the author, who termed the Veens "both rather horrible creatures." [7] That adjective is far more descriptive and suitable than others that may come to mind ("immoral," "amoral"), for the paradisial nature of Ardis requires a different vocabulary altogether. "This is a . . . howl *iz ada* (out of Hades)," writes Ada in a letter to Van, underlining the etymology of her name (p. 332). *Ad* is a Russian masculine noun for hell, *muki ada* are the torments of hell, and *ad* is of course contained in "Adam." Catching sight of Ada washing, Van notices "A fat snake of porcelain curled around the basin, and . . . both the reptile and he stopped to watch Eve . . ." (p. 60). Shortly afterward they climb "the glossy-limbed shattal tree at the bottom of the garden," where they become intimately entangled as a "last fruit fell with a thud" (p. 94). Ada claims "It is really the Tree of Knowledge—this specimen was imported last summer wrapped up in brocade from the Eden National Park" (p. 95), but theirs would instead seem to be a Fortunate Fall. [8] Innocence still prevails, and the distinction between good and evil remains ambiguous and unarticulated in the premoral world of their glimmering garden. In regaining Paradise, Nabokov has miraculously succeeded in retelling a story so old that it becomes utterly new and "infinitely richer" than the first one, as Jorge Luis Borges says of Menard's *Don Quixote*. [9]

Nabokov is the most allusive and linguistically playful writer in English since Joyce, and like *Pale Fire* and *Lolita,* his new novel abounds in amusing anagrams, delightful minor parodies and pastiches, countless multilingual puns and literary jokes. The range of reference is wide, including Rimbaud, Verlaine, Sir Richard Burton, Marvell, Melville, Chekhov, Casanova, Flaubert, Verne, Pushkin, Housman, Aksakov, Fet, Lermontov, Pasternak, Blok, Dostoevsky, Pascal, Shakespeare, Poe, Faulkner, "Heinrich Müller" (Henry Miller), Freud, Bergerac, "Pompier" (Malraux), Henry James, "Lowden" (Lowell + Auden), James Jones, Scott, "Norman Girsh" (Podhoretz), "Norbert von Miller" (Mailer), Dickens, Dumas, and Sirin. Many of these allusions are not fundamental to the design of *Ada,* but they are good fun. A few examples will suffice. Because some of T. S. Eliot's verse does not establish him as a Semitophile, Nabokov ironically describes a "Mr. Eliot, a Jewish businessman" (p. 5), who later meets the late-blooming banker (Eliot's early vocation) Kithar Sween (whose last name evokes Eliot's "Sweeney"), author of *"The Waistline,* a satire in free verse on Anglo-American feeding habits" (p. 506). "Old Beckstein's *Tabby"* alludes to Steinbeck's *Travels with Charley* (p. 403), while Kingsley Amis appears anagrammatically in the person of "Sig Leymanski" (p. 340). *Love Under the Lindens,* by "Eelmann," combines Eugene O'Neill with Thomas Mann and plants *Desire Under the Elms* on Unter den Linden, a boulevard in Berlin. "Osberg" (Borges; an anagram) is the author of *The Gitanilla* (little gypsy), a novel reminiscent of *Lolita,* and several allusions to Osberg and his influence on Van Veen are jokes aimed at the critics who yoke Nabokov and Borges, as well as a witty refutation of Borges' breadth: " 'Tell me,' says Osberg's little gitana to the Moors, El Motela and Ramera, 'what is the precise minimum of hairs on a body that allows one to call it "hairy"?' " (p. 361). Sometimes Van Veen seems to be suffering from terminal paronomasia ("Stan Slavsky"), but usually the puns are more winning ("the ballet master Dangleleaf": Diaghilev + Nijinsky's famous figleaf). These are typical of the hundreds of nuggets buried in *Ada* (Find What the Author Has Hidden, a game for all seasons), and the process of annotating *Ada* will no doubt keep some compulsive exegete busy for at least as many years as it took Nabokov to write it.

However much it is about literature, and however literary it may be, *Ada* is primarily about life—"death-padded life," as Nabokov calls it in *Pale Fire.* At the age of ninety-seven, even a philosopher who has negated the Future may be prompted to explore the subject further. In Part Five, living in Switzerland (as Nabokov and his wife do now), their fantasia suspended, Ada and Van Veen contemplate their prospects for the future. Death is imagined as eternal pain, a form of madness. But wordsmith Ada "know[s] there's a Van in Nirvana. I'll be with him in the depths *moego ada,* of my Hades," she says (p. 583), again pointing to the etymology of her name and perhaps suggesting that theirs is no longer a premoral world. Early in the novel Van describes the phases of Aqua Veen's disintegration, "every one more racking than the last; for the human brain can become the best torture house of all those it has invented, established and used in millions of years, in millions of lands, on millions of howling creatures" (p. 22). Those howls are audible throughout the novel, even in Ardis, since death casts a shadow in Arcady too. "I may die tonight," says the narrator one-third of the way into the book (p. 221), and the reader is constantly made aware of the "crotchety gray old word man on the edge of a hotel bed" (p. 121). In Part Five, the nocturnal torments and terrors of old age move into the foreground of the novel. His room dominated by a spacious bedside table containing the numerous medicinal necessities of the night, Van sleeps on "one side only, so as not to hear his heart: he had made the mistake one night in 1920 of calculating the maximal number of its remaining beats (allowing for another half-century), and now the preposterous hurry of the countdown irritated him and increased the rate at which he could hear himself dying" (pp. 569-70).

The final pages of *Ada* are as deeply moving as the earlier parodies are brilliantly "inhuman." Yet these final pages also afford deep pleasures. Their comic eschatologies are consistent with the spirit that informs all of *Ada,* the spirit that is underscored by the last syllable in Ada's name when it is pronounced correctly in "the Russian way with two deep, dark 'a's"—*da!* Yes; the name includes both Eden and Hades, and the ardor of Nabokov's art, the exuberance and luminosity of his prose, is equal to the infinite riches of consciousness. "I, Van Veen, salute you, life," proclaims Van in the opening sentence of Part Five, speaking for his creator as well. The titles of many of Nabokov's novels and stories are evoked throughout *Ada*,[10] for while Van Veen is commemorating those summer "trips to the magic islet" of Ardis, a network of authorial self-references succeeds in revealing the omnipresence of Van Veen's maker [V.V.=Vladimir Vladimirovich],[11] a Prospero who magically summons up the creations of a lifetime. And like *The Tempest*, an earlier physics fiction, *Ada* is a culminating work, an act of accommodation that in the face of darkness asserts joy. It is a great work of art, a necessary book, radiant and rapturous, affirming the power of love and imagination, "and much, much more," to quote Van Veen's concluding but open-ended self-endorsement.

Notes

1. Remarked in letters to the present writer.
2. They include Michelangelo, Cranach, Brueghel, Titian, Parmigianino, Braque, Bronzino, Zurbaran, Lautrec, Gaugin, Theban frescoes, and anonymous erotica of all kinds. Van is indifferent to the plastic arts, though he does scorn "Heinrich Heideland" (p. 462), who is Henry Moore [*heide*: German for "heath" or "moor"]. Uncle Dan Veen is an art dealer and Van's father Demon is a collector of old masters, so their name may in part derive from that of Duveen, the famous dealer.
3. All page references are to the hardcover edition (New York, 1969), and will appear in parentheses in the text.
4. Hans Meyerhoff, *Time in Literature* (Berkeley and Los Angeles, 1960), p. 7.
5. The pun was first pointed out by Robert Alter in his fine article, "Nabokov's Ardor," *Commentary*, 48 (August 1969), p. 49, reprinted in *Nabokov: A Collection of Essays*, Alfred Appel, Jr., ed. (Englewood Cliffs, N.J., 1970).
6. Nabokov and Chateaubriand share many qualities as "landscape painters": a strong sense of color, a sensitivity to the play of sun and shadow, and, for all the sensuousness of their prose-poetry, a concern for accuracy and sharpness of specification that is derived from their training in the natural sciences (botany in Chateaubriand's instance, lepidoptery, of course, in Nabokov's).
7. Vladimir Nabokov, "Letters," *The New York Review of Books*, XIII (July 10, 1969), p. 36.
8. See Alter, *op. cit.*, pp. 49-50, who develops this line of interpretation convincingly.
9. J. L. Borges, "Pierre Menard, Author of the *Quixote*," in *Labyrinths* (New York, 1964), p. 42.
10. A character recalls a room decorated with a steeplechase picture of "Pale Fire with Tom Cox Up" (p. 477), and in their old age, Ada and Van translate into Russian lines from John Shade's *Pale Fire* (pp. 577 and 585). The sun of "Spring in Fialta" is mentioned (p. 477), and phrases from the poem "Ode to a Model" are woven into a letter (". . . a petite fille modèle *practicing archery near a vase and a parapet*" [p. 503]). Van's tutor gives him a copy of *Alice in the Camera Obscura* for his eighth birthday (p. 547), Nabokov invoking the

original title of *Laughter in the Dark*. "For the big picnic on Ada's twelfth birthday . . . the child was permitted to wear her lolita (thus dubbed after the little Andalusian gipsy of that name in Osberg's novel . . .)" (p. 77). Demon Veen retreats to his "aunt's ranch near Lolita, Texas" (p. 16), an actual town, doubtless boasting no bookstore or library. In one of Van's nightmares, someone says, "It's one of the Vane sisters" (p. 521), an allusion to "The Vane Sisters," an excellent story about psychic phenomena. *Invitation to a Climax* is observed on a paperback bookstand (p. 459), a title more in the spirit of *Ada* than the extant *Invitation to a Beheading*.

11. Ada is asked to treasure "a little camel of yellow ivory carved in Kiev, five centuries ago, in the days of . . . Nabok" (p. 268), and a hapless critic discerns in Van's first book, *Letters from Terra*, the influence "of an obscene ancient Arab, expounder of anagrammatic dreams, Ben Sirine [Sirin was Nabokov's émigré pen name—A.A.], thus transliterated by Captain de Roux, according to Burton in his adaptation of Nefzawi's treatise on the best method of mating with obese or hunchbacked females . . ." (p. 344). Nabokov's birthday, April 23, is also the date on which Aqua and Demon are married and Ada's husband dies. She rejoins Van in 1922, the year of Nabokov's graduation from Cambridge, his move to Berlin, and the assassination of his beloved father. Van is fifty-two, the age of Nabokov *père* at his death. Ada and Van have been separated for seventeen years, which equals the duration of Nabokov's dark years of exile on the European continent, terminated by his emigration to America in 1940, and the beginning of a happier period in his life.

Kickshaws and motley
PETER LUBIN

Mon zemblable! Mon père!
—Tiré d'une lettre particulière

As is well known, Vladimir Nabokov ingeminates.[1] The eager critic, stumbling upon those chess men and butterflies, can only remind us of the scholiast who brought to light the "skating" in *Eugene Onegin*. But even in nice details autoplagiarism is evident: twins and breeding mirrors and symmetrical threatening cretins; *audition colorée* and anagrams; names beginning with "Mc." [2]

Characters and verbal props move from book to book. Lang paints a mural in *Pnin* and a portrait in *Pale Fire*. Podtyagin returns from *Mashenka* to serve as an extra in *The Gift*. Pnin shows up in *Pale Fire*, Delalande in *The Gift* and the Foreword to *Invitation to a Beheading*. The intoxicating sob from Mallarmé mentioned once in *The Gift* haunts *Bend Sinister*. The "macédoine of accents" in *Ada* summons up not only the description of Humbert, that "salad of racial genes," but also the "kompot slov" of Pomyalovski in *Dar*. The servile fairy-tale gardener of *Dar* putters around the platbands along the Chemin de Mustrux in *Ada*.[3] *The Gift* and *Pale Fire* are two corymbs of consonants held together by a sprig of Turgenevian heliotrope (from the same bush that supplied Anna Kern's bosom?).

In *Ada* we find again vase and parapet and pillared porch, rainbows and nightmares, intolerable bliss and the mauve glans, the trumped catoptricks of dappled dawns, and those unmistakable eyeplusenems: *grim, limp, limpid, ultimate, dim, whim, megrim, akin* (and its Caribbean cousin, *akimbo*). And all of this, from theme to phoneme, is blent in the alkahest of his art.[4]

The diffident may turn to that serviceable standby, Influence. It is not hard to do.[5] Like Proust, who built on a droplet and a crumb the edifice of Memory, Nabokov has been occupied with Time and the evocation of the Past. He has walked widdershins on the wabe. Like Gogol, he is a master of unnecessary (necessary!—A.B.) digression. And he has read the late great Irish philologist, who put old books to sly uses.[6]

But his words, not his kinship to past masters, are what most enchant this reader. Begat by that enchantment, these pages are offered, dim inklings, slim synecdoche (Schenectady for New York).

I. Words

"Why do you speak of words,
When all we want is knowledge nicely browned?"

Because, Sylvia, they excite widdrim and wonder. All of them, all of them—the words hallowed by time and rhyme that he uses not "fittingly" but exactly; the decrepit words he youthens; the foreigners he naturalizes; his own lexical offspring.

He is precise, as we expect him to be, that once curator of lepidoptera, in his use of technical terms ("the parallel rail line all at once committing suicide by anastomosis"). But he is equally precise with the nontechnical. Take the honest kersey *fey,* a wordlet with an old and venerable history. From the Anglo-Saxon *faege,* it means fated or doomed to die, dying, having the air of one under a doom or spell. ("Ocymore, dyspotme, oligochronien," as Ronsard glossed it.) It is a common epithet for the kemps and menskful kings struggling on a field, gules, in the old battle poems of Maldon and Brunanburh and, later, in Layamon. Through contamination with *fay* it may also mean "able to see fairies, be clairvoyant, have an unworldly air or attitude." Latterly *fey* has been stretched to cover "bizarre, strange, coy, whimsical," and is even applied to male pale fires and outlandish dress. But Nabokov naturally uses it exactly as it should be used. We recall a passage in *Pale Fire,* perhaps the best use of the word anywhere: "the *consonne d'appui*/Echo's fey child," one instance of his noble rescue and resurrection of a word that was slowly being put to death by other writers.

The very precision we applaud annoys others. Certain critics are offended, in particular, by "obscurities" in the *Onegin* translation.* One example cited is *shippon,* the translator's rendering of the Russian *xlev.* Nabokov's reply is that there is no acceptable alternative—he rules out *byre* as too Vermontish. (Perhaps he would allow us to suggest that *barn* is too general, *cow barn* too specific, *linney* too lean-to, *vaccary* too lactic, and *mistal* too Midlands.) † Such rarities appear only infrequently in the translation, however, and when they do, it is not lexiphanic swank but humble submission that dictates their use. He fits his shadow to that of his author. He does not add the slightest flourish to the noble-winged serifs of Pushkin's paraph.

---

* Occasionally Nabokov does go overboard in that exegetical monument, his palmary and omnianic commentary. One would practically have to be the Negus Professor of Geez or at least an Associate in Amharic to decipher "Pushkin, griffado Pushkin, whose quatrayle had hunted ashkokos and kaberus across the zimb-infested ambas of Ethiop."
† The Russian lines (*EO,* IV, 41) are "na utrennej zare pastux/ne gonıt uz korov iz xleva" which become "no longer does the herdsman drive at sunrise/ the cows out of the shippon." *Cow barn* would not only call forth an unseemly echo but would lose the sense (latent in *shippon* through usage and false etymology) that the *xlev* may just possibly be used for other animals. Dahl says there are "cow, calf, and sheep" *xleva.* A *xlev* is also a pigsty.

His passion for exactitude is necessarily coupled with a love of synonymy. Without a large bag of words, the wordman is incapable of providing the right word for the right occasion. When there are semantic equals, rhythm and sound determine choice. If *whin* won't fit, *gorse* or *furze* might do. If it is a time for Elizabethan flyting and digladiation, one may grow wrathful with an unctuous mome and let fly *cudden* and *dawkin* and *mooncalf*. If it is a matter, say, of Kinbote's catamites and urning-yearnings, it helps to have *ingle* and *gunsil, bardash* and *pathic,* in verbal reserve. Most of Nabokov's resources, of course, are not at all rare or recherché. He is a master of the familiar word. But when he does embrace a neglected one, "it lives again, sobs again, stumbles all over the cemetery in doublet and trunk hose, and will keep annoying stodgy gravediggers" as long as literature itself endures.

His words delight us not only because of their splendid fit, but because they are splendid words. *Pale Fire* gives us *marrowsky* and *stillicide.* The first (Medical Greek, Gower Street dialect, "distant metathesis"—in short, Spoonerism *avant le maître*) is accorded a spurious etymology in the Index, and this sanctions our own etymology for *stillicide,* as a word derived not from the Latin for a "dropping drop" (*stilla* plus *cadere*) but from the Anglo-Latin for "killing the stillness." The list continues. *Borborygmic* (used twice in *Ada,* high frequency for a word seldom met outside the pages of Anthony Burgess or Valéry Larbaud)— the stomach rumble-and-grumble. *Woodwose,* the tawny faun who romps with the mays and fays of Middle English ferly-tales. *Grimpen, thumbkin, peba, stang, gowpen, versipel, laund, arval, dudeen, ignicolist, menald, inenubilable, rizzom, nenuphar, ackers, barleybreak . . .*[7]

Nabokov's neologisms vary in their eligibility for English adoption.[8] His best is the celebrated *nymphet*—no longer merely "a young nymph, *Poetic*" but with a new, unforgettable meaning, also *Poetic.* A word completely his own, and akin to *nymphet* in its formation, is *iridule,* created by the addition of a hypocoristic diminutive to *iris. Iridule* emblematically evokes Nabokov's vibgyoric passion, his spotting of beauty in ugliness, the peacock feather on the dismal plain. This I think of as the "rainbow-in-the-puddle" theme, and it applies not only to the pied beauty of Nature but also to the magic discovered in the dun mundane (a sports headline; the nacreous buttons on a tobacconist's vest; a paragraph in some little known book by Lane or Longinov). Browning's door is preserved in the library of Wellesley College.

Some of them will not last. The Zemblan *coramen,* a sweet parliament of vowels, is phonetically winning but neither fills a vacuum nor has evident motivation in the language. Similarly, those words which are invented to serve as props on Antiterra— *dorophones, jikkers, ivanilich*—are part of that world and it would be unfortunate if, as with Tolkien's boring hobbits, a cute little cult of Antiterra developed (with maps, and vocabulary, and sinchilla mantillas). That is not likely to happen.

Then there are the words in other tongues which cry out (we think they are crying out) for incorporation into our own incomparably rich wordhoard. In the Free City of English, residents do not as often experience that sense of lexical lacunae, of sad lacks, that subjects of other languages do, and we can rightly glory in the butterfly of an open unabridged Webster. Somewhere in those alternate layers of Anglo-Saxon and Latin and other tongues, in that happily imperfect palimpsest, there are words for almost everything. They may be archaic, or Scottish, or slang, or nonce-words from Heywood or Middleton, but they are words in an English dictionary nonetheless. Still there are gaps, and Nabokov fills such troublesome chinks whenever he has the chance. *Kurortish* (occurring once in *Bend Sinister,* twice in *Lolita*) is the stolid German *Kurort* (a general term for a balneological resort) plus the likable English *ish.* Better is *sun blick* (in *Ada*), which anglicizes and sublimes its source—not Russian *solnečnij blik,* but rather their common stirps, German *Sonnenblick.* And here we are immediately offered an additional gift of *zajchik* for the same sun-bunny ray of reflected light.[9]

The loan blend *otsebyatinate* differs from the above examples in that it involves not only the addition of an English suffix, but also the turning of a Russian noun (*otsebyatina*—defined miserably in my Soviet dictionary as "one's own concoction") into an English verb.* It is the action of putting in something from one's self. Thus the word can be applied to the padlibbing paraphrast or translator, the gay betrayer of a hapless and helpless original.

Carpalistics, like *otsebyatinate*, is born of a need peculiarly Nabokov's. It was defined in *Pnin* as the sum of the "Russian shrugs and shakes . . . the movements underlying such Russian verbs—used in reference to hands—as *mahnut', vsplesnut', razvesti*." It is more specific than *kinesics*, the generalized study of gesture, and does not overlap *pasimology*, the science of the gestures that do not accompany and enrich speech but clumsily substitute for it. *Carpalistics* may even subsume the most common *Soviet* gesture, the vetitive waggle of forefinger. The word is not necessary, of course, to describe hands-in-pockets *amerikantsï*.

Suctorialist was first and last used (by Nabokov) in an April 24, 1949, review of a French novel for one who "reads and admires such remarkably silly nonsense as the 'existentialists' rig up." An ugly word, an ugly idea, and we may leave it, along with that novel, back in 1949.

It is enticing, this game of foreign exactions and domestic inventions. Anyone can play. For immediate enrollment in English I suggest *capicue* (from Spanish *capicúa*), the numerical equivalent of a palindrome. It has a clean etymology, coming from *caput* (head) and *cola* (tail). 14,841 (the number of books in Ardelion Veen's library) is a *capicue*. So is 343 (a perfect cube of a number!), the sum of humdrum days, *budni*, full of hectic vacancy, of tohu-bohu and carpediurnal carnality, that are left in a leap year if we remove the 23 that lie between April Fool's Day and Shakespeare's Birthday.

As a neologism I proffer the portmanteau *vendective*. The

---

* The *same* dictionary unwittingly alludes to Joyce's "comedian Capuchin" when it defines "polnolunie" as "fool moon."

good lexicogenist will see at once that the father, stepfather, and father-in-law of this word are *vendetta, vindictive,* and *invective.* That Ephraim Blueprint, incorrigible word-coiner, proposed it as the only appropriate epithet for the articles in the transatlantic journal *La Révue des Bévues, or Malice in Blunderland* (Founding editor: A. E. Housman; Present editors: V. V. Nabokov and A. Z. Vozdam). Fierce wielders of the obelus, enemies of pushpin traductions, lovers of the dim detail, for better than half a century the editors have been the scourge of careless scholiasts and degenerate grammarians.[10]

II. Phrases

> *"There is figures in all things."*
> —HENRY V

The reader soon learns to discern Nabokov's repetitive verbal arrangements, his syntactic tics. The lovely penultimate sentence in *Lolita,* for example, summons up other synaesthetic three-and-four cola periods. The "all X and Y" formula is also a favorite.[11] And there is that subspecies of *hyperbaton* (the "disorder" figure) known as *tmesis.**

Tmesis in antiquity was defined as the "cutting" (from Gr. *temnein,* to cut) of a (compound) word by the interposition of another word. In the first example below, the noun "cerebrum" is split open; in the second, the verb opens to envelop Venus in her own cloud.

Saxo cere cominuit brum (Ennius)
et multo nebulae circum dea fudit amictu (Virgil)

The classical definition is repeated by the English authors of the Renaissance rhetorical handbooks. Sherry in *Treatise of Schemes and Tropes* offers this instance:

---

* There are those who consider these to be figures of fun and who applaud Hugo's effusion,

> Syllepse, hypallage, litote
> frémirent; je montai sur la borne Aristote
> et déclarai les mots égaux, libres, majeurs

but I do not.

"Hys saying was true, as here shall appeare after," for hereafter.[12]

As some English metricians unthinkingly employ classical terms of prosody, so some rhetoricians are timidly subservient to the ancients' classification of the figures—it makes for the same muddle. The hallowed definitions simply will not do for English. We see this with *tmesis*. In the first place, a language that is preponderantly mono- and oligosyllabic has fewer words that can be sensibly split (than, say, Greek or Latin). Secondly, words cannot be cavalierly ordered in our anaptotic tongue.[13] English dictionaries follow Sherry in illustrating *tmesis* with compound words.

Examples of *simple tmesis* in modern languages:

a lady of impeckandpeckable taste (possible advertisement)
en petit couragé (a favorite of Pushkin in his postal prose, recombining
the elements of the Petersburg French phrase "petit encouragé")
Balticomore (in *Ada*, p. 124. The "co" stretches Maryland from the Baltic
Sea to Lake Como.)

But this does not cover the case that is most common in English, and that deserves taxonomical recognition, *phrasal tmesis*. An expression rather than a word is ruptured by an alien verbal insertion. The original phrase may range from adjective-plus-noun to complete sentence. "Ultimate dim Thule" qualifies as *phrasal tmesis* since "Ultima Thule" and its variant "ultimate Thule" are recognized expressions.

Nabokov is fond of this figure. He employs four varieties. Type I results from the simple interposition of a word or words in a fixed phrase (identical with the "ultimate . . ." example):

1. **"I'm all enchantment and ears"**   (*Ada*, p. 71)
2. **"the Old and rotting World"**   (*Lolita*, p. 85)
3. **"safety gold pin"**   (*Ada*, p. 124)

1) is a happy example of both *tmesis* and the "all X and Y" formula mentioned above. 2) and 3) are examples of the most common subspecies. A semantic petticoat is slipped on between

the naked noun and its clothing epithet. The resulting frou-frou is quite satisfying.

Type II consists in the intercalation of a word or words and a twist to either or both terminals. Thus, if "La Belle Dame Sans Merci" were to undergo tmetic transformation type II, we might describe the Wife of Bath, that foul-mouthed rixatrix, that atterling and shrew preserving her viraginity at all costs, as "a beldam sans any mercy." Or a changeling might be defined as a "lost-and-fairy-foundling." Nabokov employs type II in Ada's reply to Van, " 'That's all bluff and nuns' nonsense!' " ("stuff" to "bluff"; insertion of "and nuns' ").

A third type is straightforward *phrasal tmesis* except that the intervenient words form still another fixed expression with one of the limital elements. In *Ada* "the Arctic no longer vicious Circle" is a good example. The topographic phrase ("Arctic Circle") is coldly severed, and the verbal interloper couples with the second segment to form the cliché "vicious circle." This *tmesis* may be likened to a moiré pattern or a cereal-box toy; looked at one way, it is a geographic, looked at another, a figurative expression.

Lastly, there is a type of *tmesis* in which the original phrase is apprehended as an idiom (and therefore fit to be split) only within its particular context. The phrase has no more significance in common speech than do "characters" in a book outside of their cultured medium. We find in *Lolita* "an enchanted and very tight hunter" (p. 268). By the time "enchanted hunter" is put on the tmetic chopping block it has been repeated so frequently (once even as "Ted Hunter, Cane, N. H.") as to be accepted as a full-fledged expression.[14]

Why does *phrasal tmesis* attract Nabokov? Could his use of the figure in English have something to do with the habit of loose word order in Russian? Certainly he offers us the best opportunity for studying the individual speech-act *(la parole)* in relation to the system of the language *(la langue),* since there are two tongues and only one writer, thereby conveniently minimizing such ordinarily troublesome difficulties as chronology, biography, and "poetic school." [15]

Or could we perhaps relate the figure to a more general technique? Nabokov manipulates, remanipulates, obmanipulates the smallest details as well as the "themes and motifs." Isn't *phrasal tmesis* a syntactic equivalent of those "specious lines of play" his books are filled with? Fyodor does not hold that conversation with Koncheyev, not the first time we "overhear" them, not the second. Pilgram never makes it to Andalucia or Taprobane. Humbert does not drill his dolly. Glum Van does not empty the contents of the cartridge into his skull. *Tmesis* similarly surprises. It is the greater deception writ small. The mind apprehends the terminal words which it expects to find juxtaposed, and then must accommodate the alien phonemes thrust between. But this is just a start at explanation. "Questions for study and discussion," to quote an old poet, still remain.

Repairing to surer ground, we should not forget that rare brand of "anticipatory" or "proleptic" *tmesis* which Nabokov has induced in other, earlier writers. Here a phrase is perceived as being tmetically cleaved only in retrospect, for remote reasons the original author could hardly have guessed. Thus Shakespeare commits *tmesis* when he has the ghost of Hamlet's father announce:

> The glow-worm shows the matin to be near,
> And 'gins to pale his ineffectual fire.

III. Paragraphs

> *Miryachit': (Russian Miryachit', inf.) to be epileptic (Pavlovsky). A peculiar nervous disease observed in Siberia and in some non-European countries, the chief characteristic of which consists in mimicry by the patient of everything said or done by another.*
>
> —OXFORD ENGLISH DICTIONARY

The Department of Linguistics boasted three members. Waggish Asst. Professor William McPed had transcribed (clicks and all) the Lumba tongue, spoken by at least ten thousand Malumba men, women, and children somewhere between Zambia and Zululand ("to purify the language of the tribe," quipped quick-witted Bill.) The head of the department and occupant of the Harry Amurath Chair in Slavic was Roman Lefshets, much noted and footnoted since his pioneering work (at age 19!) on "Some Phonemic Phenomena of Sandhi and Futhorc."

A prodigious worker, a fine scholar, Lefshets had tried his hand at every branch of his youthful science, and everywhere he had left his mark. He had analyzed juncture in Glossic and Braille. He had composed grammars of Gilyak and Bats. He had decoded the "Bezumnij Yazik" of the Petrograd Pentad (Walter Lighthorse, Alec Twist, Anna Eckmate, Barry Parsnip, and Cosmo Breadline, as McPed anticly called them). He had invented "Phonemic Verse," a system of prosody based not on the hoary and unscientific principles of accent or syllable, but on the up-to-date method of a uniform number of phonemes per line. Hundreds of his former students were now famous professors in great universities. The Turko-Dutch scholar Derzha Veen (who with his sister had arrived in America just after the war, two penniless but eager orphans) had been his pupil. As had Oleg Shurin, brother-in-law of Derzha (Oleg had married Dazha, or Dasha, or Sasha, Veen during a dull moment at the World Congress of Poetics, in Boston, in 1956).

Lefshets had also taught Fritz Auspumpen, the world expert on runic neumes and brother of Visiting Lecturer (from Merkin College) Hans Auspumpen. Hans, a cunning linguist in his own right, was doing a really bangup job on the bilabial fricative (again a bit of sinwit, eh, Bill?). But the old man was close to retirement, and there was only one graduate student (shared with Auspumpen), a pale-faced Indian girl, Miss Diana Moonbeam from Ça Ira, Virginia . . .

Excerpts from the interview

Famous writer and a rather fatuous interviewer:

R.F.I.: There are a number of readers who are beginning to regard you as a sage on all sorts of subjects, even political ones. Do you think that despite your disclaimers you may in fact have a profound *non-literary* effect?

N.: No, no. At least I hope not. As I have said elsewhere, "Je ne suis pas un petit télégraphiste." I wouldn't know how to give a spiritual massage. I pass the metaphysical buck. I bypass the museum of general ideas (which is to your left as you stroll down University Avenue). I cannot be linked to any cult of organized non-thought. I have no yen for yurodivies. I do not delight in the Vedic verities of Vishnuland. The stale truths of Mediterranean profundits leave me cold. And the fact that the title of my last Russian novel, transliterated, is DAR, and the title of my latest English novel is ADA, has no political implications whatsoever.

I.: I wonder if in your life, if not in your art, you can dissociate yourself so completely from current events?

N.: But I do not. I am perfectly aware of the virtues of the United States government, quite apart from the simple fact that it keeps us all from being caught smack in the stipe of a mushroom cloud. I was completely taken by the stellar exploits of those brave astrofellows, landing in the Tranquil Sea, so low in albedo, so lovely in name, dimmest and sweetest of the moon's maria. And I understand the need for dealing with the latest coup in Kumquat and the thorny problem of industrial melanism. But movements, manifestoes, model mayors of model cities—these aspects do not interest me.

I.: What about organized religion? In your autobiography you mention the ceremonies of the Russian Orthodox Church. In the commentary to *Pale Fire* you refer to "the numberless thinkers and poets in the history of human creativity whose freedom of mind was enhanced rather than stunted by Faith." In the poem itself you reveal a religious sense of mystery, as when you write,

"This life may be a rough draft of the next/To which we have the footnotes, not the text."

N.: Oh, when I was young and in Russia, I went to church occasionally. Purely for the sights and sounds—the icons, the greybeard priests, the slow swing of the thurible and the melismatic wail of the women. As for the sterner offerings of non-Russian varieties, I am perfectly content to take the good works without the faith. One doesn't have to travel in Dante's circles, after all, to appreciate those far-from-terse rhymes, and I am also fond of those tender madonnas and frail angels. In that respect I am a strict omnist. But the rest of it—going to hear a good reverend read from His latest work (Rome: The Godly Head), the tedium of worship, the bother, sin and holy toast—*that* doesn't interest me. I prefer to respect the wishes of the anonymous donor of existence.

I.: You have written that "Poets never kill" and that "the murderer is *always* his victim's inferior." In *Despair, Lolita, Pale Fire,* and *Invitation to a Beheading* you come out clearly against the taking of human life. Do you think your own private brand of morality inescapably informs your novels? What about the general problem of Good and Evil in contemporary fiction?

N.: I never think about it. Speaking as a reader, I never enjoyed the chaste chapbooks of the Charskayas and Victorian novelists of my youth, and I do not experience the ecstasy of evil that is so attractive to French suctorialists and in which American *pizdatel'stvos* are now doing such a thriving business. I prefer books that are neither Bowdlerized nor Baudelairized.

I.: Speaking of Baudelaire, many of your heroes are perverse madmen who certainly require some kind of care. You often mock the "Viennese witch doctor" and the "frauds" in the "Signy-Mondieu" crowd, and I relish that observation of Humbert Humbert, that the difference between the rapist and the therapist is merely a matter of spacing. But isn't it true that psychiatry, or rather its excesses, is not a threat any more, and that you may be beating a dead horse? And doesn't some of it have value? In both *Lolita* and *Ada* you brilliantly explore the interrelation of sex and psyche yourself, and it is surely true that some of our best young novelists owe a great deal to Freud.

N.: That haplographic calembour of Humbert (bis) is one of the few things he says that I do agree with—and by the way, you abridged it charmingly. Sex and psychiatry make dismal bedfellows. In point of fact sex is a very dull subject, but I try to make it interesting. The well-paid young ladies of the Venus Villas offer treats for every taste, and thither repairs my male hero (between sips, or rather dips, of his leman-Ada) to engorge himself on a smorgasbord of orgasms. These resorts and kurorts, Humbert's longings, and the passion-play of Vaniada have nothing to do with the grotesque and ridiculous business that recent story-tailors and typewriters have made of it.

I.: What are you working on now?

N.: At the moment I am preparing a book of essays on various writers, mostly from my university lectures. I may call it *Potions of Eisell.*

I.: Could you say something about them?

N.: Well, in my essay on Joyce I begin with *Ulysses*. I focus on the hapless wittol Bloom—much more interesting than hobbledehoy Dedalus. I steer clear of old Greeks. I correct a few mistakes—a spelling error in Nighttown, an anachronism in one of the maternity hospital parodies, that sort of thing. I dwell on the sybotic and Ithacan episodes, of which there is a delicate hint in poor Humbert's tentative approximations, and on that nightfest of the whimsy (the author's, not Bloom's). I deplore the excesses of Molly's *verzücktes Jasagen.* Then I move on to Joyce's last book, that unfortunate attempt at twin-twinning the oddity (as he might put it). A Plurability Canto, a Romany Fleuve (bits of shelta float here and there in it), and a damp disaster. There are five or six other essays, but the cat is already crawling half out of the bag.

I.:   Before we leave the subject entirely, can you tell me if any living writers will be discussed?

N.:   I am thinking of including a short piece on that Argentinian maker of transcendental pastels, whose name critics so curiously connect with mine. I still admire his arcane grammars and irretrievable sunsets, the fire and algebra of his fictions. And some of his formulas are quite good—as that definition of Infinity in "The Book-shop of Isidor Circle": "ese lemniscato espantoso y sem-piterno" (Infinity, that dreadful and everlasting lem-niscate). What a splendid evocation of olamic nausea. The lunfardo-loaded tales, however, are nothing but local color and lexical slumming. Now I am really afraid that grimalkin may escape.

I.:   What have you been doing aside from writing? Reading? Traveling?

N.:   I wander, nightly, in the enchanted realm between Marlowe and Marvell. Then, a few minutes of the old palpebral cinema, the ultimate dissolve into a rainbow mist, and finally a wretched imitation of sleep. As for other journeys, in connection with the above little essay I did make a short field trip to Ireland. Dun cows, and green meads, and the particolored animated rubrics in the Book of Kells. I ran to the pub of Davey Byrnes. I walked to 7 Eccles Street. I limped to Glasnevin Cemetery. I crawled to the Hill of Howth. In short, I was the most dutiful of Dubliners.

I.:   While we're on the subject of travel, would you ever consider returning to America?

N.:   I look forward to visiting North American shores this summer, and will pass a few weeks at a seldom frequented interlacustrine retreat in southern Ontario. There, between Lake Quirke and Lake Panache (the *inner* pair) I plan to spend ack emma hunting butterflies and pip emma reading my favorite American authors, Webster, Scudder, and Gray. The last, as your readers may be interested to learn, has just been revised by the botanist Leon Pasternak (no relation to the prize-winning novelist), best known for his unforgettable saga of some Old Worldly members of the pea family, *Medicago.*

I.: During that visit, will you be making any arrangements to deposit your papers with a library?

N.: Absolutely not, because no manuscripts, galleys, rough drafts, or penultimates exist. In this I have been ruthless. The misery of pilcrows, the crude products of blunt invention, the limp iambus of a private passion—none of this, not a shim or a shadow of it, should be left behind. I have destroyed my every version except the last. No notecards to *Lolita* nor *nabroski* to *Dar.* There will be no variorum edition of *Pale Fire,* with commentary by divers hands. Galasp and Colkitto will not argue over the Fair Copy of *Ada.* There is no reprieve for those fey pages. They will burn. They are flammable. They are inflammable.

I.: From your own recent experience, do you have any further thoughts on literary criticism? Any final advice to literary critics?

N.: Literature dealt with on a taxonomic basis is not in my line, to use a favorite expression of Count Vronsky. All of those labels, donnish dog tags, exquisite etiquettes which are welcome for certain specimens won't do for books. Viktor Shklovskij, formerly a fine critic, author of *The Knight's Move,* once coined the term "ostranenie" or "making strange." American Slavists are quick to use it. But is it to refer to Tolstoy's naive Natasha alone? It might just as well apply to the metaphysical conceit. A pun makes strange, and so does a paragram, or even a slip or a lipograph, as guests at a certain literary dinner have reason to know. What doesn't make strange, estrange, strangify in a book, if the author is a genuine artist? No, leave those terms alone. Avoid textbook truth. A fine nib and a nimble wit—that's what you want.

What is our passion? What do we love?
LETTERS OF F. K. LANE, P. 327

The dark star that rose over Russia fifty-two years ago is still almuten, and the publication of his books under that disaster is still, as the Russians say, a rainbow hope. A political exile from the thugs and grobians of Soviet Rus, he came to America, where lilacs and lindens also flourish, and the Meschacebé flows. A lexical exile, he presented his Nearctic muse with many splendid druries.

The world of books offers us one unpalatable writer imitating another, examples of müllerian rather than batesian mimicry. But year after year, by way of recompense, in vendective review, in limpid iambs, in the pomp and surquidry of his prose, this fabulous tarand continues, as the Americans say, to deliver the goods.[16] We are thankful for Vladimir Nabokov, ornament of the age and Shakespeare's current avatar.

Notes

1. His revamping of traditional themes (the "double," the love-triangle) and forms (the work-of-art-and-its-commentary) has been marked and re-marked. Perhaps too much remarked.

2. Twins, doubles, and enantiomorphs: Floyd and Lloyd ("Scenes from the Life of a Double Monster"), Felix and Hermann (*Despair*), Wynn and Twynn (*Pnin*), Pauline and Paul ("The Ballad of Longwood Glen"). Onymic twins: the unnamed narrator and his namesake ("Conversation Piece, 1945"), two Walter D. Veens and two Van Veens (*Ada*). Symmetrical threatening cretins and caryatides: Rodion and Rodrig (*Invitation to a Beheading*), Ekwilist operatives (*Bend Sinister*), Gustav and Anton ("Korolëk").

All of whom demonstrate, as Dobchinsky and Bobchinsky and Tweedledum and Tweedledee before them, that reduplication is the essence of farce.

Audition colorée and anagrams: Nabokov's works, *passim*. "Mc-" names (favored by Nabokov as the Gaelic equivalent of the Russian patronymic?): Charles McBeth and Mrs. McCrystal (in *Pnin*), Jim McVey and President McAber (in *Pale Fire*), McCoo, McCrystal, and McFate (in *Lolita*), Mr. McMath (in *The Real Life of Sebastian Knight*). And at Cornell (in the equally real life of the Nabokovs) a house was rented from the MacLeods (McCloud) at 957 East State Street.

3. "Must Trucks-Must Rux" punplay on the Chemin de Mustrux in *Ada*. "Mak-s, luk-s," says the "skazočnij ogorodnik'" in *Dar*, sounding the name of the Berlin emporium Max Lux.

4. We might list a few more of the many "bits of colored glass" that Nabokov reconfigurates in his kaleidoscope with each new *vstryaska*. The Estotiland of the ingenious Zeno and Milton is the latest in his appropriations of fabulous and frigid holarctic lands (Ultima Thule, Nova Zembla) in the distant northern corners (*v uglu*, in the igloo) of our globe. The unbroken apple peel that emblemizes genius in "Restoration" recalls *Dar:* "Očistit' moë yabloko odnoj polosoj, ne otnimaya noža." Favored adjectives appear again and again with unexpected partners. *Animated*, for example, invigorates *merkin* (in *Lolita*), *mutton* (notes to *A Hero of Our Time*), and *mysteries* (*The Real Life of Sebastian Knight*).

Luck may assist the shake. A cooperative muse permits Nabokov to link all three of his past epigraphs (the oak from *The Gift*, the cat from *Pale Fire*, the author of the *Mashenka* motto) in one pun. *Quercus ruslan chat.* is planted for friends of Ruslan and Lyudmila in *Ada*. A heliophobic shrub, the Uncommon Laburnum, is sometimes found around this tree.

5. It may be more difficult with Nabokov for he does not limit himself to the pets of the seminar and the review. His crotchets and carriwitchets lead him to the farthest stacks in the Library of Serendip. We find the exploratory prose of Grigorij Efimovich Grum-Gržmajlo (*Opisanie putešestvija v zapadnij Kitaj; Zapadnaja Mongolija i Urjanxajskij kraj*) lifted into *The Gift*, and the epistolary prose of F. K. Lane (Wilson's Secretary of the Interior) pilfered for *Pale Fire*. Also, we should be mindful of Mikhail Nikolaevich Longinov, author of *True Anecdotes from the Life of Prince Repnin* (St. Petersburg, 1865), mentioned by Nabokov in class on April 2, 1957, and alluded to elsewhere.

6. With Proust he shares a fondness for cattleyas and faded, rather than sempiternal, roses.

From Gogol's *Nevskij Prospekt* he borrows the trick that twins Kraevich (*The Gift*), Conrad (*Laughter in the Dark*), and Andersen (*Pnin*). In *Pnin* there is the digression following a telephone ring:

> Technically speaking, the narrator's art of integrating telephone conversations still lags far behind that of rendering dialogues conducted from room to room, or from window to window across some narrow blue alley in an ancient town with water so precious, and the misery of donkeys, and rugs for sale, and minarets, and foreigners and melons, and the vibrant morning echoes.

A problem is posed—the verisimilar rendition of a Belled chat—and before we realize it we are taken from the telephone to a "blue alley in an ancient town," then at last to those succulent, plump, irrelevant melons. This recalls Gogol's *vprochem* device. Similarly, those quick fictions that live and die between commas, the Aeolian harps in *Lolita*, the Egyptologist Samuel Schonberg in *Pnin*—are akin to Gogol's bootophilic soldier and his other everlasting ephemera. Nabokov's lyrical digressions (e.g., the moment of punning tenderness when Fyodor onymically apostrophizes Zina in *Dar*) may also be linked to Pushkin and to Sterne, that aposiopetic tease and master of the dash—whose sentimentally jailed bird, by the way, is recaptured by Humbert.

Joyce is to be detected in the obvious spots (the three or four passages in *Lolita* similar to passages in *Ulysses* and *Finnegans Wake*, the "Winnipeg Lake" rivermaid in *Bend Sinister*, the gloss to 1. 615 of *Pale Fire*). From Bloomsday, too, may come "seasand" (*Ada*), "Leopold O'Donnell" (*Pale Fire*),' the helbeh for fenugreek (*Pnin*), and even the "clip and kiss" in *Lolita* and *Ada*. This last formula, while very old, is probably borrowed from the song of Romany chib in *Ulysses*. (Nabokov might also have found it, though, in Chaucer's *Merchant's Tale*, or earlier, at 1. 42 of the Anglo-Saxon poem "The Wanderer," a tale of silence, exile, and kenning.) And when Humbert, lying beside his sleeping nymphet in the "tremors and gropings of that distant night," says

> And so, in between tentative approximations, with a confusion of perception metamorphosing her into eyespots of moonlight or a fluffy flowering bush, I would dream I regained consciousness, dream I lay in wait.
>
> (*Lolita*, p. 121)

his "tentative approximations" indicate another bedroom scene, another logodaedal weave of words:

> The visible signs of antesatisfaction?
> An approximate erection: a solicitous adversion: a gradual elevation: a tentative revelation; a silent contemplation.
>
> (*Ulysses*, p. 734)

But the tracing of parallels can be "a form of insanity,' 'as the *EO* Commentary puts it, so I will slip out of the ruelle and terminate here these notes-to-my-own-queries.

7. The notarikon continues . . . *orbicle, kinbote, ophidian, vagitus* . . . but back to *grimpen,* one of the three words that puzzle Hazel Shade. (The other two are *sempiternal* and *chtonic*—a wayzgoose version of *chthonic*.) Her text is "some phony modern poem," and with "Toilest" as a hint, we recall the pastiche of "Gerontion" and parody of "Ash Wednesday" in *Lolita,* and the rebuke in the *EO* commentary. We seek and find all three in "Four Quartets," *grimpen* in "East Coker," *sempiternal* in "Little Gidding," and *chthonic* in "The Dry Salvages." Unlike the last two, *grimpen* is not a websterword. Allusive Nabokov! Persevering, we discover clues that lead us to Doyle and the Baskerville Hound: Sherlock Holmes at 1. 27, and Eliot's "Lines to Ralph Hodgson Esquire" (which echoes Johnson's epigraphic cat and contains 999—the number of *Pale Fire* lines—canaries). And in that masterpiece about a modern descendant (or so it seems at first) of the barghests and guytrashes that once haunted the heath and moor of the mind, we come upon the Great Grimpen Mire. But Goethe, too, whose Erlking rides ominously into the poem, can be linked to *grimpen.* Hazel Shade's suicide takes us back to another famous literary self-slaughter, Young Werther's. In the second edition of the *Sorrows,* Goethe prefixed an admonitory verse motto with the line "Warum quillt aus ihm die grimme Pein?", and thereby he joins Doyle and Eliot in the darkling *grimpen.*

A pleasing gloss on *grimpen* can be found in the work of the great toponomasiologist Eilert Ekwall. Had Nabokov read "Some Notes on English Place-Names containing Names of Heathen Deities" (*Lund Studies in English,* XXXIII), he would have found that in Grimsby or Grim's Dyke or Grimthorpe the "grim" element comes from the Old Norse for Othinn or Odin, *Grimr,* "a person who conceals his name, literally, a masked person, and refers to Othinn's well-known habit of appearing in disguise." And the Russian for make-up is *grim.* Thus the mummery of Kinbote's king, as well as the torment of Hazel Shade, is suggested by *grimpen.*

8. The laws for neoterisms are few. Does the new word answer a felt need, snugly filling a verbal vacuum? Has it been well defined by the word-smith? Is it suspended in a solution of chaste, eminently respectable, even venerable vocables? Because of this last requirement the mortality rate is very high. Hence, in the dictionary of *hapax legomena* I am indolently compiling I rarely admit entries from *Finnegans Wake* or from such inkhorn cacozealots as Gomberville and Urquhart. Urquhart, incidentally, who turned into English the immense tools and stools of the puny rhypographer, also presciently provided us with a remarkable parody of Joyce:

> Thus for a while their eloquence was mute, and all they spoke, was but with the eye and hand; yet so persuasively, by virtue of the intermutual unlimitedness of their visotactile sensation, that each part and portion of the persons of either, by ushering the tacturiency of both, made the attrectation of both consequent to the inspection of either, here was it that passion was active, and action passive, they both being overcome by other, and each the conqueror.

9. *Stingles,* like *sun blick,* is an Antiterran word (for the sensation of tactile chromesthesia) that should be in our sublunar vocabulary. It conjures up Nabokov's fascination with rainbows, iridules, *audition colorée,* his little essays on the retinas of other poets (Lermontov, the *Igor Tale* minstrel), his own attempts to rouse us from our minuthetic stupor. While on the subject of colors, we could mention two color words, *vair* (Fr.) and *izumrud* (Russ.), both outside the traditional polarities of White-Black (white the tint of innocence, black the taint of sin) and White-Red (Pure-Wanton, with its accompanying poetic botany: "So chaste she was that lilies were her roses.")

Vair (fr. Latin *varium,* variegated) describes Lolita's eyes in Humbert's plaint. It is frequently used in medieval French literature. In the *Chanson de Roland,* in the chantefable of *Aucassin et Nicolette,* in the lays of Marie de France, the pucelle's eyes are always *vair.* The meaning has vacillated between blue, grey, and blue-grey (in Ronsard it even comes out a homonymic green) and at times it is no more than a counter for "bright, sparkling, radiant." In the Nabokov-Kahane French edition of *Lolita* her *vair* glims become *gris.*

Frederic Godefroy's *Dictionnaire de l'ancienne langue française* contains the illustrative example "La nature des mauvais est tozjors vaire et movable." "Vaire et movable" is, of course, Virgil's "varium et mutabile semper femina" (perhaps better known in the Gershwin version: "A woman Is a Sometime Thing"). François Ier translated this as "Souvent femme varie/Bien fol est qui s'y fie," which line is then borrowed by Humbert for another part of his song to fickle Lolita.

Vair is also a squirrel fur. It covers a pair of slippers in *Ada* and the shoes of Cendrillon in Pnin's contribution to the corrected fairy tale (to be found in Littré and elsewhere). They "were not made of glass but of Russian squirrel fur—*vair* in French . . . which . . . came not from varius, variegated, but from *veveritsa,* Slavic for a certain beautiful pale, winter-squirrel fur." Pnin's loyal etymology reinforces the sciurine theme of the book.

Finally, *vair* is a party-colored fur of heraldry, properly azure and argent. It recalls the very title *Bend Sinister,* the "gules and purpure" of "Spring in Fialta," the Zemblan *sampel.*

Aquiver with sense, *vair* becomes more than a verbal eyespot.

Izumrud (Russ. for emerald) is one frequently repeated "lapidary epithet."

Gerald Emerald unpleasantly mocks Kinbote's maxillary russet, and the orarian Izumrudov, Gerald's skiagraphic projection in the camera obscura of Kinbote's mind, assigns Gradus his victim. *Izumrudnaja* (adjectival form) is the trial bench on which Cincinnatus "did not dare sit"; *izumrudnïe* the gloves of the eerie poet-narrator, a "magician with a bird's head," of *Slava;* emerald are the slippers—no, I mean earrings—that dying Martha demands of Dreyer. In a more recent poem a similitudinous *izumrud* contains poison (aqua tofana?): "I kak ot yada v polom izumrude,/Mrut ot iskusstva moego." And the cigarette case Lucette carries on her deathday is studded with emeralds.

Emerald, emerald green, and green do not in general wear an associational halo of exotic, threatening, funest, though there is that famous example of a grim green in another, earlier invitation to a beheading, *Sir Gawain and the Green Knight.* An English-speaking, Russian-knowing reader might notice the mru-mru stammer (*izumrud, mrut*) in the quoted lines above, might supply by subaudition both the similar consonantal collocation (s-m-r-t) in *smert'* (death) and *smaragd* (the other Russian word for emerald) and the initial echo of *izumrud with izumit'* (to astonish, amaze), and thereby draw some easy conclusions. *Izumrud,* however—according to my Russian informants—does not send such a message from Russian tympanum to Russian brain. Not that writers do not associate particular letters or sounds with particular colors, or themes, or even precious metals. A gold star essay could be written, for example, on zetacism in Fet. But it is clear that the American sesquilinguist must be wary of that mysterious entity, the Russian Word.

10. In a sillier vein, we might submit *ambiamb* for the false spondee of iambic poetry (if we agree with Nabokov that in metrical verse there are no true spondees). The reduplicative nym nicely mimics the dizzyrambic daze of prosodists on this very point.

11. Three-or-four cola synaesthetic periods: "I am thinking of aurochs and angels, the secret of durable pigments, prophetic sonnets, the refuge of art" (*Lolita*); "This is the flower whose odor evokes with timeless intensity the dusk, and the garden bench, and a house of painted wood in a distant northern land" (*Pale Fire*); "And someday we shall recall all this: the lindens, and the shadow on the wall, and a poodle's unclipped claws tapping over the flagstones of the night" (*The Gift*). An abridged version: "this graceful, fragile, tender young woman with those eyes, that smile, those gardens and snows in the background . . ." (*Pnin*); "this sky, these boughs, this gliding facade" (*The Gift*); "dark pictures, thrones, the stones that pilgrims kiss/Poems that take a thousand years to die" ("A Discovery"). The colometrist will notice the rhopalic expansion in the cola. All X and Y: "all bed and bidet" (*Lolita*), "Nijinsky (all thighs and fig leaves)" (*Lolita*), "all Adam's apple and heart" (*Lolita*), "Hunter Road, all dump and ditch" (*Lolita*), "all honey and hum (*Pnin*), "all wrinkles and bawling mouth" (*Speak, Memory*), "all icefall and rubble" ("Lance"). All X and Y and Z: "all rocks and lavender and tufted grass" ("A Discovery").

12. Quoted in Sister Miriam Joseph, *Shakespeare's Use of the Arts of Language* (New York, 1966), p. 295.

13. Since Russian word order is so much freer than that of English, and since it is difficult for me to identify fixed expressions in Russian, I have avoided examples from that language. Still, there are such self-evident instances as the glittering serpentine intrusion of "Sovetskaya susal'nejšhaja Rus" ("Soviet tinsellated Russ," "Soviet pinchbecked Rus") in *Stixotvoreniya*, p. 35. In translating a Russian phrase there may be tmetic expansion of the original. "Pis'mo napisano v beznadežnom padeže" becomes "The letter was written in the most hopeless and heartrending of all possible cases."

14. Sometimes more than a single book may be necessary as proper back-

drop for the perception of *phrasal tmesis.* Only the compleat reader of Nabokov will be struck by the multiple *tmesis* that swarms out of this unlikely bike: "A very busy though oligotropic bee (an epenthetic but not a distant northern bee)." The example, which implicates Sumarokov, Bulgarin, Delvig, and Pushkin as well as English authors, could have been held in skeptic abeyance, but as a remarkable roommate of mine once observed, "Les mots sont les abeilles pour l'esprit."

15. *Rhyme* in different tongues has been studied. A schoolboy knows that the *Onegin* stanza, with its epicene rhyme scheme, is difficult to reproduce in English, and he knows why. But there have been few comparative studies of the exploitation of tropes and figures (schemes of grammar, schemes of construction). Any such study would require a redefinition of the old terms to include the variety found most often in weakly inflected English. *Polyptoton* (*paregmenon*) or rootplay is rich and frequent in Russian, and when not pronominal (as in Pushkin's "Ja vas ljubil . . .") usually involves suffixes: "Zvezda s zvezdoju govorit' "; "Žena molčala i muž molčal." In English *polyptoton* is very poor. Shakespeare is fond of it, but the most he comes up with is three forms of a root word as in Sonnet 40 where "love" appears (a total of 10 times) in the singular, plural, and possessive. The play on three roots in the following example constitutes a veritable orgy of *polyptoton* in English: "The Greeks are strong, and skillful to their strength,/Fierce to their skill, and to their fierceness valiant." The type which I think deserves nomenclatorial status is "ablaut" or "apophonic" *polyptoton,* as in *A Shropshire Lad:* "I tell a tale that I heard told."

16. I am thinking of mammoths and madonnas, the secret of durable figments, the refuge of heart.

Playback
LUCIE LÉON NOEL

As I start out on my Proustian errand in an effort to recapture the past and recall the brief London period when we were a young and comparatively gay group, I am aware that with the écart of almost fifty years everyday events may well have taken on a nostalgic patina. Once the moment has flown, an insignificant trifle will become a precious possession, something to treasure forever. But despite the passage of time, the memories of the short years following our individual "escapes" from Bolshevik Russia remain fresh and sharp.

Let us turn back to 1919. We were all very young at the time, and carefree (regardless). Naturally we took ourselves seriously. We felt we knew most of the answers. In fact we knew very little and certainly nothing of what life had laid in store for each one of us. Maybe this was just as well. People at the time were just emerging from the horrors of World War I. It had ended on November 11, 1918. And we, Russian émigrés, were just "coming to" from the nightmare of the Revolution. The first years of terror, of famine, and persecution had taken a heavy toll from most families. Though from every walk of life, the large group of Russian émigrés were all bound by one common denominator: we had fled our country. Our existence had been shattered, there was nothing to explain. Everyone was in the same boat. Grateful to be alive, our families often had to start from scratch and make the best of circumstances. Most of the older people were living in the past. Directed by self-sacrificing parents, prudent relatives or kind friends, the younger generation was guided in the right direction, towards education—to schools, colleges, universities, whenever possible.

Some families had suffered more than others, some had a little money in Europe, but the majority had nothing. Financially speaking, the Nabokoffs' case seemed particularly distressing. They had escaped in 1919. Volodia (as he was familiarly known, a diminutive for Vladimir) was the eldest of five children. His parents were living. His father was a remarkably attractive man, highly regarded for his liberal ideas. But the fabulous fortune and "grand train" described in *Conclusive Evidence* (and the revised edition, *Speak, Memory*) had become a nostalgic memory. The *famille* Nabokoff (they spelled their name with a double *f* at the time, as did Mr. Nabokoff senior's brother, Constantine, who was our last Ambassador)—the Nabokoff family, helped no doubt by kind friends, lived in a small house in Elm Park Gardens.

However, quite soon both Volodia and his brother Serge found themselves at Cambridge University, Volodia at Trinity, and Serge at Christ's College. At the time a large group of young Russians, men and women, were to be found both at Oxford and Cambridge. I can still recall the names and faces of each of them, a veritable cross-section of the aristocracy, the intelligentsia, and the bourgeoisie. Today many of them have made good, having become professors, readers, lecturers, scientists, economists, and archaeologists, but none has reached the heights of fame and fortune as has Vladimir Nabokov.

It was Ambassador Constantine Nabokoff, Volodia's uncle, who drew my cousin Clarence's attention to his two nephews, both at Cambridge. My cousin served under Nabokoff at the Embassy during his convalescence period following a bad leg wound obtained in the war. The signing of the armistice solved my cousin's desire to rejoin his battery in France. Instead he went back to Cambridge, to Trinity, where his studies had been interrupted by the war. Before he left, Constantine Nabokoff told him about his nephews (Volodia was at Trinity) and they soon became good friends.

In a letter received this week, in answer to my query, my cousin recalls "having looked out for them, as our old friend Constantine Nabokoff had told me they were at Cambridge. Having met V. N., the following also became my friends: his brother Serge, Nikita Romanoff and Kalashnikoff. I did not meet the others to whom you refer.

"The Nabokoffs, Nikita and I frequently were in my rooms and I remember we often went on the Backs (the river in Cambridge) in a punt. I remember, I think it was K. taking a tennis ball and serving it into the river. We all roared with laughter when it bounced back onto the bank. . . . What we all used to talk about I cannot recall. Almost fifty years is a long time. What we did, what games we played, what sports they joined in, I do not recollect. I believe tennis was one of their games.

"We were all very happy together. Alas, this is all I can recall. I wish I could see them again."

Besides Volodia and cousin Clarence at Trinity, Serge (his brother) was at Christ's and my own brother, Alec, at John's. I had long pondered on the mysteries of the British academic calendar. At half-term or other frequent puzzling intermissions, they would all troop down to London "for a few days in town," delighted to be "down" for a week or so. Boat-race night led to an invariable scuffle in Piccadilly circus. But for me this also meant happy reunions, teas and tennis, literary discussions and intellectual pursuits.

No two brothers could have been less alike than Volodia and his brother Serge. At that time, however, they went around together. While Volodia was the young *homme du monde*—handsome, romantic in looks, something of a snob and a gay charmer —Serge was the dandy, an aesthete and balletomane. Volodia's conversation was gay and amusing and even when he was serious, there was a kind of lilt of laughter, a soupçon of malice at the back of his voice, as if he were relishing some private joke all his own. Serge was tall and very thin. He was very blond and his tow-colored hair usually fell in a lock over his left eye. He suffered from a serious speech impediment, a terrible stutter. Help would only confuse him, so one had to wait until he could say what was on his mind, and it was usually worth hearing. He was, amongst other things, a connoisseur of poetry, theater, and particularly ballet, and an asset in any salon or gathering. Usually he attended all the Diaghileff premieres wearing a flowing black theater cape and carrying a pommeled cane.

Volodia at the time was slender and had a natural elegance of his own. When in London he wore a navy blue suit and a canary yellow Shetland sweater which became him remarkably well. (Today whenever I see a yellow sweater I always remember Volodia.) He played quite a good game of tennis, preferably up at the net, where he liked to "lob" the ball, placing it maliciously, just out of reach. We all had lots of fun and the tennis parties were sometimes held at Queen's Club. I preferred a hard court; the others had become used to playing on beautifully rolled English grass courts.

One day, about April 1920, I received a note from a charming lady who enjoyed entertaining young people and who had a house on Onslow Square with a tennis court in the square. It was an invitation to lunch which I accepted at once. She wrote: "Paul will be there and both Nabokoffs. We can have some tennis." (The author of this note was to become my sister-in-law, for fifteen months later I married her brother, Paul Léon.)

Volodia was particularly gay and happy to be "down" for a few days. At that time in London, no one of our small group could have suspected Volodia would one day become the *monstre sacré* he is today, or that he was endowed with this many-faceted genius.

At that time, I was deep in Proust. Joyce had not yet been heard of. I had not yet read Kafka. I read nothing of Nabokov's until about the late twenties. His writing, so different from the young man we had known at first, seemed almost frightening. It was hard to believe that this youth, who seemed so in love with life, could, with dexterity of a vivisectionist, delve so deeply into the darkest recesses of the human mind and soul.

In 1921, Paul Léon and I married and came to live in Paris, settling two years later in the apartment I still live in. Our London group of friends, the students and others, had all dispersed. The Nabokoff family had moved eventually to Germany, where life at the time was the least expensive in Europe. London had become the dearest city of all. Paris was possible for meager Russian budgets, but mainly because it was possible to eke out a livelihood, and at the time things were less formal than in London. For some years, only occasionally scraps of news reached us about the Nabokoffs, through mutual friends and relatives of theirs. And then one day, new tragedy struck their family: Volodia's father, Vladimir Dmitrievitch, one of the most highly regarded liberal politicians, had been struck down by an assassin's bullet intended for an ex-Russian premier, Professor Paul Milioukoff, who was delivering a lecture. Nabokoff Sr. saw the man aim and jumped in front of Milioukoff and stopped the bullet. He died immediately. Russian émigré circles were dumbfounded and shattered.

Perhaps it was the years Nabokov spent in Germany that gave him a dark approach to people and life. The time and distance that had separated us had obviously created a gap in our relationship. We heard he had married an intelligent Russian girl. It was some years before we saw him again in Paris. And then in 1938, Volodia, Véra (his wife) and their young son,

Dimitri, came to Paris. His brother Serge had been living here for some years, and was eking out a livelihood by giving Russian and English lessons.

Volodia and his family had found a flat in the rue Boileau in Auteuil, a residential section of Paris. Almost every Russian loves living in France, however hard his material circumstances might be. Everyone lives as he pleases, managing the best he can, and you don't have to "keep up with the Joneses." But Volodia simply could not acclimate himself to the French way of life. To us the family appeared profoundly miserable for the entire period of their Paris sojourn. It was with the greatest joy that they received all necessary permits and papers enabling them to leave for the United States, thus escaping the war and the ensuing debacle, the Fall of France. In America they found a new home and once again Nabokov enjoyed working.

Knowing they were in Paris was extremely pleasant for us. Sixteen years had gone by since the London days. My husband was currently working on several important subjects. Deeply involved with James Joyce (his work, his legal affairs and personal matters) he had other manifold interests. Rousseau and Constant were his *violons d'Ingres*. Sociology was his specialty, and he had been elected secretary to the Archives of Juridical Philosophy and Social Jurisprudence. That did not leave much time for very much else. We must, on looking back, take into account that both Joyce and my husband agreed there was a great "sweetness of life" in meeting one's friends on a café terrace (café life was formerly an essential part of the Parisian's day) and discussing, over a glass of wine or apéritif, the latest book, a new play, the latest art exhibit, or simply exchanging ideas. At that time current events could be ignored by no one. Time was running out and the storm clouds of war were gathering fast.

One day in 1938 Volodia asked me whether I would like to go over his first manuscript in English, a novel he had written in the small bathroom of their apartment. It was entitled *The*

Real Life of Sebastian Knight. I was of course delighted at his suggestion. I had just finished a similar job for our dear friend Alexander Troubnikoff, ex-curator of the St. Petersburg Ermitage, who had written in English an essay on the famous Van Dyke collection in England.

So Volodia started coming over several afternoons a week, around 3 p.m. He was always on time. He was most anxious that this first novel in English should sound neither "foreign" nor read as though it had been translated into English. We both sat at the large mahogany desk and worked for several hours each time. I would read out a sentence and see how it sounded. Most of it read amazingly smoothly. Occasionally a word had to be changed, or a more suitable synonym sought. Sometimes one word was better than two. We would argue the point, and I might delete my suggestion, or he would capitulate. He would then read it out again, in his deep baritone, and I would listen. We had a little trouble with certain passages, but the author knew exactly the manner in which he wished to convey his thought. With most passages we had no trouble at all.

I was so entranced by the sheer magic of the story that I could hardly wait to see how it would all end. Every evening I would tell my husband about it. I was fascinated by its intricacies, the manner in which the novel unfolded, and by the subconscious element, with the true "inside story"—with its tragic yet whimsical overtones and the continuous puzzling *dedoublement* of the protagonists (recalling Andrey Bielyi's *Petersburg*). Yet I had a lurking suspicion that this prestidigitator, this conjuror with words and language, might after all be making fun of his reader. Then came the haunting, inevitable Nabokov "twist" ending.

The enchanted spell of our working hours was broken all too soon. But one day, towards the end of our collaboration, there was an epic occasion that almost ended in catastrophe. My husband and I found that it was our turn to reciprocate the many dinners we had enjoyed at the James Joyces' and also at the

215

Eugene Jolas's. Both couples were close friends, and friends of ours, too. Eugene and Maria Jolas were publishers of the avant garde magazine *transition*. They were first to publish Joyce, and sections of *Work in Progress* appeared from time to time in their magazine. Later *Work in Progress* became *Finnegans Wake*.

My husband loved nothing better than entertaining at home. Despite our limited means, the spirit of Russian hospitality was ever present. This time my husband suggested a roast goose, flanked by baked apples, "for a change. By the way," he added, "Volodia Nabokov says he would like to meet Joyce."

The "goose with apples" is a familiar Russian-style dish, generally served around Christmas. The only obstacle was that I knew our small French oven could never hold a large bird. The answer was our baker, or rather Madame la Boulangère, who would pop it into the oven and have it ready for the appointed hour. Our business was to remember to pick it up at the right time, otherwise it would be burnt to a cinder.

On the appointed morning I went to the large food store in our quarter, Couté's. My husband had admonished me "to be sure and pick something nice and plump, with a blue vein in its neck." He had been told that was a mark of quality. I found my bird. It cost 93 frcs., quite a high price at the time. The vendor promised to have it dressed, trussed and ready for roasting. It was to be delivered around three o'clock.

I had to hurry home because we were expecting a charming American friend to lunch, Mary Reynolds. She lived in Paris and her lovely house and garden were a meeting place for writers and artists. An early Calder mobile hung in her dining room window and swayed with the summer breeze. Marcel Duchamp was one of her closest friends. Mary's favorite hobby was tooled leather book-bindings. She presented me with one as a "memory book" to which most of our friends in the arts have contributed. This includes Volodia Nabokov. He composed a kind of palindrome in Russian: "the only sentence, Lucia," he wrote, "that in the Russian language can be read from right to left." Here it is on page 218, in Volodia's handwriting and reproduced from my album, followed by my own phonetic transliteration of the Cyrillic characters.*

Mary went home after lunch, and soon Nabokov arrived for work. Somewhat later, around 3:30, there was a ring at the doorbell, and the maid entered carrying a huge box of chocolates. No card was attached. Who in the world would have sent that, we asked each other. Maybe Mary, on her way home? Before the box reached the room in which we were working, my husband and son, Alexis (in France, school is out Thursdays, so it may have been the reason for his working at home that afternoon) had sampled most of the chocolates, squeezing them to see what kind of filling had been used. They pronounced them "very mediocre," as they brought them in for us to sample. A little later the maid appeared, somewhat disturbed: the goose had not yet arrived. I stopped work to phone and check. Couté's assured me the goose was on its way. At 4:30, still no goose. Another phone call and the staggering news that a box of candy had been delivered instead of the goose, for some quite inexplicable reason. Our work on *Sebastian* was over for the day. I had to rush over to Couté and retrieve La Mère l'Oie, found peacefully tucked under the counter. The baker's wife lived up to the occasion, but dinner was a little late that night.

Strangely enough, a couple of years earlier, Mrs. Maria Jolas had had a similar experience with her Thanksgiving turkey when "the turkey lost its liver in the Place St. Augustin." I am quoting

---

* The inscription above the title reads: "The only poem in Russian literature that can be read from right to left!" Translated literally, the meaning of the poem is:

"The Cossack"

I was eating moose meat, swooning . . .
Aeolus was plucking aloes, laurels . . .
The latter [said] to him: "Oho! He knows
How to pluck!" He [said] to them: "I am the minotaur!"

V. Sirin
II–'39

The title and all four lines (a quatrain of trochaic tetrameter, with the rhyme scheme aBaB) are perfect palindromes: the same words are formed whether they are read forward or backward. But the claim that this is the *only* palindromic poem in Russian is an exaggeration. Palindromes were very big with 17th-century poets of the Simeon of Polotsk school; there are examples by Derzhavin, and in 1920, Velimir Khlebnikov wrote a 408-line historical narrative poem, *Razin,* with every line a palindrome.

Единственное въ русской литературѣ стихотвореніе,
которое можно прочесть справа налѣво!

Казакъ

Я ѣлъ мясо лося, млѣя...
Рвалъ долъ алоэ, лавръ...
Тѣ ему: ого! "умѣстъ
рвалъ!" Онъ имъ: "я — минотавръ!"

В. Сиринъ

II·39

**Edinstvennoie v rousskoi literatoure stihotvorénie kotóroe mójno prochést
sprava nalievo!**

KAZAK

**Ia iel miáso lóssia mléia
Rval eòl alòe lavr
tiè emoú: Ogò, ouméet
rvat! On im: Ia minotàvr**

V. Sirin
11 '39

from a *Comeallyou,* published as *Pastimes,* by James Joyce, who immortalized the occasion with a hilarious ballad in the Irish spirit.

But it was on the Night of the Goose that Nabokov met Joyce. On being introduced it seemed to me that Nabokov was or seemed distant and appeared bored. It may have been timidity. After all, here was a young writer still on the threshold of fame and acclaim, confronted with a world-renowned author. My husband and I both felt bad that our friend Nabokov seemed so stiff and formal, so unlike the man we knew and loved and admired. From a recent interview, I see Nabokov admits having chatted with Joyce the entire evening but was unable to recall anything that was said.* Unfortunately neither can I, for two very good reasons. Firstly, I was completely engrossed in taking care of my guests, serving coffee and drinks later. And secondly, with the Jolas's and my husband present, I did not have to worry about keeping the conversational ball rolling, they would take care of that. I can still see them all sitting at our table (the mahogany table at which Joyce and my husband worked on *Finnegans Wake* for twelve years). We had put in the extra board so eight people would be comfortable. Today I wish I had been more attentive.

A little while before the Goose Dinner, Nabokov had brought two of his earlier novels to us and had inscribed something in each one. I often smile as I read on the flyleaf of one, in Russian: "Read it, please, both of you, and no skipping."

Now, before drawing the curtain on bygone days, I want to say: "Many Happy Returns on your seventieth birthday, my dear Volodia."

---

* Alfred Appel, Jr., "An Interview with Vladimir Nabokov," *Nabokov: The Man and His Work,* L. S. Dembo, ed. (Madison, 1967), pp. 39-40.

[2. Reminiscences]

Nabokov in the thirties
NINA BERBEROVA

Before me lies my calendar of the year 1932:

October 22.	Nabokov, in *Lat. News,* with him in a cafe.
October 23.	Nabokov. At Khodasevich's, then at Aldanov's.
October 25.	Nabokov. At Struve's lecture, then in the Cafe Danton.
October 30.	Nabokov. At Khodasevich's.
November 1.	Nabokov.
November 15.	Evening of reading by Nabokov.
November 22.	Lunch with Nabokov at L'Ours [1] (called for me).
November 24.	At the Fondaminskys'. Nabokov read new things.

This essay appeared in somewhat different form in *The Italics Are Mine,* copyright 1969, by Nina Berberova, published by Harcourt, Brace & World, Inc.

I see him entering the editorial offices of the Russian émigré paper in Paris where I then worked writing short stories, reviewing books (mostly Soviet), collaborating on the "movie-page" on Fridays, sometimes rushing to replace a reporter at the courts, or interviewing someone, or printing a poem, and of course— typing. He was then thin and erect, with long narrow hands, a neat tie, a flying gait, and that "Petersburgian moist 'r' " which was familiar to me from childhood: on my grandmother's side every other person has it. Merezhkovsky has it. And the old count Kokovstev still "gargles his throat" when he says "the late Emperor of Russia."

In front of the entrance to the metro Arts et Métiers in the building of the *Latest News,* we sat and talked on the terrace; this was one of the last days of terrace-sitting: brown foliage of the plane trees, rain, wind, evening lights in the early dusk of a lively Paris square; music blaring, people rushing. Not so much talking about: Who are you? More about: What do you like? Whom do you love? (What do you *feed* on?)

In the *Latest News* he was in these years a newcomer. There was in Paris a stratum of Russian émigré intelligentsia who entertained him enthusiastically: these were people who knew him from childhood, friends of Vladimir Dmitrievich, his father; Russian liberals, among them Miliukov, Vinaver's widow, former members of the Petersburg Masonic lodge, diplomats of Tsarist Russia, colleagues of Konstantin Dmitrievich, Nabokov's uncle, Russian ambassador in London before the Soviet government sent to England its representative. For them he was still "Volodia"; they remembered that he *always wrote verse,* a prodigy, so it was no wonder that he was now publishing his work, although it was not always understandable to everyone (a strange common Russian criterion).

Thus on the premises of the *Latest News* everybody came to look at him and Miliukov (at whom in 1922 two hoodlums had aimed their pistols and whom Vladimir Nabokov Senior shielded with his body so the bullet killed him and not the man for whom it was intended. Miliukov invited him into his office for a while, and later in a grand manner introduced him to us.

The two visits to Khodasevich's place (which six months ago had been my place as well, but was no longer), in clouds of cigarette smoke, tea drinking, cat petting, proved a projection of Godunov-Cherdyntsev's dialogue with Koncheev, that dialogue that later found its way into *The Gift*. I was (and still am) the only person who witnessed this strange phenomenon: the reality of an event (October 23 and 30, 1932, rue des Quatre Cheminées, Billancourt, Seine, France, from 4 to 6 p.m.) which was to become a fantasy—never wholly realized in the pages of the novel, only imagined, and consumed in its dreamy depth—a result of Godunov-Cherdyntsev's solitary insomnia.

I had already heard of Nabokov in Berlin in 1922. Yuly Aikhenvald, literary critic of the Russian newspaper *Rudder,* spoke to Khodasevich of him as of a talented young poet. But his verse of that time did not interest Khodasevich: it was a pale and at the same time self-assured scanning of verse, as was written in Russia by cultured amateurs, sounding nice and imitative, recalling no one in particular and at the same time everyone. Here is one (1921) with echoes of Blok:

> The black horse beneath its blue net,
> The splash of the snowstorm, the call of the snowstorm,
> Eyes burning through the hoarfrost
> And the moisture of her cloudy furs.

Pseudo-popular (1922):

> Before me, behind me, you are everywhere,
> Ah, you stand everywhere, unforgotten,
>
> and your soul is an unharvested cornfield.

And later of course Pushkin (1927):

> Those knives and pots, and various jackets
> From nameless wardrobe here and there;
> Alone in strange positions were
> The crooked bookstalls in the markets,

> Congealed, hiding scores and scores
> Of treatises on alchemic lore.

Five years later his "University Poem" flashed in *Contemporary Annals*. There was not only lightness in it, but virtuosity as well; but there was still no personality. Then his first story "Mashenka" came out; neither Khodasevich nor I read it then. Nabokov sometimes wrote criticism of verse in *Rudder*. In one review, incidentally, he mentioned my *liveliness* and spoke very sympathetically both of me and of Ladinsky as the "hope of Russian literary Paris." (Not long before, Aikhenvald had written in the same periodical a long article about one of my poems.)

Once, in the midst of a conversation in 1929, one of the editors of *Contemporary Annals* announced all of a sudden that in the coming issue of the magazine there would be a "stupendous thing." I remember how all pricked up their ears. Khodasevich was skeptical of this adjective; he did not have too much faith in Mark Vishniak's taste; the elder prose-writers took the news with a certain discomfort. I was already then publishing prose in *Contemporary Annals,* and suddenly felt a burning curiosity and very strong agitation: Indeed! If this were only the truth!

"Who?"

"Nabokov."

Slight disappointment. Disbelief. No, this man will very likely not become "the émigré Olesha." [2]

I was the first to write in the Parisian Russian daily about Olesha (I am proud of this). It was the summer of 1927, when *Envy* was coming out in the Soviet monthly *Krasnaya Nov,* and I was writing for the newspaper a weekly chronicle of Soviet literature. It was thought that Khodasevich wrote it, but in fact I did, signing it "Gulliver" (on Thursdays in *Renaissance*), and thus in great secrecy contributed to both competitive newspapers —which, of course, would have been quite impossible to do openly. I did this for Khodasevich, who said that he was incapable of reading Soviet magazines and following the rise of new talents. This remained a secret for everyone right up to 1962, when a doctoral candidate at Harvard,[3] writing a dissertation on Khodasevich, told me he had learned from Professor Gleb Struve that Khodasevich, under the pseudonym "Gulliver," wrote regular reports on Soviet literature in the newspaper *Renaissance.* I had to admit to him that Gulliver was I, but that Khodasevich, of course, edited my chronicle before printing it as his own, sometimes adding something.

Thus, in the summer of 1927 I read *Envy* and received my strongest literary impression for many years. It was and remained for me a great event in Soviet literature, very likely even greater than Pasternak's *Waves.* Before me was a story by a young, original, talented writer, very much alive in his own time, a man who knew how to write and write in a completely modern way as no one in Russia had before him, with a sense of measure and taste, knowing how to interweave drama and irony, pain and joy, and in whom literary devices combined with the inner devices of his personal inversions in an oblique presentation of reality. He depicted people without embracing the rigid laws of "realism," on his own plane, against the background of his own personal vision of the world, with all the freshness of a unique and original sight. I realized that Olesha was one of the few now in Russia who knew what an undercurrent in a text and its role in a prose work were, who had a mastery of prose rhythm, grotesque fantasy, hyperbole, sound effects, and unexpected turns of the imagination. Olesha's consciousness of his goals, and control over achievement of them, and the exquisite balance of the novel were striking. Something had been built or created, linked not to Gladkov's *Cement,* to Gorky's *Mother* and even to Chernyshevsky's *What Can Be Done?*—but directly linked to Bely's *Petersburg,* to *The Overcoat,* to *Notes from Underground,* the greatest works of our literature.

The summer of 1927, the issues of *Krasnaya Nov,* my lines in the chronicle on Olesha—all this was lodged in my memory. In the *Latest News* a review of *Envy* also appeared within a few months. People asked Khodasevich: "Is it true that it is so remarkable?" By that time he had read the novel and later, in

1931, now under his own name, he wrote about Olesha. Khoda-sevich answered that the novel was undoubtedly extraordinary. We started awaiting further books of Olesha; none came out on this level, and in the *Great Soviet Encyclopaedia* (1954) he is not even mentioned. But now he has returned to life. *If it die, it bears much fruit!*

The issue of *Contemporary Annals,* with the first chapters of *The Defense,* came out in 1929. I sat down to read these chapters, and read them twice. A tremendous, mature, sophisticated modern writer was before me; a great Russian writer, like a phoenix, was born from the fire and ashes of revolution and exile. Our existence from now on acquired a meaning. All my generation were justified. We were saved.

There was a sacred ritual at that time to finish the evening at a cafe table. And therefore after a literary reading before parting we mostly gathered either on Montparnasse, or at the Porte de Saint Cloud, or at the Porte d'Auteuil, where most people lived. Here somewhere around midnight took place the conversation about Tolstoy between Bunin, Khodasevich, Alda-nov, Nabokov, and me which I mentioned in my article on *Lolita* (*Novy Zhurnal,* 57) when Nabokov all of a sudden gave us "a piece of his mind," saying that he never read the *Sebastopol Tales,* and therefore had no opinion about them. Yes, said he, he never read that (apparently boring) "juvenilia." Aldanov had a hard time not to show his indignation. Bunin, who in his moments of rage had the peculiar ability to get green in the face, stammered some unprintable Russian anathema. Khodasevich laughed, finding the joke rather funny, taking in consideration that in Russian schools the *Sebastopol Tales* were required reading. And I learned a lesson: how in the future not to have an opinion on everything, not to read everything, not to be ashamed at not having read everything, not to respect everything.

His public readings were given in the old gloomy Salle Las-Cases in rue Las-Cases. The hall, when filled, could accommo-date about 160 persons. In the back rows the "younger generation," personally not acquainted with V.N. but having read every line of his, coldly followed his reading. The "cream" of the exiled intelligentsia (average age 40-50) accepted him with much more enthusiasm at that time. There were complaints later, especially after *Invitation to a Beheading,* that his work was becoming "incomprehensible." This reaction was of course normal, for these readers were completely alienated from literature of their century (but was it really *their* century?). As for the "younger generation," now that all this is history I might explain it in three ways: yes, there was *envy,* let us face it, chiefly among prose-writers and the group around *Numbers;* there was some *bad taste* still cultivated among "young realists" (*nomina sunt odiosa*); and finally there was their dramatic unpreparedness for the mere idea that something great, distinguished, something original, prodigious on a world scale, might emerge among the Akaky Akakieviches of Europe. . . .

I never told him my thoughts about him. I knew him well in the thirties when he began to visit Paris (from Berlin) and when finally, before the war, he settled there with his wife and son. I gradually got used to his manner (not acquired in the U.S.A., but always there) of not recognizing people, of addressing Ivan Ivanovich, after knowing him many years, as "Ivan Petrovich," of calling Nina Nikolaevna "Nina Aleksandrovna," the book of verse *In the West* "On One's Ass," [4] of washing from the face of the earth someone who had been kind to him, of mocking in print a man kindly disposed to him (as in his review of Aldanov's *The Cave*), of taking something from a great author and then saying he had never read him. I know all that now; here, however, I am discussing not him but his books. I stand at the "dusty crossroads" and look at his "royal procession" [5] with thanks and the awareness that my generation (including of course myself) will live in him, that it did not disappear, did not dissolve itself between the Billancourt cemetery, Shanghai, New York, and Prague. All of us, with our entire weight, be we successful (if there are such) or unsuccessful (a round dozen), rest on him. *If Nabokov is alive, it means that I am as well!* [6]

I hear someone inquiring derisively: Well, well! Why do you think that you are a participant in the whole story? Didn't you say (and with that finality of judgment that sometimes so irritated even the people that liked you)—didn't you say many times that everyone is his own man, that Pushkin, Gogol, Tolstoevsky, and others, not to mention the twentieth century, were their own men, and were not at all connected with that prodigious Russian people? What have you and your generation to do in all this? Was Nabokov preoccupied with the redeeming of his generation if he could not distinguish Ivan Ivanovich from Ivan Petrovich? And did not recognize him not only on the street but even in the Fondaminsky salon? Nabokov is very much alive and will live, indeed, but no one has yet said that in his shadow anyone else will survive—or among them you yourself.

And to that I reply: Yes, every man is his own man, a world, a hell, a universe, and I do not at all think that Nabokov will drag anyone with him into immortality. Some people do not deserve immortality, some people do not deserve it in his shadow, some people (myself included) loved life too much to have any right to survive in the memory of posterity, loved life more than literature and fame, the feeling of being alive more than immortality, and the "half-mad ecstasy of activity" more than the results of this activity, and the path to the goal more than the goal itself. Nevertheless, in the perspective of the past and the future, Nabokov is the answer to all the doubts of the exiled, the persecuted, the insulted and the injured, the "unnoticed" and the "lost"!

Nabokov is the only Russian writer (both within Russia and in emigration) who belongs to the *entire* Western world (or the world in general), not Russia alone. The belonging to one specific nationality for such as he has no meaning and plays no role: native language—for Joyce, Kafka, Beckett, Ionesco, Jorge Luis Borges, and for Nabokov—has ceased to be what it was in

227

the narrow nationalistic sense of eighty or a hundred years ago. Mere language effects related to native parlance and dialectisms that do not rest on other elements of a work are of no paramount interest and value, either for the author himself or for the reader, in modern literature.

In the last thirty years in Western literature—or rather, at its summit—there are no longer French, British, or American novels. Even earlier what was written best often became international, from Strindberg's *Confession* to Wilde's *Salomé* and from Conrad to Santayana. It is not only immediately translated into other languages, it is often printed simultaneously in two (or three) languages, and moreover it is not infrequently written in a language other than the one in which, as it were, it should have been written. In the final analysis it is incontestable that there exists in the world a minimum of *five* languages in which one can in our time express what he wants to the entire Western world. In which one of these this is done is then not so essential.

But Nabokov does not only *write* in a new manner, we learn from him to *read* in a new way as well. He (like some others) creates a new reader. In modern literature (prose, poetry, drama) he has taught us to identify not with heroes as did our ancestors, but with the author himself, in whatever disguise he may hide from us, in whatever mask he may appear.

Let us, however, return to the basic myth of Nabokov the Expatriate, which was gradually transformed by him into a chain of symbols. I want now to follow this chain: it concerns the problem of poetic *creation* and the problem of *Russia* and leads by a different path to the image of "pale fire," to the core that contains Nabokov's theme and where we find the catharsis of a whole life. "But I have no right to speak more in detail" ("The Glory" of Nabokov, 1942), for I am not here writing a study of his work, but am only giving an outline for reflection on his myths, his basic theme, and the development of the chain of symbols.

Here are some citations:

The soul studied oblivion in vain:
In a dream the problem was solved.

....

What was I thinking about for so many years?
(1938)

It is time. Still young, we are leaving
With a list of still undreamed dreams,
With a final, hardly visible Russia gleaming
On the phosphorous rhymes of our last verse.
(1938)

Let me go! I implore you!

....

One who freely abandoned his homeland
is free to howl about it on the summits,
but now I have descended into the valley,
and now do not dare to come near me.
I am ready to hide forever
and live without a name. I am ready
in order not to get together with you even in dreams
to turn down all dreams.
To drain my blood, to mutilate myself,
to not touch my most beloved books,
to exchange for any dialect
all that I have—my tongue.
(1939)

"Your poor books," he said casually,
"Will hopelessly waste away in exile. Alas!
These three-hundred pages of idle belles-lettres
Will scatter . . .
. . . Your poor books
without soil, without path, without ditches, without threshold
Will fall off into a void . . .
(1942)

Verlaine had been also a teacher somewhere
In England. And what about Baudelaire,
Alone in his Belgian hell?
(1942)

From the nomadic, the idly straying ones
I crawl away.
(1943)

The last drop of Russia
has already dried up! Enough! Let's go!
But we are still trying to sign
with that crooked-beaked post-office pen.
(1943)

Insomnia, your stare is dull and ashen,
My love, forgive me this apostasy.
(1945)

When I saw in the fog
....
That which I preserved
For so long . . .
I imagine now the twittering
....
and the railroad station,
....
And further on
All the details . . .
....
I feel like going home,
I am longing to go home.
....
I have had enough . . . May I go home?
(1951?)

Did the grey winters wash away
The unique outlines? Is the echo
All that remains of the voice? Or did we
   Arrive too late?
Only no one greets us! In the house
There is a grand piano, like a tomb on the North Pole. That's
Swallows for you! Can one believe that besides
   Ashes there could also be a thaw?
(1953)

There is a dream. It recurs like the languid
knock of one immured. In this dream
with a pick I work in a huge hole

and find remains in the depths.
And with a lantern I light up in them
the trace of an inscription and the bareness of a worm.
"Read! Read!"—my blood cries to me:
R . . . O . . . S . . . I cannot see the letters.
(1953)

The shadow of a Russian twig will sway
On the marble of my hand.
(Undated, not later than 1961)

Beyond a doubt all is about only one thing, all is connected and fused, and however much Nabokov assured us that a strawberry seed in his tooth prevented him from enjoying life (as his namesake, another Vladimir Vladimirovich, Mayakovsky, assured us that a nail in his shoe was more nightmarish than a Goethe fantasy, and Dostoevsky's hero demanded that the world collapse if "I have no tea to drink"), it dawned on us long before what precisely prevented him from enjoying life, and we needed no other confessions. In his Belgian hell, in his Ravenna, he remembers, and is tormented by, only one thing:

Oh, swear to me to put in dreams your trust
And to believe in fantasy alone!
(*The Gift,* 1937)

I saw him for the last time at the beginning of 1940, when he lived in an ugly bare flat (in Passy), where I went to visit him. He had the grippe but was already getting better. There was hardly any furniture. He lay pale, thin, in bed, and we sat at first in his bedroom. Suddenly he got up and led me to the nursery, to his son who was then about six or seven. On the floor lay toys, and a child of exceptional beauty and refinement crawled among them. Nabokov took a huge boxing glove and gave it to the boy, telling him to show me his art, and Mitya, having put on the glove, began with all his child's strength to beat Nabokov about the face. I saw this was painful to Nabokov but he smiled and endured it. This was training, his and the boy's. With a feeling of relief I left the room when this was over.

Soon he left for the U.S.A. His first years in America were not easy, then he made one step, another, a third. *Lolita* was obviously already begun in Paris (in Russian): Aldanov told me about it in 1939, told how Nabokov read several chapters to a selected group and what these chapters were about. Then *Solus Rex* became *Pale Fire,* and *The Gift* was finally translated. In 1964 his comemntary on *Eugene Onegin* (and his translation) came out, and it turned out that there was nothing to compare them with: there was not and never had been anything like them, there were no standards that would help us to judge the whole thing. Nabokov himself invented the method and carried out the work in accordance with it: Pushkin was exalted and—undermined. *The Igor Tale* was translated, commented upon, and—called into question. He "commented on," "exalted," and "undermined" himself—as is evident from the citations above of his verse of twenty-four years.

The burr of his Petersburg enunciation, the blond hair and bronzed, fine face, the thinness of the agile, dry body (sometimes clad in a tuxedo Rachmaninov had given him, tailored, as Nabokov put it, "in the period of the Prelude"): thus he was in those years, before the war, in our final Paris years. He walked about as if drunk with himself and Paris. Once during a conversation of ours Nikolai Felzen was present, but I fear he was unable to insert even a single word: we did not give him a chance. Another time Nabokov invited me to lunch in a Russian restaurant; we ate blinis and rejoiced in life and each other, or more exactly I rejoiced in him (this I know) and *perhaps* he rejoiced in me (though why invite me to L'Ours if he did not?). At Fondaminsky's, where he stayed when he came to Paris, after a reading of his we once sat for a long time in his room and he told about the way he then wrote his novels (reflecting a long time, slowly accumulating, and then, all of a sudden, rushing to work for entire days, getting rid of everything inside himself, and afterwards again slowly reflecting, checking, polishing). This was the time when *The Gift* was being written.

He had begun to fill out and had started growing bald when I saw him again in New York at his last Russian reading, and he tried to appear nearsighted so as not to have to answer greetings and shake hands. He recognized me and bowed from afar, but I am not convinced that he was bowing precisely to me: the more I think about this bow, the more it seems to me now that it was not addressed to me at all, but to the unknown bearded gentleman sitting behind me, or perhaps to one of the three fat ladies sitting in front. . . .

Notes

1. For details about that Russian restaurant see *Ada,* pages 410-13. L'Ours in *Ada* is mentioned a couple of times as a swanky nightclub with people drinking champagne, eating caviar and enjoying tsigan music. In our time it was a nice middle-class "blini-and-pelmeni-place."

2. Olesha, the author of *Envy,* and Nabokov were, by the way, born in the same year, 1899.

3. The translator of my autobiography.

4. *Na Zapade—Na Zadnitse.*

5. Blok to Vyacheslav Ivanov.

6. L. Tolstoy, "Master and Man": *"Zhiv Nikita, znachit zhiv i ya!"*

Nabokov at Cornell
MORRIS BISHOP

It must have been in 1941 that the word Nabokov first entered my consciousness, with a faulty pronunciation. I was enchanted by certain stories, now classic, in the *Atlantic Monthly,* treating of Russian life in Berlin with a new sharpness of perception and a new beauty of phrasing. Some of the sentences still return to comfort me in the clairvoyance of a midnight waking. At about the same time Philip Moseley, then Professor of Russian History at Cornell, spoke to me of Nabokov as a man we ought to get at Cornell. The name was not unknown hereabouts; Vladimir's cousin Nicholas was the rather startling Professor of Music at nearby Wells College. And Vladimir himself came to Ithaca to address (very successfully) the undergraduate Book and Bowl Club in 1944 or 1945. (I don't know who arranged this; I was absent.)

Shortly after the war I was appointed Chairman of a Committee charged with finding a Professor of Slavic Literature. The Committee "surveyed the field" and "examined credentials." It found a number of worthy candidates, with the proper advanced degrees and lists of scholarly publications. It found also Nabokov, writer of fiction, curator of lepidoptera at Harvard, and part-time lecturer on creative writing at Wellesley. His only critical work was his study of Gogol, which was regarded as brilliant but eccentric. It was all very irregular. He had no record of graduate study, no advanced degrees. Nevertheless the committee invited him to Ithaca, and was charmed by his person and impressed by the range of his knowledge and the acuteness of his judgments. Though certain forebodings were expressed, the committee offered him an Associate Professorship of Slavic Literature; he came to Cornell in 1948 and remained, as Professor, until 1959.

In the role of Professor, he offered an intermediate reading course in Russian Literature and an advanced course on a special subject, usually Pushkin, or the Modernist Movement in Russian Literature. Adoring as he did his beautiful Russian language, he was revolted to hear it befouled by ill-prepared students. He was personally offended by inherited Polish and Ukrainian accents and by native American splutterings. (But *que voulez-vous?* Most of the students had had only a year's Elementary Russian, and one can't blame Elementary Russian for being elementary.) Vladimir would not accept the teacher's usual recourse—if the students aren't up to the work imposed, reduce the work to the students' competence, and don't upset yourself.

As his Russian classes were inevitably small, even invisible, he was assigned a course in English on Masters of European Fiction. He chose as subjects his own darlings—Dickens, Flaubert, Tolstoy, Joyce—and interpreted them with the penetration of a scholar and with the familiarity of a creator participating in others' acts of creation. The course rapidly became celebrated. Good students were enthralled; they gained the sense of admittance to the writer's mind, the privilege of watching him at work in his study. Some, to be sure, were baffled by the lecturer's changes of pace, epigrams, farcical interludes. Some found his *obiter dicta* incomprehensible or disturbing. Those who had been taught to genuflect at the name of Freud were shocked to hear mention of "the Viennese quack."

It is pleasant to have promise of the publication of the lectures.

In all his work Vladimir was nobly seconded by his wife, tall, queenly, already white-haired Vera. She accompanied him to class, read examinations and term papers, and, it is said, substituted for him, at need, as lecturer. She typed his manuscripts and letters, managed the household, drove the car, carried the burdens of everyday life on a small budget in a provincial town. Her unceasing effort was to procure for him time and peace for his writing. But she was no mere secretary-housewife. She was his chief literary counselor; in fact, I suspect the only literary counselor he heeded.

Materially the Nabokovs' situation was merely tolerable. Most faculty members come from bourgeois, even petty-bourgeois, backgrounds. We have the habit of small economies; we cut our own grass, replace our own washers, paint our own floors. The Nabokovs had known two extremes: first opulence, then privation in mean Berlin furnished rooms. They had had little training for life in the complacent middle. The typical professor and his wife have inherited some furniture and have accumulated more. But the Nabokovs, twice fugitives into exile, had no accumulations. Thus they were forced to camp in the homes of faculty members away on sabbaticals and grants. Every year, often every term, they would move. But they never complained; rather they delighted in the frequent change of scene. They took pleasure in constructing the character of their absent hosts from the artifacts of their homes—the objects of art, the books, the mechanical robotry, the minglings of pretension and makeshift. Many results of this exercise in domestic archaeology appear in *Pnin* and *Lolita*.

I was fascinated not only by the range and depth of Vladimir's knowledge but by his exclusions. He had small interest in politics, none in society's economic concerns. He cared nothing for problems of low-cost housing, school consolidation, bond issues for sewage-treatment plants. He got the news not from the *New York Times* but from the *Daily News,* quivering with wickedness, lust, and bloodshed. He subscribed for a time to Father Divine's periodical, revelatory of a lurid, exalted world. His study was rather of human behavior and misbehavior than of the pratings of men in power.

For Nabokov the Cornell years were fruitful. In addition to stories and poems for the *New Yorker* he wrote *Pnin, Lolita, Conclusive Evidence, The Song of Igor's Campaign, Eugene Onegin,* and a number of articles on lepidoptera. He wrote in longhand, often no doubt with joy, more often, certainly, with pain and strain. The wonderful similes, the shimmering adjectives had to be captured at the cost of long ambushes, ending in triumphant swoops of the net. In the midst of composition he would sometimes appear, shaking, in the office, to confess that he had not slept all night; words and phrases had done demonic dances in his mind till morning. There was no use telling him to slow down, to take it easy; the creative spirit demands suffering of its adepts, sometimes even human sacrifice.

I need not speak of Nabokov the writer, the teacher, or the scientist. But appreciation of Nabokov the scholarly critic has been somewhat scamped. The editing, translation, and annotation of his dear Pushkin occupied him in those hours of low tension when the Muse was coy, the weather bad, and the butterflies dormant. He talked eagerly of his mighty edition, while, with a natural *pudeur,* he would seldom mention his fiction and poetry in progress. He conducted endless explorations into the literary and personal background of Pushkin, read the forgotten French critics, such as La Harpe, and minor poets of the eighteenth century, and wrote enormous commentaries on Russian prosody, on Pushkin's Abyssinian grandfather, on the formalities of the Russian duel. The manuscript grew and grew until it stood waist-high, and comprised, at a rough computation, 650,000 words, in Russian, English, and French. When Vladimir at length bore it to the Cornell University Press, the Director, Victor Reynolds, was aghast at the estimated cost of publication. He undertook to produce the book, but stipulated that the Press might also publish the translation of the text separately, without royalty to the author. Vladimir was outraged that he should receive no financial reward for all his work and retrieved the manuscript. One may sympathize with both parties—with the Press's desire to recoup itself somewhat on a gigantic money-loser, with Vladimir's insistence on the author's right to monetary recognition of his work. The book was, of course, eventually published in four handsome volumes by the Bollingen Series, which loves to lose money.

But Ithaca may be best remembered in the Nabokovian record as the birthplace of Lolita. I grant that I was much disturbed by the circumstances. I knew the main theme; I knew that the book was turned down by a number of publishers, far from squeamish, but unwilling to risk prosecutions, condemnations, perhaps even abridgment of their personal liberty. When *Lolita* appeared in 1955, in Paris, under the imprint of a pornographic press, and was soon banned by the startled French authorities, my disquiet sharply increased. I could see in the mind's eye a flood of angry letters from alumni to the President of Cornell: "Is this the kind of scoundrel you have at Cornell teaching my daughter? I shall immediately remove her and cancel my subscription to the Alumni Fund." But fortunately few Cornell alumni keep abreast of literary news from Paris. And by 1958, when *Lolita* was published in America, a number of other daring works had appeared, and the battle for freedom of expression had been fought on other terrains. *Lolita* was presented as an important work of art, not as a titillation for the solitary. The angry alumni had drained their spleen; Cornell's President, Deane Malott, wrote soothing letters to complainants, and filed away their expostulations. The explosion I feared did not occur.

But I still suspect it would have occurred in 1955; the three-years delay in American publication saved Vladimir, and Cornell, and me, from a noisy and perhaps disastrous confrontation.

On the whole, I think the Cornell years were useful for the artist. He gained security, time for abundant production, and knowledge of the American background, which he turned splendidly to account. He immersed himself in the mainstream of American bourgeois culture, and thus learned a whole subject-matter. The Cornell experience was a good thing for Nabokov; his presence was also a very good thing for Cornell.

Nabokov as teacher
ROSS WETZSTEON

"I want you to copy this down exactly as I draw it," Vladimir Nabokov instructed us, after explaining that he was going to diagram the themes of *Bleak House*. He turned to the blackboard, picked up a piece of chalk, and scrawled "the theme of inheritances" in a weird arching loop. "The theme of generations" dipped and rose and dipped in an undulating line. "The theme of social consciousness" wiggled crazily toward the other lines, then veered sharply away.

Nabokov turned from the blackboard and peered over the rims of his glasses, parodying a professorial twinkle. "I want you to be sure to copy this exactly as I draw it."

After consulting a sheet of paper on the lectern, he turned back to the blackboard and scrawled "the theme of economic conditions" in a nearly vertical line. "The theme of poverty," "the theme of political (the chalk snapped under the pressure, he picked up another piece and continued) protest," "the theme of social environment"—all leaping and dipping wildly across the blackboard. Some people simply can't draw a straight line.

Again he peered at us, over his shoulder and over his glasses, in silent reminder to copy this "exactly."

And finally he scrawled the last "theme" in a neat dipping curve, a half-moon on its side, "the theme of art," and we suddenly realized he had drawn a cat's face, the last line its wry smile, and for the rest of the term that cat smiled out of our notebooks in mockery of the didactic approach to literature.

I think of that incident whenever I read a critical analysis of Nabokov's novels—all those "thematic lines" darting wildly over the pages, up and down and crisscrossing, explaining everything, everything (to borrow a Nabokovian inflection), but lacking that final neat line, that Nabokovian smile, that "theme of art."

But the most Nabokovian aspect of the anecdote is that I'm not at all sure it really happened. I "remember" it as clearly as any number of anecdotes from his course ("By the way," he explained in casual audacity, seeming to exaggerate his Russian accent to heighten the effect, "Joyce made only one error in English usage in *Ulysses,* the use of 'supine' instead of 'prone' "), but it may very well be one of those sharp, bright, crystalline "memories," lifted from a dream, imposed by imagination, of something that never happened.

Nabokov's reputation as a novelist, scholar, translator, and lepidopterist is unassailable, but not many people know that he was also a great teacher (on the other hand, those of us who took his courses in the early '50's didn't have the vaguest notion he'd written a single word of fiction). Of course everyone has had a "great teacher"—usually that kindly, white-haired gentleman whose orderly affection for our favorite subject gave intellectual justification to our incoherent raptures—so in jotting down some of my memories of Nabokov as a teacher, I've tried to exclude the merely eccentric and personal, leaving only those reminiscences which might illuminate his novels, or perhaps even provide a footnote for the 21st-century scholar who will write a book on the four great novelists of the 20th century: Joyce, Proust, Nabokov, and Fulmerford.

"Great novels are above all great fairy tales," he would begin —or rather, he begins, memory being present tense—and already, only a sentence in, and a decade and a half late, I realize that foggy memory and sketchy notes are going to make any kind of systematic development or accurate quotation impossible.

"Literature does not tell the truth but makes it up. The first literature was the boy crying wolf . . ." "Wolf! Wolf!" Nabokov would cry out, then pause. "But no wolf. Something between the nonexistent wolf and the boy . . . the dream about the wolf . . . the shadow of the invented wolf . . . Literature!"

"Art is useful only when it is futile," he would read (but he was such a superb actor, one of the basic requirements of a "great teacher," that no one knew he wrote out his lectures, word for word, down to the wryest "asides"). "The artist is a sublime liar. . . . Art is not 'about' something but is the thing itself. . . . Art is not a simple arithmetic but a delicate calculus. . . . In art, the roundabout hits the center. . . . Life is the least realistic of fictions."

And then, in a gambit he was to use as many as three or four times a term, he would refer to "the passion of the scientist and the precision of the artist," pause for a moment as if he hadn't heard himself quite right, then ask in a mock-baffled tone: "Have I made a mistake? Don't I mean 'the passion of the artist and the precision of the scientist'?" Another pause, peering gleefully over the rims of his glasses, as if awaiting our answer—then "No! The passion of the scientist and the precision of the artist!" —a phrase which could well stand as an epigraph (if one were allowed half a dozen) for his own work.

"Great writers invent their own world," but "minor writers merely ornament the commonplace"—and he would also refer to "minor readers," particularly those who (a uniquely Nabokovian mixture of delight and scorn would come into his voice) "identify with the characters."

One should always hear this special tone of voice in the mind's ear when reading his sarcastic remarks about philistines, for he seemed even more amused by than disdainful of bourgeois vulgarity, and remarks that seem devastatingly snide in cold print seemed almost affectionate in his warm lectures. He particularly enjoyed reading bad literature aloud—"I can't stop quoting!" he would chortle in glee as he read from the masterpieces of socialist realism.

"There are two million words in this course," Nabokov would say, explaining that the novels added up to a million words but that we were to read them—"every single one of them"—twice, the first time merely to get such trivial concerns as "plot suspense" out of the way. I recall a comparison to painting—one should approach a novel as one approaches a painting, not going from left to right but taking in the whole, a simultaneous totality of experience. But just to make sure, he made a point of giving away the plots in the first lecture so that the poshlosts among us . . .

Poshlost? He would look up, mimicking surprise that we didn't know the word, then explain that it was a peculiarly Russian word (as untranslatable as "corny," with as many specific instances and as little specific meaning as "camp"), a kind of subtle vulgarity, not crude or coarse, but verging on sensitivity, sensitivity with a slight tinge of mold—Olivier's *Hamlet,* for instance, with its "Freudian staircases," or "the great ideas," or the novels of Thomas Mann. (We quickly learned that he was a master of the parenthetical putdown, the seeming "aside" which is all the more devastating because the parentheses give it an invulnerable position in the sentence. Everyone is familiar with his description of Lawrence as "a pornographer," his disdain for Dostoevsky ("memoirs from a mousehole"), but his wittiest assassination was reserved for Hemingway: "I read a novel of his in 1940. I can't quite remember the title . . . 'Bulls'? 'Bells'? 'Balls'?")

But to return to the way to read novels: What makes a good

reader? he would ask rhetorically, giving us a list of ten to choose from, beginning with "belongs to a book club" or "has seen the movie," and ending with "likes to browse in the dictionary." The proper answers, of course, were imagination and memory and the dictionary. And since this list was itself verging on poshlost (he flirted with philistinism not because he wanted to possess it but simply because he liked to see it having a good time) he would suddenly, vocally raising a forefinger, utter one of those aphorisms which seemed so eccentric at the time (the weird juxtaposition of words caused, no doubt, by the fact that "he probably doesn't know English well") but which linger in the memory precisely because of their odd flair: "Let us worship the spine . . . the upper spine . . . the vertebrate tipped at the head with a divine flame!"

(In retrospect, it seems that Nabokov was telling us how we should someday read his own novels, and telling us in a steady stream of aphorisms at that, but of course those are the two spurs to my memory.)

After the initial lecture on good literature and good readers (the course was taught in Goldwin Smith Hall, by the way, a fact which might be of interest to anyone doing research into the sources of the names in *Pale Fire*), we were told to be sure to bring our copies of the novel to the next class, for the first lecture on each novel consisted largely of a long list of corrections of the inevitably wretched translation.

"Turn to page 15, line eight—cross out 'violet' and write in 'purple.' 'Violet,'" he would blurt out in a kind of disdainful glee. "Imagine, 'violet,'" he would almost quiver in delight at the exquisite vulgarity of the translator's word-choice.

"Page 18, third line from the bottom—change 'umbrella' to 'parasol.'" He would hold up the book like something damp and greenish found under the sink: "This wingless Penguin . . ."

I almost remember the translation corrections better than the novels. In *Madame Bovary,* for instance, "steward" became "butler," "fluttered" became "rippled," "pavement" became "sidewalk"—but was Rudolf Emma's first or second lover? Never mind. The course was about Emma's eyes, Emma's hair ("smooth" to "sleek," "curved" to "dipped," "head" to "skull").

"Caress the details," Nabokov would utter, rolling the r, his voice the rough caress of a cat's tongue, "the divine details!" "General ideas" were anathema to him—because he knew too much about the differences between things to generalize about anything; because, as he wrote in *The Gift, the word "cosmic" is always in danger of losing its* s.

And so, studying for exams (which is what college was in the '50's, certainly not "getting an education"), we would simply memorize the colors, telling each other that last year he had asked: "What color was the bottle containing the arsenic with which Emma poisoned herself?" (brown?).

And speaking of exams, the mock horror with which—no, not mock horror, for though "the horrified professor" was one of his many roles, roles always played with a subtly gleeful irony, this time he was genuinely aghast—the horror with which he returned our papers one day; for nearly half the class, baffled by his accent, had referred to somebody's "epidramatic" rather than "epigrammatic" style, a willingness to parrot what one doesn't understand that is still my private if trivial symbol—along with the fact that his course was called, appallingly, "dirty lit" (*Anna Karenina! Madame Bovary!*)—for the under-25 generation of the Eisenhower years.

Vera Nabokov was as legendary as her husband, breathtakingly beautiful, regal, and dignified (I still think of her hair whenever I hear the phrase "White Russian"), attending all his lectures, always seated in the front row—presumably in order to rush to his side with some sort of pill in the event of a heart attack (recalling, or foreshadowing, in this least autobiographical of authors, the attacks suffered behind a lectern by Timofey Pnin and John Shade). Or at least that was the rumor, and rumor, as someone has written, is "the poetry of truth."

But "the enchanted eyes of nostalgia" (Nabokov on Gogol) are carrying me far from that pledge to write down only those memories which might illuminate his novels. (I wish I could work in that day when a bee flew in the window and the entomologist gently rebuked the fears of his students—"just a humble bumblebee"—but it won't fit.) (And speaking of entomology, it turns out that Gregor Samsa wasn't transformed into a cockroach after all, as most people, especially New Yorkers, assume, but into a beetle, a domed beetle, a winged beetle, in fact; and Nabokov told us something neither Gregor nor Kafka knew—if he'd wanted to escape, all Gregor had to do was fly out the window.)

Nabokov was a great teacher not because he taught the subject well but because he exemplified, and stimulated in his students, a profound and loving attitude toward it. Of course his eccentric personality intrigued us (as a matter of fact, he was considered a kind of Pnin-figure), but his vivid enthusiasms entranced us, and we emerged from his course not so much "educated" as transfigured. Nabokov didn't "teach" novels, he gazed at them with such joyful and tender devotion that they became for us what they already were for him—"shimmering prisms."

Lolita and related memories
JULIAN MOYNAHAN

I.

During the summer of 1955 the temperature rose above 95° Fahrenheit on at least seventy days and toward late August there were three major, hurricane-related floods—in the Connecticut valley, along the lower Housatonic River, and in the Delaware valley. About September 1, I pulled a mud-splashed U-Haul trailer into Princeton, N. J., after making my way from Amherst, Mass., along a series of battered and buckled highways and byways, established my young family in a dank faculty tenement on University Place, and repaired to the Princeton English Department in McCosh Hall with the intention of introducing myself around as one of the new English instructors.

Of course, nobody was there, except an assistant secretary or two, so I turned nervously and began to inspect a long row of mail cubbyholes. I was pleased to see that my name, misspelled in the now-obligatory Daniel Patrick Moyn*i*han fashion, was already in place and that my cubbyhole was jammed tight with a package wrapped in plain brown paper. I carried the package over to the office counter and began unwrapping it with noisy ostentation. As three green paperback volumes bearing the imprint of a famous Parisian publisher of pornography came to light, my social confidence ebbed. Princeton was, after all, the Presbyterian Vatican, and Princeton English Department assistant secretaries were, quite likely, intense gossips. I carried my package outside and completed inspecting its contents while sitting on a stone sundial in the midst of a scorched lawn. I found out later that only Seniors were supposed to sit on the sundial. I never did get on with that job. If I had known enough then to read the omens right I might just have turned around and gone back to Massachusetts; as in fact my wife suggested we do after she looked over our grimy apartment and completed a rough head count of the cockroaches in it.

The three volumes were first editions of *The Ginger Man* and of *Lolita*, volumes I and II. They stayed in my possession for the next thirteen years, until, like a fool, I mailed a lot of my books home from London in loosely wrapped packages to get the cheap postal rate, and some learned thief employed by either the British or American postal service filched just those three. I suppose they are moving onward and upward in the second-hand book market somewhere. Wherever you are, Sebastian and Dolores, pursuing your careers of pleasure and pain, I want to say "Hi!"

A remembering, omens adumbrating fate, and the symmetry— of arrival and departure by international mail in a brown package tied with hempen cord. I have got to be talking about Nabokov, and I am. I took *Lolita* home and read it. (I had already read *The Ginger Man*, then called *Sebastian Dangerfield*, when Donleavy was finishing up the manuscript in Boston around 1952.) I read *Lolita* again, parts of it aloud to my wife. Then she read it, reread it and began reading parts of it aloud to me. We loaned it to a young graduate student in Music named Michael Sahl. After a few days he came back and read parts of it aloud to both of us. We took turns reading it to each other. Then another new English instructor, Bob Whitman, came in and we showed him the book. He browsed through it and read out loud the poem beginning:

> **Wanted, wanted: Dolores Haze.**
> **Hair: brown. Lips: scarlet.**
> **Age: five thousand three hundred days.**
> **Profession: none, or "starlet."**

All four of us thereupon proceeded to faint with sadness and pleasure.

I must say that Maurice Girodias back in 1955 played it very cool in the matter of advance publicity and advertising. There just wasn't any. Until Graham Greene wrote his famous letter to *The Observer* and until Harvey Breit picked up the scent and offered some misleading rumors about *Lolita* in his column of literary chat in the *New York Times Book Review,* all that we owners could do was speculate and enjoy.

My first speculations were spectacularly off-target. I thought V. V. Nabokov's young nephew or cousin—perhaps that bright young man I had been acquainted with at Harvard and who pretended he was going to work in Wall Street after graduation—had written it. Clearly it came from the other side of what is now called the generation gap and clearly it could never be published in America. The distinguished lepidopterist, Cornell professor, Gogol critic, novelist, memoirist and "ruined millionaire" White Russian, Vladimir Nabokov, couldn't have composed it because . . . because he was a New Directions author, see? And who would want to put his neck on the block of public censure in middle age, sacrifice a second career, after so much exile and loss, by bringing out a mad demonic masterpiece with a small French publisher whose legal and censorship problems in his own country were a matter of world-wide notoriety? It was all right for Donleavy, who was just a kid, but something else again for V. V. N., man of historic pedigree, sometime fellow of the Harvard Entomological Museum, friend of Harry T. and Elena Levin.

But then I remembered that the Harvard undergraduate Nabokov's first name almost certainly was not Vladimir and had to admit to myself that no member of this proud clan would ever stoop to theft of another Nabokov's name and reputation. *Lolita* was, after all, from the pen of Vladimir Vladimirovitch Nabokov, of Vyra Estate, St. Petersburg, and all those later domiciles in Germany, England, France and America that lie westward of his Eden. I began to see that the main thoroughfare of the American novel was going to be torn up by *Lolita* just as though it had been hit by flood and fire, that all the rules and recipes for American fiction—merciful heaven!—were going into the furnace to be changed and renewed by a Great Russian. In truth, I only guessed a little of this at the time. Mainly I was content to lurk with my much-thumbed copy of a hot book in two volumes and wait for the huge change in the American literary weather that would soon move in from an easterly direction. Yay! Vee Vee! Yay! Hurricane Lolita!

II.

Two further points, the first about how I started with Nabokov and the second concerning where I stand with his work now.

I studied Russian at Harvard during the latter part of the Second World War. I was a middling student of the language at best. Dr. Leonid I. Strakhovsky was our Pnin and I shall never forget how he would make us construe Acmeist poems printed on mimeographed sheets and would weep when he spoke to us about the death by execution of his beloved master in poetry, Nikolai Gumilyov. Dr. Strakhovsky was a firm pedant with a strongly flavored personal style, an imagination turned toward the pre-revolutionary past, and a rich emotional nature. Something of the same combination, raised to the level of towering genius, characterizes Nabokov. One day while I was preparing for my undergraduate oral in Slavic Lang. & Lit. I came across Nabokov's study of Gogol on the new books shelf of Widener Library. I checked it out and read it at a sitting. It made me laugh out loud five times and I was also delighted by his remark that it would take an Irishman to produce a really satisfactory English translation of *Dead Souls*. I have been reading Nabokov with a strong bias in his favor ever since and am still awaiting the Anglo-Irishing of *Dead Souls*.

And now my last point. The great theme in Nabokov is not that of the past recaptured, and for me he is simply floundering in a moral and metaphysical quagmire when he insists, as he has been wont to do in recent years, pronouncements and works, upon the omnipotence of his or anyone else's creative thought. Nabokov's great theme, which he shares with the Beethoven of *Fidelio* and the Gluck of *Orfeo* and *Alceste*, is that of married love. In *Fidelio,* when Leonora penetrates to the dark dungeon where Florestan languishes in fetters and brings him up to light and freedom, she is acting out, in all the tenderness and courage of uxorious passion, a great moral positive that I find, either fulfilled or blighted, in all of Nabokov's major work. The connection is between loving and making free in a bond of two against the loneliness of exile, the imprisoning world, the irredeemable nature of time, the voidness of eternity. I am thinking of *The Gift,* that great wedding song, of widower Krug's agony of loss in *Bend Sinister,* of the sinister parodies of wedded states in *Kamera Obskura, Lolita,* and *King, Queen, Knave,* of Tatyana's blighted marriage hopes in the Pushkin translation, of the poor prisoner in *Invitation*—that mock-*Fidelio*—cursed with a foolish unfaithful wife, of old John and Sybil Shade in *Pale Fire,* whose life together is such an irritating unfathomable mystery to the mad solitary neighbor spying on them from the shrubbery.

I end on that note, the note of the happy couple. Knavish Franz, the nephew in *King, Queen, Knave,* sees such a pair just before he aids Martha in her abortive murder plot against her husband, Dreyer. They are unknown to him but not to us:

The foreign girl in the blue dress danced with a remarkably handsome man in an old-fashioned dinner jacket. Franz had long since noticed this couple. They had appeared to him in fleeting glimpses, like a recurrent dream image or a subtle leitmotiv—now at the beach, now in a cafe, now on the promenade. Sometimes the man carried a butterfly net. The girl had a delicately painted mouth and tender gray-blue eyes, and her fiancé or husband, slender, elegantly balding, contemptuous of everything on earth but her, was looking at her with pride; and Franz felt envious of that unusual pair, so envious that his oppression, one is sorry to say, grew even more bitter, and the music stopped. They walked past him. They were speaking loudly. They were speaking a totally incomprehensible language.

The language, naturally, is Russian. It is also the language of the highest truth that Nabokov has known and cleaved to during the dedicated work of a lifetime.

Nabokov's Russian readers

ELLENDEA PROFFER

When talking with Moscow and Leningrad intellectuals, one remembers with some amusement the Afterword to Nabokov's Russian translation of *Lolita*. Nabokov indicates that he does not really expect the novel to be read by Soviet readers and even intimates that imagining such readers verges on metaphysical contemplation. In fact it seems that almost every person seriously interested in literature that one meets in the Soviet Union has read at least two works by Nabokov, and *Lolita* is almost always one of them. I am sure that even the most well-informed watchers of the Soviet literary scene would be surprised at the current popularity of Nabokov in the USSR. As in the West there are even members of the Nabokov cult. One way or another (tourists, diplomats, Russian travelers), Russian translations of Nabokov's works [1] get into the Soviet Union, and in cases where they have not yet been translated Russians do it themselves. Manuscripts of *Pale Fire (Blednoe plamya)* and *The Real Life of Sebastian Knight* (only the first half) are already circulating. These are done not by professionals, but by devoted readers.[2]

Lolita is especially popular, and as I was told repeatedly, it is the first of Nabokov's novels to circulate fairly widely. Pragmatic "materialists" can best understand just how popular the book is by considering the fact that among private book traders (who rarely use money), it is worth an equivalent of about twenty dollars. This means, for example, that a collector can trade the Phaedra Press edition for a first edition of Andrei Bely's *Petersburg* or Mandelstam's *Tristia*. And, as a curiosity, it might be noted that a Russian *Lolita* is currently more in demand than a Russian *Doctor Zhivago*.

Less interesting than the private discussions of Nabokov, but more unexpected in a way, are the few official statements concerning Nabokov. Until recent years Nabokov barely existed as far as Soviet criticism was concerned. True, in 1926 a certain V. Volin quoted the poetry of a certain V. Sirin in an attack on émigré poetry.[3] After a thirty-year hiatus Nabokov's name appeared in the *Literaturnaya gazeta* (*Literary Newspaper*) when *Lolita* was misleadingly summarized. Also in the late 1950's Tvardovsky (the current editor of *Novy mir*) mentioned Nabokov's memoirs briefly. This seeming ignorance of a major American writer (something that has happened many times in the Soviet Union until the last few years) attained its peak when in 1964 M. Mendelson's *Sovremenny amerikansky roman* (*The Contemporary American Novel*) failed to contain a single reference to Nabokov. After all this it is no surprise that other standard reference works on American literature, such as Zasursky's thick volume on the twentieth century, fail to mention Nabokov—even though all of his English novels (except *Ada*) were in print before these critics published their books. Apart from a paragraph on *Lolita* by Inna Levidova—a sensitive but orthodox Soviet critic—there has been nothing about Nabokov in the literary periodicals during the last several years. Given this context, it was a shock to read the following in volume five of the *Short Literary Encyclopedia,* published in 1968:

Vladimir Vladimirovich Nabokov (1899–   )—Russian-American writer. Son of V. D. Nabokov, a leader of the Kadet Party. Finished the Tenishev School. Published his first collection of poetry in 1916. From 1919 he has been in emigration, where in 1922 he finished Trinity College (Cambridge). He achieved literary recognition after the publication of the novel *Mashenka* in 1926. N.'s works bear an extremely contradictory character.[4] Among his most interesting works are the lyrical novella *"The Return of Chorb"* (1928), the long story *The Defense* (1929-30), which depicts the life tragedy of a phenomenal chess player, the novels *Laughter in the Dark* (1932-33), *Despair* (1934, separate ed. 1936), the stories "The Little King" (1933) and "Cloud, Lake, Tower" (1937) which reflect the process of spiritual bestialization of the bourgeoisie in Germany as it was becoming Fascist. In the novel *The Gift* (1937, separate ed. 1952) N. presents a tendentiously distorted picture of N. G. Chernyshevsky. N.'s books are characterized by literary snobbism, replete with literary reminiscences. His style is marked by excessively refined "estrangement" of devices and the frequent use of mystification. These same features are also characteristic of his lyrics. In N.'s prose the influence of F. Kafka and M. Proust can be felt; such is the novel *Invitation to a Beheading* (1935-36, separate ed. 1938) in which N. describes the nightmarish existence of a little man surrounded by the monstrous phantasms of the contemporary world.[5] Such are the features which made possible the "denationalization" of the work of N.—who in 1940 began to write in English. Since that time he has lived in the USA where for some time he taught literature in universities. Among his books of this period are the reminiscences *Conclusive Evidence* (1951, Russian translation, *Other Shores,* 1954), the erotic best-seller *Lolita* (1955), the novel *Pnin* (1957). He translates Russian classical poetry into English. In 1964 he published a translation of A. S. Pushkin's *Eugene Onegin* in four volumes with extensive commentaries. (O. Mikhailov, L. Chertkov)

This article is followed by a brief and incomplete bibliography of Nabokov's works (*Bend Sinister,* for example, is not mentioned) and several references to literary criticism (including Khodasevich and Updike). Although it is easy to criticize this article, in the context of orthodox Soviet critical writing it is remarkably complete and objective. For the uninitiated this may seem hard to believe, but it is true; in fact the next volume of the encyclopedia has been delayed because the first ones have been repeatedly attacked for "objectivism."

But there are other encouraging developments, however few. One surprising "official" sign is that a scene from *Invitation to a Beheading* (the relatives' visit to the cell) was read and discussed at a provincial university during an evening devoted to émigré literature. One university seriously considered publishing an article on this novel in its "Scholarly Notes" series.

Of course, there is no objective way to measure Nabokov's popularity among Soviet readers; one is forced to extrapolate on the basis of the readers one meets or hears about. But I think that certain conclusions are fairly safe. First of all, almost everyone seriously concerned with literature (critics, translators, teachers, a few students, most poets and prose writers of stature) has read Nabokov—*Lolita, Invitation to a Beheading* (which has circulated in photo-copies for several years), and quite often *Dar (The Gift)*. Second, Nabokov's admirers are found much more often in the under-40 age group. Readers over 40 usually consider his works *omerzitelny* ("disgusting"); they are put off by the subject of *Lolita* ("I suppose such psychopaths exist, but why write about them," or "I'm sure the author himself must be sick in just that way"). This group has particularly strong feelings about the aesthetic relation of art to reality, and all Soviet age groups tend to feel that literature has a didactic function. The older generation, having lived through countless tragedies, cannot sympathize too easily with a writer who "wastes" his talent by describing mad men and bad girls. This group of readers tends to hold another symptomatically Russian view of art: "A bad man cannot write a good book." After they have read about a few of Nabokov's murderers and freaks, and after they are offended by Nabokov's brusque manner in print ("literary snobbism"), they assume that this is an accurate mirror of his character and conclude that he could not possibly write anything good. Added to all this is the reproach that Nabokov

"At that instant [at age four], I became acutely
aware that the twenty-seven-year-old being,
in soft white and pink, holding my left hand, was
my mother, and that the thirty-three-year-old
being, in hard white and gold, holding my right
hand, was my father. Between them, as they
evenly progressed, I strutted, and trotted, and
strutted again, from sun fleck to sun fleck, along
the middle of a path, which I easily identify today
with an alley of ornamental oaklings in the park
of our country estate, Vyra, in the former
Province of St. Petersburg, Russia. Indeed, from
my present ridge of remote, isolated, almost
uninhabited time, I see my diminutive self as
celebrating, on that August day 1903, the birth of
sentient life" (Vladimir Nabokov, *Speak, Memory*
[New York, 1966], p. 22). Above, "The oak
avenue in our Vyra park, now seventy years old.
Photographed in June 1969," notes Nabokov.

Nabokov's father, Vladimir Dmitrievich Nabokov (1870-1922), aged thirty-five, with his son, aged seven, St. Petersburg, 1906.

Photo of Leon Bakst's pastel portrait of Vladimir Nabokov's mother, Elena Ivanovna Nabokov (1876-1939), in 1910, aged thirty-four.

Vladimir Nabokov's mother, c. 1925, Prague.

Grandmother Marie Nabokov, née Baroness von Korff, c. 1900.

The Rozhestveno Manor (50 miles S. of Leningrad on the
Luga Highway, above the river Oredezh) inherited by Vladimir
Nabokov from his uncle Vasiliy Rukavishnikov (in 1916),
photographed in 1967 by a friend of a friend.

The Nabokovs' St. Petersburg house, of pink granite and featuring
Italianate ornaments, at 47 Morskaya (now Hertzen) Street.
The photo was sent to Nabokov by Professor S. Kosman of the
Institute of Economics, Antwerp, Belgium, in 1964.

Cambridge University,
1922. From left to right,
Robert de Calry,
unidentified bobbie,
Vladimir Nabokov,
unidentified student, and
Peter Mrozovsky. (Photo
courtesy Lucie Léon Noel)

"V.N. aged twenty-one in
Berlin with handbag of
unremembered young lady,"
notes Nabokov.

Два поколѣнія русской литературы.
Чествованіе И. А. Бунина в Берлинѣ.

Русская колонія Берлина отмѣтила пріѣзд лауреата Нобелевской преміи по литературѣ, И. А. Бунина публичным чествованіем.

На эстрадѣ знаменитаго русскаго писателя привѣтствует I. В. Гессен, бывшій руководитель кадетской партіи и редактор газет „Рѣчь" — в Россіи и „Руль" — за рубежом. Аплодируют: справа — поэт Сергѣй Кречетов, слѣва — талантливѣйшій из молодых зарубежных русских писателей, В. В. Сирин.

The above appeared in *Rubezh,* No. 15 (324), April 8, 1934, p. 7,
Easter Edition, published in Harbin, Manchuria. The original heading reads:
"TWO GENERATIONS OF RUSSIAN LITERATURE. I. A. Bunin
honored in Berlin." The caption reads: "Berlin's Russian colony observed
the arrival of the Nobel Prize laureate in literature with a public ceremony
in his honor. On the podium, the famous Russian writer is being greeted
by I. A. Hessen, the former leader of the Constitutional Democratic Party
and editor of the newspaper *Rech*—in Russia and *Rul'*—abroad. Shown
applauding: on the right—the poet Sergei Krechetov; on the left—the most
talented of the young Russian writers abroad, V. V. Sirin" [Nabokov].
(Translated by Simon Karlinsky)

Vladimir Nabokov with his son Dmitri
(b. 1934) on the *plage* at Cannes, 1937.
(Photo by Véra Nabokov)

Nabokov, 1938, aged thirty-nine, Menton,
French Riviera.

is a cold writer, that he does not love his creatures. One young poet went so far as to say that although Nabokov might have inspiration, "even Nabokov's inspiration is cerebral."

Most of these complaints are ones that also come up in Western criticism, so it is not surprising that some Russian readers would react similarly. What is surprising is that younger readers, and some older ones, read Nabokov without even thinking about his political views—in fact few of them are even aware of Nabokov's dislike of the Soviet government. Thus Russian appreciation of Nabokov is, as it should be, free of any political considerations. I was stunned to hear a very "official" literary personage declare proudly that "only a *Russian* could have written *Lolita,*" and that the ability to sharply analyze *poshlost'* (a peculiar kind of vulgarity) is a special gift of Russian writers. The slightly disaffected young people all read Nabokov and discuss him quite openly. The more orthodox also read him, but one such girl (a young teacher at Moscow State University) told me that she kept *Lolita* hidden on the back of the shelf in the bookcase. However, she was over-cautious, because even the reading of manuscripts is so widespread among members of the intelligentsia that it could hardly be construed an act of political disaffection—the people simply like to read good books.[6]

There are a few people in the Soviet Union who have actually managed to read almost all of Nabokov's prose works (even they are amazed to learn that Nabokov has written a substantial amount of poetry)—a feat that requires both luck and ingenuity. Opposed to the informed readers are the incredibly ignorant teachers (usually of English) who have read only one or two of the novels in English and are surprised to learn that Nabokov had ever written in Russian. And there are even a few dim *littérateurs* who read only the Russian novels and do not know that Nabokov has written in English. Curiously enough, the one item that is the most difficult to obtain in the Soviet Union is the Nabokov *Onegin*—all teachers of Russian literature whom I met knew *about* it, but not one of them had ever *seen* a copy.

The most interesting discussions of Nabokov currently focus

on *Lolita,* and the things Russian readers catch sometimes escape American readers. For example, one well-known young poet who had read *Lolita* only in Russian pointed out a parody which few of Nabokov's American commentators have noticed —the poem Humbert reads to Quilty in the next to the last chapter ("Because you took advantage of a sinner") is a play on Eliot's "Ash Wednesday." Those who really like *Lolita* come alive when Nabokov's name is mentioned. One elderly scholar said she was astonished that such a subject could be both beautiful and tragic. A young translator enthusiastically read favorite passages (such as the execution of Quilty) and even quoted sections from memory. A professor of Russian literature (who by chance had finished *Lolita* the day we were introduced) argued furiously with his wife—she attacked the "what" of the novel and he defended the "how."

Even Nabokov's most ardent fans dislike the Russian translation of *Lolita.* It is sad to report, but almost without exception Russians find Nabokov's translation clumsy and even ungrammatical; they express surprise that the author of *Dar* and *Priglashenie na kazn'* could write so poorly.[7] Of course, part of this is due to the fact that contemporary Soviet Russian is quite different from the Russian Nabokov once wrote, and there are many things that he might not know (for example, that ordinary Russian for "popcorn" is simply *popkorn*). But it was melancholy to hear a translator of poetry quote several lines of *Dar* from memory, then hold up the Russian *Lolita* and say, with a sigh, "He has forgotten . . . he has forgotten."

On the other hand, virtually all Russians regard the prose of *Dar* and *Priglashenie na kazn'* as unique in the history of Russian literature. *Dar,* especially, is the favorite in this respect (and there is little humorless grumbling about the treatment of Chernyshevsky). *Speak, Memory (Drugie berega)* is read with great interest, but many people complain about Nabokov's attitude toward other writers (Russian discussions of literature tend to be too solemn), particularly Bunin. Several people complained about *Speak, Memory* from another point of view, saying "it isn't really an autobiography—you can't tell anything about him from it." As Nina Berberova has observed, that is almost the point. But, to be sure, Russians know almost nothing about Nabokov's life. Each time I met one of his admirers I was deluged with questions about what exactly Nabokov has written, what writers he likes, what kind of person he is, where and what he taught. *No one* knew that he has lived in Switzerland for the last several years.

So far *Ada* has had only a handful of Russian readers, most of whom gave enthusiastic reviews. Naturally, the Russians have great fun with the setting, language, and allusions. The parodies are appreciated even in their English garb—whether it be Aksakov's *Family Chronicle* and Lermontov's *Demon* or Grigoriev's guitars and Pasternak's physician. In two cases my copy was handed back to me with eyes heavenward, followed by the Russian thumbs-up gesture reserved for good food and pretty girls, and a drawling, smiling, "Vot eto—da-a-a!"

Nabokov's future in the USSR is easier to hope for than predict. The fact that he is an émigré, the nature of his public statements on the Soviet Union, and the subjects of many of his novels all contribute to the continuing silence about Nabokov. However, during the past decade many writers whose works are considered anything but exemplary, writers who were abused unanimously for many years (Kafka, Camus, Beckett, Faulkner) have been published for the first time in the Soviet Union.[8] Of course, in Nabokov's case publication would mean admitting that a major Russian writer has been ignored for four decades; but if this process of discovery typical of the 1960's continues, it is conceivable that in the 1970's there will be some discussion of his works in the journals. This is a necessary preliminary to the publication of any previously unacknowledged writer. After that one hopes that Soviet editors will realize they should not leave themselves in a foolish and embarrassing position where visiting writers can ask, as John Updike did during his visit at the Union of Soviet Writers on Vorovsky Street a few years ago, "Why don't you publish Nabokov?"

Notes

1. Recent Western reprints of Nabokov's Russian novels are not uncommon in Moscow; Chekhov Publishing House versions are rarer. And of course many Russians read English. None of the main Moscow libraries lists Nabokov in the open card catalogue, but each library has one or more sections called *spetsxran* ("special repository") to which certain specialists are admitted if they are politically reliable.

2. There is, for example, a little old lady in Moscow who has translated dozens of Agatha Christie novels; she does nothing but sit in her apartment and type them out.

3. See *On Literary Guard,* No. 3 (1926), pp. 20-23.

4. In Soviet jargon this sentence means Nabokov's work does not fit into any of the neat oversimplifications used to abuse or praise all writers. Orthodox minds will take it as meaning there are both good things (the depiction of evil Fascist Germany mentioned further) and bad things (literary snobbism, refinement). More sophisticated people realize this is a way of talking about the unmentionable.

5. This Soviet jargon indicates (to translate roughly) that everywhere in the modern world outside the bloc of brotherly socialist countries life is hell.

6. Now even Soviet "middle-brow" readers (journalists, undistinguished members of the writers' union) who are perfectly orthodox read such things as Zamiatin's *We*.

7. One linguist told me he found *Lolita* fascinating because it was written in a kind of dead language.

8. Among the American writers first published in the last decade are Salinger, Updike, Cheever, Styron, Heller, Carson McCullers, Harper Lee, and Shirley Ann Grau.

Three meetings
STANLEY ELKIN

I met him, of all places, in western Kentucky in the, of all seasons, summer of, of all times, 1941. I was curator of a highway zoo and snake show gasoline station complex on U.S. Bypass 97 eleven miles west of Humphries. I don't flatter myself that Vladi stopped because of the wonders collected there. There was a gas war and Dmitri had to use the Men's. (Nor am I showing off when I use the pet name. A gracious and democratic man, Vladi instructed me to call him thus not five minutes after we had met.)

You know how it is with these highway zoos. The specimens are scrawny and seem somehow *sideshow,* freakish reductions, bestial lemons teetering on the brink of some evolutionary misstep. Well there's good reason, but it isn't what you think. You mustn't be too hasty to blame the curator. Nobby understood this. (Never a formal man, he instructed me to call him thus not ten minutes after we had met.) He knew the debilitating effect of the tourists on the fauna. It is the stare they bring, a glazed gaze between boredom and boldness on them like pollen, like the greasy dust of the last state line, like fruitflies and parasites on the oranges and plants between Arizona and California. What can you do? You can't have them wash their faces first. It's a ruinous hypnotism, this wear and tear of the eyes. With their fixed look they can intimidate even the healthiest animal, and over the course of a season actually impoverish it. (I've seen the rich oriental rug of a snake's second skin turn to a moldy scab under this gaze.)

I accompanied Boko through the menagerie—not one to stand on ceremonies, he ordered me call him after this fashion not seventeen minutes after we met—and watched as he grew sad contemplating my failing beasts. Every so often he would shake his head and punctuate his unhappiness with lush Cyrillic *tch tch's* which would have been beautiful had I not guessed at the torment behind them. When we had toured all the corrals and pens he looked significantly toward a woman tourist with New Hampshire plates who was depressing my porcupine.

"There's your trouble," he said.

"I know, but what can I do? It can't be helped."

"Have them wash their faces first," he said gently.

"That's brilliant. It just might work, Boko."

"More rasp on the *k* sound. It takes a strong *h*."

Struck by the incisiveness of his recommendation, I serendipitously offered to show him my butterfly cases. (I did not know who he was at this time, but there is something in a curator's temperament or even in a caretaker's or guard's which makes him always keep something special in reserve which the ordinary public never sees. This is universally true. Remember it the next time you visit the top of the Empire State Building or go out to see the Statue of Liberty. We don't necessarily do it for the tip, mind.) It was a standard collection made somewhat exceptional by the inclusion of two rare specimens—the Bangelor Butterfly and the highly prized Lightly Salted Butterfly.

I could see that Boko was very excited. "Where did you come upon this?" he asked animatedly, and pointing with a shaking finger to the Lightly Salted Butterfly. "I have searched in Pakistan and sought in Tartary. I've been up the slopes of Muz Tagh Ata and down Soputan's cone. I have stood beneath Kile's waterfall and along the shores of Van. I must know. Where?"

"In the meadow."

He revealed who he was and gave me his card and said that if there was ever anything he could ever do for me I should look him up.

And that was the first meeting.

I saw him a second time in Venezuela after the war. We had met in Cair at a boatel, or marina, where we had both gone independently to be outfitted for an expedition up the Orinoco in search of the most fabulous and legendary creature in the entire species—the Great Bull Butterfly. (The highway zoo had failed due to the construction of a new interstate and a settlement of the gas war. With the acceleration of construction on the Federal Highway System many small curators were out of a job in those days. There is no more room for the little man, it seems. Many former highway zookeepers—those who have not been absorbed by larger institutions—have been driven by their love of display and the diminished outlet for their talents to exhibitionism and been arrested.) We decided to join forces. It was Uncle Volodya who suggested it. (Never an uncompassionate man, he had seen that the rasping *kh* sound was giving me the sore throat and permitted me to call him thus.) By now I knew his reputation and his great work in lepidopterology and would have been too shy to put forth the idea myself. I was sitting in the boatel sipping an Orinoco-Cola and reading.

"What are you reading?" Uncle asked. I hadn't noticed him, but recognized him at once. I didn't know if he would remember me, however, and so did not presume to remind him of our first meeting.

"Oh," I said, "it's a birthday card. Today is my birthday.

Have you ever noticed how a birthday card always arrives on your birthday? Never a day early, never a day late. My people are in far-off Kentucky, yet the card was in this morning's mail." It was the longest speech I had yet made to him. He was clearly moved, and I have reason to believe that it was on the strength of this insight that he asked me to accompany him on the Great Bull Butterfly hunt.

We set out next morning and for the next five weeks assiduously traveled downstream, searching along the banks by day and camping by night. We encountered many strange and rare larval and pupal forms, together with some lovely eggal forms I had never before seen, but nothing approaching the mature imago we sought. Perhaps the natives were mistaken in their descriptions, I thought, never daring to voice my suspicions aloud of course. Or perhaps, I thought racistically, they lied. Maybe the Great Bull Butterfly was a Wild Goose Chase. As I say, I never said this, but one night I was sitting glumly in front of the campfire. He noticed that I was not playing my saxophone.

"You're not playing tonight, Shmoolka. Why?"

"It's the reeds, Uncle," I lied. "I've worn out the last reed."

"That's not it. What? Tell."

"Well, if you must know, I think the expedition will fail. I think it's a cruel hoax."

"A hoax, Shmoolko?"

"We've been searching five weeks, and if you can't find a diurnal creature in broad daylight in five weeks—"

"Diurnal be damned," he shouted suddenly, falling unconsciously into his fabled alliteration. "You've given me an idea. What if—what if the Great Bull Butterfly is *nocturnal*? If he were, then of course we wouldn't have found him. Shmuel, I think that's the solution, I think that's it." Before I could even reply, he was on his feet and off into the jungle. He darted heedlessly across the path of a black cat and gave it bad luck. I followed breathlessly. We found it that night.

But, alas, we had been gone longer than we had expected. The bearers had run off. We were low on supplies. The trip back to Cair was upstream against a heavy current made more dangerous by the torrential rains. We had no more food. We had eaten my last saxophone reed the day before. I don't think we could have lasted another twenty-four hours, but we were found at the eleventh hour by natives—Uncle puts it at the eleventh hour; I don't think it could have been past ten-thirty—who fed us and promised to conduct us back to Cair the next morning. They knew a shortcut.

"Why are you so hung up on butterflies, Nuncle?" I asked at campfire that night after marshmallows.

"Shmuel, that's because they're a metaphor is why."

"A meadow flower?"

"A metaphormorphosis."

"I met a fire more for us? A meaty forest?"

"Call me Steve."

"But why *butterflies,* Steve?"

"Lepidopterology—don't you hear that word leper in there? They're the outcasts, you know. They're exiles. Like me. Anyway it wasn't always butterflies; for a time it used to be squirrels and swordfish. Then for a while it was pinto ponies. But I've been east and I've been west, and I think butterflies is best."

"Could you speak about them?"

In the glow of the fire his face seemed serene and very sad.

"Like ur-airplanes they are," he spoke suddenly. "Lopsided glider things riding turbulence like the snowflakes. Heroic, heraldic. Bug pennants, bucking, choppy flags of the forest."

"That's beautiful," I told him.

"Also, if you keep one in your pocket it's good luck."

"Call me Ishmuel."

And that was the second meeting.

Odyssey of a translator
IRWIN WEIL

I first came to know Nabokov's work in 1948, when I read his book on Gogol, a book which then justified the title of its publisher, New Directions. A few years later, while working at the Library of Congress, I had the luck to learn more about Nabokov and his family, from a most remarkable man and an old acquaintance of Vladimir Dmitrievich Nabokov, the author's father. This extraordinary mentor and teacher was Evgenii Mikhailovich Kulischer, a former Petersburg lawyer and a penetrating historian of population movements—also one of the best storytellers of old Russia, trained by the master of anecdotes, the Petersburg super-lawyer Karabchevsky. Both Kulischer and Karabchevsky are well worth separate notice as fascinating and instructive examples of the Petersburg mentality at its best. V. V. Nabokov has indicated that his father considered a question settled when

"Kulischer said that. . . ." Kulischer had been close to the Nabokov family in the pre-Revolutionary days when Russian liberals still dreamed of a Russian monarchy limited by a Parliament modeled on the British system. Those liberals considered such a goal quite attainable in Russia, and they rejected the radical arguments which claimed, among other things, that the conditions of Russian history made parliamentary democracy impossible there. To the strident claims of those who proclaimed that they would allow "no one to the left of themselves," Kulischer and Nabokov replied: "Da, levee zdravogo smysla"—"Yes, farther left than common sense."

V. V. Nabokov, as author and translator, owes a great deal to this background. His father was the Foreign Editor of Russia's most prestigious liberal newspaper, and he showed the political and cultural anglophilia of his milieu. The son had an unusually strong exposure to English language and culture, through tutors, family associates, and all the unusual resources of a prominent and liberal family. His early mastery of Russian and English, his experience as an émigré who mastered the linguistic and cultural codes of several nations helped produce literary works which demonstrate, in many unusual ways, issues relevant to the art of translating.

The pains of traveling between cultures are well known to Nabokov. He has spent several periods as a tutor and a teacher, trying to help others bridge a part of the cultural gap that he himself has crossed. He can undoubtedly appreciate the irony in the situation that Pushkin described so well, fixing the genesis of the "outchitel," the teacher, forced to focus all of his experience upon a situation for which it is ill-designed.

"Ma foi, mon officier . . . ia slykhal o nem malo dobrogo. Skazyvaiut . . . chto vse trepeshchut pri ego imeni, chto s uchiteliami (avec les outchitels) on ne tseremonitsia i uzhe dvukh zasek do smerti. . . . Menia on vypisal iz Moskvy chrez odnogo iz svoikh priiatelei, koego povar, moi sootechestvennik, menia rekomendoval. Nabodno vam znat', chto ia gotovilsia bylo ne v uchitelia, a v konditery, no mne skazali, chto v vashei zemle zvanie uchitel'skoe ne v primer vygodnee. . . ." * (Pushkin, *Complete Works in Ten Volumes*, Moscow, 1957, Vol. VI, p. 279)

"Ma foi, mon officier, I have heard little good of him. They say . . . that everyone trembles at his name, that he does not stand on ceremony avec les outchitels [Russian word for "teacher," said by a Frenchman], and he has already whipped two of them to death.

". . . He recruited me from Moscow, through one of his friends, whose cook, a fellow countryman of mine, recommended me. You might wish to know that I was not educated as a teacher but as a candy maker, but I was told that in your country the teacher's profession is fabulously paid. . . ."

This incident is from Pushkin's novella, *Dubrovsky*, when the bandit protagonist, who had previously been cheated out of his estate, accidentally meets a French tutor and arranges to buy his identity in order to forward a plan of just revenge. The real tutor, shortly afterwards, is mis-identified as a German by one of the ignorant Russian drivers. Nabokov, too, has obtained cultural and material estate, or its equivalent, back again. He knows how one behaves "avec les outchitels," and his metamorphosis, as a writer and critic, like that of the candy maker turned outchitel, took adequate revenge on those who would mis-identify him as did the ignorant Russian driver in Pushkin's story: witness the caricature of the blind President of "Waindell University" who tries to say something about "the Russian gentleman."

In both his artistic writing and his criticism Nabokov has dealt with problems of transferring idioms and cultural manners from one national context to another. He did this most directly, and effectively as a critic, in his article about the pains and difficulties of translating Pushkin. In his usual manner, Nabokov also used the article polemically, to propound his notions of what translation should, and should not, be. He increased the anticipation of his version of Pushkin's most famous poem by loftily declaring at the end of the article: "And when my *Onegin* is ready, it will either conform exactly to my vision or not appear at all." It must

* In quoted passages and phrases I use the Library of Congress transliteration system; it is least confusing to the general reader, and it is clear to specialists.

be remembered that the article was published ten years before the actual appearance of Nabokov's translation.

In the body of the article, Nabokov writes:

> **I recollect the sea before a storm:**
> **O how I envied**
> **The waves that ran in turbulent succession**
> **To lie down at her feet with love!**
>
> **Ya pomnyu more pred grozoyu:**
> **Kak ia zavidoval volnam**
> **Begushchim burnoy cheredoyu**
> **S lyubov'yu lech k eyo nogam** [1]

Nabokov then continues with his commentary and explanation to the English-speaking reader:

Russian readers discern in the original here two sets of beautifully onomatopoeic alliterations: begushchim burnoy . . . which renders the turbulent rush of the surf, and s lyubov'yu lech—the liquid gasp of the waves dying in adoration at the lady's feet.

(*Partisan Review*, Fall 1955, p. 510)

In the above passage's confident, almost prosaic translation, and in its magnificent English rendering of the Russian reader's normal, internal reaction, the highest level of literary perception and taste is obvious. It is extremely difficult to explain to the English-speaking reader the basis of Pushkin's high reputation, but Nabokov has done it here cleanly and neatly. Let him who considers this an easy task try it himself! This being said, the problem of Nabokov's own extended translation of *Evgenii Onegin* is a far more complicated one. In order to understand what he accomplished directly as a critic and translator, it is also useful to consider what he accomplished on this issue indirectly, as an artist. I shall first deal with somewhat simpler, more elementary problems as they appear in some of his stories and novels.

Basically, the usual translator of quality is a person with considerable literary ability in his native language, who responds to an ultra-linguistic challenge [2] to his literary imagination. An occasional critic or linguist will sometimes translate a passage or phrase into a foreign language, but such attempts seldom make artistic pretensions; or, perhaps more accurately, under such circumstances, the fewer artistic pretensions the better. Nabokov is among the very few authors and critics whose own artistic works deal with problems of translation. They do so directly, when the characters and situations involve translators and their problems. They also do it indirectly, when the consciousness of the author, or that of the character created by the author, crosses back and forth between America and Europe, between English and one of a number of Continental European languages.

I shall take a number of examples from several works by Nabokov—all of them give impressive artistic examples of his ability to make such crossings. The most famous and widely read is *Lolita:* a European who clearly talks and reacts like a European carefully listens to, and plays back, the American scene and language. Nabokov manages a very European intrusion into the American spoken language when Humbert is in the midst of aroused passion, a time and situation when the normal man is perhaps least master of his conscious use of words:

> . . . and I laughed and addressed myself to Haze across Lo's legs to let my hand creep up my nymphet's thin back and feel her skin through her boy's shirt.
>
> But I knew it was all hopeless, and was sick with longing, and my clothes felt miserably tight, and I was almost glad when her mother's quiet voice announced in the dark: "And now we all think that Lo should go to bed." "I think you stink," said Lo. "Which means there will be no picnic tomorrow," said Haze. "This is a free country," said Lo. When angry Lo with a Bronx cheer had gone, I stayed on from sheer inertia, while Haze smoked her tenth cigarette of the evening and complained of Lo.
>
> (Crest Edition, p. 44)

Two separate effects immediately strike the reader here. One experiences the epic American struggle between mother and daughter, continuing unabated before the very eyes and glands of the nymphet chaser. Lo's words and her mother's replies are familiar to those who listened to teenagers at that time. On the other hand, one also hears a faint hint of Russian syntax in "When angry

Lo with a Bronx cheer had gone . . ." The insertion here of "with a Bronx cheer had gone" reminds me immediately of L. Tolstoy's favorite type of syntactic insertion: "Eto ego nikomu ne nuzhnaia rabota"—literally "This is his not to anyone not necessary work," i.e., his useless, vain work. It is interesting that Nabokov himself straightens out this syntactic oddity in his own Russian translation of *Lolita,* and he combines it with a circumlocutory explanation: ". . . serditaia Lo, ispustiv tak nazyvaemoe 'Bronksovoe uri' (tolstya zvuk toshnogo otvrshcheniia) . . ." (Phaedra Russian Edition, p. 36). Literally re-translated, this says: ". . . the angry Lo, having let forth a so-called 'Bronx hurrah' (a thick sound of nauseous revulsion) . . .". In some ways, Nabokov's English renders the complications of Humbert's European subconscious better, and more efficiently, than Nabokov's Russian rendering of the same phrase. It is the splicing of the European original with the American language medium that creates the effect: Humbert's marvelously skewed language. In this particular example, at least, the same art does not work in reverse, from English to Russian, even though the author is going into his "own" language.

There is another kind of American idiom equally well absorbed by the art of *Lolita:* American officialese, the jargon of those who would try to use the appearance of indirect, uninvolved description to mask the lack of real connection between their language and their feelings:

. . . Charlotte remarked that Jean Farlow, in quest of rare light effects (Jean belonged to the old school of painting), had seen Leslie taking a dip "in the ebony" (as John had quipped) at five o'clock in the morning last Sunday.

"The water," I said, "must have been quite cold."

"That is not the point," said the logical doomed dear. "He is subnormal, you see. And," she continued (in that carefully phrased way of hers that was beginning to tell on my health), "I have a very definite feeling our Louise is in love with that moron."

Feeling. "We feel Dolly is not doing as well" etc. (from an old school report). (Crest Edition, p. 77)

The contrast between the deadly accuracy of "logical doomed dear" and the almost deliberate sloppiness of "we feel" and the lame quip—all affect the health of Nabokov's protagonist and the reader's perception of officialese trying to stand in place of real human sensibility. This parallels Nabokov's almost always deft insertions about fads; the reader sees an example here in the parenthetical phrase about "the old school of painting." All these things together show a truly rare penetration into the American language by a foreign artistic perception.

Nabokov has written about some of this eloquently and directly in memoirs and in personal notes. He has also dealt with it in another artistic form, with a gentleman named Pnin. In the book by that title, we have a kind of translator's reverse English on what Nabokov did in *Lolita:* Humbert's experience showed the American language confronting the foreign-trained sensibility, while Pnin's showed the Russian sensibility confronting the American language. This is made clear and unforgettable by such details as Pnin's regret that English quotations from Shakespeare can never match the richness and power of the Russian originals in his memory from childhood. It is also expressed beautifully in Pnin's unique understanding of the speech by the American pencil sharpener: "Ticonderoga, ticonderoga."

Whatever Pnin perceives of his students and his college is again bent through the perception of the endearing Russian accent in English. In the process of refraction, it is naturally distorted; yet, Pnin's distortion, like that of the good translator, comes very close to the essence of the situation. The young gentleman who has "entombed" a large number of languages and is on the way to another entombment with Russian; the young lady who gushes about the ease of learning the alphabet so that one is reading *Anna Karamazova* in a few easy lessons; the movies showing happy, tractor-driving collective farmers bursting into attractive song (bringing on Pnin's tears, in spite of himself)—all smack of the nonsensical, but very dear, innocence of the enthusiasts in elementary Russian classes. They form a relatively happy and harmless sector of the American university, to which Nabokov's satire is entirely appropriate.

But Pnin experiences other aspects of American university standard practices which are neither so dear nor so innocent. A man can lose his livelihood and his professional life quite casually in an American university—as one of my Soviet Russian friends once asked me, in a shocked tone: "Skazhite, a pravil'no li avtor Pnina izobrazhaet zhizn' v amerikanskom kolledzhe?" ("Tell me, does the author of *Pnin* depict life in an American college truthfully?") His reaction was, I believe, very close to that of Pnin, this time without tears, when he understood the awful truth. And, if I am not completely mistaken, I see some embarrassment in the narrator of the story, an embarrassment which must in some way be connected with that of the author, when he must confront the crestfallen and rightfully resentful Pnin. Waindell College, like many others, can be painfully cruel and insensitive.

But it is Pnin forcing himself on American reality that brings a Russian accent to American English. He and his compatriots settle into a vacation in upstate New York (or adjacent New England) as if it were a Russian woods, the home of the lovely summer dachas. Pnin even wields the croquet mallet with the elan of a dachnik. The gossip of his group of friends quite naturally includes a swipe at "Vladimir Vladimirovich" and his butterflies, as well as literary conversation about Sirin, heralding the author's presence among the Russians in America. Their banter about Pnin turns him into the Russian version of an American: he owns an automobile and a suit—"Avtomobil', kostyum—nu pryamo amerikanets . . ." (p. 121, Doubleday Edition). Their remarks make Pnin a close part of American reality, a Russianization of the United States.

This is in contrast to Pnin's confrontation with Joan Clements, his landlady, and a native American. Here, Nabokov prepares an embarrassment similar to the one suffered by his own protagonist at the end of the collection of stories: Pnin is suddenly forced to break down, admitting for once his inability to understand the vagaries of American washing machines, which are not supposed to take sneakers, his incomprehension of American humorous cartoons, and, finally, his inability to keep the affections of his own wife and son. "I haf nofing left," he wails, "nofing, nofing" (Doubleday Edition, p. 51). It hurts because it is true. He is a decent man, whose intentions toward the world are nothing but beneficent. Fate has stripped him of everything, in spite of his very best efforts, and he can only express his bafflement with incorrect phonetics (fighting "th" as he must fight everything else in the universe). The laughter we have experienced before now turns to lead in our throats, and Pnin becomes by no means an exclusively comic protagonist. And all of this is done by a very slight use of Russian phonetics in English—combined with a very rare author's sense of balance in a comic story.

Presenting the protagonist as a would-be critic and translator, Nabokov moves between two views of Pnin as a comic figure: the character seen from an emotional distance sufficient to produce laughter at his expense, and the character seen very closely, so that he elicits the reader's empathy. In Pnin's grammar class, the narrator introduces a series of nonsensical phrases—"Mama, telefon! Brozhu li ia vdol' ulits shumnikh. Ot Vladivostoka do Vashingtona 5000 mil'." [3] ("Mama, telephone! Whether I walk along noisy streets. From Vladivostok to Washington is 5,000 miles.") In the midst of this nonsense, which can certainly be applied to Pnin's fate, is the first line of one of Pushkin's exquisite poems, which the narrator describes quite seriously:

In a set of eight tetrametric quatrains Pushkin described the morbid habit he always had—wherever he was, whatever he was doing—of dwelling on thoughts of death and of closely inspecting every passing day as he strove to find in its cryptogram a certain "future anniversary": the day and month that would appear somewhere, sometime upon his tombstone. (Doubleday Edition, p. 68)

Pnin then takes over, and continues, with the usual pedantry of the teacher:

"And where will fate send me," imperfective future [Russian grammatical category], "death," declaimed inspired Pnin, throwing his head back and translating with brave literality, "in fight, in travel, or in waves? Or will the neighboring dale"—dolina, same word, "valley" we would now say— "accept my refrigerated ashes," poussière, "cold dust" perhaps more correct. "And though it is indifferent to the insensible body. . . ." *(ibid.)*

While poor Pnin acts with the "brave literality" of translation which his creator will later defend in all seriousness, the situation turns against him with a cruel, satiric twist. Pnin laughs at Pushkin's mistake about the date and time of his death, while Pnin's students laugh at the "ominous crack" "emitted" by Professor Pnin's chair. But the poem comes back a few pages later, when Pnin is ascending the Library stairs, "V boyu li, v stranstvii, v volnakh? In fight, in travel, or in waves? Or on the Waindell campus? Gently chomping his dentures, which retained a sticky layer of cottage cheese, Pnin went up the slippery library steps" (Doubleday Edition, pp. 73-74). Thus does Pnin recall the infinitely sweet pain of that poem, with the courage of literal translation, and with cottage cheese sticking to his dentures. The teacher fights no less valiantly than the poet.

This is Nabokov's way of dealing with one of the most moving poems in the Russian language, whose final line about "indifferent nature" became doubly famous after Turgenev used it in his final elegy to the spirit of Bazarov, in the scene with Bazarov's parents at the graveyard, near the end of *Fathers and Sons*.[4] Nabokov does not mention the latter scene in *Pnin,* but he does have one of the young American girls recall one of Turgenev's prose poems when she talks with Professor Pnin. And the evocation of the poem's pain becomes first a comic presentation of Pnin, only to turn about and again capture the reader's sympathy for the character and the mode of translation. This is one of the most unusual and evocative uses of Pushkin's poetry; it occurs while Nabokov presents a parody of his own serious ideas about literal translation.

In the previous two books, Nabokov has explored different ways in which a foreign sensibility and the American language interact with each other. Humbert observes and wreaks his some-times perverted will upon the American reality around him. Pnin achieves a different penetration of the American language: he resists its attempts to affect him, thereby forcing some of his own Russian sensibility on the American scene. Indeed, the narrator relates the final irony that the very people who wish to mock Pnin end up resembling him by conscious imitation. Meanwhile, Pnin is blithely unconcerned whether or not his style fits the situation around him. With the situations in *Lolita* and *Pnin*, Nabokov has shown the two different cultures combining by moving in different directions—the European pressing upon the American, and the American pressing upon the European.

In another book, Nabokov carries the interpretation of the two languages even a step further. *Pale Fire* contains a scene in which perfectly correct English is used to describe the effect of a Rus-sian speaking a particular dialect in Russian. Here, the foreign sensibility is not pressing upon the American scene, nor is it resisting the American language; the description is relaxed and scholarly:

Nitra and Indra (meaning "inner" and "outer"), two black islets that seemed to address each other in cloaked parley, were being photographed from the parapet by a Russian tourist, thickset, many-chinned, with a general's flashy nape. His faded wife, wrapped up floatingly in a flowery écharpe, remarking in singsong Muscovan "Every time I see that frightful kind of disfigurement I can't help thinking of Nina's boy. War is an awful thing." (Lancer Edition. p. 105)

This description, written by King Charles (who calls himself "Kinbote") is part of his narration-miscalled-commentary on a "poem in heroic couplets" written by the American poet John Francis Shade. King Charles will later on indicate (Lancer Edition, p. 174) the vogue that a certain kind of Russian once had in his court, and among his ancestors, but in this passage he catches the lilt of the Moscow dialect. The fleshiness of the Russian, his Slavicized "many-chinnedness" (with, perhaps, the further pun on the word "chin" in English and the Russian word *"chin,"* meaning "rank"), his faded, floatingly wrapped wife—all of these qualities pinpoint the Moscovite, especially through the eyes of a dyed-in-the-wool Petersburger like Nabokov. The singsong quality of Moscovite speech, with its heavy Southern Russian phonetic admixture, stands in marked contrast to the more clipped Leningrad (a later incarnation of Petersburg) intonation, which makes jumps in pitch much closer together than those of Moscovite speech. I myself have heard Moscovites say the three syllables of the word "khorosho" in a pitch variation that changes as much as a full octave; while in Leningrad, one hears the interjection "pravda?" ("n'est ce pas?" "nicht wahr?"), going ever so slightly upward in pitch, the phonetic equivalent of a slightly raised eyebrow. Nabokov has brought this to the printed page in English, very slightly Slavicized, to be sure, but nevertheless good, rich literary English. I do not know of any other writer, at least in the United States, who has achieved this feat. Nabokov's achievement, with his unblemished English matching the mastery of the Russian over his native language, is perhaps clearer if one contrasts it to Bernard Malamud's stylistic lapse in *The Fixer*. He uses incorrect English syntax in the dialogue representing Jews in the Ukraine speaking their own native language. Whereas Nabokov makes the distinction between Pnin speaking a foreign language with an accent and the Russians speaking their own language correctly, Malamud asks his reader to accept the facile assumption that Yiddish speakers always use incorrect syntax, regardless of whether they are speaking their native language or a foreign tongue.

Nabokov, of course, has liberally sprinkled the text of *Pale Fire* with Russianisms meant either to dazzle or confuse the reader. He has Charles use Zembla and Nova Zembla to refer to his native land, and then the critic disingenuously tells us "that, in fact, the name Zembla is a corruption not of the Russian zemlya, but of Semberland. . . ." (Lancer Edition, p. 187) When the King asks himself the time, he says "kot or" (p. 101), which obviously refers to the Russian "kotoryi chas?", with another pun on the latinate use of the root or/hor. I am not sure what quality to ascribe to such linguistically mixed salt and pepper effects: they are both clever and affected—some readers find them intriguing, others find them annoying. But, again from the point of view of translation, it shows how Russian can be brought into reasonably straightforward English in an almost completely integrated fashion. By this time, the reader notes that poor old Pnin has been reduced by his colleague's observation, to a "regular martinet in relation to his underlings . . . that grotesque 'perfectionist' . . ." (p. 112). The prosperity of the American "outchitel" has not dealt kindly with the old man.

Nabokov's mastery of English in Russian, Russian in English, and many, various degrees of their interpenetrations is somehow reminiscent of the sentence from the murder scene in *Lolita:* "I rolled over him. We rolled over me. They rolled over him. We rolled over us." (Crest Edition, p. 272) "Ia perekatyvalsia cherez nego. My perekatyvalis' cherez menia. Oni perekatyvalis' cherez nego. My perekatyvalis' cherez sebia. (Phaedra Edition, p. 277) Again, with "sebia" Nabokov is forced away from a literal rendering of "us." There is another way in which Nabokov's efforts roll over each other in a way that confuses pronouns and persons. Nabokov parodies at great length the academic commentator who talks and writes at great length. We are all, unfortunately, familiar with the academician's disease of writing far more abundantly than the author of the original work: the two-hundred-page commentary on the fifty-page work. The reader of *Pale Fire* could easily be aware that the parody came from an author who was working on two thick volumes of commentary to accompany his translation of Pushkin's slim volume, *Evgenii Onegin,* the cornerstone of nineteenth- and twentieth-century Russian literature. As always with Nabokov, it is hard to draw any line between parody and self-parody.

The American reader should also understand that Pushkin was a great master at combining languages, levels and layers within the Russian language, and fantastically disparate styles and sources from all over European literature. Like Nabokov, he was well aware of syllables in foreign languages with Russian meanings, such as the Russian word for "sleep" *("son")* in the novelist's name Richardson. Like Nabokov, he knew how to tease the people he considered heavy pedants among his readers, thereby immortalizing old Admiral Shishkov, head of the "lovers (and therefore protectors against foreign influx) of the Russian language," to whom the poet apologized for not being able to translate the English word "vulgar," evidently a concept inappropriate to Pushkin's Russian. One could pile up such analogies to Nabokov's approach, endlessly; in short, if anyone could make the American and English reader begin to understand Pushkin's genius, surely Nabokov could.

The actual appearance of Nabokov's four volumes of translation and commentary immediately stimulated a controversy in American and English intellectual journals. For a time, it seemed that the controversy might raise Western interest in Pushkin to the level of the already existing interest in Tolstoy and Dostoevsky. Such a result would be entirely appropriate, since the three of them are the giants of Russian literature. (Nabokov, of course, would disagree with the placing of Dostoevsky among them; in this case, his literary judgment is mistaken.) Unfortunately, the polemic did very little for establishing a strong Western interest in Pushkin—his name was, perhaps inevitably, swallowed up by the ensuing polemic, which centered around the reputations of several contemporary critics.

The actual translation is puzzling to those who do not know Pushkin well in Russian. Nabokov quite literally carried out his intention of direct, straight translation, "unbegrimed and unbeslimed by rhyme." Forsaking what he considers the insulting notion of the translation which "reads well," Nabokov sets out to render the literal sense, and even order, of Pushkin's own words. The translator even exulted in the title of faithful pony. When the Russian uses an archaic word, Nabokov does not hesitate to find an equally archaic word in the appropriate English dictionary, or embedded in the text of an old English or French poem.

For the student of Russian, Nabokov's literal translation, together with his voluminous notes, comments, allusions, developments of theorems related to poetry and rhythm are suggestive and fascinating. One can learn something from almost every line. His regal dismissal of all other attempts at translation and commentary are reminiscent of the words he put in Kinbote's mouth. But wounded fellow critics and translators need not necessarily take umbrage at Nabokov's condescending criticism: they are in good company—Pushkin himself sometimes receives similar treatment. One of the commonly popular stanzas from *Onegin* is Pushkin's contrast of two wines, the sober, friendly Bordeaux, and the sparkling, mistress-like Aï; Pushkin rhythmically catches the distinction between the two wines by lilting over Aï's qualities in four parallel lines:

> **K Ai ia bol'she ne sposoben;**
> **Ai liubovnitse podoben**
> **Blestiashchei, vetrenoi, zhivoi,**
> **I svoenravnoi i pustoi.**

He then contrasts Bordeaux's friendly steadiness, ending with an almost shouted cheer, in a rhyming couplet including the wine's friendliness ("Long live Bordeaux, our friend!").

> **Il' tikhii razdelit' dosug.**
> **Da zdravstvuet Bordo, nash drug! (Chapter Four, Stanza XLVI)**

To this invention, Nabokov groans: "Both this and the previous stanza, XLV, are very poor, bubbling with imported platitudes." (Vol. II, p. 483)

For the general reader, who does not know Russian and has no hope of reading Pushkin in the original, Nabokov's oeuvre is probably not very useful.* When Pushkin divinely describes his own work, at the very beginning, he does so with a rhythm and

---

* Except, perhaps, as a kind of writer's laboratory to help clarify the genesis of *Pale Fire*. In that novel, Nabokov satirizes many of the academic mannerisms he takes more seriously in his work on *Onegin*.

alternation of sounds that set a standard for the highest pinnacles of nineteenth-century Russian literature, a period unsurpassed in the history of European literature:

> No tak i byt'—rukoi pristrastnoi
> Primi sobran'e pestrykh glav,
> Polusmeshnykh, polupechal' nykh,
> Prostonarodnykh, ideal'nykh,
> Nebrezhnyi plod moikh zabav,
> Bessonits, legkikh vdokhnovenii
> Nezrelykh i uviadshikh let,
> Uma kholodnykh nabliudenii,
> I serdsta gorestnykh zamet.

However literally correct Nabokov's following clipped lines may be, they simply cannot convey, or even hint, to the non-Russian-reading person the universe of feeling contained in the lines.

> But so be it. With partial hand
> take this collection of pied chapters:
> half droll, half sad,
> plain-folk, ideal,
> the careless fruit of my amusements,
> insomnias, light inspirations,
> unripe and withered years,
> the intellect's cold observations,
> and the heart's sorrowful remarks. (Vol. I, p. 91)

Nabokov has claimed that when a literal translation does not convey the desired original spirit, something is wrong with the original. It seems to me the above lines cast some doubt on that claim. My case would of course be stronger if I could offer a better translation of the same lines. Since the creation of good poetry is beyond my capability, I must ask the reader either to rely on his own knowledge of Russian or to accept my word.

It is, of course, child's play to show up the flaws in almost any translation of a major poetic work. In all justice, one might add that Nabokov himself has engaged in this child's play with the translations by almost everyone else. But the real problem of translation is not to show the weaknesses of other translators in specific places; it is, rather, to produce a superior solution of the same difficulty in that particular place. Nabokov has done this without peer or rival in his commentaries, but he has not done it for the English reader in his translation. He has, of course, given a brilliant demonstration of his theory of literal translation—and this may well be the lesson he had in mind for the academics whom he parodies and mimics so mercilessly, and so effectively, in almost all his work.

In the postscript attached to his own Russian translation of *Lolita,* Nabokov has written the following uncharacteristically modest words (translation mine):

I am only troubled now by the jangling of my rusty Russian strings. The history of this translation is a history of disillusion. Alas, that "marvelous Russian" which, I always thought, constantly awaited me somewhere, blooming like true spring behind hermetically sealed gates to which I kept the key for so many years—that Russian turns out to be non-existent. And behind the gates there is nothing, except charred stumps and a hopeless autumn vista; the key in my hand is more like a lock-pick.

(Op. cit., p. 296)

He then proceeds to some conclusions, based on six months' work, about the various categories of experience rendered more easily in Russian and in English; e.g., extreme feelings, whether coarse or tender, come out very well indeed in Russian, while restraint comes out well in English understatement. In general, Nabokov contrasts the different circumstances in the historical developments of the two languages. He considers the young genius of the Russian language in the contrasting light of the English language's mature freedom.

Nabokov has undergone a vast odyssey and exhibited an indomitable spirit, vitality, and love for much of the best in poetry and literature. His "charred stumps" are very often transformed by the power of his imagination into the kind of flowering very much appropriate to his own metaphor of spring.

Notes

1. The attentive reader will notice that Nabokov does not use any of the standard systems of transliteration, which he undoubtedly considers excessively pedantic. Nor does he bother to strive for internal consistency: he puts in, or omits, the Russian "soft sign" as it pleases his fancy and his purpose, and he chooses to instruct the readers about the correct pronunciation of the Russian "e" with diaeresis, rather than to render the vowel literally, in his use of "eyo."

2. For a more complete reference to this notion, beautifully worked out by the Russian poet Valerii Briusov, see my article on artistic translation in *TriQuarterly*, No. 8, Winter 1967.

3. Again, Nabokov uses his own capricious system for transliteration, different from his other usages.

4. The first and last stanzas of Pushkin's poem, written in 1829:

> *Brozhu li ia vdol' ulits shumnykh,*
> *Vkhozhu l' vo mnogoliudnykh khram,*
> *Sizhu l' mezh iunoshei bezumnykh,*
> *Ia predaius' moim mechtam.*
>
> · · · ·
>
> *I pust' u grobovogo vkhoda*
> *Mladaia budet zhizn' igrat',*
> *I ravnodushnaia priroda*
> *Krasoiu vechnoiu siiat'.*

Notes on the translation of *Invitation to a Beheading*

ROBERT P. HUGHES

V. Sirin's novel *Priglašenie na kazn'* made its first, serial appearance on the pages of the leading Russian émigré journal, the Paris-based *Sovremennyja Zapiski (Contemporary Annals)* in 1935-36 (volumes LVIII-LX). The integral text came out in book form in 1938. The Russian original, outfitted with a perceptive introduction by Julian Moynahan, has recently been republished, in a paperback format designed for easy (and presumably clandestine) entry into the land of its creator's birth, in Editions Victor (Paris, 1966); the author's own name, now world-famous, replaced his pseudonym. Vladimir Nabokov's *Invitation to a Beheading*, the novel in English, a joint translation by Dmitrij Nabokov and his father, appeared in post-*Lolita* 1959. The paperback edition (Fawcett Publications, Inc.) was in circulation the following year. Its latest appearance was as an expensively and sumptuously turned out "quality" paperback (Capricorn Books, 1965).[1]

Of all the translations of Sirin-Nabokov's works—by various hands, but always quality-controlled by Nabokov himself—this novel seems to have suffered least change in the process of conversion. It is basically true that "the only corrections which its transformation into English could profit by were routine ones, for the sake of that clarity which in English seems to require less elaborate electric fixtures than in Russian" (vii), and the changes made provide fascinating views of the creative process of both the original composition and its transition into English. The minor difficulty in rendering the work's title is noted in the author's Foreword.

In the naming of the work's protagonist and his antagonist, the translators were presented with a problem which they chose to disregard. M'sieur Pierre (who also appears at least once with his Russian name and patronymic, Pyotr Petrovich, 167) functions as the double—now ignoring the objections of Nabokov ("The *Doppelgänger* subject is a frightful bore") and those of his critics who so eagerly agree with him—of Cincinnatus C. This fact is emphasized in Russian in that his repeated initial "C," which, incidentally, he shares with his mother, Cecilia C., and the repeated initial "P" in the names of the man he discovers is his (own) executioner are near inversions. In a scene involving the desecration of Cincinnatus's beloved Tamara Gardens, the "grandiose monogram" of their intertwined first initials, on the evening of party and ritual farewell before the execution on the morrow, significantly, does "not quite come off" (189): ". . . *po vsemu nočnomu landšaftu rastjanutyj grandioznyj venzel' iz P. i C ne sovšem odnako vyšedsij*" (187). The translators might have chosen names for the English version beginning, for example, in "A" and "V," considering the first letter's bar no greater or less a deviation from the basic shape than the hook of "C" is different from the symmetrical "P." Readers to whom Cyrillic is not even Greek are asked to imagine the square back of a chair for the "P" and the same figure inverted and now sporting a little hooked tail near the juncture of its bottom and right-side lines for the "C." That some significance may be lurking in the names is not being discounted, but since Nabokov is not a "symbolist," one should proceed cautiously.

The English version's "Marthe" is perhaps too Frenchily elegant for the homier Russian *"Marfin'ka,"* but then any diminutive of Martha in English is too masculine and hearty for this very feminine and acquiescent creature. It is probably by chance that she bears the same name as the unlucky adulteress in *King, Queen, Knave* (1928), but it is mildly surprising that the other female character of the later novel also shares a name with Franz's envied sibling from the earlier work; another Emmy (Emmie, *Emmočka*) pops up among the lecturer's schoolgirl interlocutors in "An Evening of Russian Poetry" (1945). The ridiculous, interchangeable and interchanging trio of the jailer Rodion, the prison director Rodrig Ivanovich, and the lawyer Roman Vissarionovich (who shares a patronymic with a bloody Georgian who inspired the fear of all Russia at the time this novel was written) undergo no name changes in the transition from Russian to English. And what does the trinity of their initial syllables have in common with a German paperback series? Usually poorer in diminutives than Russian (mercifully so), the English does provide a like number of variations on the given names of these worthies: Rod and Rodka for *Rodja* and *Rod'ka;* Rom and Romka for *Roma* and *Romka.*

The Tamara Gardens are for Cincinnatus C. an image of ideal truth and beauty, the world of youth and first love to which he longs to return. Their every mention is encased in a passage of heightened perception and lyricism. The wondrously evocative prose-poetry of these passages must have posed a special problem to the translators; and here the English version falls a bit short of the Russian, even though some telling effects have been created. The difficulty begins with the name, for *tam* in Russian conveys the sense of "there (where I am not)," the opposite of the "horrible 'here,' the dark dungeon, in which a relentlessly howling heart is incarcerated" (91). In a dream, Cincinnatus C. revisits the Gardens:

. . . Izredka naplyv blagouxanija govoril o blizosti Tamarinyx Sadov. Kak on znal ěti sady! Tam, kogda Marfin'ka byla nevestoj i bojalas' ljagušek, majskix žukov. . . . Tam, gde, byvalo, kogda vse stanovilos' nevterpež i možno bylo odnomu, s kašej vo rtu iz razževennoj sireni, so slezami. . . . Zelenoe, muravčatoe Tam, tamošnie xolmy, tomlenie prudov, tamtatam dalekogo orkestra. (32)

The passage echoes with the name, the *tam*'s resound in immediate and distant context, rising in a crescendo with the band. The English is ultimately less effective, but a game and interesting try has been made:

. . . Now and then a wave of fragrance would come from the Tamara Gardens. How well he knew that public park! There, where Marthe, when she was a bride, was frightened of the frogs and cockchafers. . . . There, where, whenever life seemed unbearable, one could roam, with a meal of chewed lilac bloom in one's mouth and firefly tears in one's eyes. . . . That green turfy tamarack park, the languor of its ponds, the tum-tum-tum of a distant band . . . (17)

A few fixtures have been installed, some removed. The "firefly" complement and the location of the tears is new. The hills disappear, but a dendrologic remark on the park has been added: the translation's "tamarack" stands there because in it nestles a *tam* and the girl by whose name the park is known. The (phonetic) *tam* in *tomlenie* (languor) is irretrievable, and the double-and-a-half *tam* of the band is dulled by the distances and wilder state of the English gardens.

In a scudded, alliterative iambic line, he recalls an amorous moment with Marthe "in the shadowed seclusion of the Tamara Gardens" (62): "v tenistyx tajnikax Tamarinyx Sadov" (72). In a lengthy passage studded with incantatory *tam*'s (99)/*there*'s (92-93), Cincinnatus attempts to express in writing (cut short when Rodion extinguishes the light) his desire to shed layers of consciousness until he becomes pure being ("a pearl ring embedded in a shark's gory fat") and achieves constant existence in his timeless dream world. The translators felt compelled to emphasize even more than did Sirin the separateness of the "there" and its opposition to the "here." In the English version all *there*'s are underlined, and other languages are called upon: "There, *tam, là-bas,* the gaze of men glows with inimitable understanding; *there* the freaks that are tortured here walk unmolested; *there* time takes shape according to one's pleasure . . ." and so forth.[2]

The names of other features of cartographic interest receive less attention from the translators, although there are a couple of oddities that attract the eye: the obscenity-derived *Matjuxinskaja* becomes the contextually appropriate Matterfact Street, but at the same time comes dangerously close to getting translated; *Interesnaja Ploščad'* (Interesting Square) is transformed into the more sensational Thriller Square. Garden and Telegraph streets and Steep Avenue descend legitimately from their Russian prototypes, while the river *Strop'* flows from Russian to English with the loss only of a "soft sign."

The provenance of Upper Elderbury (108), M'sieur Pierre's supposed home-town, one of whose claims to fame is its fruit crop, is a complicated one, involving puns in and between Russian and English. *Vyšnegrad* (114) is a plausible union of (Old Church Slavic) *vyšne-* (upper, on high) and *grad* (originally, fortified place; still productive, cf., *Volgograd*), the equivalent of (Old High German) *burg,* akin to (English) borough and -bury. M'sieur Pierre's characteristic trite pun involving cherry (*višnja*) consumption in *Vyšnegrad* produces the squirm in the Russian; in English, of course, the pun depends on the second element -bury and the nearly homonymous berry, and . . . Agreed, the bark of such a pun's explanation is worse than the bite.

Nabokov's other Englished novels display a certain sympathy toward the reader's probable ignorance of Russian poetry. *Despair* and *The Gift,* for example, abound in charitable clarifications of allusions, indulgent identifications of quotations, and other such newly erected road signs and information booths to guide and comfort the inexperienced traveler. Not so in *Invitation to a Beheading*. Few readers will recognize the poem to which Cincinnatus alludes as he writes (Lenskij-like) in the chill dawn in which he expects to be led out to execution:

"... all kinds of memories come to say farewell: I, a child, am sitting with a book in the hot sun on the bank of a dinning stream, and the water throws its wavering reflection of its lines of an old, old poem— 'Love at the sloping of our years'—but I know I should not yield—'Becomes more tender and superstitious'—neither to memories, nor to fear, nor to this passionate syncope: '... and superstitious'—and I had hoped so much that everything would be orderly, all simple and neat...." (191-92)

It is Fedor Tjutčev's "Last Love" ("O, kak na sklone našix let/ Nežnej my ljubim i suevernej . . .") that produces the spasm. Nabokov does not use his own earlier translation of the poem (too much spirit and insufficient fidelity?): "Love at the closing of our days/is apprehensive and very tender./Glow brighter, brighter, farewell rays/of one last love in its evening splendor." [3]

Nor are most readers any more likely to recognize "Pushkin's lyrical duelist" (90) as Vladimir Lenskij, unless it be as the "whining weakling" that Čajkovskij made of "Pushkin's virile Lenski" in his "silly" and "slapdash" opera, loosely adapted from *Evgenij Onegin,* the libretto of which the aroused Nabokov has called "hideous and insulting." [4]

One also doubts that the translation of *kukla* ("doll," "puppet") as "dummy" *(passim)* will at first summon up the proper image for most American readers. The characters to whom it is applied are rather more obviously stupid than immediately recognizable as the author's playthings. Thus, the "theatrical" effects are somewhat veiled, even though that aspect is always present and is clearly manifested in the novel's final pages. A pedant might also question the sounds the translators' geese produce: those "discreetly gobbling" birds (214) would be mistaken for turkeys; while the Russian version's *gagakajuščij* (208; out of the onomatopoetic *gagakat',* a variant of *gogotat',* "to cackle [of geese]") is that language's accepted term for goose-chatter.

The following are examples of the individual-word and phraseological challenges presented to the translators; often enough, equivalents were found for the English version, but the original Russian probably possesses the greater number of verbal gems:

1. The spoonerism in "I didn't weep a slink all night . . ." (147) is a precise and perhaps even more effective transposition than that in the Russian: *"Vsju noč' somej ne očknul . . ."* (148).

2. " 'Take the word "anxiety," ' Cincinnatus's brother-in-law, the wit, was saying to him. 'Now take away the word "tiny," eh? Comes out funny, doesn't it? . . ,' " (102). The same terrible instrument in Cincinnatus's future was obtained in the Russian (108) by reading *ropot* ("murmur") backwards. The English printer—careless, or humorless, or both—drops the final letter when the word recurs (162, 193).

3. At the farewell party, Cincinnatus's waggish brother-in-law again engages in morbid banter: "Afraid, aren't you? Here, have a drink on the brink" (183), which is a fine phony equivalent of the pseudo-saw in the Russian: ". . . *bojazno, podi? Vot xlebni vinca do venca"* (181). The (martyr's?) crown is implicitly transformed into a wedding crown for the next bit of action; " 'Bitter, bitter, sweeten it with a kiss,' said a recent best man, and the rest of the guests joined in the chanting" (183). The original, however, is more laconic: " *'Gor'ko!' kriknul kto-to, i drugie podxvatili"* (182). The *gor'ko* gets explained, and the ambiguity of "bitter" is lost; a "best man" replaces a "somebody" to establish the event.

4. Bedazzling to eye and ear are Nabokov's alliterative discoveries. The English seems poorer in this respect, although "discrete drupes" (10) and "bad dreams, dregs of delirium, the drivel of nightmares" (34) are up to the mark of the Russian. The original, however, fairly scintillates. Cincinnatus's crime of "gnostical turpitude" is in Russian the resoundingly more infamous *gnoseologičeskaja gnusnost'* ("gnosiological vileness").[5] "[M'sieur Pierre's] crystal-bright eyes gazed politely . . ." is no match for *"Svoimi svetlymi glazirovannymi glazami on vežlivo*

gljadel . . ." (88; "With bright glazed eyes he gazed politely
. . ."). As a wave of desperation engulfs him, Cincinnatus puts
aside *Quercus,* bemoans his fate, and then senses a "leafy breeze,"
the double "ee" of which is a lesser substitute for the sonorities
of the poetic *dubravnoe dunovenie* (128; "the oak-grove's gentle
gust"), which issues naturally from his reading matter and more
"realistically" releases the "large dummy acorn" that bounces
off his blanket. "The blind stone steeps of the fortress" (164)
is equal to *"Slepaja kamennaja krutizna kreposti"* (164), and
it is also a literal translation, but the original continues *"iz
kotoroj on, kak kaplja, vyžalsja. . . ."* In *"Skrjučennyj na stu-
pen'ke, bleval blednyj bibliotekar'"* (217), the poor creature
seems indeed to be losing his dinner; and, beside it, the English
version's "On the steps the pale librarian sat doubled up, vomit-
ing" (223) is rather more delicate.

5. "A clock struck—four or five times—with the vibrations
and re-vibrations proper to a prison" (11) is a reasonably precise translation of *"Probili časy—četyre ili pjať raz, i kaze-
matnyj otgul ix, peregul i zagulok veli sebja podobajuščim ob-
razom"* (26-27); but the marvelously resonant demi-neologisms
on *gul* ("rumbling," "hum," "buzzing") and the play on the
"off on a spree, extending it, and overdoing it" potentialities of
the words that contain it are not reproduced.

"Mali é trano t'amesti," sings Marthe's brunet brother at the
family gathering (101-102). If one ignores the probably misleading but suspiciously Russian-looking fragments, *l'amitié* can
be discovered here *à l'estime;* but a patient and polyglot worker
of anagrams may ferret out in full yet another magic phrase.

The splendid verbal effects—which are at least partially exposed by a comparison of the original and a translation as well
done as this one is—are a salient and characteristically Nabokovian feature of the novel. The translators' extraordinary accomplishment has been insufficiently praised, here and elsewhere. In
the present instance, too, attention has been concentrated on some
renderings slightly less successful than others, but with the intention to illuminate and throw into relief the brilliant texture of

the original. *Priglašenie na kazn'* rightly commands its author's greatest esteem.[6] *Invitation to a Beheading* deserves only a little less.

Notes

1. The two texts compared in this paper are those of the first Fawcett and the latest Russian edition. The page numbers in parentheses refer to these two publications. The fancy Capricorn edition ($1.65), curiously enough, omits (the printer's mistake?) the work's epigraph, a line from the invented but influential Pierre Delalande. Otherwise, the texts of these two editions in English seem to be identical. The English original of Moynahan's Preface may be found in *Novel*, Vol. 1, No. 1 (Fall 1967). The system of transliteration used by academic Slavicists has been followed in this paper. Citations from Nabokov's work, of course, have been left in his own transliteration.

2. The ten-year-old Vladimir Nabokov, on the beach at Biarritz with his French playmate Colette, experienced a similar longing: "I had a gold coin that I assumed would pay for our elopement. Where did I want to take her? Spain? America? The mountains above Pau? *'Là-bas, là-bas, dans la montagne,'* as I had heard Carmen sing at the opera. . . ." *Speak, Memory* (New York, 1966), p. 150.

3. *Three Russian Poets* (Norfolk, 1944), p. 34. Vasilij Ivanovič in "Ozero, oblako, bašnja" ("Cloud, Castle, Lake," 1937) is Cincinnatus C. in another guise. When he is forcibly separated from his ideal landscape, he cries out, "Oh, but this is nothing less than an invitation to a beheading. . . ." He too is a lover and reader of the poet. A significantly disfigured line from another well-known poem of Tjutčev's proved impossible to translate, and so the English version is missing an important allusion.

4. The first four epithets are to be found scattered in Nabokov's commentary to his translation of Puškin's novel; the final pair, in "Reply to My Critics," *Nabokov's Congeries* (New York, 1968), p. 324.

5. The literal renderings (in parentheses), here and below, are meant to be only that, and they pretend to no artistic merit.

6. "An Interview with Vladimir Nabokov," conducted by Alfred Appel, Jr., *Wisconsin Studies in Contemporary Literature,* Vol. 8, No. 2 (Spring 1967), p. 152.

A new deck for Nabokov's Knaves

CARL R. PROFFER

Nabokov has said that the urge to emend grows in proportion to the length of time separating the model from the mimic. Collation of *Korol', dama, valet* with *King, Queen, Knave* supports this generalization. The novel was among the first to be written, and it is not for nothing (to use an old Russian idiom) that it was among the last to be Englished. While certain sections show the flash of the master, on the whole, and as a whole, *King, Queen, Knave* does not surmount its original weaknesses. When we triangulate to find its position in Nabokov's world, we discover that it is located near *Despair, Laughter in the Dark,* and *Lolita.* Nabokov has translated all of these novels, and the number of changes grows in inverse proportion to the author's

...ge at the time of writing. The Russian *Lolita* is marked by only a few adjustments in allusion, the English *Despair* is changed in relatively minor tonal and stylistic ways,[1] but almost every page of *King, Queen, Knave* differs from its Slavic model.

Comparing the Russian to the English, one sees that Nabokov tends not to alter simply by deletion. By far the most common kind of change is interpolation. Nabokov either "simply" rewrites, or rewrites and lengthens. Interpolations relating to *characterization* form the most important category of improvement. One senses the reviser's self-criticism in this expansion:

Believing that in such matters the details are more important than the essence, Martha . . .[2]

Believing, with so many novelists, that if the details were correct, the plot and characters would take care of themselves, Martha . . .[3]

The English king, queen, and joker are more convincing characters than their Russian predecessors. Physical description is more detailed, biographies more circumstantial, motivation more convincing. Sometimes Nabokov just adds parenthetical remarks or makes general statements more specific. In the case of Martha:

"Tom won a prize at the show. Didn't you Tom!" [(she spoke to Tom only in the presence of guests).] (p. 29)

[("First things first" and "If you want two noses, you should be content with one eye" were her favorite proverbs.)] (p. 182)

Martha, though, would refuse to come [preferring a trim suburban lawn to the most luxuriant jungle. She would only sniff sarcastically] were he to suggest they take a year off. (p. 15)

Many of the improvements in Nabokov's characterization of Martha relate to the interesting areas of sex, money, and death. Thus her ardent desire to murder Dreyer is more comprehensible to the English reader. For example, the long passage beginning, "There were those 700,000 untouchable dollars in a safe in Hamburg" and ending "at the exchange or in his frivolous transactions" (p. 114) is an interpolation. The same is true of "she urged him to accumulate more in Hamburg and gamble less in Berlin" (p. 114).

Martha's rather ridiculous sexual problem, and its connection to money, is also stated more clearly in the new version. Note, in this passage, the erotic allusion in the first addition and the alliterative coupling of the second:

This interest of hers in Dreyer's ventures did not combine organically with the new, [piercing, moaning, and throbbing] meaning of her life. She felt she could not be fully happy with such a blending [of bank and bed,] and yet . . . (p. 114)

While the Freudians have not been invited, it is nevertheless clear that Martha's antagonism towards Dreyer finds its root in sexuality. Let us take just the new details. We learn of her apparently idyllic childhood:

She used to lie on her back, and the water would lap and rock her, so delicious, so cool. [And the bracing breeze penetrated you as you sat naked with a naked boy of your age among the forget-me-nots.] (p. 214)

But then there was the wedding and the "dismal surprises" Dreyer provided on the honeymoon. After this, she tells Franz, "How can one love a man [whose mere touch makes one feel sick?"] (p. 102). Therefore she makes sex a matter of money (or promises). Nabokov provides many new details on these bargaining sessions. We also learn "that Martha regarded afternoon lovemaking as a decadent perversion" (p. 38) and that she is often prissy with Dreyer ("And will you please cover your obscene nudity" [p. 39]). The sexual antagonism is also made more obvious in this sentence:

Martha's subject was deafeningly loud, intolerably [vigorous and] vivacious; he [threatened her with a priapus that had already once inflicted upon her an almost mortal wound,] smoothed his [obscene] moustache with a little silver brush . . . (p. 178)

And finally, in the would-be murder scene, Nabokov adds a sexual suggestion:

"Twenty-five more strokes," she said with a smile. "I'll count." (Russian ed.)

"Eight more strokes," she said with a smile. "The years of our marriage. I'll count." (p. 247)

The "strokes" are metaphorical—the last strokes before the organism's terminal spasms.

There are many alterations which make Martha a more "realistic" character. Her conversations with Franz are newly calculated to arouse his interest—even in the very beginning. Thus, the passage from "I have often tried to decide" to "the exchange of ideas on life and living conditions" (p. 28) is added. And when Martha first shows up at Franz's apartment she warms his heart by saying, "I was afraid you might be ill" (p. 95), rather than "I had to get out of the rain" (the Russian, p. 94).

Finally, to show more graphically the kinds of changes typical of Nabokov's work on *King, Queen, Knave,* here are the Russian and the English versions of Martha's biography:

She barely knew him seven years ago, when her parents, who were bankrupt merchants, easily persuaded her to marry Dreyer who was getting rich with miraculous ease. He was very jolly, he sang in a funny voice, and he gave her a squirrel which had a foul smell. It was only after the wedding when her husband cancelled an important business trip to Berne —in favor of a honeymoon in Norway (and why Norway of all places?), that certain things were cleared up. (p. 66)

Her mother had died when Martha was three—a not unusual arrangement. A first stepmother soon died too, and that also ran in some families. The second and final stepmother, who died only recently, was a lovely woman of quite gentle birth whom everyone adored. Papa, who had started his career as a saddler and ended it as the bankrupt owner of an artificial leather factory, was desperately eager she marry the "Hussar," as for some reason he dubbed Dreyer, whom she barely knew when he proposed in 1920, at the same time that Hilda became engaged to the fat little purser of a second-rate Atlantic liner. Dreyer was getting rich with miraculous ease; he was fairly attractive, but bizarre and unpredictable; sang off-key silly arias and made her silly presents. As a well-bred girl with long lashes and glowing cheeks, she said she would make up her mind the next time he came to Hamburg. Before leaving for Berlin he

gave her a monkey which she loathed; fortunately, a handsome young
cousin with whom she had gone rather far before he became one of
Hilda's first lovers taught it to light matches, its little jersey caught fire,
and the clumsy animal had to be destroyed. When Dreyer returned a week
later, she allowed him to kiss her on the cheek. Poor old Papa got so high
at the party that he beat up the fiddler, which was unpardonable—seeing
all the hard luck he had encountered in his long life. It was only after
the wedding, when her husband cancelled an important business trip in
favor of a ridiculous honeymoon in Norway—why Norway of all places?—
that certain doubts began to assail her; but the villa in Grunewald soon
dissipated them, and so on, not very interesting recollections. (pp. 65-66)

The wealth of parodistic detail [4] in the genealogy of the first
four sentences is a mark of the mature Nabokov. The deceptive
shifts in focus are also typical of the more experienced writer—
thus one is led from "Papa" to the fat purser on a second-rate
liner. In just a few lines Nabokov creates a crowd of peripheral
characters that even Gogol would ogle—two stepmothers, the
fat purser, a handsome cousin, a fiddler, and just for fun, an incinerated monkey.

The ground for Martha's demise is more carefully prepared
in the revision. In the Russian her bad heart is mentioned only
at the very end—which makes it appear a lazy author decided
only then to kill off his Anna. Three new passages provide the
proper preparation:

[The great Dr. Hertz had told her a couple of years before that her
cardiogram showed a remarkable, not necessarily dangerous, but certainly
incurable abnormality which he had seen only in one other woman, a
Hohenzollern, who was still alive at forty, and] now it seemed to Martha
. . . (p. 198)

What could she care [about neuralgia, bronchitis, irregular heart beat?]
(p. 249)

[A pain, of another musical tone than intercostal neuralgia or that strange
ache which a great cardiologist had told her came from a "shadow behind
the heart" entered . . .] (p. 251)

The sections describing her delirium at the dance (pp. 252-53) and her delirium in bed (pp. 266-67) are completely rewritten and expanded.

Like Martha, Franz is a considerably more interesting and carefully drawn character in the new version. Also like Martha, he is not very attractive. We learn that he enjoyed kicking his mother's dog (p. 30) and that he shot stray cats for fun (p. 51). Narrative comment on his cowardice and emotional cretinism is interpolated:

[A high-strung and abject coward in matters of feeling (and such cowards are doubly wretched since they lucidly perceive their cowardice and fear it), he could not help cringing when,] with a banging of doors [in a dramatic draft,] Martha and Dreyer entered . . . (p. 105)

But [emotional energy had never been his forte and] he said nothing . . . (p. 214)

Franz's original fascination with Martha is made more explicit, and the whole affair between them is foreshadowed by additions to the first chapter. The descriptions of her reflect his reverence:

. . . he glimpsed the swell of her tense tongue in the red penumbra of her mouth and the flash of her teeth [before her hand shot up to her mouth to stop her soul from escaping . . .] (p. 11)

During his days with the Dreyers, Franz is continually concerned with external appearances; the first two paragraphs on page 80 are added to describe his real and his psychological underwear. Franz's biography, like Martha's, is fuller and more suggestive. Repeatedly, details of his childhood, unpleasant reminiscences of his mother, are added and expanded:

[How strange to recall the cluttered attic of his youth! His mother at the Singer machine while he tried to sleep. How could he have endured it so long?] (p. 55)

She questioned him about his childhood, his mother, [a dull theme,] his native town, [an even duller one.] (p. 83)

He talked about his school, about the dust and the boredom, [about his mother's indigestible pies,] and about the butcher . . . (p. 83)

[He imagined his mother's fat florid face and dyed hair]. . . . His love for his mother was [never very deep but even so it was] his first unhappy love, [or rather he regarded her as a rough draft . . .] (pp. 93-94)

—the rest of this paragraph is an interpolation. Other details on this page (94), such as the kissing of Christina, are also new. But perhaps the most intriguing of the biographical interpolations is the addition of an allusion to Franz's life *after* Martha— a sudden shift which occurs only once in the novel, an unexpected view of the future:

In those days [—which as a very old and very sick man, guilty of worse sins than avunculicide, he remembered with a grin of contempt—] young Franz was oblivious to the corrosive probity of his pleasant daydreams about Dreyer's dropping dead. (p. 138)

Nabokov leaves us to puzzle over what "worse sins" his knave might commit.

Although Dreyer is more poetic, he changes less in translation than do the other members of Nabokov's courtly triangle. But in his case, too, the focus is sharper, the detail more telling. In Sirin's novel Dreyer's biography is less detailed, his blindness to the plots of his wife less pathological, and his own love affairs more vaguely suggested. For example, Dreyer's Christmas conversation with Martha (from "as he vomited in the deserted square" to "hopelessly bad stenographers, both of them," p. 147) is new in the English. Here it is typical of Nabokov that what is suggested as a monstrous joke—Dreyer should try Ida and Isolda—turns out to be a jolly past accomplishment. Ida and Isolda are unnamed and unmade in the Russian variant.

Dreyer's boredom and dissatisfaction with the mundane career he has made is more convincingly explained in another new passage:

Secretly he realized that he was a businessman by accident and that *his* fantasies were not salable. [His father had wanted to be an actor, had been a make-up man in a traveling circus, had tried to design theatrical scenery, wonderful velvet costumes, and had ended as a moderately successful

tailor. In his boyhood Kurt had wanted to be an artist—any kind of artist—but instead had spent many dull years working in his father's shop. The greatest artistic satisfaction he ever derived was from his commercial ventures during the inflation. But he knew quite well that he would appreciate even more other arts, other inventions.] What prevented him from seeing the world? He had the means—but there was some fatal veil between him and every dream that beckoned to him. [He was a bachelor with a beautiful marble wife, a passionate hobbyist without anything to collect, an explorer not knowing on what mountain to die, a voracious reader of unmemorable books, a happy and healthy failure. Instead of arts and adventures, he meanly contented himself with a suburban villa, with a humdrum vacation at a Baltic resort—and even that thrilled him as the smell of a cheap circus used to intoxicate his gentle bumbling father.

The little trip to Pomerania Bay was in fact proving to be quite a boon for everybody concerned, including the god of chance (Cazelty or Sluch, or whatever his real name was), once you imagined that god in the role of a novelist or a playwright, as Goldemar had in his more famous work.] Martha was getting ready for the seaside . . . (pp. 223-24)

Goldemar (Vladimir?) is the author of *King, Queen, Knave*—his god chance is a mere rumor ("sluch" is the Russian for "rumor").

Dreyer's harshly accurate opinions of others are also sharpened in the English. Thus, he always addresses Franz "whom he had filed away in his mind long ago under 'cretin' with cross references to 'milksop' and *'sympathisch'* " (p. 169) with absentminded geniality. Such opinions are formed in a process which Nabokov explains in detail. Comparison of the two versions shows how the mature Nabokov makes up for his youthful "haste of thought" and "sloth of word":

The observant, sharp-eyed Dreyer would cease looking sharply after between him and the object he was examining, the image of that object seen by him was formed, an image based on the first sharp observation. After he had grasped the new object with one glance and correctly evaluated its peculiarities, he no longer thought about the fact that the object might change of its own accord, assume unforeseen characteristics, and no longer correspond to the conception of it which he had formed. Thus, from the first day of acquaintance he had thought of Franz as an amusing provincial nephew . . . (p. 104)

Luckily for Franz, his observant uncle's interest in any object, animated or not, whose distinctive features he had immediately grasped, gloated over and filed away, would wane with its every subsequent reappearance. The bright perception became the habitual abstraction. Natures like his spend enough energy in tackling with all the weapons and vessels of the mind the enforced impressions of existence to be grateful for the neutral film of familiarity that soon forms between the newness and its consumer. It was too boring to think that the object might change of its own accord and assume unforeseen characteristics. That would mean having to enjoy it again, and he was no longer young. He had appreciated the poor bloke's simplicity and vulgarity almost at their first anonymous rendezvous in the train. Thenceforth, from the first moment of actual acquaintance, he had thought of Franz as of an amusing coincidence in human form: the form was that of a timid provincial nephew with a banal mind and limited ambitions. (p. 106)

The comparison with which Nabokov ends this paragraph is also slightly altered: "Thus an [experienced] artist sees only that which is in keeping with his initial concept" (p. 106). This particular *artistic* ability is, however, a human shortcoming. And Dreyer's lack of humanity is underscored in new remarks made by his former mistress, Erica. For a week after their meeting Dreyer is overcome by a "tender melancholy" and when he recalls her indictment of him as an egotist who is "touched not by the blind man but by his dog" (p. 235) he is strangely uneasy:

When he went to bed that night he could not go to sleep [—an unusual occurrence.] (p. 235)

This is one of the few times that Dreyer has any normal "human" doubts. For the most part he is a frustrated artist who thinks: ". . . every instant all this around me laughs, gleams, begs to be looked at, to be loved. The world stands like a dog pleading to be played with" (p. 177).

A pungent and gory category of additions to *KQKn* is formed by what can be called, hesitantly, "dirty details." The English version of the novel is more frankly and grotesquely ribald than its Russian draft. While it is true that death and murder are important themes, it sometimes seems that scatology precedes eschatology. Nabokov has interpolated so many toilets that the novel could be called "Royal Flush" as well as "Bright Brute." Apart from the uretic additions, Nabokov also intermixes explicit references to homosexuality (p. 93, etc.), simultaneous incest (Ida and Isolda), masturbation (p. 13, pp. 83-84), menstruation (p. 86, p. 133), prophylactics (pp. 97-98), a douche bag handed down from generation to generation (p. 102, p. 220, pp. 225ff.), and suggestions of necrophilia (p. 192). The profusion of new private parts calls to mind a madman merrily decorating a Christmas tree (see p. 147) with male genitalia (see "Greedy," p. 103). A few examples should suffice (the Russian version is given first):

Martha came out of the bathroom in an orange peignoir.
Martha came out of the bathroom stark naked. (p. 158)

They were no longer sitting on the couch . . .
They were no longer coupling on the couch . . . (p. 152)

. . . they grew used to . . . the disapproving creaks it emitted when they sat down on it . . .
. . . they grew used to . . . the disapproving creaks it emitted in rhythm to their ebullient love-making . . . (p. 121)

. . . it seemed strange to her that Dreyer was still alive . . .
. . . it seemed strange to her that Dreyer had not been destroyed by her lover's thrusts . . . (p. 200)

In non-sexual subdivisions of this category, one might put the new enthusiastic allusions to mucus (p. 4, p. 157), the incinerated monkey, and Martha's amusing amputee.[5]

In all of these descriptions Nabokov's gusto instills disgust—which, along with humor, is presumably his goal. The seduction section in Chapter Five is perhaps the best example. The entire scene (pp. 96-97) has been rewritten, the long passage beginning "He made for the door" and ending "His vocabulary was even more primitive" being essentially an interpolation. It is at once a boisterous and a brutal scene. If one compares it to the initial adulteries in *Madame Bovary* or *Anna Karenina,* one can see quite clearly how much harder Nabokov is on his heroine than were the two earlier moralists. The world of *King, Queen, Knave* is a cold realm of despair and laughter in the light (Franz at the end), a world of black and blue humor.

In Nabokov's reincarnation of *King, Queen, Knave* he makes more insistent use of foreshadowing, false foreshadowing, and repeated motifs. For example, on her wall Martha has a daguerreotype of her grandfather:

. . . a long since deceased coal merchant [who had been suspected of drowning his first wife in a tarn around 1860, but nothing was proved.] (p. 36)

Also in the realm of tonal foreshadowing are such newly added references as the kitchen full of knives and cleavers (p. 134) or the silk lining of Martha's coat which is "as crimson as lips and flayed animals" (p. 95). More pleasant are the sexy strawberries (pp. 2, 3, 11, 16, etc.) of which Franz is reminded by Martha's flicking tongue (p. 11)—the same strawberries for which Dreyer lusted at the station (p. 2), but which he could not get, for fear of meeting his sister Lina (Franz's mother)— in which case he would have been *introduced* to Franz, thus spoiling much of the narrative fun and suspense in the opening chapters.

It is curious that *all* references to the movie house being built near Franz's apartment,[6] all references to Goldemar and his play *King, Queen, Knave,*[7] and all references to the film *King, Queen, Knave* which is to premiere at the movie house [8] are new in the English version of the novel. For example, this passage is an interpolation:

A little farther he . . . saw . . . a tall house . . . its first story was ornamented with a huge picture, advertising the film to be shown on opening night July 15, based on Goldemar's play *King, Queen, Knave* which had been such a hit several years ago. The display consisted of three gigantic transparent-looking playing cards resembling stained-glass windows which

would probably be very effective when lit up at night: the King wore a maroon dressing gown, the Knave a red turtleneck sweater, and the Queen a black bathing suit. (p. 216)

The court cards are our heroes, of course. Martha buys the black bathing suit on page 224, and Franz's turtleneck turns up on pages 250 and 269. The play was a hit "several years" ago when Erica happened to see Dreyer (p. 172), and the movie premiere is timed to follow the last day of the novel. July 15, in keeping with Nabokov's fetish for the fatidic, is the day on which Lermontov was killed in a duel.

However, the purpose of these parallels remains unclear to me. We are told that Dreyer divides into two in Franz's mind, the second Dreyer a purely schematic double—no more than "a stylized playing card, a heraldic design" (p. 177). What does this mean? Some commentators have toyed with the idea that Nabokov's goal was to create a world of cardboard figures, a world where *things* predominate. We are even told *King, Queen, Knave* is a kind of *nouveau roman*. But the sophisticated psychological characterization Nabokov uses, especially in the English version, makes this fashionable claim look ridiculous. Indeed, the heavy reliance on *specified* motivation, "narrated monologue" *(erlebte Rede)*, and interior monologue is not characteristic of the *nouveau roman*. The frequent detailed description of *things* is the only characteristic Nabokov's work has in common with contemporary French novels—and this is a purely superficial resemblance.

As the author notes, many of his changes are designed to surmount youthful sloth of word. There are stylistic changes on virtually every page, some of them quite extensive. This is particularly true of the last six pages, which are completely recast.[9] Except that they are more extensive, these cuts and rewritings resemble those made in Nabokov's revision of *Despair*. Similes are cut: ". . . top hats and black coats like corks on water" (p. 44), ". . . a roly poly creature with a wart-like burdock on her cheek" (p. 7) [changed to "with false teeth"]. Similitudes are added: "She had now thrown the pink shawl over her shoulders and [like a woman in some old-fashioned romance, gazed at him . . .]" (pp. 86-87), "From its threshold he would fire [half a dozen times in quick succession, as they do in American movies]" (p. 179), "Dreyer noisily folded his paper [as if wrapping a bird in it]" (p. 214), "In that very name . . . there was something that excited him [like the romantic names of good wines and bad women]" (p. 13).

Metaphors are interpolated everywhere: ". . . leafing through an old picture magazine and stopping [at the messy death of a riddle]" (p. 110). "[Now she saw that some kind of atrocious dreamland was encroaching upon her charts"] (p. 197). "Martha [accustomed to the fireworks of his face], saw his cropped moustache twitch . . ." (p. 33). The plain "she imagined" becomes "[The magic lantern of fancy slipped a colored slide in]—a long sandy beach [on the Baltic] where they had once been [in 1924] . . ." (p. 211).

Frequently Nabokov manages to retain both precision and alliteration (*blesk stekla* = gleam of glass, p. 23), but often the translation is somewhat messy (as in *jarche i nerazborchivee* = the messier and muddier, p. 36), and—most often—his English is more heavily instrumented than the original:

neposlushnyj i chudakovatyj = **wayward and wacky (p. 41)**

arxittekturnye skladki = **architectonic perfection (p. 77)**

legkim vzmaxom voobrazhenija = **deft dabs of his facile fancy (p. 22)**

istoshnym koldovstvom = **manic magic (p. 63)**

There are many puns added to the English version—particularly puns based on German names such as Wasserschluss (p. 33), Hertz the heart specialist (p. 198), and Schwimmer the gay swimmer (p. 79). There are other new phonetic games as well. "The clock ticked" *(Tikali chasy)* is changed to: "The clock tocked rather than ticked, the tock dicked and docked" (p. 128).

The plays on "Gutter-Perchers" (pp. 117, 207) are new. The appearance of anagrammatic Nabokovs—Mr. Vivian Badlook, Blavdak Vinomori (winedark sea)—is another innovation.[10] And still other names are changed: Grün becomes Willy Wald (green woods), the rowboat changes from "Fairytale of the Sea" *(Morskaja skazka)* to "Lindy" (see pp. 15, 244, 249 and index to *Keys to Lolita*); Ida and Isolda are completely new characters; Sarah Reich, who has her own husband problem (pp. 107, 108, 126, 216, 234), is not named in the Russian.

There are many stylistic features which can be studied more easily by comparing the two versions. Neutral Russian phrases become examples of peculiarly Nabokovian English: "obsolete socks" (instead of "old" or "worn-out," p. 33; in Russian *postarevshie*), "tangible tooth marks" (p. 29, *sledom zubov*), "a plausible street corner" (p. 23, instead of "likely"), or "mnemonic tricks" (p. 33, for *nabljudenija*, meaning simply "observations"). The syntax sometimes suffers from its Russian descent: "He carefully wiped with a special square of cloth his glasses . . ." (p. 16). ". . . she was the wife of the man on whom depended his whole fortune" (p. 27). The narrative tone is also somewhat different in the English version. Narrative exclamations are more common (*Kazalos', teper'*, meaning "It seemed that now" is changed to "Aha!", p. 22), the narrative "our" is more common ("our three holidayers," p. 249, are simply "they" in Russian), and many parenthetical comments—or non-parenthetical ones—are interpolated. For example:

In the cafe [where he presently joined our two farcical schemers,] Martha . . . (p. 234)

Martha, [strictly adhering to every rule of adultery,] pressed the side . . . (p. 115)

In his later works Nabokov loves beauty and beast combinations, proximity of poets and monsters. This is reflected in the style of his novels and can be discovered by comparing early versions to late ones. For example, Franz dreams of accosting a prostitute and (in Russian) "starting a conversation with her" (*razgo-vorit'sja s nej*). In translation this becomes "start a brilliant and brutal conversation" (p. 47). "She was so beautiful" becomes "She was so sinful and beautiful" (p. 159). In Russian Franz becomes simply "tame," in English "by now quite tame and bloodthirsty" (p. 156). Note these additions:

... bouquets of [blood-brown] flowers. (p. 225)

A hollow-diamond ring, filled with [rainbow] venom ... (p. 162)

... how easy to breathe, [to kill, to love.] (p. 212)

The silk lining was crimson, [as crimson as lips and flayed animals, and smelled of heaven.] (p. 95)

For in Nabokov's world, heaven is always in hell, or hell in heaven. Thus, on another level, Lolita is both Eve and Lilith, Ada is from hell, fathered by Demon, but *mère de souvenirs*.

Literary illusions, allusions, and parodies are important in this novel as in all of Nabokov's prose. For example, the generalization, "The first chapter of a journey is always detailed and slow. Its middle hours are drowsy, and the last ones swift" is based on a reversal of a famous Pushkin poem (*Telega zhizni*) which contains a pungent Oedipal obscenity. The remark about houses of exactly the sort that his fellows had (p. 35) is a paraphrase of a well-known moralism in Tolstoy's "The Death of Ivan Ilych," and the caterpillar-crunching gardener (pp. 182, 225) is from Chekhov's "The Black Monk." The Russian, *Veshchi ne ljubili Franca* ("Things didn't like Franz") exactly parallels a famous line from the beginning of Olesha's *Envy* (1927), which Nabokov surely had not read yet. In 1968 he makes it: "Not only animals, but so-called inanimate objects feared and hated Franz" (p. 229). Allusions to *Dead Souls* and *Candida* are added in the new version (Dreyer's reading, in German and English), as is the following passage:

[Not that she experienced any special constraint. She was no Emma, and no Anna. In the course of her conjugal life she had grown accustomed to

grant her favors to her wealthy protector with such skill, with such calcula-
tion, with such efficient habits of physical practice, that she who thought
herself ripe for adultery had long grown ready for harlotry.] (p. 101)

Emma Bovary and Anna Karenina—as Nabokov notes in his
preface. There are so many parallels between these works, especially *Madame Bovary*, and *King, Queen, Knave* that it would be
hard to list them all. The visit to the variety show (in *KQKn*)
where part of *Lucia de Lammermoor* is played mimics a visit
to that same opera by Emma and company. The domestic details related to Franz's love-nest, the slippers Martha brings,
their concern over "our" room are all parodistic versions of
Flaubert (see especially, *Madame Bovary*, Part III, Chapter 5).
There is even a rowboat motif which goes through Flaubert's
novel (Emma enjoys her lover in a bed shaped like a boat)—
this may be the source of Nabokov's inspiration for the rowboat
sequence.

From this rather hasty survey, it should be apparent that the
English *King, Queen, Knave* is in effect a new novel. Nabokov
made some of the same kinds of changes when revising *Despair*,
but on a much smaller scale. Furthermore, the extensive revisions
dealing with characterization in *King, Queen, Knave* are not
paralleled in Nabokov's work on *The Defense, Despair, The
Gift*, or least of all, *Lolita*. If we take into consideration the
example of *King, Queen, Knave* and the generalization with
which I began this essay, it would appear that we should expect
the English versions of *Mashenka* and *Podvig* to be quite different from the Russian originals.

Notes

1. On Nabokov's revision of *Despair* see "From *Otchaianie* to *Despair*,"
Slavic Review, XXVII, 2 (June 1968), 257-67.

2. To make the examples accessible to all readers, I have provided literal
translations of all the quotations from the Russian version (Berlin, 1928)—
using Nabokov's lead wherever possible. Curiously, for most of the novel the
page numbers of the Russian and English editions are almost identical.

3. Hereafter, when quoting, I have put into *brackets* all passages *new* in the
English version: V. Nabokov, *King, Queen, Knave* (New York, 1968). All page
numbers are in parentheses following the quotations.

4. Compare Papa beginning his career as a saddler to Humbert's father in the opening of *Lolita,* or the irrelevant "a lovely woman of gentle birth whom everyone adored" to Gogol's equally irrelevant godmother Belobrushkova "the wife of a police officer, a woman of rare virtues" in the biographical part of "The Overcoat."

5. "That morning [a cripple] walking in front of her had slipped on the bare ice. It was frightfully funny to see [his wooden stump erect while he sprawled on his stupid back]." (p. 126. In Russian this is not a cripple, but a "middle-aged lady."

6. See pages 48, 52, 54, 99, 132, 137, 147, 198, 215-16.

7. See pages 172-75, 216, 224, 261.

8. See pages 216 and 261.

9. Note, for example, the changes in the last paragraph:

> [Franz marched to the open window. Dreyer crossed the road and sat down on a bench under a tree. Franz closed the window. He was now alone.] A woman in the next room, [a miserable tramp whom a commercial traveller had jilted,] heard through the [thin] wall what sounded like several revellers all talking together, and roaring with laughter, [and interrupting one another, and roaring again in a frenzy of young mirth.] (p. 272)

10. In other works Nabokov has scrambled himself as Vivian Darkbloom, Vivian Bloodmark, Vivian Calmbrood, Vivian Damor-Blok, and Baron Klim Avidov.

Anya in Wonderland: Nabokov's Russified Lewis Carroll

SIMON KARLINSKY

In the Russian version of his autobiography, Vladimir Nabokov tells us that he translated *Alice in Wonderland* into Russian during his free-lancing days after returning to Berlin from his studies at Cambridge and that he was paid the sum of five American dollars for the job. In both of the English versions of the autobiography (*Conclusive Evidence* and *Speak, Memory*) he supplies the additional information that five dollars was "quite a sum during the inflation in Germany." [1] The translation, signed with the pen-name Nabokov used during his European period, V. Sirin, was brought out in Berlin in 1923 by an émigré publishing house named after the legendary bird of Russian mythology,

Gamaiun. The slim volume was illustrated with S. Zalshupin's drawings (remote and pseudo-cubistic variations on Tenniel). Unlike earlier and later renditions of Carroll into Russian, it is called *Anya v strane chudes* (*Annie in Wonderland*), instead of the traditional *Alisa v strane chudes*.

Of the two Russian versions that preceded Nabokov's, the best known one was done by the poet Polyxena Soloviova (1867-1924), daughter of a famous historian and sister of the great philosopher Vladimir Soloviov. Her version, signed with *her* pen-name, "Allegro," appeared in 1909. Mlle Soloviova's command of English appears to have been less than perfect; but like all intelligent translators of Alice, she bravely faced the obvious difficulties of conveying in another language Carroll's games with logic, his complex puns and parodistic transformations of familiar nursery rhymes. In her renditions of the verse parodies, on the whole the most successful part of her translation, Polyxena Soloviova resorted to the method also used in the better German and French versions of Carroll.[2] Instead of translating Carroll's parodies of English poems not known to her Russian readers, she would select some appropriate piece of verse that all Russian children would be sure to know and then proceed to use it as the basis for a parody of her own, hopefully similar to Carroll's in intent and effect. In actual practice, however, while Carroll's brilliant parodies mock the flabby and didactic poems taught to English children during the Victorian era, the verses with which Russian children of the early 20th century (and their Soviet counterparts today) would be most familiar were selected fragments from 19th-century Russian classics, mostly Pushkin and Lermontov, endlessly anthologized and traditionally memorized by the Russians practically since their infancy.

Thus, to translate the very first parodied poem in the book, "How doth the little crocodile/Improve his shining tail" (a parody of Isaac Watts's "How doth the little busy bee/Improve each shining hour"), Polyxena Soloviova made an imaginative adaptation of a fragment from Pushkin's "The Gypsies" about "God's little bird" who "knows neither care nor work"[3] (very popular with Russian children), ingeniously substituting "God's little crocodile" for Pushkin's original bird. Equally imaginative, but less successfully brought off, are her substitutions of a passage pertaining to Peter the Great from Pushkin's "Poltava" for "You are old, Father William," and of Fyodor Glinka's song about the dashing troika which rushes along the frozen river Volga in the winter for the Lobster Quadrille ("Here comes the dashing little fish,/A whiting, [rushing] over the gravel, toward the waves").

In his interesting book on the art of translating poetry, Efim Etkind, the foremost Soviet theoretician in that field, chides Polyxena Soloviova for introducing native Russian material into Lewis Carroll [4] (not realizing, obviously, that she was following a time-honored, internationally accepted practice). While his strictures, taken as a whole, seem a bit pedantic, Etkind does score one valid point. Since in Soloviova's version, Alice lives and goes to school in England, she is not likely to have heard of the Pushkin (to say nothing of Fyodor Glinka) originals used as the basis for the verse parodies; thus, the humor of these adaptations becomes a bit meaningless, especially within the framework of Lewis Carroll's kind of strict internal logic.

Vladimir Nabokov (who must have been familiar with Soloviova's translation, for he used the same Pushkin fragment she did as the basis for the crocodile poem) might have had an objection in mind similar to the one Etkind was to make four decades later. While the Nabokov translation is for the most part scrupulously exact, he subjected the Carroll masterpiece to a procedure no other Russian translator of the work had ever tried: naturalization. The name Alisa has a decidedly foreign sound in Russian, so he renamed the little heroine Anya, the usual affectionate diminutive of Anna. Her friends Ada and Mabel are here Ada and Asya (some exegete should be able to make *something* of this); the French-speaking Mouse did not come over with William the Conqueror, as in Carroll, but was left behind during Napoleon's retreat from Moscow. The White Rabbit's door plate

W. RABBIT now reads NOBLEMAN KROLIK TRUSIKOV (i.e., Rabbit, son of Rabbit), his maidservant Mary Ann is Masha, his retainers Pat and Bill speak a Russian peasant dialect and are named Petka and Yashka (since Bill is a lizard, the choice of name provides a punning dividend on the Russian word for that reptile, *yashcheritsa*). In addition, the address for sending mail to the gigantic Alice's right leg acquires a pre-revolutionary Russian aspect and the "dry" history passage about William the Conqueror recited by the Mouse just before the Caucus Race is replaced by a quotation from some 19th-century history text about Vladimir Monomakh's successors to the Kievan throne.

This almost exhausts the list of changes made by Nabokov in order to move the locale to Russia. The Duchess and the Queen, in this new context, acquire an air of foreign, non-Russian royalty, imported from some translated fairy tale. Yet, by this modest, on the whole non-emphatic geographical change, Nabokov gains the uncontested right to exploit Russian proverbs, puns and poets in order to devise full-blown equivalents of Lewis Carroll's verbal and parodistic riches.

Mikhail Lermontov, a poet much memorized in Russian schools, provides the point of departure for several of the verse parodies. His most famous poem, "The Cossack Lullaby," is cleverly and rather sadistically distorted in the equivalent of the Duchess' "Speak roughly to your little boy" ("Howl, my beautiful baby/And if you sneeze, I'll slap you!"); Lermontov's "Borodino" provides the point of departure for "You are old, Father William" ("Tell me, uncle, is it for nothing/that they consider you so very old?"); and the beginning of still another Lermontov poem, "There are words whose meaning/Is obscure or insignificant . . . ," torn out of the philosophical context of the original, provides an unexpectedly apt replacement for the Duchess' moral maxim "Take care of the sense, and the sounds will take care of themselves." The opening line of Pushkin's "The Song of the Vatic Oleg" is stunningly (and punningly) transformed into the first line of " 'Tis the voice of the Lobster," while a popular ditty about a

313

Siskin getting drunk in the Fontanka district of Saint Petersburg is carefully and thoroughly transformed into "Twinkle, twinkle, little bat!"[5] As could have been expected, Nabokov has a field day with the Griffon's and the Mock Turtle's web of puns. In some cases, the double and triple levels of meaning achieved (Nabokov's equivalent of "uglification," for example) are richer and more unexpected than the Carroll originals.[6]

Beyond his success with parodies and puns, Nabokov's version of Carroll is remarkable for its beautifully caught and conveyed tone and diction of the original. If it is not the perfect translation it could have been, it is because it does contain pages not equal in imagination and fidelity to what Nabokov had done in the best and most successful passages. *Anya in Wonderland,* we must remember, was translated by a very young man, working for money and possibly trying to meet a deadline. Still, with a few subsequent revisions, the book could have easily become one of the finest translations of *Alice* into any language. Even without these revisions, it is by far the best one that exists in Russian. And yet, apart from a few copies in the largest libraries of the Western world, it is also one of the least available versions of *Alice.*

There was something of a hiatus in publications of Lewis Carroll in the Soviet Union in the 1920's and -30's (connected, possibly, with the anti-fantasy trend in Soviet elementary education at that time). From 1946 on, however, there have been at least five editions of a translation by one Aleksandr Olenich-Gnenenko, originally published in Rostov and later taken up by the Moscow publishing houses.[7] This is an extremely clumsy translation (Alice's realization of her *faux pas* with the Mouse—"Oh, dear!"—is understood to mean "Oh, my darling!" and the Pigeon's disbelieving "A likely story indeed!" is read to mean "A fine predicament indeed!"), which waters down the puns and disregards the parodistic implications of the verses.[8] Yet, this is the *Alice* that Soviet children have been reading in the last two decades (with politically slanted introductions which tell them that Carroll's book exposes the social inequities and absurdities of

English life and that at the end of the book Alice acquires a new dream: "to see her country changed for the better and freed from all the things that astounded her in that 'Wonderland' " [9]).

Lewis Carroll's art, like that of Chekhov, can apparently survive a great deal of harsh treatment at the hands of inept translators and still convey something of its essence to the reader. For the near future, Olenich-Gnenenko's awkward, misshapen *Alisa* seems fated to remain the standard *Alice* in Russian, while Nabokov's warm and witty *Anya* stays in exile on foreign bookshelves. Were she allowed to return to the country of her spiritual origin, *Anya* could easily supersede the ungainly incumbent. At present, such a return appears a dream, as remote and curious as those of Carroll's Alice.

Notes

1. *Speak, Memory,* New York, 1966, p. 283.
2. On different approaches to translating *Alice in Wonderland,* see Warren Weaver, *Alice in Many Tongues,* Madison, 1964.
3. This fragment from Pushkin's verse tale achieved an almost independent existence as a separate nursery rhyme. On speculations about its possible derivation from Chateaubriand's *Le génie du Christianisme,* see my article "Pushkin, Chateaubriand and the Romantic Pose," *California Slavic Studies,* II, 96-107.
4. E. Etkind, *Poeziia i perevod,* Leningrad, 1963, pp. 346-51. Etkind discusses the translations of Carroll's verse parodies into Russian by Polyxena Soloviova, Aleksandr Olenich-Gnenenko, and Samuil Marshak. Nabokov's translation, being the work of an émigré, is either not known to Etkind or deliberately ignored.
5. This particular transformation is the subject of a rather lame exegesis in Weaver, *op. cit.,* pp. 90-91. Weaver's help in matters Russian was not all it should have been. His preposterous reconstruction of the Russian subtitle of the 1879 edition of *Alice* as *A Dream in the Kingdom of a Maid* (p. 61) is based on a distorted entry in Sotheby's catalogue that read "Son v tsarsve deva." A moment's thought is all that it takes to see that this is a misprint for "Son v tsarstve detstva," i.e., "A Dream in the Realm of Childhood." Nabokov's pen name, Weaver tells us, was either V. Sirin or B. Sirina, depending on the transliteration used.
6. Nabokov's equivalent of "reeling and writhing," for example. He switches around the initial syllables of the Russian verbs for "to read" and "to write," *chitat'* and *pisat',* to obtain *chesat'* and *pitat',* i.e., "to scratch" (or "to comb") and "to feed." The second half of Nabokov's Russian pun was later combined with its original in Carroll to produce "feeding upon you, writhing against you" (*Ada* p. 118).
7. See Weaver, pp. 130-33, for publication data. The translator's name is systematically cited in the genitive case.
8. Etkind, *loc. cit.,* makes a devastating case against Olenich-Gnenenko's clumsy and at times unpronounceable renditions of Lewish Carroll's verse.
9. V. Vazdaev, introduction to *Alisa v strane chudes,* translated by Aleksandr Olenich-Gnenenko, Khabarovsk, 1961.

The cypress veil
W. B. SCOTT

> Sit farther and make room for thine own fame,
> Where just desert enrols thy honored name,
> The Good Interpreter. Some in this task
> Take off the cypress veil, but leave a mask,
> Changing the Latin, but do more obscure
> That sense in English which was bright and pure.
>
> > ANDREW MARVELL, "To His Worthy Friend
> > Doctor Witty, Upon His Translation of
> > the 'Popular Errors.'"

> ". . . a baldheaded suntanned professor in a Hawaiian shirt
> sat at a round table reading with an ironic expression on his
> face a Russian book." PALE FIRE, Commentary on line 949.

> ". . . an old, happy, healthy, heterosexual Russian, a writer in
> exile, sans fame, sans future, sans audience, sans anything but
> his art." PALE FIRE, Commentary on line 1000.

Alexander Pushkin (1799-1837) wrote his "novel in verse,"
Eugene Onegin, during the 1820's, and completed it early in the
1830's. The eight chapters of the final text first appeared separately; the first complete edition was that of 1833. In 1837, a

This article first appeared in the Winter 1965 issue of *TriQuarterly*. It is
reprinted here with occasional unsignaled changes in the text and the notes,
and with additions to the notes signaled by a double asterisk **.

very short time before Pushkin was fatally wounded in a duel, the "third edition" (second complete edition) was published at Saint Petersburg. (This edition is photographically reproduced in volume four of Professor Nabokov's work discussed below.) Since that time there have been many more Russian editions, both Tsarist and Soviet, as well as editions in Russian published abroad, and translations in various languages.

Eugene Onegin has been seven times fully translated in English; three of these translations (those by Arndt, Kayden, and Nabokov) have appeared in recent years.[1] Two of them [2] attempt to reproduce Pushkin's tricky fourteen-line iambic-tetrameter stanza, Professor Arndt going so far, or so far out, as to keep the exact rhyme scheme and the exact alternation of masculine and feminine rhymes. Kayden, while regularly using certain rhymes, is a bit more relaxed.[3] Professor Nabokov, "a professed literalist," aims at a line-by-line rendering, with careful attention to the meaning and function of every word, and with a hint of the iambic rhythm, but without the rhymes; this for reasons which he vigorously states and restates. He is scornful of what he calls "the disastrous versions of *E O* in English doggerel," [4] and men-

1. To these might be added the prose translation of eighty-nine stanzas (selected from the 400-odd stanzas of the poem) in the Pushkin volume (edited by John Fennell, 1964) of the "Penguin Poets"—that useful paperback series which combines texts in the original languages with footnote translations—plain prose trots for the benefit of those of us who have forgotten too much or never known enough.

2. Walter Arndt's (a Dutton Paperback, New York, copyright 1963), and Eugene M. Kayden's (Antioch Press, Yellow Springs, Ohio, 1964).

3. Pushkin's unvarying rhyme scheme is: a B a B c c D D e F F e G G (lower-case indicates feminine rhymes, upper case masculine). Kayden eases off to: a b c b d e f d g h i h j j; he does not worry about the masculine and feminine rhymes.

4. See especially his note (III. 183) to stanzas 17 and 18 of chapter eight. In his Foreword to volume two (II. 3-4) Professor Nabokov lists the "four 'English,' 'metrical' translations mentioned in my notes and unfortunately available to students. . . ." These are by Lt.-Col. Henry Spalding (London, 1881); Babette Deutsch (New York, 1936 and 1943); Oliver Elton (London, 1937); Dorothea Prall Radin and George Z. Patrick (Berkeley, 1937). "Even worse than these," Professor Nabokov adds, "is a new version, full of omissions and blunders, by Walter Arndt . . . which reached me after this Commentary was in press, and too late to be subjected to detailed comment." Professor Nabokov finally had his chance to make this detailed comment, in *The New York Review of Books* for April 30, 1964 ("On Translating Pushkin / Pounding the Clavichord," pages 14 and 15). It is a savagely disparaging as well as detailed comment, and one's heart almost goes out to Professor Arndt, who is allowed a

tions (II. 257) his own, "first and sinful, attempt at rendering *E O* in rhyme."

Of these recent works the most important by far is this in four

---

reply ("Goading the Pony") on page 16 of the same issue—a reply in the outraged and bitter tone of a man who has just been set upon in an alley, and who, after staggering to his feet amidst the upset garbage cans, old fish-heads, and broken bottles, lurches about throwing a few game shadow punches. Professor Nabokov is then given a couple of stickfuls of type in which to have *his* final say. (When will *The New York Review of Books* publish an issue that is nothing *but* replies, counter-replies, counter-counter-replies, and so on, all springing from a single review?)

** *Some later developments:* Professor Arndt's translation was re-issued as a *"Second Printing, Revised."* In the Preface to this revised printing he added an imposing list of names of "friends and senior colleagues" to whom he owed "a debt of gratitude for helpful comments." He added also, mildly, that "several emendations were suggested by Vladimir Nabokov's criticism at various times."

In *TriQuarterly* Number 8 (Winter 1967), Professor Arndt returned to a tougher stance in the notes to his translation of part of *Faust*. Here he takes issue, not sparing the acid, with Professor Nabokov's ideas about translating verse; there is a passing swipe at "a wax museum piece like Nabokov's *Onegin*, which has its own gruesome charm." In still another issue of *TriQuarterly*—whew!—(Number 13, Spring 1969) he published a sizable fragment of his translation of Pushkin's *The Bronze Horseman;* it would probably not please Professor Nabokov. But in the notes there is no attempt to warm over the old feud.

After the appearance of many reviews pro and con his *Onegin,* Professor Nabokov published a "Reply to My Critics" in *Encounter* for February 1966. Although he gives the back of his hand to such as Robert Lowell (a back of the hand which flashes again in *Ada*), he saves his biggest gun for old friend Edmund Wilson and that critic's lengthy piece on the *Onegin* in *The New York Review of Books* (July 15, 1965). There is no room, even in this note, to summarize Professor Nabokov's counterblast, which deserves the attention of every thoughtful student of polemic prose. It is enough to say that certain MLA editors would experience a gratifying shock of recognition at Professor Nabokov's characterization of Mr. Wilson's tone as a "mixture of pompous aplomb and peevish ignorance." Much of what Professor Nabokov had to say about Mr. Wilson in his "Reply" (including this phrase) had first appeared several months earlier in an exchange of letters in *The New York Review of Books* (August 26, 1965)—a letter from Professor Nabokov about Mr. Wilson's review; the canonical reply to this letter from Mr. Wilson; letters from half a dozen other people, the most amusing of them from Stephen P. Jones of Noank, Connecticut, suggesting that Mr. Wilson's article had in fact been written by Professor Nabokov "as an appendix to *Pale Fire*." But the flawless jewel of this exchange is this by Mr. Wilson: "I am glad to be enlightened about *stuss,* a word which is not included in the *O.E.D.* (I never use Webster). . . ."

(In counterattacking Mr. Wilson Professor Nabokov had defended the use in his translation of certain rare or curious words, among them "stuss" [the card game]—and also "dit" (for "ditty") and "mollitude." These last two words turn up again (and "stuss" might too, in another careful sweep of the book) in grandly-catch-all *Ada,* along with many other long-time Nabokovian motifs, tics, tricks, games, gimmicks, jokes, loves, hates—"dit" on page 412, "mollitude" on pp. 353 and 473.)

volumes [5] by Professor V. V. Nabokov (1899–   ), the well-known lepidopterist [6] and (self-styled) nonmammalogical taxonomist (III. 231).[7] The four volumes, beautifully printed and

5. *Eugene Onegin* / A NOVEL IN VERSE BY *Aleksandr Pushkin* / TRANSLATED FROM THE RUSSIAN WITH / A COMMENTARY . . . Bollingen Series LXXII, Pantheon Books, Bollingen Foundation, New York, 1964. Volume one contains a Foreword, an elaborate Introduction, and the text of the translation. Volume two contains the Commentary on chapters one through five. (Professor Nabokov translates and comments on not only the published text but numerous rejected variants.) Volume three contains the Commentary on chapters six through eight, plus a Commentary on the fragments of "Onegin's Journey;" which are usually published with the poem, plus a reconstitution of and Commentary on the so-called "Chapter Ten." This volume also contains two Appendixes—the first a lengthy biography (highly speculative) of Pushkin's maternal great-grandfather, the "African" Abram Gannibal (that is, Hannibal—the Russian custom of trans-literating Roman and German "h" as "g" has produced over the years such confections as Goratsi [Horace], Geyne [Heine], Genri [Henry], Gitler, Garry Gopkins, Gumbert Gumbert, and Garrison Gayford). The second Appendix is a series of elaborate "Notes on Prosody," with particular attention to the iambic tetrameters of *Onegin*. The Russian tetrameter, says Professor Nabokov (III, 497), "is a solid, polished, disciplined thing, with rich concentrated meaning and lofty melody fused in an organic entity: it has said in Russian what the pentameter has said in English, and the hexameter in French. Now, on the other hand, the English iambic tetrameter is a hesitating, loose, capricious form. . . ." Volume four has an excellent Index, plus the handsome photographic reproduction (mentioned above) of the 1837 *"editio optima."* At the beginning of each of the first three volumes Professor Nabokov publishes his "Method of Trans-literation," a note on the Old-Style calendar, and a list of bibliographical abbre-viations and symbols.
  ** Its author's own translation of *Lolita* into Russian has appeared since this note was first published (Phaedra Publishers, New York, 1967). In it Gumbert Gumbert figures conspicuously.
  6. Author of *Neartic Members of the Genus Lycaeides Hubner* (1949). He has also published a study of Gogol (1944), which in this present work he characterizes as "a rather frivolous little book with a nightmare index (for which I am not responsible) . . ."; volumes of personal reminiscence, poems and short stories; and novels in Russian (subsequently translated). Professor Nabokov reminds his reader, on the rear flap of the dust-jacket of each volume, that he is "also the author of several novels in English"—these novels are not named, but this is an allusion, perhaps, to such works as *Lolita* (Paris, 1955; New York, 1958) and *Pale Fire* (1962).
  7. "Taxonomy" and related words are favorite words, perhaps key words, with Professor Nabokov, whose precise classificatory turn of mind and love of exact detail are admirably reflected throughout this work, as they are celebrated in a poem of his called "Discovery" (1943), where he recounts his finding "in a legendary land / all rocks and lavender and tufted grass" a kind of butterfly "new to science":

> I found it, and I named it, being versed
> in taxonomic Latin; thus became
> godfather to an insect and its first
> describer—and I want no other fame.

In his note to chapter seven, stanza 15, line two—a line which involves "a cockchafer, a scarabaeoid beetle"—he writes, "why Miss [Babette] Deutsch bound, easy to hold and to read, cost, boxed, $18.50. This is a lot of money, but the books should be more than worth it to

(a) serious students of Russian;

(b) frivolous students of Russian—i.e., those (the writer of these comments, for instance) who have let a one-time acquaintance with the language shamefully slide, and whom Professor Nabokov drives back to the text;

(c) amateurs of learned commentaries, whether or not they know any Russian. Professor Nabokov's hundreds of pages of "casual notes" (his phrase, III. 183) are packed with information, bibliographical, linguistic, literary, prosodic, biographical, autobiographical, historical, natural-historical, geographical, culinary, gustatory,[8] sartorial, etc., all aimed at making clearer and richer our understanding of Pushkin, but also of considerable interest on its own account. In his Commentary (III. 43 ff) on the foolish-tragic duel (chapter six) in which Onegin kills his friend Lenski, Professor Nabokov treats his reader to a detailed and fascinating discussion of "the classical duel *à volonté* of the French code," then goes on to a full account of the duel in which Pushkin suffered his own fatal wound (January 27, 1837). There are similarly interesting excursions, long or short, into such matters (among many) as "the banking game" (i.e., faro), the Wandering Jew, children's games: "The Scottish and English barla-breikis (barley-bracks, barlibrakes, barleybreaks, with 'barley' meaning a cry of truce) does not differ essentially from the Russian *gorelki,* both being country games of tig, tag, or

---

should think fit to transform a coleopterous insect into an orthopterous one ('One heard the crickets' slender choir') is incomprehensible. . . ." (The exiled royal professor-narrator-commentator of *Pale Fire* tells how he "descended by parachute from a chartered plane . . . near Baltimore, whose oriole is not an oriole." [Commentary on line 691.]) According to *The Encyclopaedia Britannica* (1957), "oriole" is "the name applied in Europe to the members of the family *Oriolidae.* The golden oriole *(Oriolus oriolus)* is an occasional spring visitor to the British Islands, but has rarely bred there. . . . The name is applied in America to the *Icteridae* family."

8. "The European beefsteak used to be a small, thick, dark, ruddy, juicy, soft, special cut of tenderloin steak, with a generous edge of amber fat on the knifeside. It had little, if anything, in common with our American 'steaks'—the tasteless meat of restless cattle. The nearest approach to it is a *filet mignon.*" (II. 149) *"Baranki,* 'bangle buns,' are known commercially in the U. S. as 'bagels' (through the Yiddish)." (III. 274)

tick," the color crimson (an excellent note), the varieties of romanticism (II. 32 ff—an impressive taxonomic exercise), the Decembrist movement, botanical fine points,[9] and so on. All this

9. Professor Nabokov is unfailingly strict (see his comment, cited above [footnote 7] on Miss Deutsch's crickets) with those who, out of ignorance or sloppiness, miss the precise meanings of natural-historical terms. An elaborate note (II. 324 ff) on the berry called *brusnika* in Russian (and "lingonberry" by Professor Nabokov in his translation) informs us that dictionaries, "and the harmful drudges who use them to translate Russian authors, confuse the lingonberry with its blue-fruit ally, *Vaccinium myrtillus* Linn. . . ." These harmful drudges turn up again in an even longer note (III. 11 ff) on (Russian) *cheryomuha,* "the racemose old-world bird cherry." This racemose bird cherry lacks such a specific English designation . . . as would be neither pedantic nor as irresponsible as the nonsense names that harmful drudges carefully transport from one Russian-English dictionary to another." In the detailed comment on Arndt's translation mentioned above (footnote 4) Professor Nabokov once more trots out his indispensable switch on Dr. Johnson's famous lexicographical joke: ". . . the harmful drudges who compile Russian-English dictionaries have at least, under *cheryomuha,* 'black alder' i.e. 'alder buckthorn,' which is wrong, but not so wrong as Arndt's [alder]." Can this sort of thing also be an echo of that unending if largely subsurface war which rages in modern-language departments between the Natives and the Foreigners?—to the extent that *anything* can be said to *rage* in modern-language departments (the Natives in this case being foreigners, and the Foreigners natives). In *Pale Fire* (commentary on line 949) the Zemblan gunman, Gradus, on his way to New Wye aboard "the small and uncomfortable plane flying into the sun . . . found himself wedged among several belated delegates to the New Wye Linguistic Conference, all of them lapel-labelled, and representing the same foreign language, but none being able to speak it, so that conversation was conducted . . . in rather ordinary Anglo-American." (If, on the contrary, Gradus [or Professor Nabokov] had entered a hotel elevator during a convention of the Modern Language Association he might have found himself wedged among many rather small-sized people chattering animatedly in Spanish.) Professor Nabokov himself appears admirably as well as enviably at home not only in Russian and English, but in French and (presumably) German. Indeed, one of the most important contributions of his Commentary is to make unmistakably clear the debt of Pushkin and other Russians of his time to French poets and French translators, and to point out the numerous gallicisms in the Russian of *Onegin.* ". . . in Pushkin's day Russian writers knew the literatures of England, Germany, and Italy, as well as the works of the ancients, not from original texts but from the stupendous exertions of French paraphrasts. . . . The gentleman author, the St. Petersburg fashionable, the ennuied hussar, the civilized squire, the provincial miss in her linden-shaded château of painted wood—all read Shakespeare and Sterne, Richardson and Scott, Moore and Byron, as well as the German novelists (Goethe, August Lafontaine) and Italian romancers (Ariosto, Tasso), in French versions, and French versions only." (II. 158) One can only admire, without really envying, the prodigious reading in usually inferior, vapidly conventional French literature of the 17th, 18th, and early 19th centuries to which Professor Nabokov's task condemned him.

** Professor Arndt's "revised printing" clings (page 142) to the alders and acacias (these acacias setting up the rhyme "Horatius" mentioned below in note 16).

As one gets to know it better, Professor Nabokov's Commentary seems even richer, even more fun to ramble in; for other reflections on its excellences see makes much better as well as much more instructive reading than ninety-five percent of the novels [10] (including some of Professor Nabokov's own) and ninety-nine percent of the literary criticism that one somehow gets mixed up with.

(d) students of prosody (maybe). Professor Nabokov is fas-

Professor Appel elsewhere in this issue. The long discussion (III. 9-13), mentioned earlier in this note, of the *cheryomuha* or racemose old-world bird cherry is a good case in point, although it begins rather sadly: "Among some fifty college students whom I once happened to ask (in planned illustration of the incredible ignorance concerning natural objects that characterizes young Americans of today) the name of the tree, an American elm, that they could see through the classroom window, none was able to identify it. . . ." Ada's creator endows his heroine with his own scrupulousness in these matters, and with his taxonomic passion, to the occasional distress of poor Van Veen.

10. One would be mad to even pretend to discover in Professor Nabokov's Commentary anything remotely suggesting the shape of a novel; it is *Pale Fire* which so strikingly blends the theoretically disparate forms of prose fiction and learned commentary. Still, Professor Nabokov is not one to keep villains and fools and some sense of drama entirely out of his notes. In alluding to previous commentators on *Onegin* he is almost casually scornful of D. I. Ciževski (*Evgenij Onegin, Edited with Introduction and Commentary*, Cambridge [Mass.], 1953): "D. Chizhevski's careless compilation . . ." (II. 80); ". . . the comic naivetés in [Ciževski's] running, or rather stumbling, commentary . . ." (II. 221). He saves his biggest bombs for Soviet critics in general ("Sovpushkinists," he calls them [III. 297]), and the Soviet critic N. L. Brodski in particular. Brodski's commentary (*Evgenii Onegin / Roman / A. S. Pushkina . . .* Moskva) runs in its third edition (1950) to 408 pages (including end-notes) of closely packed discussion; although elaborately illustrated, it *is* rather depressing to look at or through. In Professor Nabokov's pages Brodski begins to take on a silly-sinister character not unlike that of the killer Jakob Gradus ("alias Jack Degree, de Grey, d'Argus, Vinogradus, Leningradus, etc.") of *Pale Fire:* he (Brodski) "attempts to prove by the forced cards of specious quotation . . ." (II. 48); he "goes on to rant sociologically . . ." (II. 114); ". . . it is funny to follow uninformed but wary compiler Brodski's maneuvers . . . to circumnavigate the issue without revealing his ignorance" (II. 246); he is "the incredible Brodski" (II. 262); "The incredulous reader is reminded that Brodski's book is 'A Manual for the Use of High-School Teachers'! . . ." (II. 253); he is ". . . that Soviet toady, in his servile eagerness to prove that Pushkin was a solemn admirer of revolution . . ." (III. 363). Other potential fools and villains of the Commentary are only hinted at in passing: they bear such names as Stendhal: his "much overrated *Le Rouge et le noir* . . ." (II. 90); his "paltry literary style" (III. 115); and Dostoevski: ". . . Ann Radcliffe (1764-1823), whose Gothic megrims, in various translations, so influenced Dostoevski—and through him the lady's ghost still troubles the sleep of English, American, and Australian adolescents." (II. 357) "Fyodor Dostoevski, a much overrated, sentimental, and Gothic novelist of the time . . ." (III. 191); "Dostoevski the publicist is one of those megaphones of elephantine platitudes still heard today, the roar of which so ridiculously demotes Shakespeare and Pushkin to the vague level of all the plaster idols of academic tradition, from Cervantes to George Eliot (not to speak of the crumbling Manns and Faulkners of our times)" (III. 193).

cinated, obsessed even, by prosodic minutiae,[11] and may have done a kindly service to his fellow prosodomaniacs who have no Russian by transliterating all citations in Russian, with acute accents to mark the stresses.[12] Having "been forced to invent a simple little terminology of my own" (III. 499) for discussing prosodic matters, he betrays in his Commentary a most sensitive ear for the subtle modulations of Pushkin's iambics, and for all sorts of sound-effects.[13]

Who reads English translations of *Eugene Onegin?* A safe sort of answer would include

(a) the translators themselves *("Exegi monumentum . . .");*

(b) their most loyal friends and relatives;

(c) semi-captive and captive readers—e.g., teachers of and students in Russian literature-in-translation courses;

(d) publishers' editors (?); proofreaders;

11. Like Fyodor in his novel, *The Gift* (New York, 1963), which was first published complete in Russian in New York (1952), although it was written in Europe during the 1930's. See especially pages 172 ff of the Popular Library paperback edition (pages 170 ff of the Russian edition).

12. The reader with some (or a lot of) Russian may be surprised and at first, perhaps, snobbishly vexed or saddened by the absence of the Cyrillic alphabet. But one soon gets used to the transliterations, which follow a clear and sensible system. (In the Index under Khrushchev we are told *"see* Hrushchyov." On seeing it we read, "Hrushchyov/[incorrectly] Krushchev, Nikita Sergeevich . . ." So in *Pale Fire,* commentary to line 949: "Hrushchov [whom they spelled 'Khrushchev']. . . ." Professor Nabokov makes clear his own feelings about the Cyrillic alphabet: "This writer fervently hopes that the Cyrillic alphabet, together with the even more absurd characters of Asian languages, will be completely scrapped some near day." (III. 399. n.) (What makes an alphabet or "Asiatic" characters "absurd"? Professor Nabokov does not say.) He looks forward (III. 492) to ". . . the revised, and romanized, Russian script of the future. . . ."

** In *Ada* there is passing mention of "the old Cyrillitsa, a nightmare alphabet which Dan had never been able to master." (84. It should be added that Dan is not the brightest character in *Ada.*) There is much transliterated Russian in such works as *Pnin, Ada,* etc.

13. With all his devotion to Pushkin and *Onegin,* Professor Nabokov is by no means sentimentally admiring of everything; he can find fault with his poet when he has to. So (for example) he points out in the phrase *vragi Giména* ("enemies of Hymen"; chapter four, stanza 50, line 9) a "cacophonic clash of consonants (*gi-gi*) unlike anything else in *E O.*" (II. 486) Professor Nabokov's own (English) consonants (especially "p") at times do curious dances: ". . . a queer strain of triviality impairing the pounding of its profundities" (II. 236); ". . . in consequence of which the puzzled police pestered Pushkin and arrested the possessors of his MS copies" (II. 483); ". . . the criticism is more applicable to insipid Virgil and his pale pederasts . . ." (II. 55).

Who else? A casual questioning of a few bright, well-read people of my acquaintance has so far turned up no one who has, well, really *read* this work. One knows about it, and/or about the opera ("Chaykovski's silly opera"—Professor Nabokov, II. 333). But somehow or other, one has never got around to reading it, or even to feeling ashamed of not having read it; consequently one does not have to pretend to have read it; in these respects it is in a different category from certain other great works of world literature, which it would be idle to attempt to list here.

Why should this be? Is there something about *Onegin* that makes it lose much of its effect in translation? Is it the lack of an important "myth," a strong story, a powerful idea? Or is such a question merely stuffy? *Onegin* has a story, of course—a story with characters who are part (so we hear) of every Russian's experience—Onegin, Tatiana, "poor Lenski," forgetful Olga [15]— a story with hopeless love (of its heroine for the jaded worldly hero, and at the end—too late—of this hero for the by-now-married heroine), a fatal duel. Yet the interest and charm of *Onegin* are not mainly in its qualities as a story or even in its "psychology," but rather in the wonderful game that Pushkin plays with words and feelings—in its variety of tones, its Byronically chatty digressions, its mixture of tenderness and fun,

14. In his excellent poem, "A Girl in a Library," Randall Jarrell brings in Pushkin's Tatyana Larina as a sort of revery-interlocutor; then proceeds to subtly merge her with Chekhov's Lyubov Ranevskaya.

15. Professor Nabokov, in his discussion (II. 280-81) of Tatiana and Olga as "types" (a notion he does not take very seriously), tells us that in "Soviet literature, the image of Tatiana has now been superseded by that of her sister Olga, now grown buxom, ruddy-cheeked, noisily cheerful. Olga is the good girl of Soviet fiction; she is the one who straightens things out at the factory, discovers sabotage, makes speeches, and radiates perfect health."

** It might be added here, *re* "Chaykovski's silly opera," that Professor Nabokov in his "Reply to My Critics" (see above, additions to note 4) is even more severe on this work: ". . . why should I be forbidden [by Mr. Edmund Wilson?] to consider that Chaykovski's hideous and insulting libretto is not saved by a music whose cloying banalities have pursued me ever since I was a curly-haired boy in a velvet box?"

of transposed poetic commonplace and fresh imagery, of the conventionally Arcadian and the "real," its subtleties of rhythm and sound (so exhaustively analyzed by Professor Nabokov)—all those qualities that in the translations often seem thinned-out to a sort of mild watery borshch-cum-Byron, as the long stanzas monotonously plod on.

Are these new translations likely to change matters, if matters are as I've just been assuming? Probably not, even though Arndt's is published as an attractive and relatively inexpensive paperback, which a good many people may buy out of some vague untroubled sense of obligation, and which a few will at least dip into here and there. The difficulty is that the two "literary" versions (paraphrases, as Professor Nabokov disparagingly uses the term), while the products obviously of undoubted love and considerable labor, are just not much fun to read: they are dutiful and respectful, laboriously sprightful, and rather flat. Professor Nabokov's, on the other hand, is explicitly and even truculently *not* "literary":

. . . to my ideal of literalism I sacrificed everything (elegance, euphony, clarity, good taste, modern usage, and even grammar) that the dainty mimic prizes higher than truth. Pushkin has likened translators to horses changed at the posthouses of civilization. The greatest reward I can think of is that students may use my work as a pony. (I. x)

Kayden's verse is relatively more tolerable than Arndt's, whose insistence on following Pushkin's metrical scheme without deviation is in the end self-defeating. Even a poet might be licked by this problem (although a true poet would most likely simply throw Pushkin—or anyone else—overboard, as, say, Robert Lowell does Racine; this can be a dangerous procedure—witness Lowell's *Prometheus,* or Pound's notorious rape in cornball-Poundese of Sophocles' *Women of Trachis.* Yet the result at least has some sort of existence on its own terms, as the well-intended academic exercise in translation is not likely to, hovering as it does between two worlds, or stools, as the case may be). Professor Arndt is not a poet; his obligatory eking-out of Pushkin is not compensated by any extraordinary qualities of his English, and his rhymes are often plain bad.[16] In both his version and Kayden's the iambic tetrameters tend to jog-trot on the level of "I've measured it from side to side/But only God can make a tree."

Talk about translating and translations [17] and translators has

---

16. Examples (numbers refer to pages): "from the ball . . . the capital" (20); "stacks have puffed . . . blue smoke aloft" (20); "Where torrid southern blazes char / My own, my native Africa (26); "hardened . . . ardent" (40); "belittle . . . riddle" (40); "mists afar . . . *je ne sais quoi* (41); "islands . . . silence" (41); "begging . . . Onegin" (43); "day does . . . invaders" (62); "pages . . . outrageous" (98); "abandoned . . . command, and" (133); "acacias . . . old Horatius" (142); "With basins, dishes, crocks, and jars, / And sundry old etceteras" (179); "cribbing . . . Gibbon" (214); "Onegin . . . begging" (218). "Old Horatius" is typical of Arndt's curious infelicity. The allusion is to the poet Horace (not to Horatius at the bridge), but the Latin form in English pronunciation is labored (to fit the meter) and silly in its effect: What speaker of English ever calls Horace Horatius? (Kayden also has a meter-saving Horatius: "Like sage Horatius . . .") Or consider this Arndt couplet, from stanza one of chapter eight:

> One spring, when swan cries set aquiver
> The placid mirrors of the river . . . (195)

Swans can be noisy creatures, but these seem unusually and even desperately plangent—cousins, perhaps, to those who were, in the famous old hymn, reserved for the dons. Professor Nabokov's "pony" has "in springtime, to the calls of swans, / near waters shining in the stillness. . . ." Kayden has (Wordsworthily)

> I wandered lone to watch the swans
> And hear their cries above the lake . . .

Arndt's ". . . the fareway's whiteness / Is thawing into muddy slush . . ." (216) has an odd golf course flavor to it. "Fareway" here translates *ulitsa* (street) as on page 115 it does *put'* (path, way, road).

** These rhymes remain in Professor Arndt's "revised printing." As for Professor Nabokov, true to his convictions as an "incorruptible literalist" (III. 10), he promises in his "Reply to My Critics" to revise his translation in the direction of even greater literalness and plainness: "My *EO* falls short of the ideal crib. It is still not close enough and not ugly enough. In future editions I plan to defowlerize it still more drastically. I think I shall turn it entirely into utilitarian prose, with a still bumpier brand of English, rebarbative barricades of square brackets and tattered banners of reprobate words, in order to eliminate the last vestiges of bourgeois poesy and concession to rhythm."

Still, with all his rejection of "poesy," Professor Nabokov's version has its own cranky life and even (at moments) charm—not necessarily "gruesome" (Professor Arndt's word—see above, additions to note 4). The poet may take the "poesy" out of his work but he can't take himself out of it.

17. A few useful works on translation: Georges Mounin, *Les belles infidèles,* Paris, 1955 (a lively "Défense et illustration de l'art de traduire"); Theodore Savory, *The Art of Translation,* London, 1957; Reuben A. Brower (editor), *On Translation,* Cambridge (Mass.), 1959—eighteen essays on everything from

been going on for a long time now, and seems likely to go on for a while longer; the subject has generated over the centuries many sayings, some serious some frivolous—*traddutore traditore, une traduction est comme une femme,* and all the rest. Everyone likes to get in the act. And it is hard sometimes to avoid the feeling that much writing *about* translating is not only more interesting and better worded than the same writer's own translations, but tends to form a minor branch of literature, along with letters, diaries, travel books, occasional cookbooks, interviews with literary personages, better-than-average accounts of sports events (their classical archetype the great fake report of Orestes' death in Sophocles' *Electra*), record-album blurbs, collected columns by newspaper pundits, sermons, and so on—especially when it (the writing about translating) involves a sprightly-learned self-justification or second-guessing, as it often does.

"The Poetic Nuance" to "Automatic (Transference, Translation, Remittance, Shunting)"—in short, translation by machine; William Arrowsmith and Roger Shattuck (editors), *The Craft and Context of Translation,* Austin, 1960; Anchor Books, 1961—sixteen essays, some of them originally presented as lectures in a University of Texas symposium.

** A book that should have been listed in the original note is *The Poem Itself,* New York, 1960 (edited by Stanley Burnshaw; associate editors, Dudley Fitts, Henri Peyre, John Frederick Nims), now available as a Meridian paperback.

Since this note was first published, discussions of translation have zoomed on, in all the familiar directions. Among recent publications concerned with the subject one is bound to mention handsome (in all senses) *Delos / a Journal on & of Translation,* published at Austin by the portentously named National Translation Center, and involving among many talents some of those which also at Austin help produce the liveliest of learned journals, *Arion*—itself full of translations and articles about translation, mostly of classical but occasionally of modern writers.

The author of this note has received to date (late June 1969) two issues of *Delos,* both rich in good things—translations, articles, reviews, lists of translations in progress; answers (in *Delos* 2) to a very detailed questionnaire on "The State of Translation." The thirty answers range alphabetically from W. H. Auden ("A 'trot' is like a pair of spectacles for the weak-sighted: a translation is like a book of Braille for the blind") and William Burroughs to Richard Wilbur and Juliusz Zulawski.

Delos 1 contains among numerous treasures an interview with Robert Lowell by D. S. Carne-Ross, which has this by Lowell: ". . . there must be a hundred people in America who could do a readable translation of Tolstoy. But they couldn't do Pushkin; probably no one could do Pushkin unless they did it in prose the way Edmund Wilson did 'The Bronze Horseman.' But then he's a prose writer."

In that same extended note in which we meet the racemose old-world bird cherry and the harmful drudges, Professor Nabokov cites (III. 13) a couplet from a poem by Sir John Denham (1615-1669): [18]

> **That servile path thou nobly do'st decline**
> **Of tracing word by word, and line by line.**

A few lines later Denham further praises his friend, who

> **Foording his [the original author's] current, where thou find'st it low,**
> **Let'st in thine own to make it rise and flow.**

Professor Nabokov will of course have none of this: he gladly chooses that servile path, with a passing sneer at "those noble paraphrasts whom Sir John Denham praised. . . ." [19]

During the years towards the middle of the seventeenth century when Sir John Denham was praising his friend Fanshawe, Andrew Marvell wrote the lines to *his* worthy friend, Doctor Witty (or Whitty), from which the epigraph to these reflections was taken. Marvell's poem goes on, after the lines already cited:

> **So of translators they are authors grown,**
> **For ill translators make the book their own.**
> **Others do strive with words and forced phrase**
> **To add such lustre, and so many rays,**
> **That but to make the vessel shining, they**
> **Much of the precious metal rub away.**
> **He is translation's thief that addeth more,**
> **As much as he that taketh from the store**
> **Of the first author.**

Between the positions set forth in these two specimens of amiable old-fashioned complimentary verse the arguments about

18. "To Sir Richard Fanshawe upon His Translation of *Pastor Fido*." (See *The Poetical Works of Sir John Denham*. Edited with notes and introduction by Theodore Howard Banks, Jr., New Haven, 1928, pages 143-44.)

** In citing Denham's poem Professor Nabokov mentions Dryden's Preface to *Ovid's Epistles,* where these lines of Denham are approvingly quoted. In this Preface Dryden discusses three kinds of translation: "metaphrase," "paraphrase," and "imitation." He is kinder to paraphrase and imitation and less kind to the third sort of translation than metaphrastic Professor Nabokov.

19. Professor Nabokov gave the title "The Servile Path" to his article in the volume *On Translation* (see above, footnote 17). The various sections of this article now form part of the Commentary on *Eugene Onegin*.

translation continue to rage. What's the answer? Of course there is no single or simple one. We will continue to have "paraphrasts," noble or ignoble, in spite of Professor Nabokov—the main drift of translation (especially of verse) seems to be that way—and their paraphrasing will sometimes please and perhaps instruct. But since most of us are at the mercy of the translators (and since the translators and the critics skirmish so furiously among themselves) it is not a bad idea to keep our fingers prudently crossed, and to be grateful to rebarbative Professor Nabokov, or to such a crotchety scholar as the late Professor Joshua Whatmough: ". . . if Mr X must translate, say, the *Antigone* of Sophocles into English, the title page should read, 'The Antigone of Mr X, with reminiscences of Sophocles,' which is what in fact it would be." [20] From their position of special privilege, well-earned or not, the translators can upstage us, put us on terribly (and themselves too), if we let them.[21]

20. Joshua Whatmough, *Poetic, Scientific and Other Forms of Discourse,* Berkeley and Los Angeles, MCMLVI, 265 (in the chapter "Confessio Fidei").

21. For example—but there are wheels within wheels within wheels here!—Professor Robert Corrigan, in his essay "Translating for Actors" (in *The Craft and Context of Translation*—see above, note 16) writes as follows (Anchor Edition, 144): ". . . there are some things that are lost that need not be. For instance, in all the published translations of *Uncle Vanya,* the shooting is botched. The typical translation reads: *Let me go, Helen! Let me go!* (Looking for Serebryakov) *Where is he? Oh, here he is!* (Fires at him) *Missed! Missed again!* (Furiously) *Damnation—damnation take it . . .* (Flings revolver on the floor and sinks into a chair, exhausted).

"Not one translator has seen that in the Russian Vanya does not fire the gun, but he *says 'Bang!'* He has become so incapable of action that even when his whole life is at stake he cannot act but substitutes words. Here is a case where the meaning of the play has been drastically changed by the translator's failure to see that Chekhov's conception of that ghastly moment is truer than our more simple-minded logic."

There are several things to be said about this (Professor Corrigan's rather *écoeurant* critical tone aside):

(1) This "typical" translation is virtually word-for-word Constance Garnett's (a detail which Professor Corrigan tactfully omits)—with one important exception: she *does* have the word "Bang!" (the usual translation of Russian *bats!*) after the stage direction "Fires at him."

(2) Before Vanya rushes in with the gun, chasing Professor Serebryakov, we have already heard a shot offstage—a shot which Professor Corrigan retains in his own version: what about Chekhov's conception of *that* ghastly moment? The Russian stage direction which in this "typical" translation is rendered "Fires at him" is *strelyaet v nego,* which in fact means "fires at him" or "shoots at him." In making it "pointing the revolver at Serebryakov" (as he does in his version) Professor Corrigan props up his own case at some cost to the facts.

Well—enough for the moment of these reflections and re-reflections. Have a look at Professor Nabokov's *Onegin*—read it side by side with Professor Arndt's and all the others. Better still, learn enough Russian to use it as the trot which its maker insists he intended it to be. Roam about in his Commentary—however arrogant, reactionary, pedantic you consider some of his passing glances at un-admired authors (or however dubious some of his enthusiasms, e.g., Chateaubriand—see III. 98.) [22] His very outrageousness may help to keep us on our toes, since it is combined with learning and love of learning, and love of and respect for precise detail. [23] Would there were more like him. Or—does madness lie that way?

> Now I shall speak of evil as none has
> Spoken before. I loathe such things as jazz;

---

(3) It is not improper to assume—as all the other translators of the play seem to have done—that desperate Vanya, in this sad-farcical travesty of a big dramatic showdown, *after* missing again with the gun frustratedly exclaims "Bang!" (which all the translations, typical or not, do have).

** I don't know how many new translations of *Uncle Vanya* have appeared since Professor Corrigan's. The most important (assuming more than one) is certainly Ronald Hingley's in volume three (1964) of *The Oxford Chekhov*. In his Preface Hingley lists Professor Corrigan with other translators whose versions he has "closely examined," but his own treatment of the great curtain scene of Act III remains staunchly uncorriganated: "[*Fires at him.*] Bang! [*Pause.*] Missed him, did I? Missed him again, eh?" And so on.

(Of course, one has one's reservations about Professor Hingley's version too—his extreme anglicizing of the names, etc.—h-m-m-m-m.)

22. It would be a pleasure to be able to pick a few holes in his display of learning; perhaps someone better qualified than I has done so, or will do so. I must be pitifully content with a few incorrect page references, and with the fact that Goethe's "marvelous *Auf allen Gipfeln*" (II. 235 and Index) is in fact "Über allen Gipfeln."

** In "Reply to My Critics" Professor Nabokov thanks John Bayley of *The Observer* for calling attention to this same slip. The writer of this note is happy in the knowledge that he never saw that issue of *The Observer,* and that all eight lines of Goethe's little poem popped into his mind as he came upon Professor Nabokov's *"Auf"*—[AUF?!]. He no longer was sure what the rhyme-word "Wipfeln" meant, but the poem had been tucked away in his unconscious all these years, a small by-blow of an early, abortive affair with the German language.

23. "In art as in science there is no delight without the detail, and it is on details that I have tried to fix the reader's attention. Let me repeat that unless these are thoroughly understood and remembered, all 'general' ideas (so easily acquired, so profitably resold) must necessarily remain but worn passports allowing their bearers short cuts from one area of ignorance to another." (I. 8)

The white-hosed moron torturing a black
Bull, rayed with red; abstractist bric-a-brac;
Primitivist folk-masks; progressive schools;
Music in supermarkets; swimming pools;
Brutes, bores, class-conscious Philistines, Freud, Marx,
Fake thinkers, puffed-up poets, frauds and sharks.
    —*Pale Fire, a Poem in Four Cantos,* lines 923-30

These are, to be sure, ill-fated Professor John Shade's lines.
Still . . .

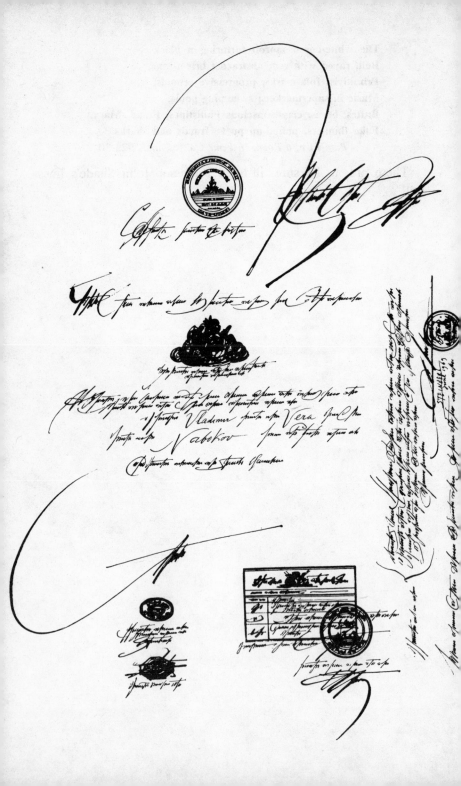

[4. Tributes]

En plein vol
17 IV 69

My dear Baron,

You write so infrequently that it's almost an impertinence to protest against such an exquisitely selective intermittency. Believe me, my dear fellow, it's not the rarity of your epistles that gives them their price. But the distance from which you write, the ingenuity of indirection with which you call forth the latent intelligence of the postal service, and, if you will allow me to remark on it, the singular angularity of your fist, all invite me to believe that not every word you dispatch into the smoke and stir of this low pinfold actually gets here. A return address now and then would also facilitate our correspondence. As it is, my responses must often be made in these somewhat public terms— *ad urbem*, if not exactly *ad orbem*, and our correspondence can scarcely escape the shabby look of a *pis-aller*.

You inquire with an excess of flippancy (surely unnecessary as between old friends) regarding the character and sentiments of "my former colleague N."—they are, of course, sentiments that I could scarcely fail to realize you would find wounding. Let me remind you, first, that having served in the same university with a man is scarcely a better title of intimacy than having crossed the ocean on a large boat with him. The quarters are relatively cramped, to be sure; but the monotony of the scenery, the hypnotic susurration of the wavespeech, and the rigid compartmentalization of the structure all militate against genuine conversation. Yet it is true, I have had a certain amount of casual acquaintance with N. Still, I am afraid you are unlikely to derive much comfort from my assurances that he is a man of courtly manners, lively wit, great personal charm, and as much kindliness as is compatible in our present wretched century with high literary standards. (One could perhaps speak of the sour cream of human kindness.) No doubt you will tell me with disgust that these are the vague, honorific terms in which one commends a second-string diplomat to be *chef de bureau* in a banana-republic consulate. True enough: I speak only of preliminaries. But in fact it's often struck me that, setting aside for a moment the unhappy issue of your direct encounter with N., there's a quality to his imagination which you, of all people, should find congenial; I'll *versa* this *vice* in a moment. But to illustrate with an anecdote. Imagine, if you will, the long, gray New York State winter, a provincial town swirled over by snow-devils for four solid months of the year, the daily grimness of muffled faces and frostbitten imaginations. In the midst of this frozen landscape, as a result of the ice, and while actually performing the most menial of domestic chores, it was my destiny to fall from a moderate altitude and dislocate my right shoulder. In due course it was repaired, and after an interval I returned, with a fine triangular sling and a flapping sleeve, to my chores at the academy —and to the usual barrage of facetious remarks about my athletic incompetence, my infuriated students, and so on and so forth—academic wit on these topics being, let me assure you, no more deft or delicate than the military badinage with which you were familiar. Only my colleague N. said a memorable word. Meeting me, wounded, in the corridor, he flung up both hands, and cried in spontaneous delight: "Ah-hah, a duel!"

Spontaneous delight, my dear Baron, there you have it; my former colleague N. has a notable tendency to admire architectural fiction of a superlative inevitability, but his own style is something else again—something rarer and more precious, I venture to think. This can be said without the slightest diminution of the appreciation due Flaubert, Joyce, and Proust—none of whom is, indeed, remarkable for unpredictability, or the finely improvised sense of excess. N. actually goes farther than this (but he is a man of great critical *brio,* even in his taste for what others would think square or stolid), and has been known to express a lurking tolerance verging on fondness for that emphatic Christian rhetorician whom you in your time so heartily disliked. (I am confident you will appreciate knowing that, by the malice of history, he is best remembered for having baptized a beefsteak.) But, by a paradox to which I can do no more than point in stupefied admiration, N.'s fiction rejoices precisely in those bold transformations, those sudden modulations from one key of fantasy to another, those audacious leaps and gestures of abrupt imaginative imbalance which were your own special delight.

He has spoken of your work, I confess, with an asperity, an almost perverse inaccuracy, which in your position I should doubtless find hard to forgive. To refer to your fictions as *femme-de-chambre* romances when it was precisely *against* the anticipations of the *femme-de-chambre* romance that you deliberately played, suggests a *parti pris* that I find quite as deplorable as you must yourself. But two considerations enter here. In the first place, you must reflect that the man's genius lies in the extreme, the comically unstable, the *up;* it is no accident, surely, that the *hauteur* of M. Humbert merely prolongs the ultimate gesture of Cincinnatus C. in "rising above it all." N. has an extravagantly witty eye and a supreme sense (quite indispensable in a novelist, however suspect in a critic) that things are good for what he can make of them. And then it's apparent that the appreciative faculties which might have led to a better estimate of your work have been—as it were—mainly directed toward one of your later and more remote contemporaries, a Scythian fantasiast named Gogol. Like all sharp satiric eyes, N.'s have a great gift of variable and selective focus; and he has found such richness of comic inspiration in the example of Gogol that one could almost (were it not, of course, for old friendship) find it in one's heart to forgive his unfairness to yourself.

I should feel more distinctly apologetic for this left-handed, halfhearted, collapsing defense if it weren't all too apparent that in the world of letters a reputation may suffer quite as much from the wrong sort of friendly support as from a frank, swashbuckling attack. Consider only the whole tribe of translators, and the sort of wrong they daily perpetrate out of pure friendship. But as this may well be an awkward topic between us, let me simply assure you of my continuing respect and admiration for both yourself and "my former colleague N.," along with my sense that when you finally meet (and it's my earnest, selfish desire that that day may be long delayed), you will find between you better grounds for mediation than could ever be discovered by

Your humble, obedient servant,

R. M. ADAMS

À: M. le Baron de Stendhal
Les Champs Elysées, quelque part (4ème étage)

To Vladimir Nabokov on his 70th birthday
That nymphet's beauty lay less on her bones
Than in her name's proclaimed two allophones,
A boned veracity slow to be found
In all the channels of recorded sound.
Extrude an orange pip upon the track,
And it will be a pip played front or back,
But only in the kingdom of the shade
Can diaper run back and be repaid.

Such speculations salt my exile too,
One that I bear less stoically than you.
I look in sourly on my lemon trees,
Spiked by the Qs and Xes of Maltese,
And wonder: Is this home or where is home?
(Melita's caves, Calypso's honeycomb.)
I seek a cue or clue. Just opposite,
The grocer has a cat that loves to sit
Upon the scales. Respecting his repose,
One day he weighed him: just 2 rotolos.
In this palazzo wood decays and falls;
Buses knock stucco from the outer walls,
Slam shut the shutters. Coughing as they lurch,
They yet enclose the silence of a church,
Rock in baroque: Teresan spados stab
The Sacred Heart upon the driver's cab,
Whereon, in circus colors, one can read
That *Verbum Caro Factum Est.* Indeed.
I think the word is all the flesh I need.—
The taste, and not the vitamins of sense,
Whatever sense may be. I like the fence
Of black and white that keeps those bullocks in—
Crossboard or chesswood, Eurish gift of Finn—
The "crossmess parzel." If words are no more
Than *pyeoshki,* preordained to look before,
Save for their taking *chassé,* they alone,
And not the upper house, can claim a throne
(Exploded first the secular magazines
And puff of bishops). All aswarm with queens,
Potentially, that board. Well, there it is:
You help me counter the liquidities
With counters that are counties, countries. Best
To read it: *Caro Verbum Factus Est.*

ANTHONY BURGESS

Nothing is more heartening than to see a great writer become more and more audacious. *Ada,* like most novels breaking new ground, is uneven. Moreover, Nabokov doubtless indulges too often the impulse to parody conventional serious fiction, those "classics" which can be as deadly as subliterature. At times we lose the double voice, and seem to be floundering in the thing satirized.

But the book begins and ends with the highest fictional satisfactions. The twelve-year-old Ada is a creation of incorrigible love, but also of professional expertness. The great *trouvaille* was for Nabokov to endow the sexually attractive nymphet with a loving and lovably pedantic interest in nature, and with his own mature wit and own beautifully precise descriptive language. The reader who is drawn to Ada, or who delights in Van's and Ada's sexual explorations, has not been "trapped" by a wily, secretly moralistic author. Not even Colette rendered fleshly textures and tones with such grace. The children of Henry James are charming too, and speak well, in "The Turn of the Screw" and "The Pupil," but are hardly allowed to experience these delights. Ada and Van achieve and later remember the adolescent's erotic heaven that many aspire to but few fully enjoy; and almost none seem to remember. Elsewhere in *Ada* Nabokov may be having his satirical fun with sex or with sex novels. But these early chapters are true triumphs of erotic literature; or, perhaps, of "life" held at precisely the right distances from the narrative eye.

Near the end (Part Four), by contrast, Nabokov offers a meditation on Time in the purest and richest philosophical prose. But philosophical with the most personal accent, the most vivid twists and turns! It is a rare pleasure to read such English as this, to listen to such a voice. At the end of this section, in another moment of great satisfaction for the reader, the aging lovers are seen to triumph (after a momentary rebuff) over whatever Time "is" or is "like."

Ada is of course a novel to be reread, and it will be harried in many seminars. But no amount of professional rereading should dim these first exceptionally pure pleasures.

ALBERT J. GUERARD

Vladimir Nabokov is not only a great novelist, poet, critic, translator, and polemicist, but he is also justly renowned as the man responsible for bringing me to Cornell University as temporary successor in teaching his courses, circa 1958. He offered me sherry, a place to nap, and laughter in the light before my interviews with deans and chairmen. He guided me faithfully through hours of torment, past stormy martinis and across rocky lunches, my hand in his, my footsteps following his galoshes through a heavy Ithaca snowfall. In casual conversation he quoted generously from my novel, *The Man Who Was Not with It;* I was speechful with gratitude. He offered me part of the royalties from *Lolita* if I could formulate a sentence using every letter of the alphabet once and only once and, to be helpful, supplied a fine opening word: "Sphynx, —" He gave me his annotated copy of *Dr. Zhivago,* which he called "Dr. Van Cliburn." He asked if I realized that T. S. Eliot spells "Toilets" backwards (it doesn't quite). We discussed at some length the significance of the repeated refrain "U.P." in *Ulysses.* He said he was writing a book on James Joyce. I said he should write more novels. When he left for Europe, he promised to write to me daily for the rest of our lives.

Years later I did an interview with him for *Paris Review* and spent a week with him in Montreux for an article in the *Saturday Evening Post.* I was afraid of imposing on his time, but he seemed to finish his day's work before I got up in the morning and he would awaken me with suggestions for curious outings.

He was a genial host, a lumbering good walker, a spouty swimmer, a relaxed companion, and he denied many of the things I later wrote about him. I seem to recall that he was in a high mood of generosity; he even forgave Dostoevsky. He expressed great fondness for Lyndon B. Johnson, Leo Tolstoy, and everybody at Cornell; his hatred for Maurice Girodias was joyous and vibrant; he dealt with Edmund Wilson as an old friend who had somehow not turned out.

One afternoon—to give an idea of our concerns during that Swiss Indian summer period, nostalgic, affable, and expense-accounted—we discussed the problem of hair on the body and the dangers of tweezing in the nose. Later I sent him a Swiss noseclippers from San Francisco. He wrote personally to the editor of the *Saturday Evening Post* to deny some of the conclusions I had come to, such as that he did not write many personal letters. He may have been irritated by my balanced adoration in the pages of that popular, now-dead magazine, but I was only trying to be a decent interpreter for the mass of folks out there in subscriptionland. I believe he is a genius, a never-ending source of joy, informal spasms, and intelligence, but he hasn't written to me every day for the rest of our lives.

HERBERT GOLD

Waiting for Ada

> There is always another, one more,
> one *last* Grand Hotel: far-fetched, far-flung,
> but built to last. At least penultimate, surely,
> Rimini's Grand Hotel du Miroir
> stares down its methodical rivals,
> modest interlopers on the English Parade

where all the pretty kiosks pointed
once as a matter of course to this
thermal term, this nearly pearly nougat-textured
art-nouveau pavilion readied now,
renewed this rainy April, for what
will never again be more than an off-Season.

Inside, I edge past the furniture,
oppressed by giant boudoirs no one
ever sulked in, knowing you would be at home here
—Hotel du Miroir! what better place?
working wickedly away, when all
I can manage is to scavenge the lounge for books
and read till the rain relents: albums
of sepia views, and a German Guide
to what our Air Force left of Malatesta's will—
these cannot beguile a mind obsessed
by what they bear eyewitness to: life
as it merely passes is so much time wasted.

And time saved? In store for me, once home,
your ardors loom, unspeakable loves
which ransom not by being beautiful or true
but by liberating us from *this*—
panoramas and preconceptions,
the places and the past we cannot recover
or truly possess save in the form
we give them. I leave all Grand Hotels
to you; the fishy photos slide away, the Guide
to Rimini lies: Nothing exists,
and Never has existed always.
The rain stops. The Adriatic glows. Ada, I come!

RICHARD HOWARD

341

Your invitation to Vladimir Nabokov's birthday reaches me in England, and it was in England, nearly fifteen years ago, in Oxford, that I first read this great man: in the *New Yorker,* the Pnin story where the pencil sharpener says *ticonderoga, ticonderoga* and Pnin bursts into tears during a flickering Russian film. It was another fictional universe, or at least a stunning intensification of the ordinary one, and it has been one of the steadier pleasures of the fifteen years since to catch up on the considerable amount of Nabokov then in English (including the miraculous *Speak, Memory*) and to keep up with the ample installments of reincarnated Russian and newly spawned American that have been issued through an untidy assortment of publishers, ranging from the elegant Bollingen Press to a miserable little bindery called, I think, Phaedra. Though I may have nodded here and there among the two volumes of notes to *Onegin,* I have not knowingly missed any of the rest; for Nabokov is never lazy, never ungenerous with his jewels and flourishes, and his *oeuvre* is of sufficient majesty to afford interesting perspectives even from the closets and back hallways. I have expressed in print my opinion that he is now an American writer and the best living; I have also expressed my doubt that his aesthetic models—chess puzzles and protective colorations in lepidoptera—can be very helpful ideals for the rest of us. His importance for me as a writer has been his holding high, in an age when the phrase "artistic integrity" has a somewhat paradoxical if not reactionary ring, the stony image of his self-sufficiency: perverse he can be, but not abject; prankish but not hasty; sterile but not impotent. Even the least warming aspects of his image—the implacable hatreds, the reflexive contempt—testify, like fortress walls, to the reality of the siege this strange century lays against our privacy and pride.

As a reader, I want to register my impression that Nabokov does not (as Phillip Toynbee, and other critics, have claimed) lack heart. *Speak, Memory* and *Lolita* fairly bulge with heart, and even the less ingratiating works, such as *King, Queen, Knave,* show, in the interstices of their rigorous designs, a plenitude of human understanding. The ability to animate into memorability minor, disagreeable characters bespeaks a kind of love. The little prostitute that Humbert Humbert recalls undressing herself so quickly, the fatally homely daughter of John Shade, the intolerably pretentious and sloppy-minded woman whom Pnin undyingly loves, the German street figures in *The Gift*, the extras momentarily on-screen in the American novels—all make a nick in the mind. Even characters Nabokov himself was plainly prejudiced against, like the toadlike heroine of *King, Queen, Knave*, linger vividly, with the outlines of the case they must plead on Judgment Day etched in the air; how fully we feel, for example, her descent into fever at the end. And only an artist full of emotion could make us hate the way we hate Axel Rex in *Laughter in the Dark*. Not to speak of towering creations like the father in *The Gift* and Dolores Haze. If we feel that Nabokov is keeping, for all his expenditure of verbal small coin, some treasure in reserve, it is because of the riches he has revealed. Far from cold, he has access to European vaults of sentiment sealed to Americans; if he feasts the mind like a prodigal son, it is because the heart's patrimony is assured.

JOHN UPDIKE

A day, a country home

Homage to Vladimir Nabokov

This true estate:

There is time here for the sea
To die in waves slow as eyes,
Where the sound of each dying
Holds to the ear like hunger.

You walk along the pebbles
Of the shore. The high leaves
Lap at the late sun like dogs
Hot from the romp, the chase.

The water moves like a freed circle,
Spiraling into froth, into foam,
As the stone darkens and gleams
At each departure, wave on wave.

Is there a house through the trees,
Catching light through the leaves
Like butterflies, like the sun
Too bright to see, like the day?

You see two figures far down the shore,
A young man, his young blond wife,
Examining the stones, pocketing
A few bright pebbles, watching you.

The sun touches the edge of the day
As gingerly as hands, as fingers,
Your shadow slips long into the aspens,
Into their shade, clear to the golden walls.

R. H. W. DILLARD

Mr. Nabokov's tent

Tributes between poets, chess champions, couturiers—and novelists—are always hopefully contubernal. All such donors really yearn for others to see that the honored one lives in a tent *they* share. Therefore, I am grateful to Nabokov for having made the only kind of tent that interests me—one that nobody else, except as a reader, *can* share.

I've no intention of describing what Nabokov has made. Not because critics and other mad anthropophagi haven't tried. Because Nabokov fully describes his world in the act of making it. Which is as it should be, for any world-without-end worth making. And he does it rather better than anyone else.

I am convinced, of course, reading, that he does it for me alone. This is *our* joint paranoia, a lovely affaire. Who else would be limber and zestful enough to follow him? Whom else can I trust better to know, as I do, that language is not the surface of life, but the surfacing *of* life?

Few writers convince me that word-life exists. Or that they themselves exist truly and naturally in it—like, say, Wittgenstein, who exists perpetually in the act of convincing me that he is a homeless word seeking to be Wittgenstein. For many, a word is what you use, not what you are. For some, language is a vessel, into which realer life is shamefully drained. When I see a writer thinks of "words" as the inner dirt *of* life, or embroidery *on* life, or a weak separation *from* life—I have trouble believing in the life he talks about. He hasn't proven the existence of mine. But with Nabokov I can believe very seriously in the existence of us both.

So doing, I give thanks for certain sympathies that strengthen and redeem mine. I know that life came before Freud did, and literature also. He too loathes any reversal of that order. He laughs at symbols, for being the sounding brass and tinkling they are. And thinks of women not as symbol or topic, but as another part of the civilization. He writes for the most intelligent reader alive—who may just possibly not be himself. And he knows that "literature" comes first—for any writer who views life as the very process of seeing and saying why that is so.

I wish him all joy of his book-seventies, and thank him for all that I have had of him. I think I thank him most for seeing and writing double, always from the keen sensation which comes of knowing the double identity and indemnity between hymenopter and hymenopterist. Orphaned early, he has made me laugh the harder at everything relative. And in the lingua franca that counts.

HORTENSE CALISHER

The ordinary is, too

1. The advantages of not being born in America are, in 1969, so numerous, so new, so exciting, one might conclude—erroneously—that thirty years ago, when Vladimir Nabokov came to the United States, none at all existed. But just a brief enumeration of a few merely negative advantages dispels the possibility of any misapprehension: for example, Nabokov, on the planet Europe, was born free of Norris's pits and Dos Passos's typography, with immunity against feelings of guilt or treachery about this freedom. Like, say, a man from Rome visiting Texas and being asked his opinion of the Roman statues in a millionaire's garden, Nabokov could smile, shrug, and be mum about The Dreiser of firm unyielding native granite, or The Hemingway cast taut-throated in bronze carefully engraved (like medieval armor) with remarks and best sayings—about codes and being tested and behaving bad (or good). A gentleman encapsulated in European manners and ideas would be forgiven his provincial responses to even so respected a teller of the American tale as Fitzgerald if he wondered, "What were they all doing in Paris then anyway?" or "Who, one must ask, caused their Crash?" Nobody in unrepentantly unilingual America would expect a serious answer to Faulkner's question, "Why do you hate the South?" from a man-of-many-languages.

Encompassing these advantages and a good thousand others was Nabokov's ultimate freedom to write novels or chase butterflies without joining the pursuit of that terrifying indigenous unwinged American thing, The Reality. When the furl-browed city boys charged past with upheld nets, Nabokov could Pnin it quaintly and quietly, and not even ask what or whom the collectors were after.

Nor did Nabokov have to subscribe to the Ideology of Reality or its article of faith which holds that not The Messiah but The Novelist will one day free American mankind. Just as Americans brought up on Hearst cartoons could dismiss the intellectual as a butterfly-chasing professorial nut, so Nabokov, barely looking up from his twin labors, may have formed the wrong impression of America's true-believers. Worrying one's head about the nature and meaning of reality is America's longest standing, most profound fix, deeply rooted in the actualities of American everyday life.

A man without this fix and with, instead, a rich feeling for the past, a turn for the ironies of language and situation, nuance, in-jokes, secret messages, puzzles, was just the guy to look over Disneyland emerging, and see through its facade of the normal and the ordinary. That much, of course, a Waugh or Huxley could do: Nabokov's genius went much further, humanizing what lay behind the appearance. Nabokov's perception and imagination broke through corny anticipation—his images replaced the superficiality associated with certain callings and stations. *Lolita* superimposed on a two-dimensional Disneyland cartoon (and its received truths and clichés) what children actually are and actually feel and actually do.

A butterfly man, like Keats's watcher of the skies, stares long and hard at the ordinary, knowing that one new dot or color shift may herald the extraordinary—the faithful observer's reward. But butterflymen, I take it, rarely look at moths. By taste, choice, and background Nabokov long ago declared for butterflies, a positive advantage—but also, possibly, a disadvantage. Because if The Reality is anything at all, odds are high it's a moth, and not a butterfly.

II. In *Lolita* Nabokov established himself the genius of the *seemingly* ordinary. What he has never been able to understand about America is the terrifying pervasiveness of the *actually* ordinary, which, when stared at, only declares *itself,* over and over and over. The techniques for revealing the transparent world of Humbert Humbert won't do for the constricted world of Jack Portnoy.

By 1969 we only yawn at the bowler-topped Waugh bore putting down Hollywood as the compleat American scene, sniffily implying comparison with the superior (if sagging) civilization and its elegant (if sagged) taste. The historically unworthy, we're told once again, have wrongly inherited the earth from Europe, which invented style and refinement and taste and power. It's something of a shock to hear Vladimir Nabokov, of all people, doing business at that old Hollywood one-night stand, now, in 1969, putting Mailer down—in *Time Magazine!*—and Roth, for tastelessness and mere farce. It's a shock, that is, till one realizes the America Mailer and Roth write out of and about is precisely *the actually ordinary,* that segment of American turf or moth-land Nabokov disbelieves, or consciously rejects.

Mistaking the moth-land ultimately means missing the essence of America, which, in 1969, means ignoring the present and becoming ahistorical, almost irrelevant, comfortably contemporary only with T. S. Eliot in Bloomsbury, Joyce in Trieste, Tolstoi in Old Russia. Playing the old-fashioned put-down game is also out-of-time: to be no more than amused or disgusted by the American natives is to freak out a little, if unawares—like missionaries, like Waugh, like Huxley, like Switzerland. Fifty years from now it won't make much difference, of course: fifty years from now everybody will know Nabokov's contemporary was Eliot, not Roth: history will set things right, according to sensibility, not chronology.

III. The detachment from the immediate, the urgent, those pressing anxieties which send Mailer and Lowell marching (and, from Nabokov's point of view, make them abdicate their literary roles and responsibilities), constitutes Nabokov's great strength, but not without loss: only someone with Nabokov's born advantages could have mastered the actually ordinary, someone, that is, truly free of the native American fix and hang-up. But the new American insistence on no limits eliminates the brakes of taste or tradition. American fiction now *reports* everything, *including* Jack Portnoy's constipation (which Nabokov mistakenly discounts as farce).

Ada tells us of the great distances which separate Nabokov and America 1969. Alexander Portnoy's howl and Mailer's declamations and actions belong to a naive perspective, hope, expectation, loud insistence that the present yield for men all its possibilities. Nabokov in *Ada* writes out of a sadder world, which has quite given up on the present. Nostalgia is the significant dimension of this art, and language a magical medium containing everything from lyric loveliness to sheer play. Nabokov and Roth (or Mailer) basically disagree about what Conrad called "rescue work." For Roth even Jack Portnoy's constipation and Alexander Portnoy's masturbation *must be told,* and thus rescued from burial in the actually ordinary. For Nabokov "rescue work" does more than remember things past. It makes the past recreate itself in the present, and, through art, pretends (or believes) it can coerce the present into being less moth, and more butterfly. To him Mailer and Roth are only characters in a mad American tale, who insist the sky is falling. And they, for their part, can only point him to this sky.

JACK LUDWIG

TO: V. Nabokov, Montreux, Switzerland
FROM: J. Barth, Buffalo, U.S.A.
RE: April 23

Dear Mr. N.:
Today we lost Cervantes, St. George, and Shakespeare, but recouped Shakespeare and are clear ahead by Viscount Allenby, Admiral Anson, Hazel Brown, Sandra Dee, J. P. Donleavy, J. A. Froude, Raymond Huntley, Margaret Kennedy, Ngaio Marsh, Max Planck, I like Max Planck, Sergei Prokofiev, Henry Sherek, Vladimirs Sikorski and Yourself, Dame Ethel Smyth, Shirley Temple, and J. M. W. Turner. I guess we're OK. If the chaps on Nu Ophiuchi have their scopes trained just now upon 47, Morskaya, St. Petersburg, they may catch the p. f. of your first birthday candle—unless the east curtain's drawn, Russia cloudy, or the family gone a-Mondaying to Vyra, or that tot was after all born yesterday, despite the evidence a Saturday's child.

He'll go far in time! My wish for him, before he outs that one brief candle: let today in 2899, when Earth sets about his Millennial *Festschrift,* Betelgeuse count a hundred on his cake!

Yours truly,

ЭПИСТОЛА АПОСТОЛА

Владимир! Вла-Вла! Папа Лолы!
(Пусть дерзновенен мой привет)
Те берега пусты и голы,
Где нет тебя уж столько лет!

(Недосягаем он, угрюм.
Кошмарен взгляд его альпийский.
Но старомодный тот костюм
Прекрасен, как павлин индийский!)

Американец ты, хотя бы
Последнего призыва. Но
Пора домой. В Монтре арабы
Пускай живут: тебе ж грешно.

Вернитесь к нам! (Увы! Глагол
Не в том лице, что нужно здесь.
И без того он будет зол...)
Излишнюю оставьте спесь!

Здесь Эдмунд Вильсон, Лоуелль Роберт
Певцов отечественных бьют.
Давно пора им между ребер
Кинжал вонзить! Будь дик и лют!

От Принстона и до Корнеля
Закатят громы «Здравия!»
От всех, кому так надоели
И Беккет и Моравия.

Вернитесь к нам, в наш Sodom East,
Где блудный сын семейства рот —
Горизонтальный мемуарист,
Фрейдист и умственный банкрот —

Соперничает с милой «Адой».
Ему бы лучше — ни гу-гу!
Уж лучше дантовского ада
Ему гореть в седьмом кругу!

Вот вам роман: герой, портной,
И день и ночь валяясь в ванне,
Своей умелою рукой
Играет соло на органе.

Спасите ж нас от музыканта
Уединенного! И вновь,
Назло судье и коммерсанту,
Нам правду пойте и любовь!

CLARENCE BROWN

Vladimir! Vla-Vla! Lola's papa! / (Let bold my greeting be!) / Those shores are void and nude / where there's been no you for so many years!

(Unreachable. he, gloomy. / Nightmarish his alpine gaze. / But that old-fashioned suit of clothes is / splendid, like an Indian peacock!)

Thou art American, although of the / very latest levy. But— / it's time for home. Let Arabs live / in Montreux, but you ought to be ashamed.

Return to us! (Alas! The verb / is not the person needed here: / he'll be cross enough without that . . .) / Give up superfluous hauteur!

Here Edmund Wilson, Robert Lowell / are slaughtering your homeland's bards. / It's long since time to plunge the poniard / in between their costae! Be savage and cruel!

From Princeton to Cornell / peals of "Vivat!" / will roll from all who have been so bored / by Beckett and Moravia.

Return to us, to our Sodom East, / where the prodigal son of the family of Roth— / a horizontal memoirist, / Freudist, and mental bankrupt—

competes with dear *Ada*. / Better he held his peace! / Better for him to burn / in the seventh circle of Dante's *Hell*.

Here's the novel for you: The hero, a tailor [in Russian: portnoy] / wallowing in the bathtub day and night, / plays with his skillful hands / solos on the organ.

Save us from this solitary / musician, and once again, / in despite of judge and businessman, / sing to us of truth and love!

To Basic Training in hot Texas eight years ago I took Gogol,
Gorky, Chernyshevsky, Lermontov, and something called *Pale
Fire,* which was on the same shelf at school. Just graduated, I
had no time for Lolitas, was determined to occupy my enforced
leisure with "the other Russians."

Our barracks sergeant was opposed to the idea. Not the content, but the form. Too big. We each had one drawer only for
personal effects. A library would interfere with Inspection. I
managed to hold on, randomly, to Gogol and Nabokov through
the day. But the former was confiscated along with my allergy
medicine while we were at mess.

I also had a subscription to the *New York Times.* The next
morning our sergeant held my airmail edition up before the
troops: "Airman Newman, your news is here." Then he ripped
it very carefully into four tabloids and threw them away. He did
this every mail call for three months. Even on Sundays. He
wasn't being vicious. There just wasn't any place to *put* a good
read.

So I tore *Pale Fire* from its binding and kept it pure and
scrolled in my Fatigues' long pocket like a Bowie Knife. I was
once called down at Parade Rest for this; it bulged on my
demeanor.

It frankly took me the duration to get through it. On midnight
sentry duty, the gnat-encrusted searchlight allowed me a few
fulvous pages at each end of the compound; then an about-face
to make the Absence Report.

After four months of this, we were mustered for a party on a
mesquite-studded swale between two runways. "The sun was
burning like a man." Troop transports built to raid the Ploesti
oil fields coursed on either side of us like extinct puffins. An am-
phibious tank delivered beer and watermelon. A little-known
recording star of our troop did his duty on an electric organ. He
was killed in the very beginning of the Asian wars.

In the tall razor-edged grass I withdrew what had become
a manuscript from my uniform, and discovered crazy Kinbote,

". . . plated with poetry, armored with rhymes, stout with another man's song . . . bullet proof at long last." I was sappy with
a privilege I have yet to understand. But as neither Nabokov
nor I had made our juncture up, we were now free to imagine
all sorts of things for one another. I finished off the references
and divided the naturalized Nabokov on my hips.

Obviously, this was precisely the sort of contingency between
words and experience which Nabokov always promises, always
destroys; his grandest theme. He wears like a spume those lacunae
which only shortwaist us. No writer since Dr. Johnson has so
predetermined the tone and concern which his critics shall bring
to him, no writer in English more controls those personages who
serve doubly as his characters and his ideal readers. No living
writer is more winning and less exemplary. Already, he is the
man to get out from under.

CHARLES NEWMAN

Laughter in the dark

Trying to laugh with our mouths shut is a lesson
In physics, good taste, and raw anatomy;
And since, like titters and giggles, it gets us nowhere,
We might as well let it rip, our throats lying open
Like organpipes, all the way to the belly.
But when we laugh in darkness, we'd better move
Fast, unless we want more company
Than we can use. And all of it's in the dark:
We're laughing in a dark of our own making,
And soon, over our shoulders,
We'll hear the sinister heart-failed snickering
Of our bent selves, who are no laughing matter.

DAVID WAGONER

Seven for seventy

V. N.

Nous connûmes—leasing his Flaubertian loan—
A certain number of this roving set;
But yet, that archly *fauve* and referential tone,
Opulent, triplicitous, *sauvage,* yet
Karamazov-triste, hazes, confounds. *Chez lui,*
Olives float, clouds do research, and *la pluie,*
Vagrant, sly, perfumed, settles near the bone.

RICHARD STERN

> *How pleasant to know Mr. Lear!*
> *Who has written such volumes of stuff!*
> *Some think him ill-tempered and queer,*
> *But a few think him pleasant enough.*
> —EDWARD LEAR, *Nonsense Songs*

In his Afterword written especially for the Russian reader of his own translation of *Lolita* (following upon his translation of his Afterword written for the English reader of *Lolita*) Nabokov, neither sadly nor sardonically, enumerates the "other, normal" readers of his art, and in the far-off distance there appear enthusiastic groups of young people waving their arms, but, he adds, "they are simply asking me to stand aside because they are just about to photograph the arrival of some President in Moscow." Thus a soVereigN of letters, in the midst of the huckstering of these sideshow years of our literature, anticipates the waning of his latter-day popularity, the "cult of Nabokov," with typical émigré humor of which, alas, he seems the sole representative.

So here, beyond the books themselves, is what we (perhaps I anticipate: I, at any rate) have learned from Nabokov. That fame, like time, does not exist. "And now, ladies and gentlemen, I see columnist Louis Sobel coming in . . ." intoned the announcer as Nabokov passed unnoticed to see the premiere in 1962 of Kubrick's movie made from his novel. For two decades

Nabokov's novels appeared in minuscule editions—everyone knows that now—and were praised by a still smaller circle, chiefly of fellow poets and writers. And when *Pale Fire* appeared a critic wrote in the New York Russian paper *Novoe Russkoe Slovo:* "I have always acknowledged that Nabokov is a great, even a very great master, and that he will remain in the history of literature. But for all that I have somehow had a cold, indifferent feeling towards his art. His novel *Eternal Flame (Vechnoe plamya)* has dissipated my coldness and indifference." And how could any writer survive such marrow-sucking reservations as these: Gilbert Highet worrying that "he despises us, his readers"; the usually judicious Sir Herbert Read asserting that "the talent (for genius is innocent) of a Vladimir Nabokov derives its energy from an obsessive hatred of the civilization it depicts"; and John Simon complaining "nor do Nabokov's characters have that marvelous rightness of tone that, for example, C. P. Snow's have. . . ." C. P. Snow!!

Now, of course, Nabokov has been *Time*-covered. *For book cover on novelist Vladimir Nabokov please interview Andrew Field, an American from Newark* [well, New Jersey anyway; P. Roth, however, does come from Newark] . . . *and was an undergraduate student of Nabokov's at Cornell* [sorry again] . . . *Did he have tea often with the Nabokovs as most top students did?* [of those Johnsonian afternoon soirees no survivors remain] . . . *FYI Nabokov's wife Vera is a very beautiful, intelligent lady who runs most details of the author's life . . . FYI Ada is a beautiful, sensual book, but even more puzzling than Pale Fire* [and on such sure judgment rise reputations] . . . *Has Field ever been butterfly-hunting with Nabokov? FYI You may find Field somewhat prickly.* Nabokov may be counted upon to observe the hoisting of his statue (Peter the Great seated upon an invisible horse) with disinterested amusement. There will be more solemn articles, theses, courses, books about him (and I can scarcely excuse myself here), Nabokov professors and Nabokovnik creative writing students, all of it. And Nabokov will not, really not be terribly bothered by any of it. Certainly he is the greatest writer of our time as well as our *Time* culture. But, For Your Information, he is also much more, a man with no Craft but his own craft and no values but his own. Enter young people waving their arms . . .

ANDREW FIELD

My own copy of *Lolita* happens to come not late from G. P. Putnam's Sons but early from the Olympia Press. The two-volume, sewer-green-covered 1955 edition with its quick-rot, slime binding and its heavy pollution of typos. That is the actual, physical feel of the book—much as *Ada,* at the other end of the scale, now has the black, basaltic weight in my hand of an encyclopedist's tombstone—and I mention this very minor fact of sensation to recall a time, a now forgotten time in Nabokov's career when he was struggling to gain recognition for *Lolita* above the pornography line, and when we, his avid readers, had no end of difficulty simply getting hold of a copy.

At one point I actually had brief possession of the manuscript. My wife was working for a publishing firm that was then called Farrar, Straus and Cudahy, and she brought home one evening what higher editorial wisdom had already decided must go back to the agent next day. We tried, but *Lolita* is not the kind of book that somebody can read hastily overnight, particularly both somebodies. We had to send instead to a friend in Paris. The friend wrote us later that she'd gone promptly to Brentano's with our under-the-counter order, but in that case she was unconscionably late in forwarding the contraband. It finally arrived, much thumbed through, obviously several times read, and under cover —another ironic comment, I think, on Nabokov's *émigré* status —of a UNESCO envelope.

All this seems so antiquely absurd now, what with the new

breadth of literary license that has caused even Nabokov himself to demur from the lubricity of Philip Roth's *Portnoy's Complaint*. But I would want on this occasion to remember those original difficulties that Nabokov had "placing" *Lolita* with a "respectable" publisher, and to pay him a peculiar tribute—exactly the kind he most abhors—a tribute of a socio-political nature, honoring him for the deft blow he impeccably dealt nativist comstockery in this country. We were still not that far removed from Mencken's boobocracy until his nymphet challenged all its assumptions, indeed, its very jurisdiction, in a girlishly grand manner that could no longer be put off, handled hypocritically as an aberrant matter for some juvenile court.

The fact that *Lolita* was never brought before the courts at all in this country, as she was in England, has tended to obscure this eccentric (as usual) Nabokovian effect on literary censorship. The case of *Ulysses* came long before, and those of *Lady Chatterley's Lover, Tropic of Cancer,* and *Fanny Hill* came almost too quickly thereafter. But the avoidance of any attack upon *Lolita* is, I suspect, the secret turning point. And I don't think this inaction came only because of the book's obvious "redeeming" literary qualities. It occurred equally because *Lolita* was uneasily understood, recognized in some unconscious way, as a prophetic work.

Prophetic in a quite literal sense. To reread her sad history now, almost fifteen years after "John Ray, Jr., Ph.D." released it to the world, is to catch an agonizing glimpse of present-day America in pupa. The motel culture, the coming of the teeny-bopper, our endless mobility, the malaise of sexual freedom, the corrupt beauty of plastic, even the fashion of violence are all there in the brilliant haze of this iridescent comedy. And through the haze—Dolores Haze—the "painful haze"—can also be seen the tragedy, our growing tragedy of violated—better, self-violated—innocence and adulterate adult misery. Humbert Humbert even renders a kind of verdict.

"Unless it can be proven to me—to me as I am now, today, with my heart and my beard, and my putrefaction,—that in the infinite run it does not matter a jot that a North-American girl-child named Dolores Haze has been deprived of her childhood by a maniac, unless this can be proven (and if it can, then life is a joke), I see nothing for the treatment of my misery but the melancholy and very local palliative of articulate art."

Lolita itself—H. H.'s own purging confession—can perhaps be considered just that kind of "palliative of articulate art" for our present generational scourge. Of course, it cannot cure, but it does ease, and most magnificently explain. We will probably have volume on future volume concerning Nabokov's literary art, but I think it is well to note that his prevision, his sighting of land's end in the American future—originally set aside as merely a "dirty read"—has stayed with us as an unavoidable moral presage. He wrote a tragi-comedy, a great novel, a psychological masterpiece, any of which we might happily have burned—or ignored. But what we could not ignore, even in our prudery and xenophobia, was his sibylline wisdom, the hard fact that Vladimir Nabokov came among us not only as a foreigner, an author, but as a highly accurate, and clean, and local oracle.

BROCK BROWER

Advice to a young writer

If possible, be Russian. And live in another country. Play chess. Be an active trader between languages. Carry precious metals from one to the other. Remind us of Stravinsky. Know the names of plants and flying creatures. Hunt gauzy wings with snares of gauze. Make science pay tribute. Have a butterfly known by your name.

Do not be awed by giant predecessors. Be ill-tempered with their renown. Point out flaws. Frighten interviewers from *Time*. Appear in *Playboy*. Sell to the movies.

Use unlikely materials. Who would choose Pnin as hero, but how did we live before Pnin?

Delight in perversity. Put a noun into the dictionary. Now we recognize the Lolita at every street corner, see her sucking sweetened milk through straws at every soda fountain, dream her through all our fantasies.

Burn pedants in pale fire. Accept no fashions. Be your own fashion. Do not rely on earlier triumphs. Be new at each appearance.

Age indomitably, in the European manner. Do not finish your labors young. Be a planet, not a meteor. Honor the working day. Sit at your desk.

Not all of this is possible for you. But it is possible for Vladimir N., perched on his hill in Switzerland.

IRWIN SHAW

In the Chinese boxes
The academic foxes
Pursue one another.

V. Nabokov

The maker of illusion
Sees the confusion
And smiles.

He sees his love

In the mirrors transparent
Where nothing is apparent
He resides, royally.

JAY NEUGEBOREN

Toward the end of *Ada,* Nabokov describes how his hero on Antiterra, Van Veen, falls asleep while reading "the proofs of an essay he was contributing to a festschrift on the occasion of Professor Counterstone's eightieth birthday." It's only a most casual detail in a great complex fantasy and esthetic universe, but it partakes of Nabokov's joyous and unending mockery of academicisms, in this case the academic way we seize and try to control time. To have simply reached such a rounded age, to have extended so far, like a long, perfect fragment of chronology! The passage made me hesitate to contribute to Nabokov's being turned, on the occasion of his seventieth birthday, into a Professor Counterstone. It would have been better, I thought, if we had paid these tributes on his sixty-eighth birthday or waited until his seventy-first. Something irregular, unexpected, outside the patterns.

But I suppose we have to face the fact that we live in the grip of chronology and are subject to its protocols and formalities, unlike artists such as Nabokov, who escape time, while they are being artists, by creating counterforces and alternatives. Another quote from *Ada:* "the dream-like, dream-rephrased, legend-distorted past." Such is Nabokov's territory, increasingly so as his own past piles up and offers so much more material for rephrasing and the distortions of new legend.

All writers are engaged with time, but some, the greatest I think, are committed to a kind of holy war against it. In our own era Proust, Joyce, Beckett, Borges, Nabokov. (Has anyone noticed that American novelists of this century haven't, with the exception of Faulkner, been implicated in so desperate a struggle with time, and that this might be a source of their relative inferiority?)

The particular aesthetic irony and task that Beckett, Borges and Nabokov have confronted supremely among present-day writers is, of course, that of having to find a way past what their great predecessors have laid down as road-blocks, the results of *their* conquests of time. No going back to Stendhal or Flaubert, certainly, but not to Joyce or Proust either. One way of breaking into new novelistic space—and thus into new freedom from time—is through parody, of which Nabokov is as great a master as Joyce. Parody, by announcing a clear knowledge of language's previous uses and tasks, frees writers for the assumption of the present, changing ones.

"Oh, how I sometimes yearn for the easy swing of a well-oiled novel!" the narrator of *The Real Life of Sebastian Knight* exclaims, to be answered by that voice in *Ada* saying: "old storytelling devices may be parodied only by very great and inhuman artists . . ." Nabokov is indeed very great and "inhuman." The notion that writers ought to be comfortably human has been regaining its force, after a period of decline, and writers like Beckett, Borges and Nabokov continue in their different ways to hold out the most valuable kind of opposition to it.

For what is meant by human in this context is almost always an idea of the writer as consoler, corroborator, accomplice in our plots to appease the imagination instead of trembling at it. Again from *Ada* (is seventy a "human" age at which to have one's greatest book appear?):

> **Thus the rapture young Mascodagama derived from overcoming gravity was akin to that of artistic revelation in the sense utterly and naturally unknown to the innocents of critical appraisal, the social-scene commentators, the moralists, the idea-mongers and so forth. Van on the stage was performing organically what his figures of speech were to perform later in life—acrobatic wonders that had never been expected of them and which frightened children.**

One more point in tribute. In his essay on translation, Walter Benjamin advances the theory of a universal language that underlies all particular ones, and that makes not only translation but literature itself possible. Who better than Nabokov upholds the validity of this idea? Who, for that matter, better upholds the validity of language, now under such siege and assault, language where all the "useless" truths lie: "Oh, my Lolita, I have only words to play with!"

RICHARD GILMAN

A storyteller's material being connections among people, what is he to do if he does not feel close kin to most of his fellowmen and much dislikes the social formalities which they have instituted, the customs and governments?

One thing he can do is take a nostalgic trip, as Mark Twain did in *Huckleberry Finn,* into a world where he can not only like but even love some of the people. Nabokov has done this in several either openly or disguisedly autobiographical narratives. But his verbal genius, that quirky, shifty wit which is his hallmark, is not perfectly appropriate to a visit into the gone country. He has said that his personal tragedy is having to abandon his native Russian for a second-hand brand of English. Forced to read his Russian novels in translation, I am unsure, but my strong hunch is that not even in Russian did his nostalgia find an idiom as vigorous as *Lolita*'s. Second-hand indeed!

Another thing a storyteller can do if he finds mankind hard to put up with is take a satiric trip, as Swift did in *Gulliver's Travels,* into a world where there are no personages credible enough to love, or to hate either, and where social institutions are there for the purpose of being lampooned and despised. Nabokov seems to start on this trip in nearly every story he tells, but he simply can't dehumanize his people that much. His obsessive characters do not flatten into Laputans but turn into mad game-players (*The Defense*) or scholars (*Pale Fire*). His detestation of social arrangements is usually too fastidious to engage the reader's savageness; at its strongest, in *Bend Sinister,* it reaches a pitch of pain so excruciating and unpurgeable that not even the storyteller can stand it but turns back to butterflies instead.

Another thing a narrative misanthropoid can do is estrange himself and us from his characters by his language, as Joyce does; shift the energy of the story, by the idiom of its telling, away from the people we might have become hotly connected with and toward the writer's handling of them. This, Nabokov does with famous dazzle, no one more resourcefully.

Of course there is a sort of perverseness to this: the fictional servant, language, mastering the characters; the creator interfering with his creatures' autonomy. But Nabokov at his very best is perverse indeed. "Nothing is more exhilarating than philistine vulgarity" ("On a Book Entitled *Lolita*"). What he loves straight—butterflies, his Russian youth, affectionable sex—he ornaments lavishly but not with the final flair. His pure hatred, of totalitarian despotism above all, generates more pain than story can contain—with one exception, that little masterpiece, "Signs and Symbols," whose perfection holds its anguish.

But *Lolita!* What endless riches of vulgarity and what a profusion of idiom America provided for Nabokov's aesthetic, detached fascination! In all his fiction, no love is more persuasive than Humbert Humbert's beneath his monomaniacal, criminal lechery. In no other novel does Nabokov sustain an unslackening drive so exuberantly—up to the end, at least; comic wander-tales are notoriously hard to finish well. Nowhere else is his kaleidoscopic prose as useful as in this total put-on. He is the living master of the narrative perverse.

GEORGE P. ELLIOTT

This is Nabokov's moment; Nabokov just now is king over that battered mass society called contemporary fiction. And he is king not only because of *Ada*—truly royal pleasures!—but also because he does not belong to any country but his own. *We* call him "king"—he sees nothing in political relationships, not even the mythical ones to which his genius lends itself. Ours is an age so dominated by politics, historical "necessity," the seeming total reality of social and racial conflict, that Nabokov stands out just now because he has no country but himself. He is the only refugee who could have turned statelessness into absolute strength. The penniless have-not fleeing the Crimea in 1919 has turned out to be, in his blessedly unconventional, unyielding terms, the true possessor. The torments of so many decent and even talented Soviet writers in the Hell of total obedience contrast so ironically with the freedom of our *barín*—the last and by no means the smallest of the aristocrats who made Russian literature *international*. And Nabokov's imaginary realm puts his own readers to shame, for *they* are still in bondage to actual states and cruel political abstractions.

Is Fiction the only true freedom? Who lives by a "fiction"—the slaves of political "reality" or the stateless exile luxuriating in his own imagination? And where, in this ever crueler treadmill of "progress," are *we* to find the comfort of being at home with ourselves except by escaping from fictions into Fiction? Ours is a tragic generation, for at our best we want to raise everybody, yet never has this essentially religious idea been so violated by the arrogant exclusions of politics as well as by the aggressiveness of political language.

So we who are not Nabokov, who must perhaps remain in bondage to all those "realities" that genius is right to scorn, must first of all salute him for being *free*. In an age of total propaganda for the total state, of a coercion that rests on forms of power that require another kind of genius even to understand, in the age of "society" incarnate and of its only possible hero, The Totally Obedient Man, Nabokov the Russian-American lives in Switzerland, writes in his own delightful space-time, and so ends by receiving our astonishment even more than our homage.

ALFRED KAZIN

Many respected Professeur Apple [sic],[1]

22 Mai 1969

Your lettre addressed since many month to New Wye finally catch me here in hôpital of Caurina wher I am lieng cloué au lit on acont fractturd ankle now hangd in traction, thus helploss. I in large rom with three more individus which allday bavardent about nothings, allnihgt makes loud snors, spitings, éructations, borborygmes, allso two postes of television and courants d'air.[2] Un vrai supplice and I do not evn to mention the food! Stil is my heart strong in spite what my "friend" writs about it,[3] it bumps [4] finely I am thanking you!

Pleas to for giv my writtng is not eassy in flat up on back position allso to excuse my old fontaine pen stylo which may be making som splodges,[5] pleas allso for giv my english which I have learn now manny years but writ onely few usuely with helpfull aidings of good friends, I much preffer to writting you in french or mostly in Russian, and if print I hope to be so in our beautifull *kirillitsa*[6] so méprisé by my "friend" le translittérateur! But I most not risk to doeng so!

Editor's note: The above communication was written on stationery of CAURINA UNIVERSITY: *Department of Slavic and Baltic.* On the first sheet these names are loosely canceled, and the words "Caurina General Hôpital [*sic*]" inserted in the same hand as that of the text of the letter. This letter has been transcribed, and arranged for the press, with notes, by editorial associate W. B. Scott.

1. This will be the last *sic* in these notes. Professor P.'s letter is printed here as closely as possible as it left his pen. His control of English spelling and idiom, remarkable in one so profoundly non-Anglo-Saxon, seems nonetheless at moments a bit uncertain—but there is no need to drown him in a flood of condescending *sics*! As for the handwriting, it hovers with passionate intensity (as one might almost say) between an unqualified Russian script for the occasional Russian word or phrase, and a sort of qualified Russian script for the English and occasional French. The transcriber—no expert at this sort of thing!—has done his best.

2. For Professor P.'s feelings about noises and drafts, see *Pnin, passim.*

3. For Professor P.'s heart, see *Pnin, passim.*

4. pumps [?] The handwriting is unclear.

5. splotches [?] Could Professor P. have been aware that "splodges" is in fact an acceptable alternative form?

6. the Cyrillic alphabet (in Russian script in the original). For V.N.'s animadversions on this alphabet, see his Commentary on *Eugene Onegin*, III.398-9.n., and—more recently—*Ada*, 84. For his transliterations of Russian, see his English works, *passim.*

Now most I to explan that I am sevrl year retiret, this year 1969 on 3 février julians calendrier I have become seventy one years aged. So since som years I retired from New Wye with great farwel banquet, even much locall native *shipuchnoe vino*[7] allso kind speches and songs, allso gift of expensive real lether valise en veau silver innitials! *Et voilà pour mon "friend" and all his labels.*[8] Since my retraite I am more busyer as ever, ghest lectureur to manny universités, importants savants which invit me, state university Bufalo on kind invitation Prof. Milton Shakespeare,[9] Grands Tetons Universitey, Aardvaark wher verry distinguish Professeur Barry Vélin[10] holding Cosa Nostra chair in manny langages invit to me, université California at Tehachapi,[11] Hayford Institute,[12] and actuely this term Caurina University wher last Friday I have sliped from low plateforme and casser ankle while makeng conférence on death of Ivan Ilyich. I am then caryd to this excelent but nosy[13] hôpital in police voiture ambulance with loud sirin scremming, allso flashy lihgt I am told by some students.

7. sparkling wine, "bubbly" (in Russian script in the original).
8. libels [?] See *Pale Fire,* 112, 163, 189, 200 (Lancer Books paperback). The sentence is heavily underlined in the original.
9. Professor Milton Shakespeare is Director of Advanced Sophomore Literary Hermeneutics at the New York State University at Buffalo, and a frequent contributor to *The New York Review of Books.*
10. Professor Barry Vélin is Chairman of the Department of Omniliterature at Aardvaark (amusingly, an "Aardvaark" figures fleetingly in *Ada!*), and the author of numerous books and articles, which range from *Old Sardines* (a small volume of whimsical aphorisms) to the by-now-classic omniliterary study, *The Confident Smirk in World Literature from Homer to Lo Hung Dong* (xlviii + 698 pages, New York and Calcutta, 1954; also paperback in Pétarade Books, Chicago). (Lo Hung Dong, b. 1923, the Taiwanese *feuilletoniste,* has been described by Andalusian sinologist Alfredo Graff y Ananas as "blending in his subtle *chung* [Chinese] fashion a whisper of Kafka with a scft footfall of Borges, to venture for the moment only the most obligatory names.")
11. The Tehachapi "branch" of the University of California is powerful in Russian and Bulgarian under the forceful chairmanship of Mexican slavophile Andrés del Campo y Chapucerías.
12. The Department of Languages and Literatures at the Hayford Institute of Human Engineering is headed by Dr. Bernard Mosher, whose *Zénaïde Fleuriot et le monde slave* (Toulouse, 1946) remains pre-eminent in its field. Professor P. lectured at Hayford in the autumn of 1967 on the writings of Prince Sergei Shirinsky-Shihmatov (1783-1837).
13. noisy [?] Again the handwriting is unclear.

Now you are askng in lettre to me if I mihgt contribuer to in honneur to my old "friend" numéro? Why shold I, sir? may I francly to demand? Yes of corse I know him since many years but not as he is fond to pretendng.[14] Francly is he tryng to run [15] my life as manny peuples well know this, he has bassed his pré-tendue narration on manny inventions (*vïdumki*) [16] allso on cruel mimicrys by amateur cabotins like late Cockrel,[17] who I am informmed has been strick [18] by fatale crise cardiaque whil makenng one mor *verry funy* [19] imitation, but this time *was not of myself, was of my "friend" self!!* [20] Ha! Ha! [21] C'est bien fait pour M. Cokrel!!

Evvery wher are ennemis, upping eybrous when is mention my name. Onely to say this name is enohg then the eybrous and many little small smiles, allso clins d'oeil. And who is the faute? You most know ther is onely but one single onswer! So why most I writ for your revue Tri quortrley about this "friend" be cause evvry wher are allso *true* friends who say rihgt my name with out smilling or to sneze or *"prepostrous litle explosion."* [22]

Do you know it is verity, sir, some tims in America on manny campuss I am oftn by folish peuples beng evn mistackn to be this "friend"?! Then truely am I feling like shodowe of a shade when these are sayng, O ho, you are un tel, mentiong his name, of corse then soon they allways posing same questions about that best saling yong "lady" with spainisch name, or why love I not Dostoevski?!! Stendhal?! Fomann? [Thomas Mann?] or how is

14. See *Pnin*, 185 (Atheneum paperback edition).
15. ruin [?] Either word would seem to fit.
16. So in the original—the English word followed by its Russian equivalent in Russian script and in parentheses.
17. For the late Professor John Cockerell's elaborate imitations of Professor P., see *Pnin*, 36 and (especially) 187-89.
18. stricken [?] struck [?]
19. Heavily underlined in the original.
20. Heavily underlined in the original.
21. "Ha! Ha!" inserted above the line, perhaps as an afterthought. (In Russian script in the original: "Xa! Xa!")
22. In quotation marks and heavily underlined in the original. See *Pnin*, 32.

to be cald buterflie just flitring by in air,[23] or why is my fond interst of sqrls? [24]

Une heure latter, pleas to for giv. Now have I terminatd lunch, vegtebal soupe, som things like macaroni and ches, *drozashchee zhelyonoe zhelo* [25] salade, a piece spices cake too drie, allso wek tea. One television poste now has bassbal other a senator the sound of senator seems comeng from bassbal the sound of bassball from senator, my rom compagnons I can hear chatring a bout bassbal, allso a bout chirurgicale interventions, gas, *o kateterah, kishkah.*[26] In to my memoiry sudenly comes poet Yuvenal, *zdorovii duh v zdorovom tyelye.*[27]

No, esteamd Professeur Apple, I can not see what I can truely writ about my "friend" of who the Russians books I can not finnish them or his english understand! Avant-hier while I *dremal* [28] malgré l'éternelle television and rum compagnon nose [29] som boddy has leaved to me the book Ada, I do not know may be some collègue from department Slavic and baltic Caurina université wher I am actuel visstng Emeritus professeur. Who cold be doing? Of corse evn if this *uzhasno tyazholaya kniga* [30] mihgt be in Russian I can not be reding it whil flat up on back leg suspendue in air! I have heared it is beng about the inceste well sir if inceste I need I can allwayes go back to Sofokles allso Ovide! Who is neding more of inceste? Not I to be sure! In Sofokles is the best! So manny terrble bookes now to day! This Ada, then

---

23. For some thoughts on butterflies, see *Pnin,* 128.
24. squirrels [?] girls [?] The handwriting is decidedly unclear at this point, and a bad "splodge" compounds the difficulty. In *Pnin* squirrels are more important than girls, while in other works of this author the reverse appears to be true.
25. trembling green Jello (in Russian script in the original).
26. about catheters, bowels (in Russian script in the original).
27. Juvenal's famous "mens sana in corpore sano" (*Satires* X, 356). (In Russian script in the original.)
28. was dozing (in Russian script in the original).
29. room companions' noise [?] The handwriting again! See above, notes 1 and 13.
30. terribly heavy book (in Russian script in the original).

terrble *portnoi* [31] I hear of, allso Fruits of the M L A I am told
by student to who I demand what is mening of this name but I
have attendet to manny conventions of M L A and is not true!
No, M L A is filld of veritabel genuin men! [32] Allso feuilletant
this book Ada I can see it make manny jokes about prety Chateaubriand poem [33] wich I have learn as skolboy, allso making fune
and jokes with manny other not onely my "friend's" usuel joks
such as Fyodor Mihailovich Dostoevski no doute but allso Lev
Nikolaiovich Tolstoi, Sergei Timofeievich Aksakov,[34] beatifull
Bérénice of Racine [35] Dr. Mertvago [36] *i pr. i proch.*[37]

No! Dear Sir I find that I can not writ nothing for your especial
numéro! Too many memoirys, sir! insults, trahison! Now most I
think actuely onely about my own travaux of manny years son
to be complett if it suffices the time and force.[38] Now must I stop

31. In Russian script in the original. In Russian *portnoi* means "tailor," a
fact of some symbolic significance in a recent novel whose hero is forever
taking his pants off, according to critic Norman Empson, in *Gag*, June-July
1969.

32. A vigorously loyal yet strangely cryptic statement! Attempting to reconstruct its background one images some lightminded student "introducing"
innocent Professor P. to arcane American idiom and informing him in "far
out" "deadpan" labored jest that Edmund Wilson's *The Fruits of the M.L.A.*
(1969) is an account of sexual deviation in the Modern Language Association,
rather than the collection of small devotional exercises which it is in fact.

33. The "romance," *Le Montagnard Emigré*, sung by the French prisoner
of war in Granada in Chateaubriand's story, *Les Aventures du dernier Abencerage*, figures importantly—variously altered!—throughout *Ada*: see for
example 138-39, 141, 233, 241, 428, 530.

34. 1791-1859, author of such works as *A Family Chronicle* (1856) and
Years of Childhood (1858). In an admiring account of him in *A History of
Russian Literature*, 288, Prince D. S. Mirsky links Aksakov with time and
Proust—"only [Aksakov] was as sane and normal as Proust was perverse and
morbid, and instead of the close and stuffy atmosphere of the never aired
flat of the Boulevard Haussmann there breathes in Aksakov's books the air
of the open steppe." On the other hand, the translator of *Eugene Onegin* in his
Commentary (III.139) describes Aksakov as "a very minor writer, tremen-
dously puffed up by Slavophile groups . . ." An Andrey Andreevich Aksakov is
a very minor character in *Ada*.

35. See *Ada*, 231.

36. This family name figures lightly (although a matter of life and death)
in *Ada or Ardor: A Family Chronicle* and even more lightly in S. T. Aksakov's
Semyeinaya Hronika (*A Family Chronicle*—see above, note 34). Consult the
author's (Aksakov's) interesting footnote on the name (8th edition, Moskva,
1895, 146).

37. and much much more (in Russian script in the original).

38. For Professor P.'s great work, see *Pnin*, 39.

to writ my arm is tird and I have swetty itch bitwen omoplates but of corse no norse com to my lihgtng! [39] To morowe visttng hour will I speack to my admirable étudiante Varvara Ivanovna H. about this book Ada whch I am sur she has read it no doute! It is great déception to me that she much admire works of my "friend" both Russian and in english, but allways am I tryng showng to her true beautés of *veritable great Russian litterature!* [40] *O Rus'!* [41] But dear yong Varvara Ivanovna at least knowes who am I realy in fact personely, *not* [42] by *"friendily"* [43] calomnies!

Now most I to achieve my lettre dearly most estemd Sir, manny good wish to you and I thank you, I am your most respectfuley fathfull serviteur, and with fervant handshak,

TIMOFEY PAVLOVICH PNIN [*signed*] Professor Emeritus (being corrently ocupyd with manny *great* [44] Russian writters, lecturng in Caurina univesitè distingushd Visstng Emeritus Professeur)

39. . . . of course no nurse comes when I turn on my light [?]
40. Heavily underlined in the original.
41. In Russian script in the original. A famous pun, in this context rich in overtones: Horace's *O rus!* (O country-home, *Satires,* II, vi, 60) and *Rus',* the old form of *Rossiya* = Russia. For a note on Pushkin's use of this wordplay as the motto to Chapter Two of *Onegin,* see the Commentary, II.217.
42. Heavily underlined in the original.
43. Heavily underlined in the original.
44. Heavily underlined in the original.

Contributors

ALFRED APPEL, JR., guest co-editor of this issue, is Associate Professor of English at Northwestern University. Appearing in 1970 are his *Annotated Lolita* (McGraw-Hill) and *Nabokov: A Collection of Essays* (Prentice-Hall). He is presently preparing a critical book on Nabokov. PETER LUBIN is a graduate student in Comparative Literature at Harvard University. P. M. BITSILLI (1879-1953) was a Russian literary scholar and critic who resided in Bulgaria between the two wars. He is the author of studies of Pushkin and Dostoevsky (see *Brown University Slavic Reprint IV*) and a rare monograph on Chekhov (see *Yearbooks of the University of Sofia,* 1941-42, vol. 6). VLADISLAV KHODASEVICH, poet, critic and biographer, was one of the most distinguished writers of the Russian emigration. He died in Paris in 1939 and was rehabilitated in the U.S.S.R. only in 1963. The essay published here is the first of his prose to appear in English. PHILIPPE HALSMAN received the Newhouse Citation in 1963, and the Golden Plate Award in 1967. He has published five books, and two of his photographs, those of Adlai Stevenson and Albert Einstein, were used on U. S. postage stamps. ALBERT J. GUERARD, author of six novels as well as critical books on Conrad, Gide, Hardy and Bridges, is Professor of Literature at Stanford. NINA BERBEROVA's autobiography, *The Italics Are Mine* (Harcourt, Brace & World) was published in May, 1969. She is currently teaching in the Slavic Department at Princeton University. ROBERT M. ADAMS holds the Pan-American Chair for the Study of Over-developed Countries. His current project is titled, *La Chasse au Bonheur dans la Toscane et la Venétie: une étude comparée.* ELIZA-BETH LUCIE LÉON NOEL has written extensively as a journalist, fashion reporter, critic and translator. Among her translations are Boris Simon's *Abbé Pierre's Ragpickers* and François Six's *Witness in the Desert.* Her memoir of her husband, Paul Léon, and James Joyce is titled *Story of a Friendship* (Gotham Book Mart). HORTENSE CALISHER is the author of four novels, the most recent being

The New Yorkers. A volume of essays, a collection of short stories, and a new novel are forthcoming. **RICHARD HOWARD's** *Alone with America,* a critical study of poetry in the United States since World War II, was recently published by Atheneum. **BARBARA HELDT MONTER** is Assistant Professor of Slavic Languages and Literatures at the University of Chicago. **HERBERT GOLD** is author of *Fathers, Salt, The Man Who Was Not with It,* and a number of anecdotes about Vladimir Nabokov. His new novel, *The Great American Jackpot,* will be published by Random House in 1970. **JOHN UPDIKE** is the author of five novels and four children, and lives in Ipswich, Massachusetts. **STANLEY ELKIN** is the author of a volume of short stories, and three novels, the last of which, *The Dick Gibson Show,* is just completed. **ROBERT P. HUGHES**, Assistant Professor of Slavic Languages and Literatures at the University of California in Berkeley, is co-editor of *A Century of Russian Prose and Verse from Pushkin to Nabokov* (Harcourt, Brace & World, 1967). **ROBERT ALTER** is Professor of Comparative Literature at the University of California in Berkeley and author of three volumes of criticism. **RICHARD STERN's** new fiction entitled *1968* (Holt, Rinehart and Winston) will appear in 1970. Among his other books are *Stitch* (Harper), *Golk* (Meridian) and *In Any Case* (Penguin). **ANTHONY BURGESS** has written over twenty books, seventeen and a half of them novels, and is now working on a "Structuralist" novel besides sweating blood. **MORRIS BISHOP** is Kappa Alpha Professor Emeritus of Romance Literature at Cornell University. **ELLENDEA PROFFER** is now doing research on her doctoral dissertation, "The Major Prose of Mikhail Bulgakov." **CARL R. PROFFER**, Associate Professor of Slavic Languages and Literatures at Indiana University, is author of several books, including *Keys to Lolita* and the forthcoming *Critical Prose of Alexander Pushkin.* **JOHN BARTH** is at the State University of New York at Buffalo and working on a new novel about Indians. **DABNEY STUART** is Associate Professor of English at Washington and Lee University, poetry editor of *Shenandoah,* and author of two volumes of poetry, the latest being *A Particular Place* (Knopf, 1969). **JAY NEUGEBOREN**'s latest book, *GM and Points Left,* was published by Farrar, Straus and Giroux in 1970. **GEORGE P. ELLIOTT**'s most recent book is a collection of poems entitled *From the Berkeley Hills* (Harper and Row). **SAUL STEINBERG** continues his work. **JACK LUDWIG** is currently writer-in-residence at the University of Toronto and writing plays for the Stratford Shakespeare Theater. He is the author of two novels and several critical works. **CLARENCE BROWN** is now in London completing a study of the life and poetry of Osip Mandelstam. Of his own Russian poetry, heretofore prized by a tiny circle of connoisseurs, this is the first example to appear in print. **SIMON KARLINSKY** is a member of the American Association for the Advancement of Slavic Languages and secretary of the Slavic Literature Section of the Modern Language Association of America. He currently teaches at the University of California at Berkeley. **R. H. W. DILLARD**, author of *The Day I Stopped Dreaming* and *About Barbara Steele and Other Poems,* is Associate Professor of English at Hollins College. **ANDREW FIELD**'s *The Complection of Russian Literature* will be published in 1970. **JULIAN MOYNAHAN** teaches English at Rutgers and has written a pamphlet on Nabokov for the University of Minnesota's American Writers series. His novel, *Pairing Off,* has just been published. **ROSS WETZSTEON** is a free-lance writer and critic who at present is Associate Editor of *The Village Voice,* where this essay originally appeared in a somewhat different form. **GEORGE STEINER** is Extraordinary Fellow of Churchill College, Cambridge. His books include *Tolstoy on Dostoevsky* and *Language and Silence.* **DAVID WAGONER**, Professor of English at the University of Washington, is editor of *Poetry Northwest* and author of five books of poetry and five novels, the latest of which is *Baby, Come On Inside.* **RICHARD GILMAN** is Professor of Drama at Yale. **IRWIN WEIL** is Associate Professor of Russian and Russian Literature at Northwestern University. He has taught at Moscow University and is currently writing a book about L. Tolstoy. **CHARLES NEWMAN** is author of a novel, *New Axis* (Houghton Mifflin, 1966) and the editor of a casebook on Sylvia Plath to appear in 1970 from Indiana University Press. **STANLEY EDGAR HYMAN**'s latest book, *Iago,* will be published by Atheneum in 1970. **W. B. SCOTT** is Professor of Dramatic Literature at Northwestern University. **BROCK BROWER** is now in London working as a reporter and completing a second novel. **ALFRED KAZIN** is Distinguished Professor of English at the State University of New York at Stoney Brook. **IRWIN SHAW**'s new novel will be published by Delacorte in 1970. Two sections will appear in the January and February 1970 issues of *Playboy.* He is now living in Switzerland. **JEFFREY LEONARD** is a graduate student in English at Northwestern University.

Vladimir Nabokov, distinguished lepidopterist, is also the author of fifteen novels. McGraw-Hill recently published a facsimile edition of the original Russian version of his *King, Queen, Knave,* and forthcoming in late 1970 is an English translation of his first novel, *Mashenka.* He recently completed a set of notes to be added to the paperback edition of *Ada* (spring, 1970), and is presently resurrecting several other old works, as well as composing a new novel, entitled *Transparent Things.*